Women and Patriotism in Jim Crow America

Gender and American Culture

Women and Patriotism in Jim Crow America

Francesca Morgan

The University of North Carolina Press

Chapel Hill

Designed by April Leidig-Higgins
Set in Ehrhardt by Copperline Book Services, Inc.

The paper in this book meets the guidelines for perma-
nence and durability of the Committee on Production
Guidelines for Book Longevity of the Council on
Library Resources.

Library of Congress Cataloging-in-Publication Data
Morgan, Francesca.
Women and patriotism in Jim Crow America /
Francesca Morgan.
    p. cm.—(Gender and American culture)
Includes bibliographical references (p.) and index.
ISBN 0-8078-2968-4 (cloth: alk. paper)
ISBN 0-8078-5630-4 (pbk.: alk. paper)
1. African American women—Political activity
—History. 2. Women, White—United States—
Political activity—History. 3. Women—United
States—Societies and clubs—History. 4. Women
in politics—United States—History. 5. Nationalism
—United States—History. 6. Patriotism—United
States—History. 7. Political culture—United States
—History. 8. United States—Race relations—
Political aspects—History—19th century. 9. United
States—Race relations—Political aspects—History
—20th century. 10. United States—Politics and
government—1865–1933.   I. Title.   II. Gender &
American culture.
E185.86.M585 2005
320.54'082'0973—dc22   2005005930

cloth   09 08 07 06 05   5 4 3 2 1
paper   09 08 07 06 05   5 4 3 2 1

For Chuck

Contents

Illustrations

Acknowledgments

THIS BOOK RESULTS FROM the labor of many people in addition to myself. Thousands of long-ago volunteers committed their own thoughts and those of their colleagues to paper. Those thoughts constitute this book's empirical basis. A host of my own friends, relations, colleagues, librarians, and archivists also ensured that, in the end, I wrote the book I wanted to write. Among this project's financial supporters are the University of North Texas's Office of the Vice Provost for Research, which awarded me two Junior Faculty Summer Research Fellowships and two Faculty Research Grants; my family; and a Sesquicentennial Research Grant awarded by the State Historical Society of Iowa and the Iowa Department of Cultural Affairs. For much-needed space and library privileges, I would like to thank Sara Austin at the Newberry Library and the departmental associate program at Northwestern University's Department of History.

Allowing me access to their holdings and hefting innumerable dusty volumes in the process are the staffs at the Newberry Library, the New York Public Library's Local History and Genealogy Room, the Boston Public Library, and Northwestern University's Periodicals and Newspapers Room. I also thank the archivists and staffs at the American Heritage Center, University of Wyoming; the Atlanta History Center Library/Archives; the Georgia Department of Archives and History in Atlanta; Howard University's Moorland-Spingarn Research Center; the Library of Congress's Manuscript Division; the Litchfield Historical Society in Litchfield, Connecticut; the Minnesota Historical Society in the Minnesota History Center, St. Paul; the Mississippi Department of Archives and History in Jackson; the National

Archives and Records Administration facilities in Washington, D.C., College Park, and Suitland, Maryland; the Nebraska State Historical Society's Manuscript Division in Lincoln; the New York Public Library's Manuscripts and Archives Section; the North Carolina Division of Archives and History in Raleigh; Radcliffe Institute's Arthur and Elizabeth Schlesinger Library on the History of Women in America; the Saratoga Springs Historical Museum in Saratoga Springs, New York; Stanford University's Special Collections; the State Historical Society of Iowa's Library/Archives Bureau in Iowa City; the Swarthmore College Peace Collection; the University of Kentucky's Special Collections; the University of Michigan's Bentley Library in Ann Arbor; the University of Mississippi's Special Collections in Oxford; the University of Missouri's and State Historical Society of Missouri's Western Historical Manuscript Collection in Columbia; the Western Reserve Historical Society in Cleveland, Ohio; and the Woman's Collection, Texas Woman's University. Although the Daughters of the American Revolution's central archives at its headquarters in Washington, D.C., remain closed to researchers, I would like to thank Elva B. Crawford for supplying me with material that would otherwise have been difficult or impossible to obtain.

As for insights, a conversation at the very beginning of this project with Jane McCarl about American and Confederate flags proved extremely fruitful, as did a dinner with Pamela and John Mearsheimer toward the end of this project. Commentary delivered in the U.S. History Dissertation Seminar at Columbia University, notably by Eliza Byard, Cori Field, Mike Flamm, Walter Hickel, Anne Kornhauser, Rebecca McLennan, Michelle Morgan, Mae Ngai, and Thad Russell has continued to be of use many years later. Alan Brinkley, Rosalind Rosenberg, Jean Cohen, and Silvana Patriarca defended my dissertation, meaning that they saved it and me from various embarrassments. Guiding this project further upward were a work-in-progress group at the University of North Texas made up of Claire Sahlin, Diana York Blaine, and Diane Negra; Chris Morris, Stephanie Cole, Alison Parker, and others who convened as the Dallas Area Social Historians; and the University of North Texas History Department's faculty seminar. Furnishing extremely helpful comments and suggestions, and/or sharing items from their own research, were Maurice Barboza, David Cannadine, Linda Colley, Karen Cox, Ruth Crocker, Kirsten Delegard, Joy Kasson, Nancy MacLean,

Stuart McConnell, Patrick Miller, Kim E. Nielsen, Peggy Pascoe, Denis Paz, Linda Perkins, Daryl Scott, Barbara Steinson, and Elizabeth Toon. Dear friends Alexis McCrossen, Prudence Cumberbatch, and Joan Johnson read and helped renovate the entire manuscript. I have been lucky also to have W. Fitzhugh Brundage and one who has remained anonymous read the manuscript for the University of North Carolina Press. Both put considerable time and thinking into the entire book. Both responded to each version with an admirable combination of speed and prolix, razor-sharp advice. I would also like to thank Charles Grench and Amanda McMillan at the University of North Carolina Press for steadfastly supporting this book and overseeing its completion, as well as Bethany Johnson for its copyediting.

For more than a decade, my graduate advisor Betsy Blackmar has furnished extraordinary levels of feedback. Long after I left Columbia and New York, she continued to encourage this project and its author from half a country away. Time after time, Betsy has seen patterns in my evidence that I initially did not, and she has pushed my thinking in directions that turned out to be the roads best taken. In her intellectual acuity and breadth of heart, she shines.

My mother, Mary Rhinelander McCarl—a historian, librarian, preservationist, and proudly documented *Mayflower* descendant—was my book's very earliest inspiration. She and my stepfather, Henry N. McCarl, have done much to advance my education, as did my late father, John S. C. Morgan. Rest in peace. Making this project possible in a different, more recent capacity were Daniela Faldusova and Jana Bendova, with their loving child care.

The only thing that Chuck Steinwedel, another scholar of nationalism, did not do for this project was type it. He shaped its analysis and responded to the bouts of whining and self-absorption that accompanied my writing by making me pancakes on Sundays without number. Again and again, Daniel Greene Steinwedel recharged my commitment to my project by taking me away from it.

Abbreviations

The following abbreviations are used throughout this book.

ASNLH	Association for the Study of Negro Life and History
DAR	Daughters of the American Revolution
GAR	Grand Army of the Republic
GFWC	General Federation of Women's Clubs
ICWDR	International Council of Women of Darker Races
MID	Military Intelligence Division, U.S. War Department
MVLA	Mount Vernon Ladies' Association of the Union
NAACP	National Association for the Advancement of Colored People
NACW	National Association of Colored Women
NCW	National Council of Women
SAR	Sons of the American Revolution
SCV	Sons of Confederate Veterans
UCV	United Confederate Veterans
UDC	United Daughters of the Confederacy
UNIA	Universal Negro Improvement Association
WCTU	Woman's Christian Temperance Union
WILPF	Women's International League for Peace and Freedom
WJCC	Women's Joint Congressional Committee
WPP	Woman's Peace Party
WRC	Woman's Relief Corps

Women and
Patriotism
in Jim Crow
America

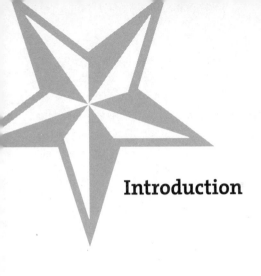

Introduction

STARTING IN THE 1880s, hundreds of thousands of women in the United States sought to instill in each other and in other Americans the conviction that they belonged to a nation. These women were black and white, native-born, educated, propertied, and mostly Protestant. They organized as women—operating, for the most part, in all-female groups. Most important, the women operated as nationalists and patriots. They promoted identification with a large imagined community that they called the United States, to which they imparted a national past and a national destiny. That community possessed borders, literal and figurative, that included some and excluded others.[1] Patriotism—a person's attachment to her or his nation—is able to exist in nationalism's absence. But patriotism often operates in harmony with nationalism, and it did so here.[2] Enriching this history of American women and nationalism are disagreements on the composition of the national community. Nation was not synonymous with country. The plural American nations the women imagined were variously coterminous with the contemporary state, a bygone country called the Confederate States of America, the white race (sometimes spanning U.S. borders), and the black race (sometimes spanning U.S. borders). All of those entities could and did embody "America" in the eyes of its beholders.

An important reason that so many women combined nationalism and patriotism, and organized to produce both in others, stems from the women's own historical moment. Across the Western world in the late nineteenth and early twentieth centuries, the nation was considered the most powerful, effective way of organizing political authority—in combination with empire and, later, as an alternative to empire. Educated Americans, especially those of a conservative bent, perceived the nation's ability to create unity as a potential remedy for a plethora of ongoing, incipient, and above all, national disorders. These included continuing sectionalist strife between the white North and the white South, mass immigration, apathy and/or corruption within the propertied classes, conflict between labor and capital, and the consequent ascent of socialism among the lower classes. Americans combined the view of nationalism as a solution to recent, new, or future political problems with older beliefs that American potency and expansion expressed God's wishes. The women's historical moment was also intimately related to the apogee of the cultural and moral authority commanded by female institutions and by groups of women. Nationalism and patriotism at the turn of the twentieth century, then, offered to female believers a remarkable opportunity to present solutions to truly national problems to truly national audiences.

Women's own readings of nationalism also explain what nationalism offered to American women. Not simply "ruling" women in the United States, nationalism's flexibility allowed women to attach multiple meanings to the relationship between themselves and the nation.[3] Women framed nationalism so that it encouraged their own political activism outside their households and, moreover, so that it assigned broad political importance to that activism. Women perceived nationalism also to honor female fertility, mothers' development of their children into members of the national community, and mothers' sacrifice of their sons to that community. Though this last reading of nationalism—stressing female domesticity and male warriors—may seem logically to demean women's public activities, that reading appealed to many women. Those women found it difficult and undesirable to separate their motherhood (actual or potential), their children's political education as citizens, and their own political lives as activists. Regardless of whether their nationalism praised domesticity or women's activism outside the home, women nationalists operated as subjects and creators of nationalism—acting on nationalism—and not only as nationalism's objects or symbols—acted on by nationalism.

Female nationalism's importance goes beyond its production by women—

notwithstanding their own political subordination as women. Female nationalism matters also because of its presentations of gender. Women in the United States forged a self-consciously women-centered nationalism. Although the term "feminine" in modern English better communicates this nationalism's ramifications for gender, I instead deploy "women-centered" to describe this nationalism because, to propertied Americans in the early twentieth century, "feminine" and "masculine" denoted tendencies generally considered innate to the sexes. Women's forms of nationalism, on the other hand, operated as attempts to uplift the women themselves and others. Uplift urged the cultivation of personal or collective qualities such as patriotism. By definition, such qualities were not innate.[4]

Women-centered nationalists posited women's moral superiority to men, including those of their own races and classes. Therefore, those nationalists considered female political activism essential to nation-building and positioned women as creators of culture, in the sense of everyday life and attitudes. The women specialized in what the literary scholar Anne McClintock calls "national fetishes"—history house museums, patriotic holidays, and monuments—which were intended to speak to all who saw them.[5] The women redrew calendars, customs, landscapes, and nationalism itself in making nationalism both tangible and visible. Women's domination, relative to men's patriotic groups and to the virtually all-male state, of that process in the United States before World War I asserted considerable cultural authority for women. I intend the term "cultural authority," as articulated by the historian W. Fitzhugh Brundage, to communicate the women's manufacturing and remolding of custom, and the women's assertion that women, as well as men, could define what was civilized and educate others in the ways of civilization.[6]

Challenging some sex hierarchies while enforcing others, women-centered nationalism illustrates nationalism's vexed relationship with feminism.[7] Though women-centered nationalism opposed particularly restrictive forms of women's exclusion from political processes, it ultimately confined its struggles against male domination to the arena of culture. While positing— and illustrating—women's ability to influence, most such nationalists initially approved the denial of political power to women—that is, women's exclusion from voting, officeholding, and other forms of direct political participation in most of the United States. In celebrating men's sacrifices on battlefields as the highest form of patriotism, women-centered nationalists also tacitly reinforced women's official exclusion from military service and therefore from first-class citizenship.[8]

Apart from possessing the above-mentioned characteristics, women-centered nationalism constitutes a spectrum. That nationalism's boldest forms, developed mostly by African Americans in the 1890s, presented women as potential leaders of races and nations, and generated histories focused on women and not merely inclusive of them. In keeping with the wealth and power commanded by propertied white men relative to other men, most of the white women found in this book practiced conservative forms of women-centered nationalism. Those forms deferred to men, past and present, in the practice of politics, while imparting considerable cultural and moral influence to women and to female institutions. Demonstrating further that women-centered nationalism accommodated a range of attitudes toward women's political activism are its adherents' invocations of "home," itself a multivalent concept. In the late nineteenth and early twentieth centuries, "home" evoked seemingly nonpolitical pursuits, such as wifehood and motherhood, and often promoted women's exclusion from political activism. Yet the trope of home also accommodated such activism. Home had nationalist implications, in distinguishing "us" from the "them" outside a nation's borders, in addition to its possessing a lengthy American lineage as a political institution.[9] Originating with the American Revolution, the concept of republican motherhood had declared a woman's patriotic education of her sons to be a form of political participation. Subsequent generations redefined the home beyond a dwelling's four walls and redefined the sons in question to mean the community at large.[10] Even those conservative women who located women in the home, then, were not necessarily renouncing the notion of female political engagement. As Americans had done for generations, such women were infusing the work done within—and outside—their own family circles with political importance, though ultimately positioning men as first-class citizens.

Combined with communism's triumph in Russia, World War I (1914–1918) radicalized—to the right—Americans who had already considered themselves patriots. Those Americans intensified their support for the male-dominated state. Many such women deemphasized the values of women-centered nationalism, which emphasized female cultural and moral authority, in favor of a men-centered nationalism that reassigned cultural and moral authority to men. I use the term "men-centered" here instead of "manly" or "masculine" because the women in question assigned increasing cultural significance to men and masculinity within their nations without wanting to become or resemble men themselves. To a new degree, men-centered nationalists treasured men in the present—men in military uniform and in new federal surveillance agencies, as well as the men who headed movements for African American civil rights and black nationalism—in addition to history's warriors. Some women who subscribed to men-centered nationalism relocated women at large on nationalism's sidelines. Others repudiated, in patriotism's name, longtime patterns of female cooperation. Yet, in contrast to some male contemporaries who believed that women's relationship to the nation should focus on reproducing it, women who believed in men-centered nationalism maintained that female political activism, within and outside the home, was vital to nationalism—as long as that activism directly served male-dominated entities such as the security state.

GROUPS OF PROPERTIED WOMEN were not the only nationalists, patriots, or supporters of the American state to communicate using symbols or material culture, including such everyday objects as furniture and food.[11] Making the work of female nationalists especially distinctive, and feminine according to its historical contexts, were its focus on the past, its emphasis on young and popular audiences, and its incorporation of foremothers, as well as forefathers, into its history and commemoration work. The results of women's labors—monuments, plaques, and flags that suffused cities and towns of all sizes—transformed the abstractions of nationalism (an imagined set of relations) into practices and helped draw the "island communities" of yore into the increasingly interconnected United States of the twentieth century.[12] Tensions among local, regional, sectional, and national loyalties were always alive even among these dedicated individuals—a major reason they constantly exhorted and Americanized each other. Precisely because they stood in the long shadows of civil war, the women made strenuous efforts to create harmony among local, regional, and national loyalties.

Despite their widespread opposition to formal political power for women, women nationalists often encountered resistance to their political influence and cultural authority. I do not intend my book's focus on women to belittle men's nationalism. Men invented such familiar American patriotic rituals as the Pledge of Allegiance to the American flag (1892) and Negro History Week (1926) (later Black History Month).[13] Exclusively male by definition, Union and Confederate veterans' organizations shaped Civil War memory and thereby the terms of national unity, in addition to ideals of manliness shared by both men and women.[14] The activities and beliefs of women who focused on nation harmonized enough with those of like-minded men for male nationalism and female nationalism to relate as overlapping circles. Women popularized male-invented holidays and rituals, and women and men both presented soldiers' sacrifices—sacrifices that women were barred from making—as patriotism's epitome. Like the various forms of nationalism practiced by women, men's nationalisms accommodated plural, conflicting ideas, notably regarding the relationship between women and nation. Some men strictly distinguished male patriotism from female domesticity.[15] Others, such as members of the Sons of the American Revolution (SAR) (formed in 1889), valued politically active women as nationalists to the point of collaborating with them, even as followers—sharing women-centered nationalism's regard for female political activism.[16]

Such overlaps notwithstanding, female nationalism in the early twentieth century merits a discrete study because of its demonstration of women's political agency; its creation of and reliance on all-female, amateur institutions; and its faith in the potency of organized women. Moreover, the areas of disagreement between women nationalists and male contemporaries are meaningful ones. Women—conservatives and progressives alike—rejected en masse the notion that women best served their nations by producing more babies and eschewing political activism. In the 1900s President Theodore Roosevelt's manifestos on masculinity had white Anglo-Saxon men combating softness in themselves and their nation by fighting for the United States's new imperial mission. Ideally, white Anglo-Saxon women would cast aside their commitments to higher education and to club life, and other distractions from the home, in favor of the large families their grandmothers had known. Also focusing definitions of female nationalism on female fertility, African American male commentators feared that falling birth rates among middle-class black women would bring about black "race suicide."[17]

STUDIES OF U.S. NATIONALISM, patriotism, and imperialism have focused on the doings of crowds, literary and scientific texts, photography on both sides of the camera, patterns of consumption, and the workings of government.[18] I base my own study of nationalism on women's voluntary associations. Especially among white Americans, female patriotic groups exceeded similar groups of men in size and dedication.[19] More important, female voluntary organizations constituted the principal vehicles of women's political activity, self-education, and thought in the late nineteenth- and early twentieth-century United States—when "the family claim" and careers for women were considered mutually exclusive, particularly in white America.[20] The political importance of women's associations, notably to progressive reform, has led scholars to expand their understandings of American political participation.[21]

An additional reason to base a study of early twentieth-century nationalism on organized women is that volunteers and their organizations dominated the translation of nationalism's ideas into everyday practice in the United States. Unlike in contemporary Europe, where governments spearheaded the "invention of tradition" so crucial to fostering national loyalties, the American initiative in historic preservation, commemoration, and efforts to assimilate the foreign-born almost always came from outside the state and—until the 1910s—from amateurs.[22] Not until World War I did the federal government begin pursuing the Americanization of immigrants. Only starting in the 1930s did the government take the lead in preserving the built environment or in systematically marking the landscape with monuments.[23] Some boundaries between volunteers and the state were permeable—as in the case of the numerous cabinet officers, members of Congress, state legislators, and local officials who were married to white women active in patriotic organizations. In addition to using family connections to advance their organizations' agenda, these wives and female relatives of political elites articulated "official" versions of history, infused with state-based patriotism, similar to those disseminated directly by governments.[24] However, the exclusion of most women from most forms of direct political participation in the early twentieth century—especially east of the Mississippi River—positions the patriotic work of even the most privileged women firmly outside the state.

WITHIN THE SPRAWLING COSMOS of women's associations at the turn of the twentieth century, a constellation of white-led groups sought to produce patriotism. My study emphasizes that constellation's brightest, largest stars—the Woman's Relief Corps (WRC) (formed in 1883), the Daughters of the American Revolution (DAR) (1890), and the United Daughters of the Confederacy (UDC) (1894)—because of their large memberships and nationwide reach and because of those organizations' explicit focus on cultivating national and American identity.[25] Women in those groups also participated in better-known women's movements for temperance; for spreading Protestant Christianity worldwide; for social reforms; in support of both major political parties; and for and against woman suffrage.[26]

Another basis for my analysis of women's nationalism is the National Association of Colored Women (NACW) (formed in 1896), the sole national network of black women's clubs before 1935. Numbering around 100,000 women at their collective peak in the 1920s, the NACW's constituent clubs did not self-consciously dedicate themselves to fostering American nationalism or patriotism.[27] They focused most on aiding and culturally "uplifting" the black poor. Treating the NACW umbrella as an exemplar of women's nationalism is potentially problematic also because of the national leadership's conservative turn in the 1900s. Subscribers to Booker T. and Margaret Murray Washington's advocacy of practical education, racial self-help, and friendly relations with whites came to dominate the organization, resulting in a loss of interest by many, mostly northerners, who were militantly critical of both Jim Crow and black male leaders.[28] This shift shaped the NACW's stances on the relationship between women and nationalism. The NACW and its internal struggles nevertheless show how a broad cross-section of middle-class black women located themselves within American and "Negro" nations. Especially significant for both kinds of nationalism, American and black, is the clubwomen's development of black history for popular audiences and young people. The NACW's history work and commemorations anticipated the activities of the Association for the Study of Negro Life and History (ASNLH) (1915) by two decades.[29]

Although black and white women nationalists generally worked separately, they should still be studied together. Women of both races articulated forms of nationalism that positioned women as cultural authorities and, later, forms of nationalism that conferred both cultural and political authority on contemporary men. Women of both races also assumed their own social and cultural superiority to others of their races, infusing womanliness with both race- and class-specific meanings.[30] The women measured their own and others' class standing in education, documentable American ancestry (in the case of many white women), and light complectedness (in the case of some black women), as well as in personal or family wealth. Appearances of sexual respectability also communicated middle-class, bourgeois, or upper-class standing—a major reason that married women in this story usually veiled themselves in their husbands' names when appearing in print. The meanings the women attributed to those intangibles and tangibles gave them the self-confidence to approach the masses of their respective races—men as well as children and other women—in order to uplift them culturally and morally.[31] Simultaneously, in 1913, black club leaders and white Daughters condemned as threats to their nations the Turkey Trot dance and other excrescences of a rambunctious, comparatively interracial youth culture.[32] Not coincidentally, that youth culture would later constitute a potent form of defiance of clubwomen's cultural authority.

Nevertheless, dominating the history of American women and nationalism are sharp differences regarding the content of the national community. Though so dedicated to unity, the white women in this story depended on and, indeed, deepened a profound division among Americans. The history of women and nationalism in the early twentieth-century United States is also a history of "race women." A term used by African Americans to express racial fidelity and commitment to racial justice, it also communicates many white women's Anglo-Saxonist pride, which sometimes amounted to a transnationalism stretching across the Atlantic.[33] White women's nationalism, and ruling definitions of national unity in general, walked hand in hand with Jim Crow.[34] That amalgam of legal apartheid and racial violence characterizing southern life between the 1890s and 1960s endured only with the approval of the federal government and the tolerance of white Americans nationwide. That combination of approval and tolerance made Jim Crow a truly national phenomenon, as did the state's own expansion of Jim Crow in the 1910s.[35] With the exception of nonsouthern contingents of the WRC, who were dedicated to commemorating the Union struggle, women's organizations concerned with nation practiced racial segregation—even, in some cases, excluding African Americans altogether—in order to reconcile North and South. In Jim Crow America, white women worked with white women, and black women with black women, to foster patriotism. Yet the connections between white women's nationalism and white women's racism are deeper than the fact of separateness from African Americans. Except for small numbers of pro-Union women whose American nation embraced all those loyal to the United States during the Civil War, the white women in this book generally viewed their nations—American or Confederate—as commensurate with their own race. Even pro-Union northerners reached out to ex- and neo-Confederates because the latter were white, but not to southerners of both races who had supported the United States in the 1860s. White women's actions confirm that Jim Crow was more than a masculine offensive by Democratic white men that subjugated white women in addition to victimizing people of color. White women, North and South, also imposed Jim Crow.[36]

Agreeing that a combination of race and documented bloodlines denoted Americanness, many white women based American national belonging on descent rather than consent—a tendency that too many scholars of nationalism have located east of the Rhine and far from the United States.[37] The Confederate States of America died in 1865, and Confederate nationalism gradually died with it. Subsequent generations of white southerners articulated ideas that constitute a discrete and therefore neo-Confederate nationalism.[38] Peaking at 100,000 members nationwide in 1924, the mostly white, hereditarian UDC was a major exemplar of race-based American nationalism, and—not coincidentally—preferred a particularly narrow variant of women-centered nationalism.[39] Among the organizations featured in this book, the UDC was alone in its refusal ever to endorse women's voting rights before they became national in 1920. The organization's consistent regard for contemporary white Democratic politicians in addition to Confederate warriors anticipated the men-centered nationalism adopted by other women nationalists in the 1910s. Yet for all its countenancing of white male supremacy, the UDC's transformations of southern everyday life, patriotic rituals, and landscapes make it vital to the history of women-centered nationalism. By planting formidable numbers of monuments (800 in the UDC's first thirty years), by funding educations for white descendants of Confederates, and by "catechizing" similar children, the women aspired to unite the white South into a national community.[40] Stopping short of reviving the notion of national independence, the women and allied male organizations demanded sovereignty for that community within the United States and regard for that community as particularly American and patriotic. Yet the prospect of living as Americans within an American nation-state with an American national destiny created apprehension among militant neo-Confederates.[41] Especially before World War I, such women placed allegiance to nation in tension with allegiance to the contemporary state.

White women also espoused a civic nationalism stressing consent— behavior, allegiance, and legal stature—rather than descent. Sometimes, the women blended civic and blood-based forms of nationalism.[42] Simultaneously stressing race, heredity, assimilation, and, most of all, support for the federal government and its policies was the mostly white DAR. Numbering 172,000 dues-paying members in 1931, the DAR embarked on pioneering historic preservation projects (250 of them in the organization's first half century) and efforts to Americanize the foreign-born.[43] To the DAR, the American nation was commensurate with the American state and empire, and patriotism therefore entailed supporting them. The organization's Americanization projects implied that immigrants from around the world and some native-born who were considered racially inferior to Anglo-Saxons (Native Americans and Mexican Americans) belonged in the national community—once they had assimilated into middle-class, Anglo American culture, down to its cooking and methods of housekeeping, and gave their allegiance to the state. The women made these determinations about national belonging from the perch of their eighteenth-century lineages—their basis for asserting the cultural and moral authority so vital to women-centered nationalism. Documenting descent from a Revolutionary fighter or supporter was required for admission to the DAR. Also demonstrating the DAR's incorporation of race-based nationalism is the organization's official exclusion, for much of the twentieth century, of "colored" women from membership—notwithstanding the presence among fighters for the American Revolution of an estimated 5,000 African Americans and of numerous whites with mixed-race descendants considered black.[44]

Such a strong commitment to race-based national unity exceeded contemporary norms. Dating from 1894, the DAR's explicit, statutory ban on black women was unique among white-led women's organizations with large, national memberships.[45] Even at Jim Crow's highest tide, most such organizations, including the WRC, stopped short of excluding African Americans altogether. The largest discrete women's clubs—the Woman's Christian Temperance Union (WCTU) (formed in 1873) and the Young Women's Christian Association (1906)—possessed multiracial if heavily segregated memberships. Also segregated, like the Protestant denominations begetting them, were women's church and mission organizations. White suffragists openly prioritized the voting rights of native-born white women at the turn of the twentieth century, yet the National American Woman Suffrage Association (1890) included small numbers of African Americans.[46]

The multiracial, white-led WRC stood for national patriotism, meaning loyalty to the recently reunified United States. The WRC was, with 118,000 members in 1894, second in size only to the WCTU among discrete women's organizations before 1900.[47] In popularizing Memorial Day, placing American flags in U.S. classrooms, and performing charity work among needy Union veterans, the nonhereditary WRC focused simultaneously on remembering the Union dead and on forging national unity with allegiance to the Stars and Stripes as the glue.[48] Its status as an auxiliary to organized Union veterans and its members' resulting solicitousness of those veterans' sensibilities help explain why the WRC preferred a conservative type of women-centered nationalism. In the 1890s and 1900s the organization's white leaders increasingly favored race-based definitions of national unity—emphasizing outreach to the white South while increasing racial segregation within the organization. That pro-Union white women, dedicated to remembering loyalty to the United States, concurred in the newly dominant, race-based definitions of national unity demonstrates Jim Crow's truly national reach and its value to white Americans who were seeking to build national unity. So do the considerable numbers of women who belonged both to the DAR and to the UDC, despite those organizations' opposing views of the contemporary state.[49]

Given white women's conflation of race with nation, African American clubwomen insisted fervently on their own Americanness or cultivated other national identities altogether. The "twoness" experienced by those both "Negro" and "American," articulated most famously by W. E. B. Du Bois in *The Souls of Black Folk* (1903), troubled his black female contemporaries.[50] Many insisted that their nation and their country were the same — an assumption also central to the nascent African American civil rights movement. Separating patriotism from conformity or obedience, and American heritage from white bloodlines, black women who adhered to American civic nationalism struggled against forms of nationalism based on race. The women instead embraced the Reconstruction-era definition of national belonging as birth on U.S. soil. Although black women did often call attention to ancestors who had fought for the United States, they did not usually view their American lineages — often centuries old — as bases of class or cultural superiority to others.[51] Black women's American civic nationalism could and did accommodate criticisms of the state. Other women subscribed to black nationalism in two forms: the strand that focused on "racial self-determination" within the United States and, increasingly, a transnationalism that sought psychic if not actual separation from the United States.[52] Adherents of both these forms of black nationalism distinguished their nation from their country and were therefore critical of the American state. Especially following the First World War, proponents of black transnationalism criticized identifying with the United States in general. Notwithstanding its Jamaican leadership and its international membership, which numbered in the millions in the 1920s, the officially all-black Universal Negro Improvement Association (UNIA) (formed in 1914) was most popular in African

America.[53] These followers of Marcus Garvey desired a race-based community that would ultimately unite under a red, black, and green flag in an African Zion.

MANY WORKS ON NATIONALISM in the United States have unquestioningly focused on male thinkers, political and military leaders, and war veterans—either underplaying or omitting women's early leadership in forging a national past for the United States and in enjoining immigrants' Americanization with a view to the nation's future.[54] The vast scholarship on women's activism in the early twentieth-century United States has had relatively little to say about nationalism or patriotism, especially conservative and/or state-based varieties.[55] Scholars of those women who organized to support existing political orders have focused usually outside the United States.[56] Conversely, discussions of women's nationalism that was opposed to such orders have been both plentiful and fruitful.[57]

Likely reasons for most scholars' cursory treatment of U.S. women's nationalism in the twentieth century are the unsavory meanings many modern-day progressives attach to American patriotic symbols and the U.S. right's use of such symbols as red, white, and blue cudgels from the First World War onward.[58] Women nationalists' bold assumption of authority regarding cultural matters and their simultaneous discomfort with female political authority challenge whiggish trajectories that have early twentieth-century clubwomen progressing from reform work to organized feminism and woman suffragism. Many African Americans did follow such paths. On the other hand, many white women asserted considerable political agency as organized women in estrangement from—and sometimes in opposition to—contemporary movements for women's rights.[59]

My study of black women's national identities contributes an exploration of African Americans' attachment to the United States. Works on African Americans' relationship with nation before the 1960s have focused overwhelmingly on black nationalism's strands of racial self-determination within the United States, pan-Africanism (solidarity with the worldwide, African-descended diaspora), and emigrationism (African Americans' desire to separate—mentally and/or physically—from the United States).[60]

Highlighting black women's American civic nationalism expands the range of meanings of American patriotic symbols, in addition to broadening perceptions of black women's activism. While many white Americans redefined national patriotism as political conformity, especially after the First World War, the American flag as interpreted by black women expressed defiance of Jim Crow—a political order that sought their own and other blacks' de-Americanization.[61]

INSPIRING THIS BOOK's chapter titles are female nationalism's backdrops —the United States's own successive incarnations in the early twentieth century. Each incarnation built on the one preceding it. Chapter 1, "The Nation," presents conflicting definitions of national unity. In the 1890s, national patriotism, state-based nationalism, neo-Confederate nationalism, American civic nationalism, black nationalism, and the female entities promoting them all constituted pronouncements on Civil War memory.[62] All these entities also stressed women's cultural and moral authority within their respective nations. Some black women went further and, in their anger at many black men's accommodation of Jim Crow, conferred political authority on women within their nations. The next chapter, "The Empire," examines the effects on organized women's nationalism of the United States's transformation from a land empire into an overseas empire with distant "possessions." The imperial wars against Spain and against the Filipino independence movement convinced white women that their own patriotic activism was valuable—to the point that the women developed an imperialism that positioned white women as civilizers. Yet the wars simultaneously reduced organized women's sense of their own patriotic importance relative to men in uniform.

The third chapter, "The State," discusses the incorporation of progressive reforms into nationalist women's programs in the period preceding World War I. White women who explicitly focused their activism on nation, and black clubwomen with nation on their minds, infused nationalism and patriotism with two major tenets of early twentieth-century reform: the effectiveness of the state and the possibility of human progress and change. Female nationalists' reform work fits within the history of gendered, women-centered nationalism because of that work's focus on youth and — in the DAR's attempts to Americanize adult men as well — its positioning of women as makers of civilization. However, progressive reform also accommodated a nationalism that, more than ever, associated citizenship and patriotism with manhood. The national emergence of a national, mixed-sex, male-led movement for black civil rights, most notably in the form of the National Association for the Advancement of Colored People (NAACP) (organized in 1909), helped foreclose black women's aspirations to leadership of the race — moral, cultural, or political.

In chapter 4, "The War," I argue that the First World War and the Russian Revolution thoroughly radicalized many American women and caused a regendering of women's nationalism. White women's men-centered nationalism did not entail the repudiation of female activism outside the home, as long as women acted in support of male-headed entities, most notably the state. Exclusions of black men from combat and of black women from volunteering overseas as nurses, in turn, helped cause many black women to subscribe to a black nationalism that conferred cultural, moral, and political leadership on men. The book's final chapter, "The Security State," shows organized women's tightening embrace of the men-centered nationalism that, for the most part, continued to accept the political activism of right-minded women while increasingly casting present-day men as shapers of patriotic culture and of patriotic morality. State-based nationalists in the DAR, in particular, turned against female reformers, with whom they had formerly collaborated, as threats to their nation. Within men-centered nationalism, white and black women articulated opposing perspectives on the government's new peacetime surveillance, which was intended to create opposition to leftism and to peace activism in the population, with white women (except for neo-Confederates) as surveillance's cheerleaders and black women among surveillance's targets.[63] Disagreements were intraracial as well as interracial. Civil rights–minded black clubwomen fiercely contested the notion that the United States was a white person's country — a belief of both Garveyite black nationalists and the revived Ku Klux Klan.

This history of women and nationalism closes in the 1930s. That decade saw the beginning of the end of Jim Crow and the decline of organized women's cultural authority regarding matters of nation. DAR leaders took Jim

Crow custom a step too far, in the eyes of many white contemporaries, when they excluded nonwhite artists from the stage of their new auditorium— Washington's largest. The black opera singer Marian Anderson's ensuing outdoor concert at the Lincoln Memorial in 1939 resuscitated an old Civil War patriotism that valued loyalty to the United States over race. Commentators as otherwise diverse as Eleanor Roosevelt and the black politico Mary McLeod Bethune forged new links between American patriotism and democracy. The women-centered nationalism so noticeable at the twentieth century's turn would never again command the same influence. Women's patriotic organizations and concerns as such did not disband or disappear, but an epoch that worshipped at experts' and professionals' feet belittled female amateurs to a new degree. Marginalized alongside the multiple incarnations of women's nationalism, until recently, have been the women and others well outside the American state who influenced profoundly political questions of nation; an appreciation of a nationalism that communicated in symbols and was often deeply sentimental (in both the emotional and the literary senses of the word); and an understanding of how women in Jim Crow America could simultaneously hail themselves as "High Priestess[es] of Patriotism" while enforcing sex and gender hierarchies—with no awareness of contradiction.[64]

Chapter One
The Nation

U.S. WOMEN BEGAN engaging in sustained patriotic activity in peacetime only in the nineteenth century's closing decades.[1] Before, women had organized as patriots in response to wars that demanded significant sacrifices from civilian populations. In the American Revolution and the Civil War, women supplied armies with funds, food, clothing, and their own labor in the absence of modern-day military supply networks.[2] Occasionally— as commemorated lovingly by early twentieth-century clubwomen—women themselves engaged in warfare. Some disguised themselves as men, as did the Revolutionary soldier Deborah Sampson, and some did not, as in the cases of numerous white and black Civil War spies and of Hannah Duston— hailed in Puritan New England for the numerous Indian scalps she brought with her in escaping capture.[3]

An apparent exception to the pattern of wartime female patriotism was the Mount Vernon Ladies' Association of the Union (MVLA). Ann Pamela Cunningham, a thirty-eight-year-old South Carolina planter's daughter with Unionist sympathies, formed this small organization of wealthy white women in 1854 in order to buy George Washington's adult home in Virginia and convert it into an inspirational house museum. A national network, the MVLA was the first of many female associations to purchase property deemed historically significant and to convert that property into a symbol intended to unify a nation.[4] These innovators directly inspired the women's nationalism of later decades. Ellen Hardin Walworth, for example, raised funds for

Mount Vernon in the 1870s and helped organize the DAR in 1890.[5] Much later, a president of the NACW called on "all patriotic, race-loving Negroes" to fund the renovation of Frederick Douglass's house into a house museum, just as "the white women saved the home of George Washington."[6] Whether MVLA women constituted peacetime patriots, however, is doubtful. The MVLA formed in response to sectional tensions that made many Americans anticipate civil war. The group therefore constituted a response to a national emergency.

AT THE TWENTIETH CENTURY'S turn, organized women were still debating how the United States should reunite after the Civil War. Ultimately winning the day was the desire of white women who favored national patriotism (attachment to the contemporary, reunified United States) and state-based nationalism to unify the nation on two bases—white supremacy and loyalty to the federal government and its laws. This race- and class-specific form of reunion assumed African Americans' political subordination in the past and in the present. Omitted from this rapprochement was the argument of militant neo-Confederates that the Confederate struggle was the sole epitome of American patriotism at the time of the Civil War. Also rejected were the entreaties of black women and shrinking numbers of white women who believed that North and South should reconcile along the lines of consistent loyalty to the United States instead of race. In an increasingly hostile racial climate, it became clear that white northerners and the federal government considered white southerners, including ex- and neo-Confederates, indispensable to the new nation and accepted African Americans' political debasement. Ultimately, black women disagreed with each other on the extent to which they should identify primarily as Americans. The study and production of black history, concerning African-descended people in the United States, bridged that intraracial division. The women's histories communicated that African Americans had long belonged to their country, and the country to them—a belief of black women who identified primarily and emphatically as Americans—while simultaneously fostering a race pride congenial to black nationalists.

Recent works on national reunion following the Civil War have included women's perspectives in addition to men's. Nevertheless, this literature focuses heavily on men's pronouncements. Organized women's struggles over the question of North-South reunion merit discussion in themselves in part because those struggles produced distinctively gendered forms of nationalism. The women and others considered young people and the past to be women's concerns. Moreover, in placing women among U.S. history's actors, the women prolonged a flourishing tradition in which amateur historians wrote about women.[7] Unlike subsequent generations, these Victorians lacked any sense of making history's women (those resembling themselves) visible. Women had not been invisible to them in the first place.

ANTECEDENTS FOR THE multiple forms of women's nationalism of the late nineteenth century, and the conversations and contests among them, extend back before the Civil War. Black clubwomen's debates on American identity possess the lengthiest pedigree of the strands of nationalism discussed in this book. In the antebellum North, even where slavery was banned, Fourth of July celebrations often culminated in white-on-black mob violence. The abolitionist and ex-slave Frederick Douglass renounced celebrating the Fourth of July in 1852, in the wake of the Fugitive Slave Act and other actions by a federal government he regarded as in the grasp of slaveholders. African Americans' patriotism toward the United States intensified with the end of slavery and with Reconstruction, however. With the first wave of emancipation in 1863, Douglass reclaimed the Fourth of July, positioning it alongside the Emancipation Proclamation's anniversary (January 1) in importance.[8]

Among black women, Union patriotism flowed easily into national patriotism. In 1867 a recently freed woman in Richmond, Virginia, urged her white teacher to display an American flag in the schoolroom, offering her own for the purpose. Following her speech, her classmates proposed a monument to Abraham Lincoln, and the women began throwing coins into a box. In the North, on Memorial Day, 1870, the Colored Women's Lincoln Aid Society of Philadelphia laid the cornerstone of a monument, projected to cost two thousand dollars, to those black men "who fell fighting to perpetuate our glorious Union."[9] Those efforts at monuments, however, came to nothing. They likely foundered, as black men's monument-building proposals often did, on the rocks of other needs: the difficulties of raising funds from a comparatively poor population; an absence of government aid (which was readily available to white commemoration efforts in later years); and ongoing debates on the appropriateness of devoting emotional and financial resources to remembering an often painful past.[10] However, the women's commemoration proposals are significant for the desires they expressed. The Richmond students and the Colored Women's Lincoln Aid Society wanted to leave permanent marks on the landscape to remind passersby of history—in this case, the Union dead, black and white—and to produce among passersby an American national identity that emphasized behavior over blood.

Later in the nineteenth century, organized black women, as such, began articulating an American civic nationalism and a black nationalism that both promoted the cultural authority of women. Black women's associations, like white women's associations, originated shortly after the American Revolution. The Colored Women's Lincoln Aid Society was among hundreds of groups formed during the early and mid-nineteenth century.[11] In the early 1890s, African Americans embarked on two additional waves of organizing— local and, for the first time, national. A major reason for these waves was the surge of racial hostility in the South, in the form of both laws and violence, marking the creation of Jim Crow.[12] A northern lecture tour by Ida B. Wells—the journalist, born enslaved in Mississippi, whose debunking of connections between lynchings and black-on-white rape kept her from returning south for thirty years—inspired numerous additional clubs to form in 1892 and 1893. These clubs and older ones coalesced into national umbrella organizations based in Washington, D.C., (1892), Boston (1895), and Atlanta (1895). These umbrellas then combined in Washington as the NACW in July 1896. The network expanded from a total of 5,000 members in its first year to an estimated 15,000 in 1904.[13] These were middle-class, educated, often professional women living in all parts of the country, including in the smallest of black communities.[14]

From the first, clubs under the NACW's umbrella performed educational and charitable work among the black poor and among black youth; protested both Jim Crow laws and violence, drawing attention to abuses of black women as well as of black men; socialized; and studied and commemorated black history. The needs of the black poor and black youth in Jim Crow America were formidable indeed. While Daughters of the American Revolution and neo-Confederate women often held patriotic essay contests among high school students, black clubwomen in the South struggled to develop high schools open to African Americans in the first place—they were nonexistent there before the 1920s.[15] While Daughters of the Confederacy stocked southern libraries with histories that met their approval, black women focused on establishing southern libraries that African Americans could enter.[16]

These and other indignities sharpened differences of opinion among African Americans regarding whether their nation was their country or their race. Some in the 1890s considered emigrating to Africa or Europe and shedding American attachments altogether. A few actually took flight.[17] Ida B. Wells was one of many who believed that racial injustice was not so un-American after all, when she characterized lynchings as "so peculiarly national."[18] Other women, however, refused to acknowledge any tension between their American and black identities, seeing in the language of national patriotism a challenge to Jim Crow (which, in contrast, was undergirded by pro-Confederate views of U.S. history) and in American ideals a refutation of contemporary racial injustice. In her twenties, when teaching on isolated St. John's Island, South Carolina, the future club leader Mamie Garvin (later Fields) put American patriotism's symbols to use. On the last day of school, her white predecessor merely had the youngsters sing and dance in their own style ("dance Sam") and invited other whites to take in the entertainment. Garvin's response to "dancing Sam"'s implied nostalgia for plantation life was to create, with her black colleague, a closing-day celebration infused with the Stars and Stripes. Aghast that her hundred-odd students had never been taught "America the Beautiful" ("Would you believe it?") or the Pledge of Allegiance, she made a special trip to Charleston, by train and ferry, to obtain an American flag. On the last day of school in 1910, Garvin and her colleague had the children put on a show, made them uniforms out of tissue paper, and led them in singing "America the Beautiful." "My school was in the United States, after all, and not the Confederacy," she recalled.[19]

THE BLACK CLUB movement's history work appealed to both American civic nationalists and black nationalists. Amateur historians among women were not the first to generate black history. Starting in the eighteenth century, African American men and women developed commemorations in the form of parades and other rituals. Often they celebrated the end of slavery elsewhere, such as in the British Empire in 1834.[20] In the late nineteenth century, male commentators consistently urged African Americans to engage in organized remembrance.[21] However, black clubwomen's self-education in black history in the late nineteenth century and their popularization of that history to audiences of young people are important in themselves. Black women's history work expressed a strikingly women-centered nationalism that positioned women as cultural, moral, and sometimes political authorities in relation to their nations.

The Washington-based writer, educator, and club founder Anna Julia Cooper, born into slavery in North Carolina, scorned in 1892 what she viewed as black men's accommodationism and failure to protect the race. "You do not find the colored woman selling her birthright for a mess of pottage," the thirty-four-year-old wrote, alluding to black men in the South who voted Democratic. She praised otherwise "ignorant" black women there who left their husbands for doing so. "[The colored woman] has been known to cling blindly with the instinct of a turtle dove to those principles and policies which to her mind promise hope and safety for children yet unborn," Cooper wrote. Her polemic, *A Voice from the South*, situated women as African America's moral exemplars and as potential cultural leaders of the United States at large.[22] The Boston editor and club leader Josephine St. Pierre Ruffin, born free in that city, reflected in 1894 on a white woman's successful effort to defeat an antilynching resolution at a national meeting of Unitarians: "America stands impotent and Europe amazed at the barbarous state of affairs in the Southern states of America. The protestations of black men have in most cases fallen flat and almost unnoticed. Is it not possible it has been left to black women to bring about the moral reform so urgently needed?"[23]

In addition to viewing women as potential national leaders, black clubwomen's nationalism in the 1890s was women-centered because of its attention to women's history, as when one woman praised Harriet Tubman as a "Black Joan of Arc."[24] A teacher in Washington, Josephine Beall Wilson Bruce was married to Senator Blanche K. Bruce of Mississippi, one of the last black southern members of Congress before the 1960s. She was also prominent in that city's Ladies' Auxiliary. In 1896 the club's "literary feature" focused almost entirely on women—Sojourner Truth, Harriet Tubman, and the eighteenth-century poet Phillis Wheatley—in order to increase members' knowledge of black history in general and of "the valorous lives and self-sacrificing deeds of those in their own ranks." The only man on Bruce's list was the slave Crispus Attucks, one of five Bostonians gunned down by British troops in 1770.[25]

Black clubwomen on both sides of the double-consciousness divide also emphasized outreach to young people—another earmark of women-centered nationalism. One club inspired into existence by Ida B. Wells's lecture tour was the Woman's Loyal Union of Brooklyn, New York. It was organized in October 1892 by thirty-one-year-old Victoria Earle Matthews, a journalist who had been born into slavery in Georgia. Declaring itself (in its motto) "Vigilant, Patriotic, Steadfast," the Woman's Loyal Union, and Matthews most conspicuously, devoted themselves to simultaneously protesting contemporary civil rights abuses and disseminating "race literature," African Americans' histories and writings about themselves.[26] Matthews announced in 1894 her plans for a "series of . . . historical primers for the youth of the race, which will . . . show that [the African] and his descendants have been prominently identified with every phase of this country's history including the landing of Columbus."[27] In 1897 Matthews helped establish the White Rose Mission, a New York settlement house catering to young black women. In addition to social services, the White Rose Mission offered "classes in race history" taught by Matthews.[28]

Women-centered nationalism's challenges to male political supremacy were inherently limited. Though they honored past women and criticized male contemporaries, women-centered nationalists who were black also lionized men as warriors and as historical heroes. Immediately following the NACW's inaugural meeting in Washington in July 1896, twenty delegates made a pilgrimage to Cedar Hill, the Anacostia home of Frederick Douglass, who had died the year before. At a time when historic sites controlled by women were unknown apart from Mount Vernon, the clubwomen announced their intentions to convert Cedar Hill into "a Mecca to which pilgrimages may be made"—an effort that would finally bear fruit two decades later.[29] More fundamentally, women pointed to men's self-sacrifice on battlefields when they argued that African Americans should be treated as the U.S. citizens they were. Standing before the Berlin consulate, the young Mary Church (later Terrell) solidified her decision to return to the United States on the basis of male ancestors who had died in every American war. Their deaths had made the United States "my country; I have a perfect right to love it and I will."[30]

Most of black women's history work in the 1890s and 1900s concerned abolitionism, the Civil War, Emancipation, and Reconstruction. The primacy of war and of political officeholding helps explain why the women focused on great men. Most of the subjects that the Boston novelist and clubwoman Pauline E. Hopkins chose for her series "Famous Men of the Negro Race" (1900–1901)—aimed at youth—were either abolitionists, Union fighters, or southern, Reconstruction-era politicians.[31] Dedicated to "the study of race history and literature among the young people," as well as by its own members, the Rose of New England Women's League in Norwich, Connecticut, brought in a Union veteran, then working as a "letter carrier" in New Bedford, Massachusetts, to speak to its class of young people in 1904. The women heralded William H. Carney as "the hero of Ft. Wagner."[32] New Englanders knew Fort Wagner, South Carolina, as the place where the Massachusetts Fifty-fourth had famously fought and died, by the score, in July 1863. However, in designating a black man "the hero," the Norwich women consciously deviated from the usual emphasis on the martyrdom of the white Boston Brahmin officer Robert Gould Shaw. Legend had it among black commentators that Carney had borne an American flag throughout the battle despite being severely wounded, and that he had told hospital workers before collapsing, "'The old flag never touched the ground, boys!'"[33]

Black women also occasionally eulogized white men who had been opposed to racism, in part to delegitimize the conviction of white unity that undergirded race-based American nationalism. Ten years before the all-male Niagara Movement celebrated the militance of John Brown—most famous for his doomed attempt in 1859 to foster slave uprisings—Mrs. T. H. Lyles of St. Paul, Minnesota, labored in his memory.[34] Too incendiary a figure to be honored by most white commemorators, Brown was considered by Lyles to epitomize "Christ-like" unselfishness. Most fundamentally, his actions at Harpers Ferry created the catalyst that ended slavery.[35] In August 1894 Lyles incorporated the John Brown Memorial Association, which intended to fund a monument for Brown's "neglected and sunken" grave in upstate New York. The governor of Minnesota offered matching funds if Lyles raised a certain amount of money.[36]

Her monument-raising efforts met with frustration after she approached black clubwomen for help in 1895. Those most interested in black history in the 1890s generally lived in the North; they prized access to elite institutions, notably to educations in the humanities; and they prioritized political rights for African Americans. More influential among clubwomen, in keeping with their focus on the black poor, were Booker T. Washington's and Margaret Murray Washington's notions of industrial education and racial self-help. With the exception of Victoria Earle Matthews, who simultaneously valued black history instruction, social service work, and other ideas of the Washingtons, that school of thought often considered "book learning" and especially the expending of scarce financial resources on statuary to be of questionable practicality.[37] The National Colored Women's Congress of Atlanta persuaded Lyles that a more suitable way to "show our esteem" for John Brown than a "marble tribute" would be to establish an "industrial training school and home for indigent colored boys" in the South in his memory. After the National Colored Women's Congress joined the NACW in 1896, NACW leaders were raising funds for the project, which was intended to honor not only Brown but his "faithful followers" at Harpers Ferry. The project was eventually aborted, however, in favor of other social welfare projects.[38] Ultimately, black women producing black history devoted much of it to praising famous men. Even in "the woman's era" of the 1890s—the high-water mark of women-centered nationalists' imputation of authority to women—most such activists conferred political power and true patriotic leadership on male warriors and heroes, black and white.

THE LATE NINETEENTH CENTURY saw white women launch massive patriotic mobilizations. Organizations formed that, unlike the NACW, devoted themselves to fostering both loyalty and unity—neo-Confederate nationalism, in the case of the UDC; national patriotism, in the case of the WRC; and state-based nationalism, in the case of the DAR. All of these schools of thought made pronouncements regarding the terms of North-South reunion and regarding the importance of women to nationalism. Initiating these discussions were white southerners who had supported the Confederacy.

By the time the UDC organized as such in 1894, many of the local organizations that became its chapters were nearly a generation old. Across the South, "ladies' memorial associations" had begun forming on the heels of Appomattox to maintain the graves of Confederate dead and, in some cases, to arrange for the reburial of those dead in their communities of origin. The women's ritualized remembrances evolved into Decoration Day, or Confederate Memorial Day. Some women sought also to create permanent reminders of the Confederate cause. The Ladies' Memorial Association of Augusta, Georgia, formed in 1868, unveiled a seventy-six-foot Confederate monument ten years later—having raised an impressive $18,000.[39] As early as 1866, ladies' memorial associations lobbied southern state legislatures for funds for their work.[40] All of these projects presented Confederates as Americanism's true heirs and protectors.

Working independently alongside the men's groups that gradually took shape as the United Confederate Veterans (UCV) (formed in 1889) and the Sons of Confederate Veterans (SCV) (1896), numerous local and state-level associations of women coalesced in September 1894 into the National Daughters of the Confederacy, which was renamed the United Daughters of the Confederacy the next year.[41] The UDC admitted Confederate veterans' white female kin, women who themselves had served the Confederacy, and both groups' documented female descendants—provided that each applicant could demonstrate her own personal acceptability by gaining current members' assent, usually in the form of signatures.[42] Among those linked to famous Confederate women was Louisa Cheves McCord Smythe of Charleston, South Carolina, president of the UDC in the mid-1900s. Smythe's mother had been the proslavery commentator Louisa McCord, famous in the 1850s for excoriating abolitionists and women's rights activists in the pages of De Bow's Review and other periodicals.[43] Considering that the desire for a white, socially prestigious organization was so basic as to leave it implicit, the UDC's founders intended the personal acceptability requirement to exclude not nonwhite or lower-class southerners but white northerners married to Confederate veterans.[44] These restrictions kept UDC numbers relatively low by the standards of national women's clubs—over 20,000 in 1900.[45]

The neo-Confederate movement drew in white, mostly Protestant women from all over the South—from border states as well as from the old Confederacy—and white southern expatriates throughout the United States.[46] Not strictly a Bourbon preserve, the movement also contained socially ambitious women from the white South's middle classes.[47] Communicating the UDC's objective of bringing upper- and middle-class women together were its elaborate social events. These allowed women who did not come from aristocratic family backgrounds to rub shoulders with those who did. Seemingly frivolous, one typical "fête" in Galveston, Texas, in 1896 featured the crowning of a five-year-old May Queen on a throne "trimmed in Confederate colors" and functioned as social glue.[48]

The neo-Confederate coalition of middle- and upper-class white women included those whose male relatives joined the new professions of the late nineteenth century and/or who participated in the South's modernization. Lost Cause activists' nostalgic approaches to the Old South did not entail opposing the South's ongoing industrialization. The Nashville-based *Confederate Veteran*, the UDC's and other neo-Confederate organizations' official periodical, reported fondly on the editor's own hobnobbing with southern business and railroad executives and resented the term "New South" for locating industrial innovations and entrepreneurial energy in the North.[49] Virginia and Georgia were the only states that outstripped Texas—where white southerners migrated in large numbers in the late nineteenth century to seek their economic fortunes—in numbers of Daughters of the Confederacy members in 1900.[50] That year, one Texas woman infused Corsicana's "five hundred oil wells" and the "enterprise" behind them with patriotic meaning.[51]

The UDC sought to produce unity among propertied white southerners as part of its broader mission to produce neo-Confederate nationalism. Neo-Confederates' frequent self-designation as "Confederates," as if the Confederacy itself still existed, communicated their intense focus on the past. As with most Lost Cause activists in the late nineteenth century, the women's fealty to the Confederacy did not revive the notion of seceding from the United States. Rather, the women sought to control perceptions of the past.[52] The UDC embodied nationalism also in contending that the Confederacy had possessed the political and cultural uniformity characteristic of a nation. Again and again, the women themselves applied that label to the Confederacy.[53] A 1907 obituary of a woman who had taught and lectured on the Confederacy asserted that its identity as a nation had outlived its defeat. "When the stars and bars were folded around the wrecked hopes of Southern nationality[,] . . . there [was] left untarnished the rich heritage of its national characteristics of blood."[54] The Confederate flag was, especially before the First World War, neo-Confederates' most cherished symbol. Fund-raisers sold a great many small Confederate flags, "each visitor being anxious to pin to his shoulder one glorious symbol of Liberty and Truth."[55]

At the same time, many neo-Confederate women resisted designating as a "nation" the country they inhabited—the United States. The UDC's very name and comparatively loose structure communicated an aversion to the trope of "nation." Despite its geographical breadth—with chapters from Philadelphia to Los Angeles to Montana by 1903—the UDC swiftly shed its original name, the National Daughters of the Confederacy. Members in Charleston were among the many who "disliked the name 'National.'"[56] Local chapters reported to the UDC's state "divisions," not to the national leadership; state divisions also determined admission to the association.[57] Yet characterizations of the relationship between nation and country varied. Moderate neo-Confederates posited a seamless relationship between Confederate allegiances and American allegiances. Within the same month, many saluted the Stars and Bars or the Southern Cross as Daughters of the Confederacy and the Stars and Stripes as Daughters of the American Revolution— an organization that conflated nation with the contemporary state, but in which these southerners also constituted a moderate wing.

By contrast, militant neo-Confederates' reluctance to identify as members of an American nation is starkly illustrated by a South Carolinian who was transplanted to East Texas. Adelia A. Dunovant's planter father had helped draft South Carolina's secession decree in 1860—the first in the country— and had served the Confederacy as a colonel. Dunovant herself never married and lived near Houston with her brother, another planter. In 1900 she was rising swiftly within the UDC.[58] Within the Texas Division, she occupied the all-important position of "historian"—not only directing members' historical studies, but exhorting them to greater heights of Confederate patriotism. That year Dunovant asserted that the United States was not a nation but a plural noun. "A nation is one political society. The United States are several political societies . . . united in a general or federal government." She went further. In "applying the term 'nation' to the United States," UDC women would be repudiating their objective to vindicate "the men of the Confederacy who fought and died in defense of the constitutional right of State sovereignty."[59] Dunovant's implication that labeling the United States a nation betrayed the Confederate dead met resistance even in the *Confederate Veteran*'s pages.[60]

Yet Dunovant's and other militants' definitions of national reconciliation were influential among neo-Confederates. True sectional reconciliation would occur only when white Americans outside the South (the only nonsoutherners whose opinions mattered) no longer treated American patriotism and retrospective Confederate patriotism as mutually exclusive. It was not only possible to be good Americans and faithful "Confederates" simultaneously, but integral to the definitions of each term. In seceding from the United States in 1860–61, white southerners had conserved the principles of the American Revolution and the U.S. Constitution in the face of northerners' violation of them, in creating an aggressive federal government and in flouting white southerners' property rights by ending slavery. An El Campo, Texas, woman wrote, "we are citizens of the United States," as the first of many reasons she defended secession in retrospect.[61] In 1902 Dunovant described northern behavior in the 1860s as "treason"—not against the Confederate States of America, but against the United States and its constitution.[62]

The history of neo-Confederate women's nationalism thoroughly intertwines with that of Jim Crow, illuminating race's centrality to the women's nationalism. Demonstrating the women's ties to Democratic political establishments—and to an increasingly one-party South—was the South Carolina state legislature, which allowed the state's Daughters of the Confederacy to house their "Relic Room" in the state capitol starting in 1901.[63] Keeping Jim Crow in place were its creators' and supporters' assertions of white intraracial solidarity, Democratic Party solidarity, imaginings of "Negro Domination" during Reconstruction, and present-day "white man's government" in the South — all of which the UDC's official journal fervently propagated.[64] The *Confederate Veteran*'s editor, Sumner Archibald Cunningham, spoke for many if not most neo-Confederate women — who were accustomed to engaging him as a speaker on special occasions — when he condoned the pogrom in Wilmington, North Carolina, in November 1898. After white mobs killed more than ten African Americans, 1,500 others later left town. Southerners, the fifty-five-year-old Cunningham remarked, "are determined upon a white man's government, and when race riot begins they may be counted and recounted to a man to maintain their part of it." Historians ascribe the bloodshed to that year's midterm elections; Cunningham later tied the massacre to black-on-white rape. Republican president William McKinley's appointment of African American men to government positions, Cunningham contended, caused them to become "more insolent than ever," to the point that "white ladies could not walk the streets in safety . . . . The men bound themselves by their sacred oaths to submit no longer, and blood ran in the street."[65]

The personal connections between leading neo-Confederate women and Jim Crow's male architects are striking. The UDC's national president between 1905 and 1907, Lizzie George Henderson of Greenwood, Mississippi, was the daughter of Mississippi supreme court justice and longtime U.S. senator James Z. George. A UDC profile of Henderson credited her father with Mississippi's 1890 state constitution, reminding readers of that constitution's innovative "franchise clause, thrusting out the ignorant vote." The first in the country to devise methods of disfranchising black men and poor white men — poll taxes and selective "literacy tests" — that withstood federal court challenges, the Mississippi constitution of 1890 was a building block of Jim Crow. It was emulated in the next two decades by Democratic state governments all across the South, with modifications that made it possible for many more white men to vote. Henderson evidently wore her parentage fondly. The *Confederate Veteran* called her mother, who cared for Confederate soldiers during the war, "as ardent a Confederate" as her father. "In this air of love and reverence for the Confederacy Mrs. Henderson grew up, ardently loyal to the traditions of her people." Decades later, with Henderson still alive, the UDC lay a wreath at the feet of her father's statue in the U.S. Capitol.[66]

Neo-Confederates' intense desire to commemorate the Confederacy as American did not ensure a united front. Serious disagreements dogged presentations of slavery and its aftermath. Starting in the early 1900s, women and men proposed sentimental monuments to ex-slaves who had remained with their former owners after emancipation. In a highly revealing turn of phrase, neo-Confederates dubbed such people "faithful slaves"—as if their emancipation had never occurred.[67] Such monuments would, in the words of a North Carolina woman, "verify the character of the Southern people and also show the true relation that existed between master and servant." Depictions of southern slavery as kind (in the belief that if slaves had been cruelly treated, they would have lived elsewhere once freed) helped form the bedrock of neo-Confederate arguments.[68] One Memphis woman, however, objected vociferously to "faithful slave" monuments on white supremacist grounds. "Instead of raising a black monument to mar any Southern city (go away and stay a year and see how black it looks already), secure an authentic list of the Southern homes desecrated by the freedman" since Emancipation. Mrs. W. Carleton Adams's replacement of the "faithful slave" with the black rapist anticipated Thomas Dixon Jr.'s slashing novel *The Clansman* (1905) and the film *The Birth of a Nation* (1915), Dixon's novel adapted for the screen.[69] Adams's arguments did not win the day in 1904, when she made them. Such apocalyptic depictions of interracial strife would harm neo-Confederates' case for contemporary race relations as congenial, for they wished to avoid any northern or federal interference.[70] Ultimately, the disagreement regarding the presentation of slavery was not resolved to the full satisfaction of either faction. "Faithful slave" monuments' many proponents did not achieve their objective for decades and, then, never on the ambitious scale they wanted.[71]

NEO-CONFEDERATE WOMEN WERE aided considerably by men, notably by Democrat-dominated state legislatures whose generosity toward pro-Confederate monument proposals deviated from their usual parsimony. Adams's and others' fears of black rapists and the UDC's loving commemorations of the Reconstruction-era Ku Klux Klan positioned white men, past and present, as protectors and therefore leaders. Yet the women simultaneously functioned as neo-Confederate nationalism's instigators. In operating, as volunteers and amateurs, in ways associated with women—in schoolrooms, in their own meetings, in "entertainments" to raise funds for monuments— women forged a conservative nationalism, centered on women, that stood for female political activism, for female cultural authority, and at the same time for male political authority. Neo-Confederate women altered hundreds of the most public of southern spaces with enduring (if mostly mass-produced) stone reminders of the Confederate cause, and they persuaded southern state legislators to create new state holidays to honor Confederate leaders.[72] They also shaped the federal government's commemorations of the Civil War.

Although overseen by a parade of northern Republican presidents between 1897 and 1913, the federal government promoted forms of national unity that were congenial to neo-Confederates on numerous occasions. The individual most responsible for the first federal appropriations for maintaining Confederate war graves was nicknamed "Mother Richmond." Born on her family's "estate" in Virginia, Janet Weaver Randolph had married a Confederate major after the war. A doyenne of commemoration in the monument-saturated city of Richmond, the Confederacy's second and final capital, she helped transform the old Confederate White House into a popular museum in the 1890s. She was, in one historian's assessment, "the UDC's most effective lobbyist with politicians."[73] Fifty-two years old in 1900, Randolph convinced the U.S. Congress to pass a law financing the maintenance of Confederate graves in Arlington National Cemetery. A 1903 law extended this support to Confederate graves in national cemeteries elsewhere in the North.[74] Federal authorities proved friendly to neo-Confederate collectives and not only to individuals. In 1906 secretary of war and future president William Howard Taft permitted the UDC to erect a monument at Arlington "to the rank and file of the Confederate army"—a project that was completed eight years and tens of thousands of dollars later.[75] The federal government went beyond merely allowing monuments to the Confederacy on federal land, even bankrolling "a granite shaft . . . to perpetuate the memory of the fifteen Confederate soldiers who died in Union prisons in Kansas City."[76]

Despite such assistance from white men, who in the 1890s generally demonstrated less interest than white women in the past, the Daughters of the Confederacy's intense focus on the past was feminine in itself. Also illustrating women-centered nationalism, particularly its special capacity to mold everyday life, were neo-Confederates' efforts to direct history education in the South, starting in 1896 in Georgia. Going beyond patriotic essay contests, the women pressured school boards to select pro-Confederate history textbooks, stocked school libraries with histories they considered appropriate, and sought to place Confederate flags or portraits of Confederate leaders in classrooms.[77] Similarly, in 1896 women in Alexandria, Virginia, convened the first Children of the Confederacy chapter—adult-supervised groups intended to instill pro-Confederate history in white, Confederate-descended children.[78]

Neo-Confederates' women-centered nationalism also informed the content of their history. The women presented white women as history's subjects, telling numerous stories of such women's sacrifices and fidelity during the Civil War.[79] In an organization whose members stood on both sides of (though mostly against) woman suffrage questions, female patriotism took multiple guises in UDC commemorations. Neo-Confederates honored mothers and wives, as such, as well as spies. A Louisianan referred to the "women of Jefferson Davis's cabinet" knowing that the cabinet had been, in fact, entirely male. She understood that white women's unpaid labor as household managers, hostesses, and symbols had enhanced their husbands' careers and was historically significant in itself.[80]

However, in keeping with femininity, as described by Ann Douglas and others, neo-Confederate women's assertion of cultural authority did not extend to claiming women's political authority or political equality with men. As lobbyists and petitioners supplicating male legislators, the women condoned a strictly gendered division of political labor that maintained white men's positions as the race's political leaders. Neo-Confederate women in the 1890s undertook their projects intending to preserve such divisions of labor, especially in relation to men of the Civil War generation.[81] In the women's eyes, the historical significance of female patriotism lay in women's relationships to men—feeding, supplying, nursing, sacrificing, mourning, and burying them, and protecting their memory from oblivion.[82]

Neo-Confederates' espousal of intensely gendered divisions of political labor sometimes extended to marginalizing themselves and other women. Regarding the monuments they bankrolled, the women considered male orators an essential element of dedication ceremonies—to the point of minimizing their own importance. At the 1907 unveiling of the massive Jefferson Davis statue in Richmond—for which Daughters of the Confederacy had raised $50,000 of the total $70,000 cost—UDC president Lizzie George Henderson "had a man speak for her" because, in her words, "a great speech should be made for the U.D.C. on this our great occasion."[83] Women in Franklin, Tennessee, led the fund-raising for a Confederate monument there through "ice cream suppers, concerts, [and] cakewalks," yet men's speeches dominated the women's accounts of the 1899 dedication.[84] To some neo-Confederates, women's nationalism was supposed to take the form of women's grooming of their sons to be citizens and patriots— a progressive idea in the late eighteenth century, a conservative one in the twentieth. A Columbia, South Carolina, woman declared in 1896, "We cannot make healthy manhood by standing in its place"; therefore, she praised Confederates' mothers for having taught their sons to sacrifice themselves.[85] In keeping with its context, in which many well-off white southerners were struggling hard to reconstitute rigid gender, race, and class hierarchies simultaneously, neo-Confederate women's nationalism promoted female political activism, female cultural authority, and definitions of patriotism that centered on the battlefield. The women reinforced the exclusion of women from first-class citizenship, even as they and other women repudiated definitions of female patriotism that focused exclusively on making babies.

With the twentieth century's arrival, neo-Confederate women continued to try to fold southern white opinion and national white opinion into a pro-Confederate consensus. A Kentuckian believed in 1901 that the goal was in sight: "The truth is sought and welcomed by patriots of both North and South." By the 1910s, neo-Confederate commentators were noting happily that "[t]he North is recognizing more and more the Confederacy's true place in history," in the words of Adelia A. Dunovant.[86] Showing that the defeated Confederacy had in fact won the peace, pro-Confederate renditions of U.S. history seeped into the upbringings of black children as well as of white ones. The club leader Mamie Garvin Fields refused to send her children to Charleston's public schools because of teachers who not only were exclusively white but "Rebbish."[87]

NORTHERN WOMEN concerned with Civil War memory emphatically counterposed their own approaches to the war to those of neo-Confederates. Members of the WRC, the leading pro-Union women's organization, cast the Civil War as a struggle between American and un-American forces—with true Americans fighting for instead of against the United States government. Pro-Union women's major contribution to the history of female nationalism was their transmutation of Union patriotism's symbols, such as the Stars and Stripes, into symbols of national patriotism. However, the women disagreed among themselves whether loyalty to the contemporary nation required transforming Union patriotism's meanings. Black women and small numbers of white women posited a seamless relationship between the Civil War–era United States and the modern-day United States, in keeping with civic nationalism's premium on loyal behavior as a basis for national unity. In contrast, the white women who set the tone for the WRC reinterpreted the symbols of Union patriotism to accommodate ex- and neo-Confederates. In subscribing to race-based definitions of North-South reconciliation, the women of the WRC promoted an American nationalism based on race.

Unlike neo-Confederate women's associations, which originated as independent entities, most postbellum associations of pro-Union women originated around 1869 from within the Grand Army of the Republic (GAR)—the dominant, multiracial organization of Union veterans (formed in 1866).[88] Female relatives of veterans who were active in the GAR formed local associations devoted to grave decoration, grave maintenance, sewing, and other forms of charity aimed at ill or disabled veterans and their families. The women decided only gradually to organize themselves on a larger scale. What began on the state level, in Massachusetts in 1879, became national with the formation of the WRC in 1883. This transition coincided with the GAR's own growth spurt.

As the GAR's main auxiliary, the WRC drew in veterans' female relatives and women who had served the United States in their own right during the Civil War.[89] While personal or family ties to Union veterans mattered in the formation of local corps—a process overseen by GAR posts, especially before 1898—the WRC repudiated the privileging of retrospective ancestry.[90] This decision resulted in a massive membership surge in the organization's early decades but would threaten the WRC's stamina as the Civil War generation began dying away. Conscious of its class and ethnic diversity—much greater than in any other contemporary female organization centered on patriotism—the WRC contrasted itself proudly to the hereditary and therefore "un-American" Ladies of the Grand Army of the Republic (formed in 1886), which was limited to Union veterans' female kin and descendants.[91] Illustrating the WRC's relative diversity were a contingent of German speakers in New York State and a group of black women in Wallaceton, Virginia, who built their own meeting house from pine boards.[92]

From the first, the WRC's membership was multiracial and, outside the South, interracial. Comprising the organization were white and black women in every part of the country (including the former Confederacy) that had sent troops to fight for the United States, a handful of Native Americans, and increasingly, white southerners married to Union veterans. With local corps in every state and continental territory, save Alabama, by 1894, the organization was strongest in New England and in the upper Midwest, with white women from those areas dominating the national leadership.[93] Not all WRC leaders were white, however. Black women held state-level offices in Kentucky (as of 1900), Maryland (1900), and the District of Columbia (1897). The entire leadership of the Department of Louisiana and Mississippi was African American. In Julia Mason Layton, a Washington, D.C., teacher born enslaved in Virginia and married to a disabled navy veteran, the WRC also had a black national officer.[94] However, to the WRC's top leaders, the organization's transcendence of racial lines was never as important as its charity work among Union veterans or its influence on white southerners.

In addition to its primary focus on Union patriotism—performing charity work among needy Union veterans, maintaining and decorating the graves of Union dead, and promoting the celebration of Memorial Day (the last Monday in May)—the WRC pioneered also in devising national patriotic rituals. The women planned to place American flags in every school-house; disseminate the observance of Memorial Day as the "nation's *holy day*"; spread the new practice (minted in 1892 in observance of Columbus's four-hundredth anniversary) of having schoolchildren verbally "pledge allegiance" to the Stars and Stripes; and, in Massachusetts in 1894, lobby for legislation to ban the marking of American flags with words or designs.[95] With this last proposal, the WRC constituted the first women's group to call on the government to eradicate what later generations would call flag desecration. Impelling these projects was apprehension at the vast "foreign" presence in the North.[96]

These national patriots also considered white southerners their audience. Efforts to segregate African Americans nationally within the WRC proved unsuccessful, as did a national president's 1906 proposal to exclude black women altogether. However, WRC leaders allowed the racial segregation of the organization at the state level in Tennessee (1890), Kentucky (1900), and Maryland (1900), despite strenuous objections from black and some white members.[97] National leaders favored fostering growth among white southerners in part because they expected that such efforts would result in more funds for indigent veterans. Many black corps in the South and in border states were relatively impecunious and worked among comparatively poor populations.[98] However, the WRC's desires to reach white southerners cannot be explained only in economic terms. These national patriots saw a chance to complete what they perceived as the Union's ultimate mission of reuniting the country.

To the WRC, the Civil War had indeed been a struggle between right — the U.S. government — and wrong — defenders of secession fighting under "the cross of human slavery," the Confederate flag.[99] However, that struggle was a thing of the past. Like white veterans on both sides, pro-Union white women increasingly boiled memories of the Civil War down to individual experiences of grief and loss and eschewed sweeping political questions. This tendency, however, contained political ramifications in itself, by promoting neutral characterizations of the other side.[100] Moreover, even those white women who called the Confederacy's actions "treason" and who celebrated the end of slavery reserved their highest praise for Union soldiers who had "planted the grand old 'stars and stripes,' as God planted the 'Tree of Life, for the healing of the nations.'"[101] The American flag now truly belonged to everyone.

White pro-Union women working on southern ground spread national patriotism among their white neighbors. This was especially evident in Texas, which attracted Yankees as well as New Southerners in the late nineteenth century. In Waco on Memorial Day, 1894, white WRC corps and GAR posts socialized with their "ex-Confederate" counterparts. Veterans and women *"all"* joined in singing 'America.' . . . No flag but Old Glory in the procession." That same year, Hattie Loring of San Antonio happily described the array of Confederate veterans and descendants at the Texas WRC convention, including "hundreds of school children, the children of rebel parents" — "we know that our work is being felt, and that we are teaching Loyalty, not only to the ones who fought against our flag, but to the rising generation."[102] National leaders and northerners shared this premium on reconciling North and South on the basis of white unity. In 1894, in thanking two white Bostonians for working as "missionaries" among black members in Florida and South Carolina, WRC president Sarah C. Mink dwelled on the Bostonians' hardships that "no one can know of living in a loyal community and among a loyal people."[103] This refrain, frequently echoed by pro-Union women when speaking of the South, overlooked the black southerners who struggled in large and small ways against pro-Confederate versions of history.[104] The "loyal people" who mattered most were white.

Not all white women in the WRC joined the chorus of conciliation. A New Yorker transplanted to Missouri called herself a "champion of the Union cause" there. While acknowledging that Missouri never joined the Confederacy, she wailed to the 1894 national convention that "[t]he elements of disloyalty in our State have combined . . . to teach our Southern youth that the war for the Union was wrong and that secession was right."[105] Yet her and others' complaints about the neo-Confederate movement did not always amount to defying race-based definitions of reconciliation. The invigoration of that movement in the 1890s angered white national patriots not only because they opposed pro-Confederate characterizations of the Civil War. Neo-Confederates also threatened to pull the attention of white southern audiences away from pro-Union women's mission of bringing them under the umbrella of nation and country—synonymous, in this case. However, pro-Union women came to agree with neo-Confederates on the bravery of the Confederate dead. On Memorial Day, 1901, WRC members decorated the graves of "brothers who wore the gray" as well as the blue. A national leader from Indiana proclaimed "sectionalism forgotten."[106]

THE WRC'S DEVELOPMENT of histories of female patriotism, its focus on young audiences, and its grounding of national patriotism in everyday practice all place it within the spectrum of women-centered nationalism. WRC leaders lobbied the U.S. Congress for pensions for "loyal soldier-women," army nurses, with limited success in 1892.[107] Its patriotic rituals aimed at young people—the placement of American flags in every schoolhouse and the celebration of Memorial Day—altered landscapes and customs in much of the country. A Minnesota corps's report that "[o]ne hundred Indian children participated in song, recitations, and parade" on Memorial Day was one of many such "success" stories.[108] Working alongside the GAR, pro-Union women developed "patriotic instruction," or the teaching of rituals regarding the Stars and Stripes, and monitored public schools' choice of history textbooks that were favorable to the Union struggle.[109]

Yet even more than neo-Confederate women, the WRC limited its acceptance of female political activism, reinforcing women-centered nationalism's tendency to impart cultural authority and influence to women while denying political authority or power to women. Women mattered to history and to the present for their relations to children and to patriotic men. Pro-Union women's homages to army nurses focused on the latter's "ministrations of mercy" to their patients.[110] Ultimately, no woman's patriotic deed could equal the sacrifices of the "boys in blue." Except for the two areas of overlap with the GAR—both relating to young people—the women observed a strict division of political labor with organized Union veterans, with the men focusing on federal pensions for Union veterans and the women focusing on patriotic rituals, patriotic instruction, and charity toward needy veterans. In keeping with its self-definition as the GAR's auxiliary, the WRC emphasized its ultimate subordination to the needs of veterans—to the point of rejecting opportunities for political visibility, such as in parades, that veterans found acceptable or even proposed.[111]

Some WRC beliefs regarding women and nationalism communicated a decidedly narrow construction of women's cultural authority. Until the sense of national emergency created by President William McKinley's assassination in 1901 resolved the question, the WRC struggled over the notion of even engaging in patriotic instruction. On the grounds of femininity, some believed that aid to needy Union veterans, the WRC's original emphasis, should remain the organization's primary expression of patriotism.[112] The women's discomfort with other forms of female activism, due in part to the organization's status as an auxiliary, would endure throughout the early twentieth century. While women's self-education in history—studying the work of both amateur and professional historians and composing and delivering history papers—was vital to other female organizations concerned with nation, including the NACW, the DAR, and the UDC, the WRC openly eschewed "literary" programs in favor of charity work.[113] This was an old-fashioned stance, by late nineteenth-century standards, on the question of what organized women should accomplish.[114] Ultimately, like neo-Confederates, pro-Union women occupied the conservative end of women-centered nationalism's range.

MANIFESTATIONS OF African American civic nationalism, black nationalism, neo-Confederate nationalism, and national patriotism among organized women at the twentieth century's turn all descended from discussions at least as old as the Civil War. In contrast, women's state-based nationalism was new in the 1890s. It originated as a dimension of Civil War remembrance. The leading exemplar of state-based nationalism was the Washington-based DAR (formed in 1890). The DAR was made up of mostly white women who were able to document their descent from soldiers, sailors, and others who had supported the American Revolution. Applicants were also required to certify (by means of members' signatures) that they were "personally acceptable." This policy demonstrates that the DAR valued documented heredity only to the extent that it aided the organization in fostering unity among white Americans from the middle and upper classes.[115] Despite the organization's eighteenth-century moniker, the DAR was a response to the Civil War, rooted in the present. In bringing together propertied white women from all parts of the country, the DAR sought symbolically to unify the United States into a nation on the bases of white supremacy and elite class standing.[116] DAR members sought also to produce in others loyalty to that nation, embodied by the state—the federal government and its laws.

Most retrospective hereditary organizations in the United States, which honored long-dead, unknowable ancestors, were inspired by the national centennial in 1876. The Sons of Revolutionary Sires (formed in 1875) and the Sons of the Revolution (1883) both emphasized socializing, as did a later constellation of groups that also prided themselves on small memberships and stiff genealogical requirements. Examples are the invitation-only National Society of the Colonial Dames of America (1891), the mixed-sex General Society of Mayflower Descendants (1897), and the invitation-only, mixed-sex Order of First Families of Virginia (1912).[117] Although many DAR women also belonged to such organizations, the DAR itself embodied something altogether different. It combined hereditarian, racial, and class exclusivity; ambitions for growth among middle-class as well as upper-class women; and emphases on women's self-education and present-minded activism more common in nonhereditary women's clubs. Strongest in the Northeast and the upper Midwest, but with chapters in every U.S. state and territory by 1912, the DAR, like the UDC, brought together white women who were eager to parade their social stature with those who aspired to climb farther up the social ladder.[118]

The immediate spur for the DAR's formation was the SAR's expulsion of its female members a year into its own existence. Limited to those able to document their descent from Revolutionary combatants or supporters, the SAR organized in 1889 when forty-one-year-old William Osborne McDowell of New Jersey led an exodus from the Sons of the Revolution. The SAR's exclusion of women in April 1890—relegating them to decorative "honorary" status—resulted from additional infighting; other SAR members intended the move in part as a slap at McDowell.[119] The SAR's change in policy also constituted, in the eyes of many women, a repudiation of female nationalism.

In July 1890 a Washington boardinghouse keeper and journalist named Mary Smith Lockwood published a protest against the SAR in the *Washington Post*. Affirming female patriotism, she pointed to an ancestor's threats in 1775 to leave her husband if he sided with the British. Inspired by Lockwood's piece, McDowell (then living in Washington) helped bring together white women who desired to organize as female Revolutionary descendants and patriots. In two meetings, in August and in October 1890, the women did form such an organization. The three who showed up at the first meeting (when a severe thunderstorm kept people away) were later designated as the DAR's official founders — a fifty-eight-year-old journalist and writer named Ellen Hardin Walworth and two government clerks, thirty-nine-year-old Mary Desha and fifty-year-old Eugenia Washington.[120] McDowell left the DAR by 1891, and his midwifery ultimately does not explain why the DAR attracted influential white women in all parts of the country to its cause of state-based nationalism. As Lockwood's protest demonstrates, such women viewed the SAR's action not only as insulting to present-day women, but as denying what they already knew, from their reading of history, to be true — that female patriotism did, could, and should take the form of organized political activism by women.

THE CIVIL WAR runs like a trench through the lives of the DAR's founding generation. The same events that represented liberation to African Americans signified catastrophe to many white Americans, especially to those whose families had experienced the antebellum South as people of wealth and prominence. Never married, Mary Desha and Eugenia Washington (a great-grandniece of George Washington) had both been born into long-powerful planter families, in Kentucky and Virginia, respectively, that later fell on hard economic times. Because Kentucky never joined the Confederacy, Desha's pro-Confederate family found a hostile atmosphere there and waited out the war in Canada. Desha herself took a strong interest in the neo-Confederate cause, helping to organize the UDC in the District of Columbia.[121] Eugenia Washington had been raised on a plantation near Fredericksburg, Virginia, and had devoted her youth to caring for her invalid father. Legend had it that Washington had witnessed the battle of Fredericksburg (1862) from a trench. Failing to evacuate in time, the twenty-two-year-old sheltered her father's body with her own as the cannons roared overhead.[122] The DAR's first organizer of chapters, fifty-one-year-old Flora Adams Darling had been born into an antiabolitionist, Democratic family in New Hampshire and had married a Louisiana planter — only to lose him to the war.[123] Cofounders of the DAR who had supported the United States in the Civil War also endured tragedy. De facto president of the DAR between 1890 and 1893, Mary Virginia Ellet Cabell came from a Virginia family who had opposed secession. In her youth, she had been a spectator at a Unionist convention. Her father and her brother later died for the United States, one in the naval battle of Memphis and the other at Vicksburg.[124] Ellen Hardin Walworth's brother, a Union colonel, was wounded in the second battle of Bull Run.[125]

Such traumas did not result in pro-Union or pro-Confederate militance but instead fueled the women's commitment to North-South reconciliation, as expressed in a focus on the seemingly neutral ground of eighteenth-century history. That era seemed to them to demonstrate the United States's internal, eternal cohesion. That "Connecticut and Virginia stood shoulder to shoulder" during the Revolution to fight a common enemy was repeated like a mantra.[126] In regional or local settings the women tended to go their own ways in defining national patriotism, as when a South Carolinian appealed in 1894 for funds for a DAR monument to the "women patriots of the Southern Confederacy."[127] At the national level, however, Daughters hoped that focusing on early America and avoiding or playing down such controversial topics as abolitionism, antebellum sectional tensions, the Civil War, and Reconstruction would unify the United States into a nation on the desired race and class terms. An Atlantan's exclamation, in a 1903 paper on colonial Georgia, that "It seems amazing that people wanted these savage Africans!" articulates the wishful amnesia that was necessary for forging national unity.[128] Unlike those neo-Confederates who wished for permanent reminders of "faithful slaves," DAR women often strove not to "see" slavery.

In keeping with the mores of race-based national unity, DAR admission policies ensured that members would be white or, at least, that none would be black. African Americans found it especially hard to prove Revolutionary ancestry according to the DAR's requirements of written evidence of births and marriages for every generation. Slaves' marriages possessed no legal standing. Black women descended from white Revolutionaries confronted the illegal, often clandestine, and increasingly taboo nature of interracial unions, let alone marriages.[129] Even so, some whose recent ancestors had been free mapped their descent from black Revolutionary soldiers. W. E. B. Du Bois, a Massachusetts native, did likewise in 1908 in an unsuccessful bid for admission to the SAR.[130] Such applications to the DAR would surely have foundered, however, on the rocks of the personal acceptability requirement. It is possible that African Americans who were light-skinned enough to "pass" as white surmounted both obstacles and gained admission to the DAR, since applicants needed to document only one line of ancestry. Surviving and available evidence, however, does not reveal such women. Instead, it reveals an even more emphatic barrier—the official ban on "colored" women altogether, dating from 1894.[131]

It would be simplistic to ascribe the DAR's exclusion of black women to racism per se. No similar blanket bans applied to Native Americans, Jews, Roman Catholics, or Latinas of Spanish descent, although many Anglo American, Protestant contemporaries considered these groups racially distinct from and inferior to themselves.[132] Small handfuls of women from the first three groups did belong to the DAR. The last was a group that one Californian aspired to draw into the organization.[133] The DAR's exclusion of black women related directly to the Civil War, after which Americans of all kinds struggled over the place of African Americans in the new body politic. These state-based nationalists of the 1890s viewed the induction of African Americans and of white southerners—into the nation at large, as well as into their own organization—as a question with an either/or answer. The women's decision in favor of propertied white southerners, in keeping with their definition of national unity as first dependent on intraracial and intraclass unity, entailed courting past supporters of the Confederacy. Not only did this pattern result in the large overlap in members between the DAR and the UDC, but it also created an overlap in ideas between state-based nationalism and neo-Confederate nationalism.

This overlap could go only so far. Occasionally, the accommodation of neo-Confederate notions menaced the DAR's goal of national communion among white elites. Some northerners considered the sight of Confederate flags hanging in the organization's auditorium in November 1912 a "desecration." The DAR's leadership had engineered the occasion—honoring the UDC by inviting it to use the DAR's facilities for its national convention that year and conspicuously socializing with the UDC on the national level for the first time.[134] Though stopping short of paying homage to Confederate wartime heroism, DAR president Julia Green Scott, a Kentucky native transplanted to Illinois and a faithful Democrat, dismissed the criticisms as stemming from other resentments of her administration.[135] While she and other officers brushed off the complaints, never again before World War II would the DAR embrace neo-Confederates on such an ostentatiously national basis.

Confirming the DAR's ties to Jim Crow, in addition to ties to neo-Confederate movements, women married to southern Democratic politicians who were linked to racial violence populate the organization's records. In Atlanta in September 1906, a white mob of 10,000 killed eleven people while attacking black neighborhoods over a period of five days. Historians ascribe the pogrom to a theatrical performance of Thomas Dixon Jr.'s *The Clansman* and the antiblack rhetoric—inflammatory even by local standards—of Hoke Smith, running for Georgia's governorship against another Democrat. His wife, Marion Cobb Smith, was a DAR national officer in the 1890s.[136] As the foregoing discussions of pro-Union women and national patriotism illustrate, however, southern Democrats did not monopolize white supremacy. The development of Jim Crow and the mores supporting it is a truly national story. By World War I, the national state, as well as the country at large, would reinforce pro-Confederate notions of history and national unity.

AT THE SAME TIME that it promoted intraracial national unity, the DAR embodied state-based nationalism in its focus on allegiance to the federal government and its policies. These women admitted no tension between state and nation. The DAR's very structure—unusually centralized—not only elevated the concept of nation but located it in the literal seat of national government. Against the dominant nineteenth-century pattern in which national organizations formed from preexisting local, state, or even national units (in the case of the NACW), the DAR organized from its Washington headquarters outward. The national leadership approved all applications for membership and appointed all organizers, state and local. State-level organizations were afterthoughts, most of them forming years later.[137]

Presenting women as shapers of culture and simultaneously reproducing some contemporary male supremacies, the DAR's state-based nationalism illustrates women-centered nationalism. This relationship can be seen in the immediate reason for the DAR's formation, an instance in which men repudiated women's patriotism in the form of public activism. As with neo-Confederates, the women's interest in the past was feminine in itself in the context of the nineteenth century—as made plain by the neglect or threatened demolition of Philadelphia's Independence Hall and other historical structures later "rescued" by the DAR and other amateur preservationists. Moreover, the Daughters positioned women like themselves as cultural authorities. Their fostering of patriotism in the population sought to alter everyday practices, notably the treatment of American flags. Also exemplifying women-centered nationalism was the DAR's attention to history's women and to women's work. DAR women celebrated "foremothers" not only for caring for patriotic men, but also for patriotism in their own right as warriors and vigilantes. DAR members in Georgia honored an eighteenth-century woman, Nancy Morgan Hart, said to have captured six British soldiers on her farm. She shot one and hanged the others with her husband when he came home from hunting.[138] Daughters also attributed historical importance to feminine labors. For example, they attributed one crucial American victory in the Revolution to a North Carolinian's cooking and her financial generosity.[139]

Indeed, some in the DAR developed a truly women-centered nationalism. These women inverted the usual designation of fighting men as the ultimate patriots by instead viewing men's historical significance in light of their relations with women and children.[140] The house museums developed by the DAR starting in the 1890s honored the entire families who had lived there and the household labor performed in them. Historical significance inhered in kitchens and pots as well as in writing desks. In 1903 the DAR came into possession of a seventeenth-century house in Windsor, Connecticut, named for the Supreme Court chief justice who had lived there in the late eighteenth century, Oliver Ellsworth. To the wife of the editor of the *New Haven Leader*, the "[r]oomy, plain, and dignified" house's importance transcended that of the great man to show "the kind of men and women who lived their upright, wholesome, austere lives within its walls."[141]

DAR members cherished George Washington, too, not only as a hero but also on the basis of how they imagined his relations with women. He was valued as a romantic suitor, a loving husband, and a caring stepfather. His wedding anniversary was marked by nearly as many receptions as was his birthday. Indeed, the Jefferson City, Missouri, DAR chapter toasted "Washington as a Lover."[142] In another telling, Washington's weeping in public did nothing to compromise his manhood. Before an audience of women at the Chicago World's Fair in 1893, Mary Virginia Ellet Cabell evoked "the tears and sobs of Washington, as he watched from afar the slaughter of his beloved citizen soldiers by the bloody Hessians! When are the tears [shed] by woman ever . . . more tender than those that flowed down the warrior's stern cheek?"[143]

Yet, as shown by the DAR's frequent praise of George Washington and other warriors, women-centered nationalists accepted many forms of sex hierarchy even as those nationalists boosted the cultural authority of women. In keeping with the organization's own considerable ties to the state and to capitalist wealth, the DAR communicated white women's historical importance and present-day potency while ultimately seating white men at the head of the nation. The literary scholar Shawn Michelle Smith has argued that in requiring members to base their applications on public documents generated by exclusively male entities such as government and military institutions, the DAR stressed a white masculine national identity that, in its logic, excluded women from political activity.[144] I argue conversely that the DAR provided cultural and moral justifications for white women's political activity. However, the DAR treasured men's wealth and power to a degree not evident even in the otherwise conservative UDC, in which a number of single women rose to state-level and even national prominence. In contrast, no never-married woman presided over the DAR before World War II.[145] The DAR's valuing of women for their relations to men stemmed directly from the organization's state-based nationalism. The state was still an exclusively male entity in the 1890s. Forms of marriage that stressed monogamy and that excluded women from first-class citizenship had long constituted units of governance in the United States.[146]

The DAR's self-supporting official founders (two widowed and two single women) and the comparatively conservative wives who came to lead the organization both believed that recruiting the wives of important men — as wives — would accomplish the objective of assembling a national female elite to buttress the state. Women with husbands high in the federal government and the military, particularly the navy, seemed especially able to transcend North-South tensions. The founders chose as the organization's first president Caroline Scott Harrison of Indiana, the wife of Republican president Benjamin Harrison, precisely on the basis of sectional reconciliation.[147] The women made no comment on the ironies presented by President Harrison's background as a Union officer or his administration's conspicuous support for federal pensions for Union veterans (a sore point with ex- and neo-Confederates).[148] Until her death from tuberculosis, the first lady functioned in the DAR in a mostly ceremonial capacity, with Mary Virginia Ellet Cabell serving as the organization's day-to-day leader. Harrison's and Cabell's successor, Letitia Green Stevenson, was married to then vice president Adlai Stevenson, who was conveniently a Democrat. It was almost certainly cofounder Ellen Hardin Walworth who praised the second lady primarily for her husband, "a man who stands preëminent among his countrymen."[149] DAR leaders' cultivation of and access to powerful men bore considerable fruit, especially in relation to the U.S. Congress. The organization paid no property taxes in the early twentieth century on its city-block-sized tract at 1776 D Street Northwest, within sight of the White House.[150]

The same conservative variant of women-centered nationalism—in which the DAR's embrace of the state necessitated a pointed regard for men's political power—is evident in the organization's membership. Not only did white women with unlettered ancestors have greater difficulty documenting their Revolutionary descent, but national, state, and local organizers valued access to male wealth and prominence above all. Organizers contacted women they wanted in the DAR for reasons of social prestige, and then sought to document their ancestry.[151] These practices resulted in a preponderance of members who were married to or related to elite men. These men possessed national stature—in the cases of industrialists, Cabinet members, and members of Congress—and local stature, in the cases of professionals, local and state politicians, landowners, and businessmen.[152] Studding DAR records are surnames that, in evoking the great men of history, undoubtedly made the organization attractive to both *arrivistes* and those already arrived.[153] Yet the DAR also welcomed the Gilded Age's industrial rich who could fulfill its requirements. Mellons from Pittsburgh, Pillsburys from

Minneapolis, Pullmans from Chicago, the daughter-in-law of the agricultural machinery manufacturer John Deere, the wife of the California railroad kingpin Leland Stanford, and the daughter of financier Jay Gould all belonged.[154] The visibility of capitalism's consorts within an organization dedicated to state-based nationalism expresses the affinity between the state and capital at the time, illustrated most starkly by the use of U.S. Army troops in the 1890s to break strikes.[155]

From its inception, the DAR's nationwide web of propertied women simultaneously embodied the interests of the state and the interests of capital and defined national patriotism in part as support for capitalism; the association aspired to form a hedge against the increasingly organized, assertive workers and farmers of the late nineteenth century. A dedicated antisuffragist from South Carolina described the DAR's duty as keeping "the land of the free . . . from getting too free."[156] In the election season of 1896, a Saratoga Springs, New York, woman disparaged the "hoarse Jacobin cries" of "the various breeds of populists and anarchists and other demagogues."[157] Indeed, the DAR began its own conspicuous efforts against flag desecration in the backwash of that same presidential race, in which the victorious Republican Party asserted that it embodied a manly state and that the opposition constituted enemies of that state.[158] In the face of Republicans' unprecedentedly lavish use of the American flag as a campaign symbol, a physician's wife in Milwaukee was horrified at newspaper reports of Democrats in northern cities tearing down Republican bunting. Reading the reports aloud to her chapter, thirty-eight-year-old Frances Saunders Kempster imagined the Stars and Stripes as the target of "rotten eggs, tobacco juice and street filth"—the effluvia of lower-class disorder. The first laws against flag desecration proposed by the DAR, an effort spearheaded by Kempster and other northerners, were directed against partisan (Democratic) uses of the Stars and Stripes, as well as against the flag's commodification by petty entrepreneurs.[159]

Much of the history studied and generated by the DAR also simultaneously reinforced men's political authority and the interests of capital, in keeping with state-based nationalism—but also in keeping with conservative forms of women-centered nationalism. From the first, warriors' battlefield deeds were the focus of most histories that Daughters consumed and composed. Men's military and political activities also dominated the DAR's historic preservation efforts. The Pittsburgh chapter legally incorporated itself in 1894 in order to own property after a member donated a building that had been part of Fort Pitt, dating from the French and Indian War, to the chapter.[160] Starting in 1896, Philadelphia's first chapter oversaw the renovation of Independence Hall, a building that had once been relegated to use as a municipal dog pound.[161]

Populating DAR histories, in addition to warriors, were people like themselves — white, Anglo American, and economically successful — and those imagined as such. Litchfield, Connecticut, was an epicenter of the early twentieth-century "colonial revival" in architecture and decoration. To evoke a "pure" American past, local elites garbed both eighteenth-century and eighteenth-century-style houses in anachronistically bright white paint. The town similarly boasted a thriving DAR chapter. A poster advertising a 1902 "colonial tea" depicted the *Mayflower* bearing a grandfather clock and other luxury furnishings to American shores. In imparting such comforts to Pilgrims — who lived, and starved, at a time when clocks constituted decorative objects for the wealthy — the women imagined early American history as an unbroken line of prosperity.[162]

The DAR celebrated capital's progress notwithstanding its potential threats to the women's own historic preservation agenda. Rarely aspiring to historic authenticity in its first decades, the DAR seldom hesitated to alter land or objects if such alterations fostered patriotism. The organization lobbied the U.S. Congress in 1914 for funds for a transcontinental, paved highway. Following the routes of the trails used by westbound white settlers, the highway would constitute "a memorial to the pioneer-patriots." Lining the highway would be newly planted trees, old taverns that had been revived, and museums of local history.[163] The relationship between industrialization and history work on the local level was also often harmonious. The Talladega, Alabama, chapter in 1900 successfully lobbied the city council for an appropriation allowing the women to "[remove] the dust" of seventeen Americans, buried where they had fallen during the War of 1812, to the city cemetery. The battlefield had "recently passed into the hands of the North Alabama Coal and Iron Company, and the Talladega Furnace stands on its site," the women explained; "consequently the burial ground . . . will be-

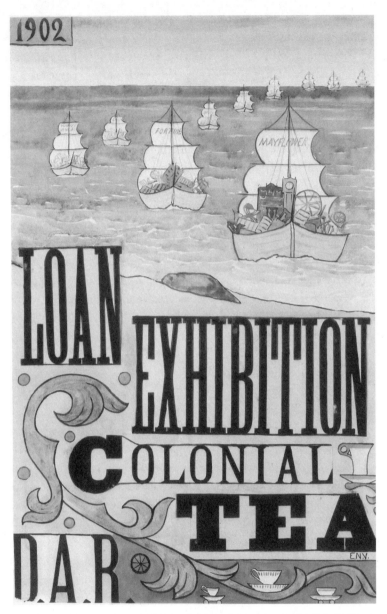

Poster advertising a "loan exhibition and colonial tea" by the Litchfield, Connecticut, Daughters of the American Revolution chapter, 1902. Collection of the Litchfield Historical Society.

come, in a few months, a waste of slag and cinders." The battlefield's annihilation was no cause for mourning or for protest. The relationship between
the War of 1812 and the North Alabama Coal and Iron Company—the
latter embodying "[t]he demands of the commercial and industrial interests
of that South, which [Andrew] Jackson and his men helped to make"—
seemed a logical and, above all, desirable progression.[164]

A less rosy view of late nineteenth-century capitalism can be found in a
Pittsburgh woman's lament that "the new industrialism," and the Pennsylvania Railroad in particular, "is steadily and rapidly blotting out the pictur-
esque and historic all around us." However, the Pittsburgh DAR's efforts to
prevent its French and Indian War–era fort from being surrounded by ware-
houses and tracks were stymied by one of its own. The member who had
deeded them the fort, Mary Elizabeth Schenley, had sold the surrounding
land to the steel magnate Henry Clay Frick.[165] In conflating nation, country, and state and in conflating the interests of the nation with the interests
of capital, the DAR reinforced white men's leadership of the race and of the
nation—affirming male political supremacy more broadly than women who
praised fallen warriors and heroes. Even so, the DAR's notions of women and
nation imparted substantial influence to white women regarding patriotism's
cultural and moral dimensions.

ORGANIZED WOMEN in the 1890s struggled fiercely over the question of
on what bases, and how tightly, to reunify the country in the wake of civil
war. To African Americans, the process of freedom was incomplete. Forms
of national unification that valued race over past and current allegiance to
one's country were proving costly indeed. White women who focused on
national patriotism anticipated harmony in a national unity based on race
and abandoned those aspects of Union patriotism that did not comport with
that definition of unity. With her husband, a former Union major, and 10,000
others, Louisa Johnson Smith of Cleveland, Ohio, attended the massive
"Blue-Gray" reunion in September 1895 at the site of the battle of Chicka-
mauga in Georgia. As she listened to veterans' speeches, Smith thought "my
heart would burst with enthusiasm and patriotism." When attending the
DAR's national convention some years later, however, she felt apprehensive

when the meeting opened with the singing of "The Battle Hymn of the Republic"—Julia Ward Howe's militant lyrics paired with the tune "John Brown's Body Lies A-Moldering in the Grave." "If you remember," Smith reminded her chapter, "this hymn was written expressly for the Civil War," and she wondered, "'Who has blundered?' But it was made all right the next morning by singing 'Maryland, My Maryland.'"[166] Sectional tensions among white Americans would endure, but they gradually lost their ability to threaten national unity. To white women outside the South, national unity seemed impossible without white southerners, and very possible— desirable, in fact—without African Americans, regardless of wealth, education, or documented ancestry.

What makes women's contests in the 1890s over the question of national reunification more than merely emulative of men's debates is the women's distinctively gendered nationalism. Women on all sides of the reunion debate —state-based nationalists, national patriots, neo-Confederate nationalists, African American civic nationalists, and black nationalists—operated on the assumption that women's innate unselfishness and generosity, stemming especially from their capacity for motherhood, made women's activism a political and moral necessity. The women viewed their projects as correctives to men's propensities toward excessive sectional or partisan conflict (from the perspective of the DAR) or toward excessive compromise and camaraderie (in the opinions of Anna Julia Cooper and Josephine St. Pierre Ruffin). Characterizing outreach to youth as a feminine duty, these very different groups of women sought to rectify what they perceived as young people's ignorance about the American past and to win them to the women's respective interpretations. In keeping with women-centered nationalism's inherently limited notions of women's political power, most women in this story accepted and reinforced normative gender divisions of political labor at the same time that they emphasized the necessity of women's political activism. Women measured acts of patriotism using manly yardsticks, with men's self-sacrifice in battle as patriotism's apotheosis. While often criticizing male behaviors, and while taking it upon themselves to reshape or invent patriotic customs and observances, most black and white women did not directly challenge male political supremacy except when it conflicted with women's collective, public activism.

Chapter Two
The Empire

FOLLOWING ITS INDEPENDENCE, the United States developed as a land empire—continually conquering and repeopling territory beyond its western border until that border reached the sea. At the turn of the twentieth century, the United States also constituted an overseas empire with distant possessions. The country annexed Hawaii and, after a brief war with Spain, Spanish island colonies (including Puerto Rico) in 1898; it suppressed the Filipino independence movement to hold the Philippines as a colony by 1902; and it continued military and political interventions in the Caribbean and in Latin America, forging an empire without colonies, throughout the twentieth century. The United States's acquisition of distant colonies and the wars accompanying that process had contradictory effects on the spectrum of women-centered nationalism, appearing to validate both its boldness and its conservatism. War and the awareness of empire heightened women's convictions that their own political activism was valuable to their nations, especially as contrasted to the place of women in masculine nationalists' ideas about race suicide. Yet war and the awareness of empire simultaneously reduced women's importance as patriots. Women who eulogized fighting men even more than before—at a time when the military excluded women from combat—reinforced men's monopolization of political leadership and of first-class citizenship.

War and overseas empire also sharpened differences of opinion among women regarding the relationship between state and nation. The imperial wars of the late 1890s and early 1900s were the first wars directly experienced by these female organizations, which had originated in peacetime. Adherents of all the major strands of women's nationalism—state-based nationalism, neo-Confederate nationalism, African American civic nationalism, and black nationalism—contributed funds and labor to the government. In the brief Spanish-American War of 1898, logistics were handled so poorly that ten times more U.S. soldiers died of disease than in combat, as compared to a two-to-one ratio during the Civil War. The government was especially dependent on the work of volunteers. White women who focused on fostering patriotism contributed badly needed supplies for caring for invalids.[1] Organized black women, including some strong critics of overseas imperialism, helped draw together the nearly 10,000 black men who enlisted.[2] The Spanish-American War marked the first time that female nurses served in the U.S. military in an official capacity. The government depended on female volunteers to locate nurses of their respective races to serve troops of their respective races.[3]

Yet following the initial flush of prowar enthusiasm in 1898, and especially after the shooting began in the Philippines in early 1899, differences in women's approaches to the state became apparent. The state-based nationalists of the DAR supported the new overseas empire in part because the very fact of war intensified the women's support for the state. Moreover, the DAR's readings of U.S. history—celebrating the westward course of land empire—caused them to believe fervently in extending that empire. There appeared no reason for U.S. expansion to stop at the water's edge. Although their rigid support for the male state inherently marginalized women politically, the women simultaneously positioned white women as civilizers and conquerors alongside white men—in distinct contrast to the male nationalists who ordered white women to attend exclusively to producing babies, and lots of them. Neo-Confederates, in contrast, were uncomfortable with overseas imperialism's embrace of American state power. However, their critical approach to the contemporary state did not result in critical approaches to male-centered patriotism. Continuing to dominate the women's vision were kinsmen garbed in Confederate gray.

Although many black clubwomen approved of imperialism in the form of Christianizing Africa, subscribers to American civic nationalism and black nationalism both countered the dominant forms of overseas imperialism. African Americans posited that the United States's new subject peoples were capable of self-government. Many women also winced at the juxtaposition between the country's overseas military adventures and African Americans' inability to obtain federal protection at home from atrocities in the South. White Americans' and the federal government's apparent toleration of Jim Crow violence caused some black women to challenge the United States's moral standing as a civilizing force in the world and to begin developing a black nationalism as an alternative to American national identity. This pattern was especially apparent in the "race" histories that women developed for black youth. Some of those histories incorporated the histories of African and Caribbean peoples then under the imperial control of Europeans or Americans. Whether they identified primarily as Americans or as part of an international, African-descended diaspora, however, black clubwomen continued to affirm black women's considerable cultural and moral authority within their nations — American and "Negro."

WOMEN-CENTERED nationalists asserted the importance and appropriateness of organized women's political activism to their nations in contrast to male contemporaries' alarms about "race suicide." Such men bemoaned women's increasing activity outside the home as a threat to the reproduction of the race, and therefore, of the nation. To Theodore Roosevelt, the lassitude of American men and of the American nation threatened the eclipse of both. The nation-as-man needed to rediscover physical labor and athleticism in the form of wars that civilized new territory — in short, to pursue a more "strenuous" life. "The woman must be the housewife, the helpmeet of the homemaker, the wise and fearless mother of many healthy children," Roosevelt argued. "When men fear work or fear righteous war, when women fear motherhood, they tremble on the brink of doom." Declining marriage and birth rates among native-born, educated, white women, when juxtaposed with immigrants' large families, seemed to threaten Anglo-Saxon governance of the United States and, therefore, civilization itself.[4] While Roosevelt was silent regarding African American women — whose birth rates had also been falling — some black men similarly worried that women's activities outside the home threatened their own race's extinction. Black women, said Thomas Baker (the first African American to earn a doctorate from Yale) in 1906, needed to be better educated than black men in order that they rear the best sons possible. In general, however, the black woman "must not be educated away from being a mother."[5] An unnamed commentator in the *Colored American Magazine*, probably editor Fred R. Moore, joined Baker. "Every woman should bear a sufficient number of children so that our race may increase and not decrease, she must bring up these children sound in mind, in body and soul, else no prosperity[,] no triumph of science nor industry will save our race from utter ruin and death."[6]

Likely due to the distinctive threats to black lives all around them—reflected in a symposium in which black doctors addressed the question, "Is the Negro Dying Out?"—women writing in the relatively staid, Washingtonian *Colored American Magazine* also warned of race suicide.[7] However, many dissented from those male contemporaries who discussed women's childbearing in isolation from politics. The women instead emphasized the political dimensions of raising children. Roosevelt's words struck a chord in Josephine Silone Yates, a forty-seven-year-old teacher and former NACW president based in Kansas City. She bewailed a broad cultural tendency "to shirk the responsibilities of parentage."[8] Another, focusing on guiding black youth past life's rough places, agreed that the prevention of "race suicide" should be central to black women's lives: "What greater, grander work would one wish than race-making and race-building?"[9]

Others dissented from race suicide arguments by contending that mothering should range far outside a home's front door. Addie Waites Hunton, a thirty-seven-year-old Virginia native who was prominent in the segregated Young Women's Christian Association, called on black women to answer "the crying needs of humanity" and study "all questions that can possibly affect the progress of the race," while also producing a strong "manhood." Female political activism—particularly black women's uplift of the black poor—constituted not only a way to prevent race and national suicide, but was also indicative of the race's progress.[10] Herself a mother of two, Yates focused her own definitions of motherhood on homemaking rather than babymaking. Her infusion of motherhood with political significance led to a ringing affirmation of female cultural authority within the African American nation.

Once "our home life" "becomes truly noble, truly inspiring, truly artistic, shall we find the young people who go forth . . . prepared to achieve success; and thus in turn they will demonstrate that the true measure of a nation's civilization and power is found" not only in "fleets and iron clads, but, as well, in the well rounded character of the individuals that compose it."[11] Women who took part in a 1907 symposium in the *Colored American Magazine* on "Woman's Part in the Uplift of the Negro Race" similarly affirmed the female cultural authority so basic to women-centered nationalism. The women located women's authority in motherhood and monogamous marriage, while simultaneously characterizing club work as important and necessary to their nations, American and black.[12]

Black women also indirectly challenged race suicide arguments in celebrating the political advancement of women of any race. In September 1898, the NACW's *National Association Notes*'s front page juxtaposed reminders of Jim Crow atrocities and news of a white woman's rise in public status—Anita Newcomb McGee's appointment, with the rank of lieutenant, as the first woman surgeon to serve in the War Department. "Now that the lines have slipped a bit," the article noted, "we hope there will be more to follow."[13] In 1901 Margaret Murray Washington eulogized Britain's Queen Victoria as embodying the progress of women. The queen—world-famous, "progressive," yet womanly—had reigned during the peak of British national greatness and had also presided over the British Empire's outlawing of slavery in its Caribbean colonies in the 1830s.[14]

Black women's refutations of "race suicide" was accompanied by an anti-imperialism compatible with both American civic nationalism and black nationalism. Those women who had newly defined black history internationally discovered in the history of the African-descended world diaspora a fighter against empire. Born in a slave revolt following the French Revolution, Haiti became the first black-ruled republic in world history. In the United States, a southerner and a northerner, working separately, fashioned the Haitian independence leader Toussaint L'Ouverture—born enslaved—into a hero for young Americans. Selena Sloan Butler of Atlanta was a Spelman Institute graduate, president of a local women's club, and the wife of a successful physician.[15] Writer and editor Pauline E. Hopkins, who was born in Maine to a Union veteran and his wife, expressed a proud identification with New England, a strong attachment to the Republican Party, and pride in her descent from black abolitionists.[16] Butler praised L'Ouverture for his "unerring resolution, military genius and precision." "For the Republic of Hayti," Hopkins wrote from Boston in 1900, "whose freedom was cemented by the martyred blood of this soldier and statesman, we feel with the late Frederick Douglass, that as the north star is eternal in the heavens, so will Hayti remain forever in the firmament of nations."[17]

NOTWITHSTANDING their own praise of motherhood, many white women nationalists and patriots lived lives that would not have pleased those who anticipated race suicide. Typifying the overall decline in births among native-born Americans, especially urban ones, during the nineteenth and early twentieth centuries, such women kept their families relatively small. My sample of 516 Daughters of the American Revolution born before 1900 who bore children shows an average of 2.72 children and a median of 2.45 children.[18] More meaningful to the history of nationalism than the facts of white women's maternity was their own defiance of race suicide arguments. Progressives and conservatives alike celebrated the increased public visibility of women like themselves and, indeed, of themselves. Some developed a women-centered imperialism that positioned white women as civilizers in their own right.

State-based nationalists found their country's overseas expansion profoundly energizing. DAR members were primed by Anglo-Saxonist racial beliefs, by eagerness (in other capacities) to spread Protestant Christianity, by their conviction that the United States had long constituted an empire, by family connections to official Washington and the military, and above all, by their fervent allegiance to the state to herald, following Rudyard Kipling, the United States's assumption of the "white man's burden" to civilize the world.[19] The DAR's national magazine cheered Americans' overthrowing of the Hawaiian monarchy in 1893: "The soul of freedom is marching on."[20] In DAR chapters in Honolulu (formed in 1897); Sitka, Alaska (1903); Havana (1907); Manila (1913); the Panama Canal Zone (1925); and San Juan, Puerto Rico (1932), missionary women and the wives of diplomats and military officers experienced overseas imperialism first hand, in addition to declaring it American and patriotic.[21]

War and overseas imperial expansion together profoundly altered the organizational culture of women's state-based nationalism. It seemed plainer than ever within the generally conservative DAR that patriotism necessitated women's direct involvement in politics. To a Coloradan, the Spanish-American War removed any doubt that the members should "[enter] more wisely into the councils of the men of the Nation."[22] Accordingly, the DAR began electing leaders for their personal qualifications and not only for their prominent husbands. To be sure, the organization continued to treasure proximity to male power. Members continued to express antipathy to "feminine politicians"—women who seemed overly ambitious.[23] The victor in the stormy 1901 DAR presidential election, Cornelia Cole Fairbanks, possessed the mandatory famous spouse. Charles Warren Fairbanks, a Republican senator from Indiana, would become Theodore Roosevelt's vice president in 1905. However, Fairbanks herself was a college graduate who possessed extensive experience as a club leader. President of Indiana's first literary club for women and the first woman appointed to the state Board of Charities, she had recently been elected director of the massive General Federation of Women's Clubs (GFWC).[24]

Before the Spanish-American War, the DAR's internal culture emphasized its members' self-education in Revolutionary history, lavish social events, historic preservation on a sporadic, local basis, and patriotic celebrations largely directed at other self-consciously patriotic white elites of documented Revolutionary descent.[25] After 1898, Daughters on a national scale began seeking the patriotic uplift of Americans at large, notably in engaging in commemoration for the first time. Only then did the women begin funding monuments, plaques, and flags that presented U.S. history, infused with state-based patriotism, to all passersby. By 1900, the DAR had also become a leader in historic preservation in the United States, at a time when amateurs generally dominated the field. All across the country, the women began setting aside property they deemed historically significant—battlefields, forts, private homes—from destruction or further alteration by others. They either bought such property themselves or appealed to state governments to do so. Among the hundreds of sites first administered or marked by the DAR, several were later deemed important enough by the federal government to be designated national parks or national historic sites: Revolutionary battle-fields and encampments at Valley Forge in Pennsylvania, Kings Mountain and Moore's Creek in North Carolina, and Cowpens in South Carolina; Independence Hall in Philadelphia; the route of the Natchez Trace Parkway in Tennessee, Alabama, and Mississippi; a pipestone quarry in Pipestone, Minnesota, sacred to the Dakota and Ojibway; the site of the Daniel and Agnes Freeman Homestead (later the Homestead National Monument) in Nebraska; the site of Bent's Old Fort in Colorado, on the Santa Fe Trail; and the Lapwai Mission to the Nez Perce in Idaho.[26]

The DAR's expansion and elaboration of its history work was intimately related to its support for the United States's transformation into an over-seas empire. DAR members came to consider nineteenth-century westward expansion as meaningful to American national identity as the American Revolution. In the words of a Tacoma, Washington, woman, the Revolution "gave us . . . the opportunity for the conquest of a continent."[27] Carrying with them the founders' values, westbound white migrants repeatedly rees-tablished the American nation. Most important, the women themselves in-terpreted the history of westward expansion as justifying the United States's contemporary overseas expansion. Both expressed God's plan for the spread of American civilization. White Americans throughout the centuries — "empire builders" — migrated to land that destiny had already specified as their own.[28]

Although it focused on socially prominent white "pioneers," the DAR did not pretend that those pioneers peopled empty lands. The women also paid tribute to nonwhites whose actions appeared ultimately to have advanced the course of American empire, eulogizing as "statesmen" Native American chiefs who had signed treaties relinquishing tribal lands.[29] Pocahontas and Sacagawea were beloved for ensuring the survival of white explorers (John Smith and Lewis and Clark, respectively), as was Chipeta, who had ruled the Ute with Chief Ouray in what became Colorado.[30] The DAR also hon-ored non-Anglophone Europeans on the grounds that they embodied the leading edge of whiteness and Christianity and that their actions assured the success of U.S. conquest. Although emphasizing Protestantism's superiority when discussing early Spanish missions, DAR women used language to memorialize Spanish colonists that they otherwise reserved for Anglo American founders. For example, the Los Angeles Daughters hailed Felipe de Neve, the first Spanish governor of California, as "scholar, statesman, [and] brilliant military leader."[31] The Laredo, Texas, DAR used similar language in honoring José Vásquez Borrego, who was credited for establishing an eighteenth-century settlement there, as "a great frontiersman, farmer, stockman," and significantly, "colonizer."[32] Mexican leaders did not receive such encomiums, most likely because Mexicans had taken up arms against U.S. conquest, but perhaps also because Mexican nationals' whiteness was in question.[33]

Writing in the DAR's magazine in 1902, a Californian considered Bernardo de Gálvez, the Spanish colonial governor of Louisiana, and his uncle José de Gálvez, Spain's visitor general, minister of state to the Indies, and later, governor of California, "great Revolutionary heroes," even "demi-gods" on a par with George Washington. The Gálvez men's defiance of British and Russian control of their respective territories in the late eighteenth century enabled the United States to conquer them later. Aside from such deeds, the writer declared, "[d]o we need any further evidence that the God of Nations has mapped out our manifest destiny?" In conclusion, she baldly linked the old land empire and the new overseas empire: "if we have come into possession of [the Philippines] it is just as logical as our coming into possession of any part of Spanish-America. The Philippines were settled by a colony from Mexico in 1564, hence were American from the beginning."[34] The DAR's commemorations of westward expansion and its support for contemporary overseas imperial expansion, then, were of one piece. Both ideas communicated the desire of state-based nationalists to unify white Americans at home into a national community and to locate that community's history within a trajectory of Anglo-Saxon transnationalism.

AS THE U.S. EMPIRE expanded across the water, the DAR developed an ambitiously women-centered nationalism that not only praised white women's political activism but portrayed white women as makers of civilization. Daughters paid respects to the explorers, fur traders, and others who were the first Europeans in the women's own localities, and they put much effort into remapping trails submerged beneath pavement, railroad tracks, and farms.[35] Yet they most cherished the layers of resettlement that indicated the presence of white women. DAR plaques throughout the United States marked communities' first schools, newspapers, churches, and substantial houses — wood "frame" or stone, as distinguished from more humble dwellings of logs, sod, or adobe. All increased their locales' resemblance to the more "civilized" ones that white migrants had left behind.[36] The organization also honored the New York–born Congregational missionary Narcissa Prentiss Whitman as the first white woman, in 1836, to cross the continent. Grace Raymond Hebard, a Wyoming historian and woman suffragist, imagined the Whitmans and their party traversing the Rockies that year on the Fourth of July. With husband Marcus Whitman carrying "the Bible in one hand and an American flag in the other," the group knelt "and took possession of the land to the West as a home of American mothers."[37] Indeed, DAR women's narratives of resettlement inverted Frederick Jackson Turner's famous and decidedly masculine praise for the frontier. Turner believed that the "continuous touch with the simplicity of primitive society" on the frontier produced "the forces dominating American character."[38] Although Daughters wrote or sponsored the first histories of many a western locality—something else Turner advocated—many believed conversely that the most meaningful aspects of the country's character, "whatever is of most permanent and abiding value[,] has come from this eastern coast of America" (in the words of a New Yorker transplanted to Colorado).[39] In celebrating their communities' increasing resemblance to those to the east, white women celebrated their communities' feminization and consequent Americanization.

Also portraying white women as shapers of civilization were neo-Confederate women. At the turn of the twentieth century, the UDC still constituted a potent political force in the South by shaping the deeply political process of commemoration, even as it reinforced white men's leadership of the race. The women's pointed conservatism regarding gender—as exemplified by a Texas leader's call in 1903 for members to lobby the state legislature by contacting "some man of influence or prominence" to petition on their behalf —did not mitigate the hostility of those men who recognized and were threatened by the women's potency.[40] The UDC's preeminence among neo-

Confederates—as indicated by its greater numbers and dedication relative to male organizations, notably the SCV—did not go unlamented by contemporaries.[41] Men and women alike perceived women's looming importance within pro-Confederate commemoration as a problem, but each assigned different causes and implications to that importance. Implicitly arguing for female moral superiority, one North Carolina woman tied "[o]ur younger men['s]" apparent apathy toward commemorating the Confederacy to their own greed.[42] *Confederate Veteran* editor Sumner Archibald Cunningham, in contrast, considered white women's status as "the sole protectors of the honor of ancestors" to be a threat to southern civilization at large. He feared that if men did not "take part in the preservation of correct history so zealously pursued by the great and grand organization of our women . . . , much of the sacrifice of a half century will be forgotten, the wealth of the best part of American manhood will be lost, and the best of our civilization will be retarded inestimably."[43] Such associations between the neo-Confederate movement's feminization and its eventual decline are questionable. White women's commemorations, focusing on altering everyday life and the very landscape not only protected the Confederacy, as neo-Confederates viewed it, from oblivion but enabled the contemporary white South to shape the terms of national unity. The achievement of race-based national unity in turn justified the country's overseas expansion.

THE DEVELOPMENT OF the American overseas empire at the turn of the twentieth century, and the wars that accompanied that process, produced varieties of women-centered nationalism among organized women that challenged some men's narrow definitions of female nationalism as rooted in reproduction and that positioned white women as makers of civilization. Yet the imperial wars also brought out women-centered nationalism's conservative aspects, reinforcing models of patriotism that placed women behind the political scenes. An Ann Arbor, Michigan, DAR leader called her young audience's attention to "how women uncomplainingly give the loved men in their home[s] to fight the nation's battles."[44] African American and white women alike measured patriotism with male yardsticks. When Mary Church Terrell boasted of the achievements of graduates of Washington's only

black high school in 1904, she began with veterans of the imperial wars—
"[t]hree of the finest lieutenants in the Spanish-American war" and one
army captain who had been "president" of a Filipino town "during the late
unpleasantness there."[45] Led by Emma Trowbridge Hart of Jacksonville,
Florida, black women launched a nationwide effort in early 1899 to fund a
$25,000 monument "to the memory of the colored heroes" of the Spanish-
American War army, to be "erected in some liberal city," not Jacksonville.[46]
White women in the DAR funded numerous monuments to Spanish-American
War heroes, as in Mansfield, Ohio, and Waco, Texas.[47] Similarly, black and
white women alike continued to direct their patriotic education efforts at
boys in particular—destined for or, in the case of African Americans, aspiring to first-class citizenship. In Norwich, Connecticut, the black women
of the Rose of New England Women's League ran what they called a Boys'
Race History Class.[48]

State-based nationalists focused in peacetime on producing loyalty to the
state. In wartime they called for unquestioning allegiance to the state. The DAR's
leadership defended the McKinley administration's conduct of the Spanish-
American War against what the organization viewed as partisan attacks—
even though congressional investigations of conditions in military camps were
damaging enough to bring about Secretary of War Russell Alger's resignation
in 1899. Revolutionary soldiers had had it worse, asserted the DAR's national
magazine.[49] Married to a patent lawyer, Alice Bradford Wiles headed the
DAR's massive chapter in Chicago, which numbered more than 700 women.
The forty-four-year-old defended the U.S. government in 1899 against al-
legations of brutality in the Philippines. She implored her audience "not [to]
be so dazzled by the brilliance of our catchwords of liberty, 'the rule of the
majority,' 'the consent of the governed' and others." Filipinos, she said, "must
learn what law and order is before they can themselves maintain it."[50]

Some women-centered nationalists went beyond praising warriors or the
government and called on those who were ineligible for military service to
emulate military hierarchies. To compare the actions and bearing of organized women to those of troops constituted the highest compliment a state-
based nationalist could pay to women, which also communicated women's
hunger for public recognition. However, such comparisons heightened the
cultural authority of present-day men and anticipated a female nationalism

truly centered on men. Reubena Hyde Walworth, a Vassar graduate who never married, was the daughter of DAR cofounder Ellen Hardin Walworth and active in the DAR herself. When she died at thirty-one of the typhus she contracted from her soldier-patients at the Long Island hospital where she volunteered, she "gave her life," said two of her fellow Daughters, "as surely as any soldier on the field of battle."[51] Following the swift U.S. victory over Spain, a South Carolinian cheered the DAR as "the Household Troops . . . . For who excels us in national pride? In soldierly discipline?"[52] In 1901, when revelations of U.S. atrocities against Filipino civilians and the use of torture were making the Philippine-American War controversial well outside the anti-imperialist press, a New Haven woman called on other Americans, including her fellow Daughters, to emulate military models of subordination. "[W]hat our patriotism lacks in this country is reverence," she insisted. "[A]s we honor the generals in battle for guiding a campaign to a successful issue, so in the world's arena, let us have the true reverence for its leading lights and the humility to make us admire them, trust them, defer to them, and follow them. This is rightly termed the truer patriotism. We know how impossible it is for the general to bring to successful issue his campaign without his common soldier, but the true soldier loves, reverences his general."[53]

Fueling state-based nationalists' support for the imperial wars was the same energy source that powered white nationalism in general—aspirations to white Anglo-Saxon world supremacy. The women's racism was not absolute. If they dreaded the prospect of millions of new, nonwhite U.S. citizens, presented by the annexation of territories in the Caribbean and the Pacific— an objection often raised by white anti-imperialists—they left that dread unarticulated. The women's definitions of national greatness, now expanded to fit the new overseas empire, won out over such fears. Gazing overseas, state-based nationalists felt a race-based affinity with Britain. With many male contemporaries, they envisioned a transnational union of Anglo-Saxon, English-speaking peoples keeping the peace in the Western world.[54] Mary Smith Lockwood, speaking for the national leadership in the DAR's magazine, hoped that an alliance with "our kinsmen over the sea" would protect what she revealingly called "the human side of the world."[55] Calling England "Our Mother Country," DAR leaders paid tribute to Queen Victoria on her eightieth birthday in 1899 by rejoicing over the reunion of "the Anglo-Saxon race in sentiment if not political bonds."[56] The next year, without any sense of irony, a Connecticut leader proposed organizing a Daughters of the American Revolution chapter in London.[57]

Another entity that stressed conservative forms of women-centered nationalism in wartime was the WRC, the standard-bearer among organized women of national patriotism. The WRC long struggled over the appropriateness of overtly political activism by women regarding patriotism. Following the Spanish-American War, a Massachusetts leader worried about how "[t]o face the serious crisis of war which now confronted me; to do what ought to be done by this large and patriotic organization of women, and yet to do this in such a way as would meet with the approval of the Grand Army of the Republic." That same year, in 1899, the national WRC convention passed a resolution to "disapprove of women marching" in GAR parades.[58] Yet the patriotic instruction of young people was condoned when, for example, the WRC distributed its "Patriotic Primer for the Little Citizen," which contained patriotic songs' lyrics, the Gettysburg Address, and excerpts from Lincoln's other speeches, in Puerto Rican and Filipino schools.[59] Women's patriotic uplift of children was acceptable even to those who otherwise longed for women to pledge their primary allegiances to their family identities.

THEIR OWN WAR WORK notwithstanding, neo-Confederate women and African American clubwomen were less comfortable with the wartime conflation of nation, state, and country. With the exception of the UDC Texas Division's tongue-in-cheek commendation of the Roosevelt administration's engineering of Panamanian secession from Colombia (on the grounds that the administration realized "the bright realms of truth attained by the Southern states so many years ago"), neo-Confederate women commented relatively little on the new overseas empire.[60] The imperial wars and the assumptions behind them no doubt constituted divisive topics in their circles. The *Confederate Veteran* took offense at the floridly reconciliationist rhetoric — for example, that celebrated former Confederate officers' service in the war with Spain — that saturated the national white press in 1898. Such rhetoric ignored what neo-Confederates saw as white southerners' steadfast American patriotism, as demonstrated by their having separated from a country and fought a government, the United States in 1860, that had repudiated Revolutionary and constitutional principles.[61] The UDC's national leadership made similar, if veiled arguments in hailing the organization's own war work and the appearance of Confederate veterans in the U.S. ranks as proof of the old Confederacy's consistent Americanism.[62]

Though marveling later at the Panama Canal, other white southerners challenged the enthusiasm for overseas expansion while still emphasizing their American identities.[63] Married to a Confederate captain who later became Georgia's state treasurer, Emily Hendree Park of Macon held state-level offices in both the UDC and the DAR. In reply to the DAR president's rejoicing in February 1900 that the Fourth of July was now celebrated in places tens of thousands of miles apart, the fifty-two-year-old Alabama native agreed that Americans "must fulfill our destiny and civilize the world." But then Park directly challenged overseas imperialism. Praising, in an aside, the Boers' ongoing "valiant struggle" against the British in South Africa, she voiced an unfashionable distaste for the "English"—attributing to them a "deadness to any but crude and violent stimulus." She concluded by opposing the United States's entanglements in Asia: "Let us beware of the unrest that follows war, and the greed that grows with gain . . . . The new reading of the Monroe doctrine . . . may lead us into dangerous complications with new and strange neighbors." Ultimately, Park enjoined the U.S. government to "forbear to throttle a single cry for freedom" in the Philippines.[64]

Combined with her standing among neo-Confederates, Park's prominence in the DAR exemplifies many white southerners' ability to harmonize Confederate and American identities by asserting the Americanism of the Confederate cause. To other, more militant neo-Confederates, Confederate identity and American identity—especially in the form of allegiance to the contemporary state—could not mesh easily. The president of the UDC's Virginia Division characterized its extensive war relief work as "extraneous" and "foreign to the work of the United Daughters of the Confederacy." She omitted the projects from her annual report to the 1898 national convention, which met shortly after the Spanish-American War.[65]

IN WARTIME AND in peacetime Jim Crow violence continued. Only a week after the USS *Maine* exploded in Havana harbor in February 1898—spurring the United States's initial decision to fight Spain—a black postmaster and his infant son were gunned down by a white mob in Lake City, South Carolina. African American commentators hoped that the lynchings would revive federal intervention against racial violence in the South, as Fraser Baker had been a government employee. Their hopes came to nothing despite the lobbying efforts of Ida B. Wells-Barnett and others. The sole remaining black member of Congress, George Henry White of North Carolina, tried to pass a resolution to give Baker's widow and surviving children "a small indemnity," but he was not allowed on the floor.[66] That fall, black clubwomen contacted his widow Laremie Baker to see if the federal government had yet sent her any money.[67]

Black male editorialists clashed over whether to declare support for the imperial wars and to continue backing the Republican Party, with some contending that black men should engage in military service in order to bolster their ability to defend themselves at home.[68] Black clubwomen also pondered questions of empire. Though they generally opposed the new overseas empire, they did not reject all the premises of U.S. imperialism. Most associated "civilization" with European high culture and Christianity. (Not until after the First World War did most black nationalists or African Americans in general cease to make that connection.)[69] At the turn of the twentieth century, some celebrated the United States's long history as a land empire. Contemplating the ruins of an early Spanish mission in California, thirty-two-year-old Sarah Willie Layten, a Baptist leader, contended that in bringing Christianity to "savages" who had lived in "barbarism," the "[k]ind padres" had brought about "the dawn of civilization on the Pacific Coast."[70] A Texan similarly meditated in 1895 on the doomed men of the Alamo—the "almost superhuman accomplishments of its brave patriots in their struggles for freedom" against Mexican forces—notwithstanding the centrality of slavery to the Texans' struggle.[71]

The Texas woman's notation elsewhere in the article that the men had not been buried, like decent Christians, but burned is especially poignant in light of what she left unmentioned—the seventeen white-on-black lynchings that had occurred in Texas in the foregoing three years.[72] Such violence helps explain why many African Americans in the late nineteenth-century South associated westward migration with their own liberation. Black men and women alike chased the western horizon. While stopping short of celebrating women as civilizers, some associated westward migration with expanded political rights for women. Reveling in the sight of women of "all nationalities" voting in Colorado in the early 1890s, a Denver woman mentioned another, newly arrived from Tennessee, who was already prominent in the Republican State League of Colorado. Lizzie M. Olden and those who had come west like her longed not only for mountain air, but for "a dwelling place where free speech would not be denied them."[73]

However, most black clubwomen's relatively benign view of American empire terminated at land's end. Most who spoke out on the subject of overseas empire opposed it, demonstrating that their patriotism did not always demand support for the state. Many believed that the United States's subject peoples were inherently capable of governing themselves. Moreover, domestic racial violence undermined the United States's position as a civilizing agent in the world. Some opposed overseas expansion as early as January 1894, when the newly formed Woman's Era Club of Boston denounced the U.S. takeover of Hawaii, which had been, until then, an independent country. With the help of U.S. Marines, white men who were descended from American immigrants had forced Queen Liliuokalani to abdicate in 1893 and had created a republican government in hopes of U.S. annexation. Headed by Josephine St. Pierre Ruffin, the Woman's Era Club praised President Grover Cleveland's refusal to agree to Hawaii's annexation, which was consequently delayed until 1898, when his Republican successor approved it. In addition to condemning "greedy" Americans in Hawaii, the women defended the patriotism of those who opposed the conquest of Hawaii as "those who place truth and justice above national gain and power." In a pointed rejoinder to white supremacy, Ruffin and the *Woman's Era* also devoted breathless society-page coverage to the deposed queen's comings and goings in neighboring Brookline, Massachusetts, where her in-laws lived.[74]

Following the outbreak of war with Spain in 1898, anger at the national state's acceptance of Jim Crow caused two very different people, who had feuded with each other, to turn normative notions of the American "civilizing mission" and normative notions of national unity on their heads. Both women focused on race-based rather than gender-based notions of civilization. The fiery Ida B. Wells-Barnett, then beginning her civil rights work, was not the only one to assert that Americans' toleration of "anarchy" and "murder" in the South would earn them "the contempt of civilization"—placing the United States outside civilization's pale.[75] In the 1890s Mary Church Terrell of Washington, D.C., had presented a less confrontational demeanor than Wells-Barnett, in keeping with the Terrells' ties to Booker T. Washington. In 1905, however, Terrell published her stinging "Service Which Should Be Rendered the South." Using language that was commonly applied to non-whites, she contended that many in the territorial United States, not in its new colonies, were in need of moral and political tutelage. Jim Crow's many cruelties had convinced her that the white South—especially its "ignorant," "vicious" white poor, on whom she and many contemporaries blamed most racial violence—required "civilizing and Christianizing."[76] Thus inverting the language of overseas imperialism, Terrell's rhetoric removed Jim Crow's vigilantes from the United States and placed them in the new antipodes, whose residents were then ineligible for American citizenship.[77]

Strongly criticizing government actions following the imperial wars, other African Americans reconceived their national identities. In 1905 Emma Frances Merritt, a forty-five-year-old teacher and principal in Washington, emphatically rejected a ruling premise of African American civic nationalism —that racial injustice constituted a sharp deviation from America's essence.[78] The histories of westward expansion and of slavery, combined with the just-concluded imperial wars, all demonstrated to Merritt that "prejudice" was in fact "inseparably linked with America" and followed the American flag wherever it was "planted." She concluded that in her own time, "Native racial differences along mental and moral lines and the natural right of a more powerful [race] to dominate and fix the status of an inferior race is the doctrine inculcated and disseminated by America throughout the entire world." The remedy lay in teaching a black history, centered on the heroic Frederick Douglass, that would instill racial pride in black children. Ultimately, Merritt intended black history to foster black nationalism, a sense of belonging to a race-based collective. She conflated her race with her nation, rather than situating one inside the other—her race inside the American nation. Her patriotism was profoundly dissociated from, if not opposed, to the American state.[79]

Numerous black women at the twentieth century's turn made arguments similar to Merritt's, that black history should inculcate race pride.[80] Other women went beyond instilling collective racial self-determination at home to adopt a race-based internationalism. Such women located African Americans within a world community of African-descended peoples. In 1900 Anna Julia Cooper of Washington, known for her particularly sweeping definitions of women's authority within their race and nation, spoke at the world's first pan-African conference, which had been organized by a Trinidadian lawyer and held in London.[81] Others linked African Americans to a glorious African past. Like many black nationalists at the time, Selena Sloan Butler of Atlanta believed modern Africa represented a decline into "barbarism."[82] In ancient Africa, she contended, blacks had "occupied a stage of civilization to which other races bowed." In 1897 Butler implored readers of a Baptist periodical to recover that feeling. The ideal result would be to have "almost every child of the succeeding generation . . . speak with as much pride of his race and the Negro blood in his veins as does the Anglo-Saxon of his race and the blue blood which comes to his veins." To Butler, the inculcation of this pride in white youth was clearly being accomplished by white women.[83] Also focusing on ancient Africa was Pauline E. Hopkins's 1903 novel *Of One Blood*, which located civilization's origins among ancient Africans, "the people whose posterity has been denied a rank among the human race."[84] In her series of articles for young people on "Famous Men of the Negro Race," Hopkins addressed the question of why her readers should interest themselves in Haiti by pointing to overlaps between African American history and the histories of others in the African-descended diaspora. In the United States and in Haiti, "brothers in blood" had fought their way to freedom. "[T]hough speaking different languages," she argued, "we should clasp our hands in friendship when we look back upon our past, when we, too, though unaccustomed to the sound or use of arms, marched to Fort Wagner and to Fort Pillow." She predicted, "As a race"—an international entity—"we shall be preserved, though annihilation sometimes seems very near."[85]

The NACW put ideas about transnational communion into practice at its

1906 convention. Two Americans who had recently worked in Africa—one in Madagascar, as the wife of the U.S. consul there, and one in Liberia—addressed the meeting. The latter, Georgia De Baptiste Faulkner, "wished there could be some way whereby direct communication, as well as transportation, could be opened between the colored women of America and the colored women of Africa; also, that some day one of our conventions might be held in Africa." Immediately following, the delegates voted in a resolution to ask the two women to start "women's clubs" in the respective countries; "the final result to be an International Association of Colored Women."[86] The next NACW biennial, in 1908, featured delegates from Liberia and Bermuda in addition to those from throughout the United States.[87] Ever after, NACW gatherings had an international component.

Black clubwomen who sought to convene women like themselves from around the African diaspora were practicing a nationalism that posited a race-based sense of community between themselves and African-descended peoples abroad. Other adherents of black nationalism promoted race pride and solidarity at home. All of these women cultivated patriotic identities other than, or in addition to, their identities as Americans. They were operating as post-Emancipation race relations neared their worst—as manifested by the tightening of Jim Crow laws and violence in the South, whites' nationwide accommodation of Jim Crow, and the United States's expansion into an overseas empire informed by white supremacy. White Americans' own race-based transnationalism, in the form of affinities with Britain, intensified those processes. Unlike the black nationalists who self-consciously distanced themselves from the American state and occasionally from their country, however, white women viewed their own desires for international racial community as reinforcing their country's glories in addition to uplifting the world. White Anglo-Saxon transnationalism did not entail alienation from the state.[88]

WOMEN'S DEBATES on the question of overseas empire show sharp differences. The expanded American empire, like a Rorschach blot, revealed in its interpreters differing assumptions about nation, the state, and race. To members of the WRC and the DAR, national unity with allegiance to the federal government as that unity's glue had always been the core element of patriotism. Accustomed to believing in manifest destiny, DAR women embraced the United States's new incarnation as an overseas empire and extended their patriotic outreach to the population at large. The imperial wars helped solidify a national near-consensus among white elites on white supremacy even as neo-Confederate women expressed skepticism about overseas empire in their continuing discomfort with state power. Emphasizing both African American civic nationalism (especially as related to Civil War commemorations) and, increasingly, black nationalism, most black clubwomen steadfastly opposed the premises of overseas imperialism even as they, like white women, supported the imperial war effort in 1898 with their labor. Black women objected to the white supremacy they knew undergirded imperialism. What all of these different groups of women shared was opposition to the variant of men's nationalism that emphasized women's fertility at the expense of women's political activism. The women were certain of the importance of female public activism and female cultural authority to nationalism. The women expressed that conviction in taking part in the early twentieth century's reform movements.

Chapter Three
The State

BETWEEN THE TWENTIETH century's turn and the First
World War, women's nationalism often walked hand in hand with desires
for political and social reform. Pondering the phrase "My country, right
or wrong" in 1901, a St. Paul, Minnesota, member of the Daughters of the
American Revolution allowed that her country could sometimes be wrong,
and she called on her audience to "[bend] all our powers to make it right."[1]
It was not only state-based nationalism, the merging of state with nation,
that portrayed the state as an agent of progress. Black women who subscribed to American civic nationalism and black nationalism, which were
both critical of the contemporary state, did the same in the course of their
civil rights activism and social work. Significantly, neo-Confederate women
did not, as neo-Confederates, engage in reform work except in relation to
the erstwhile Confederate nation's core—Confederate veterans and their
white relatives and descendants—in part because of reform work's faith
in the state. Neo-Confederate women's relationship with the state continued to be stormy because the women continued to deny that allegiance to
America must necessarily take the form of allegiance to the contemporary
state.

Women nationalists' reform work exemplifies women-centered nationalism in its approaches to the state (as no longer exclusively male), its focus on
youth, and its assertion that women could and should shape civilization. Reform work accommodated expansive definitions of female authority but ulti-

mately respected male power. White and black women-centered nationalists who engaged in reform persistently upheld normative notions of marriage and motherhood.[2] Even those limited definitions of female authority drew resistance, however—significantly, from other women. As an organization, the UDC withheld support from most child-centered reform work, partly on the grounds of its challenges to male supremacy, and it never endorsed woman suffrage before the Nineteenth Amendment's ratification in August 1920. The reformist guises of women-centered nationalism also enhanced men's political authority—more than ever before among African Americans. The emergence of a national, male-led reform movement for black civil rights, a movement that newly conflated citizenship and patriotism with manhood, closed a window in time in which politically minded black women laid claims to leadership of their nations.

WOMEN-CENTERED nationalists presented histories focused on women during the Progressive Era, as those nationalists had done earlier. A pageant put on by the Ohio Federation of Colored Women's Clubs at the 1914 NACW biennial presented the black race's evolution over time, in the United States, entirely in light of women's history. The Ohioans began with impersonations of such "great Negro women born in slavery" as Phillis Wheatley, Sojourner Truth, and Harriet Tubman and ended with "contemporaneous Negro women of distinction," with some playing themselves.[3] That same year, black clubwomen finally succeeded in altering the landscape in memory of a black woman. The Empire State Federation of Colored Women's Clubs dedicated its monument to Tubman in Auburn, New York, on a summer day in 1915, raising the monument on the unmarked grave where she had been buried two years before.[4] That the New Yorkers chose the Fourth of July as the dedication day suggests many black clubwomen's continued investment in their American identities. They pledged allegiance to a nation unified by loyal behavior toward the United States.

Also illustrating women-centered nationalism is women's reliance on symbols and artifacts and the infusion of such artifacts with sentimentality. A common practice in the DAR and the UDC was to present leaders with ceremonial gavels made of wood of historically significant provenance, such as (at one UDC meeting) "from the platform of the mortar that fired the first shot on Fort Sumter."[5] Black clubwomen engaged in the same ritual while communicating a sharply different view of the past. At the 1912 NACW biennial, Mrs. I. N. Ross of Washington gave the organization's president an oak gavel "made from the balustrade, where Harriet Beecher Stowe rested her hand in going up and down the stairs while writing 'Uncle Tom's Cabin,' Cincinnati, Ohio," as well as from wood from the Washington, D.C., house where Abraham Lincoln had lived. Ross herself had been born enslaved— and had been given, as a child, as a birthday present to her young mistress— and perceived that Lincoln's Emancipation Proclamation had freed her.[6] Crafting an interracial vision of country, Ross's homage to Stowe and Lincoln affirmed American civic nationalism.

New to women-centered nationalism in the Progressive Era were definitions of patriotism that ranged beyond allegiance to the state—notably pro-Union women's characterization of patriotism as "a broader humanity" that extended also to animals.[7] Also resulting from female nationalism's reformist turn was a new closeness to the state. Approaching the government did not, in the Progressive Era, necessarily reinforce male political supremacy as it had in the 1890s. Progressive women nationalists were not demanding unquestioning allegiance to the state and its policies; on the contrary, they operated in the belief that they and the state could together better their country. Moreover, in contrast to the late nineteenth century, in the Progressive Era the state itself did not reflexively act to protect capital, which was concentrated in the hands of men. The state now entertained some regulation of business and dissolved a few corporate monopolies. The state was also no longer administered exclusively by men. In the cases of the U.S. Children's Bureau (created in 1912) and the U.S. Women's Bureau (1920), both sub-agencies of the Department of Labor, the federal government hired small numbers of white women as policymakers. State and federal governments also enacted some policies that were desired by organized women and female professionals, such as tighter child labor restrictions and pensions for infant and maternal health.[8]

In their focus on young audiences and in their appeals to the state to help fulfill their nation's needs, African American clubwomen's reforms aimed at black youth illustrate women-centered nationalism especially well. Even in the legally segregated South, black clubwomen did not operate in estrangement from government. Creating institutions to help and uplift the black poor with the help of governments was done by American civic nationalists and black nationalists alike, and particularly by black nationalists who were focusing on racial self-determination within the United States. The Oklahoma Federation of Colored Women's Clubs was among many southern federations that lobbied state legislatures to fund facilities for black juvenile delinquents. Significantly, the Oklahomans no longer viewed the promotion of black history as conflicting with their work among the poor. They also lobbied the legislature to have "Negro history" included in black schools' curricula.[9] Black clubwomen also joined other organized women in imploring the federal government to place additional restrictions on child labor and to reduce infant mortality rates.[10]

Also exemplifying women-centered nationalism, white women pursued the patriotic uplift of white youth and of immigrants. Among female organizations that were explicitly devoted to patriotism, the DAR engaged by far the most in progressive reform. Not only were these women already accustomed to approaching the state, but their broadening definitions of white women's authority facilitated their turn toward reform. The DAR's ranks as of 1900 included the leading reformer Jane Addams. Other members reported sustaining and even creating settlement houses in which reformers lived among the poor and investigated their living conditions.[11] However, except in their quest to Americanize immigrants, DAR members were followers, not leaders, within female progressive reform. Compared to the earnestness of many in the mostly white GFWC network, which itself represented moderate strands of progressive reform, the DAR's commitment to reform, as an organization, was uneven.[12] Substantial numbers limited their other club activities to church memberships and to more exclusive hereditary groups. "You are familiar with the character of the membership of the organization," an Iowa leader sighed to the chief of the U.S. Children's Bureau.[13]

The DAR's progressive nationalism occupied the conservative end of progressive reform's vast political spectrum in another respect. In sharp contrast to women reformers who focused on the exploitation of workers and who aided strikers, the DAR's progressives (like its conservatives) were devout antiradicals to the point of opposing organized labor in most cases.[14] The

1901 assassination of President William McKinley by the self-declared anarchist Leon Czolgosz provoked a fresh wave of worries about foreigners and radicalism, notwithstanding the fact that Czolgosz was American-born. The shooting also helped propel the DAR into reform work in the first place. Except for the Americanization of immigrants—pursued in northern industrial cities starting in the mid-1890s—the DAR's reformist projects postdate the assassination. The lives of some of the organization's progressives suggest that the shooting first galvanized them into action. To thirty-three-year-old Elizabeth Cynthia Barney Buel, a college-educated writer and physician's wife living in Litchfield, Connecticut, McKinley's death made it "our duty to stamp out anarchy's fiendish and unholy cult." Buel went on to become the DAR's leading Americanizer, supervising the publication of two successive "manuals," in 1910 and 1921, that encouraged European immigrants to become citizens and to assimilate.[15]

Subsequently, within the DAR, progressives and conservatives alike resolutely opposed anything they perceived as smacking of leftism. The women blamed the violence and disruption resulting from strikes on the strikers and publicized attacks on strikebreakers. Like Theodore Roosevelt in his "New Nationalist" phase of 1910, the women supported modifying capitalism—having government curb the excesses of employers in addition to the excesses of labor—in order to save capitalism and to diminish the appeal of revolution.[16] For all its antiradicalism, the DAR's short-lived progressive incarnation commands significance because it shows that even state-based nationalism and patriotism could accommodate desires for human progress. The women themselves redefined national patriotism to mean more than "a willingness to fight for, and to maintain inviolate the special government under which one lived." Patriotism also embraced "every movement that stands for the betterment of mankind."[17]

Progressive reform, as defined by these white women, exemplified women-centered nationalism in its positioning of women as cultural authorities and civilizers. That tendency was especially evident in Americanization work. By the turn of the twentieth century, even the most conservative female nationalists considered it acceptable for women to engage in the patriotic education of youth. Americanizers favored a bolder form of female influence in also attempting the patriotic uplift of adults, including adult men. Originating locally as early as 1894 (in Illinois and in Lowell, Massachusetts) and declared a national project in 1903, the DAR's Americanization programs welcomed a wide range of nationalities into the United States as long as they assimilated—and thus exemplified a limited civic nationalism.[18] Distributing its own "manuals" for citizenship and funding and teaching classes at local schools or settlements, the DAR prepared immigrants who were eligible for naturalization—non-Asian men and unmarried, non-Asian women— for the history and civics examinations that were made mandatory for U.S. citizenship starting in 1906. The women also infused naturalization procedures with a new degree of ceremony, gathering at courthouses to greet newly minted citizens with American flags and desserts.[19]

For the most part, DAR women considered racial distinctions among Europeans to lack significance and sought the patriotic uplift of immigrants from all parts of Europe, in contrast to contemporaries who desired on racial grounds to reduce the numbers of southern and eastern Europeans admitted to the United States.[20] Starting around 1910, Daughters all over the trans-Mississippi West—in Kansas, Idaho, southern California, Arizona, and Texas —also performed "patriotic education" work among Mexican or Asian immigrants in their communities, despite the latter group's ineligibility for naturalization.[21] Such Americanization efforts, while assuming and desiring even non-Europeans' capability of change, nevertheless ultimately strengthened racial assumptions by designating white, middle-class, Anglo American culture as Americanism's yardstick.[22] Moreover, except in the West, the DAR focused on turning Europeans into white Americans. "In the children of today lies our white hope of the future," one woman remarked regarding Americanization.[23] Moreover, the women derived their considerable sense of authority over immigrants from their own documented Revolutionary ancestry. Bloodlines in themselves, they thought, imparted knowledge and leadership. Accepting foreigners from around the world into the American nation, Americanization work therefore communicated a race-based nationalism and a civic nationalism simultaneously.

Similarly positioning white women as the nation's protectors were the DAR's appeals to the state for tighter restrictions on industrial child labor, on the grounds that such labor constricted white children's opportunities and thus endangered the country. This logic conflated the nation's fortunes with those of the white race.[24] Local DAR members demonstrated interest in the topic of child labor as early as 1902 in Auburn, Alabama. In 1907 the DAR's national convention denounced "child labor in all forms." A year later, the organization formed its own national Child Labor Committee—headed by J. Ellen Foster of temperance and Republican Party fame—to oversee ongoing state-level lobbying and local efforts.[25] The DAR's Child Labor Committee later became its Committee on the Welfare of Women and Children. Among many local efforts were those of Kansas City members who visited a juvenile court in search of children under fourteen who applied for work permits. The women paid the children's families in hopes of keeping the children in school.[26] The DAR called for the creation of a federal children's bureau three years before it transpired, and it supported indirect means of combating child labor such as state-level compulsory education laws and birth registration, which were both intended to keep underage children in school. Local chapters lobbied the U.S. Congress for the passage of a ban on child-manufactured goods from interstate commerce (which bore fruit in 1916 in the short-lived Owen-Keating Act) and also later cooperated with the U.S. Children's Bureau's efforts to combat infant mortality.[27] The DAR also promoted National Consumer League boycotts of sweatshop- and child-manufactured goods.[28]

Another indirect measure against child labor was to fund schools in the southern Appalachians and Ozarks, where isolation denied white children access to public education and where economic pressures often swept those children and their families into southern textile mills. In remote Grant, Alabama, the DAR created its own school—first proposed in 1910, opened in 1924.[29] Daughters well outside the South justified their fund-raising for southern mountain schools in starkly racial terms in addition to humanitarian ones. An Ohioan hailed mountain children as "sons and daughters of Scottish kings" and "pure American white citizens who need only opportunity."[30] A Massachusetts native living in Washington, D.C., lamented that "environment," as opposed to "heredity," "crowds out the nobler qualities and pushes aside those who would, if opportunity offered, make a name and place for themselves."[31] Such language contrasts with that deployed by neo-Confederate and pro-Union women. Both groups considered similar projects among southern mountain people. Rejecting them, the UDC gener-

ally directed its scholarships after 1908 at white Confederate descendants—
not even at white southerners per se.[32] It did not escape the attention of
president Lizzie George Henderson that many "mountain whites . . . had
fought against the South" in Union blue uniforms.[33] For the same reason—
the region's support for the United States during the Civil War—the WRC
raised money for and held numerous essay contests at mountain schools
starting in 1912.[34] The Civil War–centered arguments of neo-Confederate
and pro-Union women make the DAR's racial justifications for funding
schools for southern mountain people all the more apparent.

ALTHOUGH WOMEN-CENTERED nationalism infused with progressivism
fostered a bold form of female cultural authority—condoning women's
patriotic uplift of adult men—women-centered nationalism also, as always,
incorporated elements of domesticity. Adherents opposed forms of female
authority that relocated women far from the home. Even black clubwomen's
support for woman suffrage demonstrates this tendency. In 1912 the NACW
fully endorsed women's right to vote, years before white-led women's organizations stressing nation did so.[35] While black clubwomen supported
female suffrage in part on the grounds of justice and consistency, in keeping with their goal of restoring black men's ability to vote in the South, the
women also articulated their support for women's voting rights in terms,
used also by many white suffragists, that reinforced domesticity. Votes for
women constituted "Votes for Mothers" and "Votes for Children," two
clubwomen wrote in the NAACP's magazine in 1915.[36]

Exemplifying some black women's discomfort with expansive notions of
female political authority was Margaret Murray Washington, the wife of
Booker T. Washington. The longtime editor of the NACW's *National Association Notes*, its official periodical, she published in 1912 an interview with the
president of Cornell University that relayed anxieties that women's colleges
were fast becoming "Old Maid Factories."[37] Showing that antiradicalism
was, in this period, not for whites only, she proudly characterized black
women's support for woman suffrage as "conservative." Unlike British and
white American suffragists who favored street confrontations, she boasted,
"We have not blown any houses with dynamite, nor have we been engaged

in parading the streets in men's attire." On those grounds, Washington pointedly withheld endorsement of black clubwomen's participation in the suffragist march on Washington in 1913. Four years later, the *Notes* condemned the Congressional Union (later the National Woman's Party) for its wartime demonstrations in front of the White House.[38]

Except for the WRC, which endorsed woman suffrage in 1916, white women's organizations focusing explicitly on patriotism withheld support for women's voting rights until shortly before the Nineteenth Amendment's ratification, if they endorsed such rights at all. One reason for their relative silence on the issue, amounting to a 1914 gag rule within the DAR, was that the issue's profound divisiveness threatened the UDC's and the DAR's goals of assembling white female elites.[39] When edited by cofounder Ellen Hardin Walworth, who reportedly favored woman suffrage, the DAR's magazine featured a piece on "foremothers" by the feminist firebrand Elizabeth Cady Stanton, shortly before her *Woman's Bible* (1895) created consternation among suffragists as well as among clubwomen.[40] In their eighties, the women's rights leaders Susan B. Anthony and Julia Ward Howe belonged to the DAR and promoted women's voting rights to DAR audiences.[41] Yet later "antisuffrage drives in at least fourteen states and the District of Columbia" were directed by members of the Daughters of the American Revolution in other capacities.[42] The ability to vote seemed to threaten the female cultural authority so vital to women-centered nationalism. Many also doubtlessly feared that female suffrage would mean black female suffrage and therefore black suffrage.[43]

To palliate the conflicts over the shape of women's authority, progressive and conservative nationalists both stressed dominant notions of marriage and motherhood. The Protestant Christian home, with monogamous, heterosexual marriage at its center, was a cornerstone of American national identity for women-centered nationalists in general, and a governing institution in the eyes of state-centered nationalists especially. For example, black clubwomen, pro-Union women, and neo-Confederate women all objected strenuously to indications that Mormon men were continuing to take multiple wives even after Utah outlawed plural marriage in 1896 as a precondition for statehood.[44] The DAR joined massive petition drives in 1898 and 1903 against the seating in the U.S. Congress of alleged polygamists and, in a 1906 resolution, called for the "abolition of Mormonism."[45] At stake in the DAR's opposition to plural marriage was the organization's intertwining of nation and state. Distinguishing "covenant-breaking" Mormons from "the American people," a resolution by the chapter in St. Paul, Minnesota, charged that the presence of a polygamist in Congress was "threatening the security of the American home."[46] Conversely, once the church hierarchy began truly punishing polygamy in the late 1910s, Daughters began stressing ancestral and racial commonalities with Mormons and welcomed eligible Mormon women into the organization.[47]

In addition to dividing over woman suffrage (a division that was ameliorated by a focus on protecting the American home), state-based nationalists expressed an aversion to women's political power in their Americanization work. The Americanization project affirmed gendered divisions of political labor among white Americans even as it imparted great influence to its female practitioners. Gender differentiation indicated a society's high caliber of civilization, according to then-dominant notions of civilization.[48] Instilling American-style differentiation in immigrant children—training girls in "home making and sewing and right principles of living" and boys in "civics and forms of government, and . . . patriotism and good citizenship," as the Cincinnati DAR did in 1900—was vital to their uplift.[49] The women encouraged European and white boys of all classes to aspire to social mobility. In 1915 the chapter in Menominee in Michigan's Upper Peninsula organized a club composed of teenage boys then "in trouble in the juvenile court," later attracting hundreds more. In addition to furnishing extensive leisure facilities with the help of local lumbermen, the Menominee Boys' Good Citizenship club offered classes in social and table etiquette. While many Progressive Era institutions focused on socializing working-class or poor children as laborers, especially in the case of nonwhite children, the DAR's lessons about multiple forks ritually welcomed the Menominee boys into the American elite.[50] A Cleveland woman's 1923 account of working among Italian boys in that city did the same. Her narrative of their Americanization culminated in a formal banquet and a night at the opera.[51]

The DAR Girl Home Makers' Clubs presented a contrast. This national project originated in Cleveland, in part as a remedy for the "servant problem," a perennial shortage of live-in domestic servants due to young women's widespread preference for factory work or, in fact, for any other work they could find. Elizabeth Hyer Neff developed the first Girl Home Makers' Club in 1911 among Greek, Syrian, and Italian girls at a Cleveland settlement house. She popularized the project within the DAR by invoking the recent Triangle Shirtwaist Factory fire in New York City, in which 146 workers, mostly women and girls, died because their employer had locked the exits. "On that same day," Neff lamented, "not less than a thousand doors in New York were wide open to those poor girls where they could have had homes in addition to their wages."[52]

In addition to training future servants, Girl Home Makers' Clubs sought also to turn out "American" wives. The first such club in Cleveland offered instruction in table etiquette along with how to make a potato and milk soup that caused a "parish priest" to remark (in one Daughter's recollection), "Now not so much divorce."[53] The Girl Home Makers' project expressed another principle of women-centered nationalism. Americanness inhered in domestic, seemingly mundane objects and labors, as the potato and milk soup made plain. Simultaneously, Girl Home Makers' Clubs posited a strict separation between female labors at home—female domesticity—and men's active citizenship. As putative wives, Girl Home Makers were not taught to aspire to social mobility on their own, as individuals. The DAR considered immigrant wives and mothers to be their families' most meaningful agents of Americanization—within the walls of their own homes.[54] The DAR thus ultimately limited the power to define American culture at large, and to communicate it to others in public forums, to women like themselves.

In not promoting gender differentiation among African Americans—among whom northern Daughters engaged in occasional patriotic outreach and philanthropy—the DAR affirmed the white supremacy undergirding its notions of civilization.[55] In 1913 the chapter in Oberlin, Ohio, formed a Girl Home Makers' club among "six colored boys from the delinquent room" who aspired to become professional cooks. The women aided the teenagers in gaining a livelihood and, indeed, wished them well: "Their interest is intense, and we feel sure of their ultimate success."[56] Symbolically, however, the women affirmed race-based nationalism. Even in what had been one of abolitionism's burned-over districts—even in the shadow of a white-run college exceptional for educating meaningful numbers of

African Americans, including women, in the nineteenth century—the DAR failed to acknowledge African Americans as fellow Revolutionary descendants or even to consider that it was possible to civilize black youths fully.[57] If it had acknowledged African Americans as such, the Oberlin DAR would have tutored those male Girl Home Makers in those gender distinctions associated with "civilization."

LIKE THOSE women-centered nationalists who positioned women as civilizers, female nationalists who emphasized the authority of men, past and present, continued to struggle over the concepts of home and country in the 1900s and 1910s. In the 1890s Ida B. Wells-Barnett and her antilynching exposés and Josephine St. Pierre Ruffin and her newspaper *The Woman's Era* had been nourished by collectivities of black women. Such organizational patterns began to seem old-fashioned twenty years later, and not only because Wells-Barnett's and Ruffin's outsized personalities contributed to their clashes with other women. Black male leaders were beginning to move away from Booker T. Washington's political accommodationism, supplanting women's long-held criticisms that black men were overly conciliatory. There was little space within early twentieth-century black politics for contentions such as Anna Julia Cooper's that black women were the race's rightful leaders, not least because the women themselves had difficulty living up to that notion, especially in the eyes of black men. Consequently, some black men blamed any sign of racial decline on black women.[58] Regardless of where they stood on the eternally divisive question of whether to emphasize American or "Negro" identity—American civic nationalism or black nationalism—many black clubwomen began adopting definitions of black citizenship that, more than ever, conflated it with manhood. The movement for African American civil rights itself made that connection.

For years, small groups of middle-class African Americans who were exasperated by Booker T. Washington's public toleration of Jim Crow promoted civil rights reform—as in the National Afro-American Council (formed in 1890) and the all-male Niagara Movement (1905) and its female auxiliary (1906).[59] The civil rights movement began operating on a mass, national scale at the end of the twentieth century's first decade. The catalyst for this transformation was a patriotic anniversary juxtaposed with a racial atrocity, conspicuous for its northern location. Six months before the centenary of Abraham Lincoln's birth in February 1909, a white mob rampaged through a black neighborhood, lynching two, following rumors of black-on-white rape. The violence occurred in the city where Lincoln had made his name: Springfield, Illinois. More than ever, Jim Crow seemed to demand a national and nationalist response—that is, one that asserted blacks' Americanness.[60]

Ensuing meetings led to the formation of the NAACP. One-third of those who signed the NAACP's first call to action were women.[61] Interracial, mixed-sex, and led by men (mostly white men in its first years), the NAACP embodied progressive reform in turning to the state, in the form of courts, to fulfill its objectives in addition to increasingly rallying activists on the community level.[62] The NAACP also became the premier voice of African American civic nationalism. Black members maintained constantly that national unity should be based on loyal behavior rather than on blood, and that African Americans had met those criteria for Americanness throughout U.S. history. Though the NACW's own ranks also contained black nationalists, the women's group generally made common cause with the NAACP on the question of identifying primarily as Americans, in addition to questions of civil rights activism and protest.

Before the NAACP organized, Carrie Williams Clifford, a Cleveland club leader who was also active in the Niagara Movement's auxiliary, published some forceful civil rights commentary. In a 1907 rejoinder to the white Virginian writer Thomas Nelson Page, who told northerners to leave southern race relations in the hands of white southerners, Clifford demanded, "Why, then, did this government interfere with Cuba? . . . Why were not the Mormons left to settle their questions to suit themselves?"[63] After joining the NAACP, however, Clifford headed a women's committee to raise funds for the NAACP periodical's innovative artwork—making *The Crisis* "beautiful," as its male editor put it.[64] Clifford did continue, in other capacities, to demand expanded political authority for women. She was one of a handful of black women, including Ida B. Wells-Barnett, who marched in the March 1913 parade for woman suffrage in Washington. They endured male hecklers, white suffragists' attempts at exclusion, and many black clubwomen's refusal to condone such militance.[65] Yet Clifford's fortunes within black politics in the 1910s echo those of other politically assertive women. Not until 1919 did the NAACP's board of directors include a black woman—longtime civil rights activist and NACW president Mary Burnett Talbert.[66]

Also communicating the growing importance of manhood to African American politics were W. E. B. Du Bois's ideas about gender and nation. I do not intend to suggest that Du Bois was conspicuously male supremacist in comparison to his contemporaries. The writer who anonymously attacked women's club life in the *Colored American Magazine* as detrimental to black families and to civilization shared much with former President Grover Cleveland, who condemned white women's clubs on similar grounds.[67] Against such a backdrop, Du Bois was comparatively friendly toward women's political activism. His 1909 sociological work, *Efforts for Social Betterment among Negro Americans*, remains an important source on women's club work, and after 1910 he published multiple symposia and editorials in *The Crisis* that promoted woman suffrage.[68] However, as Hazel V. Carby has argued, his *Souls of Black Folk* (1903) blamed racial subjugation on the black mother's failure to resist white men's sexual coercion and on the black man's failure to monopolize her sexuality. Presenting masculinity as the glue binding African Americans to the American nation, the work ultimately positioned black men as race leaders and as "race men."[69]

It would be misleading to build on these examples an unambiguous narrative of men's displacement of women. Men and women both articulated the struggle for African American civil rights in increasingly men-centered terms. To the extent that Du Bois did not reduce women's relationship to the nation to their reproductive capacities, his visions of gender and nationalism comported with those of many women.[70] Even women from older generations went on to praise protest as manly. Maritcha Lyons, a teacher and clubwoman from Brooklyn, New York, helped sponsor Ida B. Wells-Barnett when she first came north in 1892 and worked alongside the black history pioneer Victoria Earle Matthews. A generation later, in her late seventies, Lyons described citizenship as "the duties and prerogatives attached to unshackled manhood."[71]

In addition to imparting a new degree of cultural authority to men in the present, many black women continued to rely on men's past military service when asserting the race's American patriotism. In 1914 "colored women" in Princeton, New Jersey, announced plans to raise a "tablet to the memory of Oliver Cromwell," a black soldier who had accompanied George Washington across the Delaware River in 1776.[72] A float in a Fall River, Massachusetts, Fourth of July parade that same year emphasized men-centered definitions of national belonging even more. Young black women held up large American flags and signs reading, "With you at Bunker Hill," "With Jackson at New Orleans," "With you at San Juan Hill"—pointing to black men's self-sacrifice on battlefields throughout U.S. history.[73] Among those subscribing to American civic nationalism, women and men together developed an African American politics that was increasingly invested in manhood, manliness, and masculinity. Yet in continuing to develop monuments, black history for young people, and black histories that discussed women, black women remained within the broad spectrum of women-centered nationalism.

WHITE WOMEN's nationalism did not undergo as apparent a masculinization during the Progressive Era. The "daughters" organizations and the WRC had always been more accepting of male supremacy than black clubwomen had been. While occasionally criticizing men's greed, selfishness, partisanship, or sexual excesses, no white woman engaged in organized patriotism made claims equivalent to Anna Julia Cooper's or to Josephine St. Pierre Ruffin's in the 1890s—that white men were failing as race and as national leaders.[74] On the contrary, some white women avoided reform work entirely, notwithstanding its compatibility with marriage and motherhood. That avoidance was most evident among neo-Confederate nationalists. To these women, most types of reform work appeared to threaten white male supremacy and associated nation and state overly closely.

Neo-Confederate women's extensive fund-raising for Confederate veterans and for scholarships for Confederate descendants, combined with the women's appeals to state and local governments for assistance in funding veterans' and Confederate women's homes, constituted reform work in the sense of advocating a "welfare program."[75] Yet before World War I, the UDC generally withheld support from reforms not aimed at those of Confederate background or blood. To be sure, in other organizational capacities, Daughters of the Confederacy moved confidently with other white southern women into broad-based, progressive political activism. Cofounder Caroline Meriwether Goodlett, for example, lobbied the Tennessee legislature to raise the legal age of consent for sexual activity from sixteen to eighteen years and to fund a home for "feeble-minded" white children.[76] Some neo-Confederates also welcomed the expansion of white women's educational and political opportunities. A 1903 speech by Mary Wooldridge Latham, another Tennessee UDC leader, anticipated historian Mary Ritter Beard's *Woman's Work in Municipalities* (1915). Latham celebrated married women's property rights, white women's admission to state universities, women's establishment of "industrial and reform schools" for girls, and their community work that resulted in "public libraries, public drinking fountains for man and beast, police matrons, public parks, and clean streets."[77] Some neo-Confederates, in other organizational capacities, also went so far as to promote women's voting rights. Nellie Nugent Somerville, a woman suffragist and temperance activist in Mississippi, would win election to the state legislature in the 1920s. She was active in both the DAR and the UDC. To a suffragist audience in 1898, the thirty-five-year-old pointed out that "a disfranchised class can never be truly patriotic"—overlooking the ongoing, massive disfranchisement of black men.[78]

Occasionally, contingents among neo-Confederates favored broad definitions of reform. Mississippi Daughters of the Confederacy met in 1913 with U.S. Children's Bureau chief Julia Lathrop and "other women's organizations" regarding child-centered legislation in that state, including restrictions on child labor, the enactment of compulsory education, the establishment of a juvenile reformatory, and the appointment of women as county and state superintendents of education. The Virginia UDC promoted women's admission to the all-white University of Virginia that same year.[79] Some neo-Confederate monuments demonstrate familiarity with progressive reform at large. A Fayetteville, Tennessee, drinking fountain commemorating the women of the Confederacy communicated a decidedly twentieth-century eagerness to avoid spreading germs.[80]

As an organization, however, the UDC defined women's nationalism to exclude reform work except toward what was left of the Confederate nation.

Leaders strictly separated the cultural authority commanded by women when commemorating the Confederacy from the cultural authority of women in other, seemingly more risky areas. In 1905 UDC president Louisa Cheves McCord Smythe did not allow the Salt Lake City chapter (like the DAR chapter there, it consisted of non-Mormons) to present a resolution against polygamy to that year's convention because it "might be construed as political."[81] As always, neo-Confederates' histories treasured great white men. In the late 1900s and 1910s, the women appealed successfully to southern lawmakers to establish the birthdays of Confederate leaders as state holidays, as in the case of Robert E. Lee's birthday in Mississippi.[82]

The women also honored the all-male Ku Klux Klan, organized by ex-Confederate officers in 1866 and shut down by federal authorities during Reconstruction, although just how to honor it became subject to debate. Even those who praised Thomas Dixon Jr.'s *The Clansman: An Historical Romance of the Ku Klux Klan* (1905)—they welcomed the book as a counterpoint to *Uncle Tom's Cabin*—found it "sensational."[83] At the 1906 convention of the Florida Division, a Gainesville woman squared off against a Tampa woman who thought Dixon's novel lacked historical value. "I am proud to say that my father and brothers were members . . . and if I should ask the veterans present (I am not going to), I am sure they would agree with me, for I know most of them were members. If I live to be ninety, the one 'page in memory' of which I shall be proudest is that my father and brothers belonged to the Kuklux."[84]

Laura Martin Rose of West Point, Mississippi, felt the same. Born near Pulaski, Tennessee, where the Ku Klux Klan had formed, and keenly conscious of it, Rose published a 1909 pamphlet glorifying the Klan that raised funds for neo-Confederate projects for years. The Klan, as another leader summarized Rose's pamphlet, "was organized from the flower and chivalry of the South, to intimidate the negro through his superstition into good behavior, and to drive the carpet bagger and the scalawag from our midst. It was an absolute necessity at the time and saved the South from race war." The bloodshed of Reconstruction ("some deeds that the South regretted and tried to punish") had been committed by impostor organizations.[85] Such messages were still finding receptive ears in 1917, when the Children of the Confederacy of McComb, Mississippi, adopted the name "Ku Klux Klan

Jr." for the chapter and asked the woman who supervised them "not to let . . . other boys have that title."[86] By then, *The Clansman* had inspired an acclaimed Hollywood film.

Despite neo-Confederate women's affirmations of white and male supremacies, such women continued to draw objections from white men who were discomfited by female authority in any form. The UDC found itself red-baited more than once following the McKinley assassination because the women's heartfelt challenges to state-based American patriotism drew the wrath of Americans who emphasized fealty to the state—significantly, of men. Calling glorification of the Confederacy "treasonable," one clergyman demanded, "why not allow Emma Goldman, the high priestess, nay, the 'Daughter of Anarchy,' to address audiences also and declare the principles of anarchy to be right?" Significantly, the *Confederate Veteran* denounced the clergyman as a "Rip Van Winkle"—conspicuously behind the times.[87] Daughters of the Confederacy did not dwell on such hostility. The women regularly prided themselves on their intensity relative to their men, and they appropriated the rhetoric of the assassination's aftermath for their own purposes.[88] An effective way to communicate John Brown's villainy to schoolchildren, one Georgian thought, was to label him an "anarchist."[89] Yet twentieth-century analogies between the UDC and Emma Goldman recall some northern men's gendered belittling of ex-Confederate men immediately following the Civil War, when northerners drew attention to the untrammeled fanaticism of white southern women.[90]

Southerners, as well as northerners, objected to neo-Confederate women's assumption of cultural authority. While praising some women's partisan (Democratic) fervor, the *Confederate Veteran* doubted that white supremacy would be safe in the face of unstable gender relations.[91] Ensuing struggles among neo-Confederates over white women's demeanor and their political activism spilled over into commemoration work. In 1909 many Daughters wanted the UCV's proposed statue to the "women of the Confederacy" to praise female militancy. *Confederate Veteran* editor Sumner Archibald Cunningham did not care for the design favored by a number of women—the "defiant expression on the woman's face," "her stern hold on the flag," and "the sight of her clinched hand around the blade of the sword." He also disapproved of the motto on the statue's base, " 'Uphold Our State Rights,' " as "[t]he war is certainly over and our women are not in politics." Male neo-Confederates ultimately overruled the women by choosing a motherly figure with a miniaturized Confederate soldier draped, *Pietà*-like, in the crook of her arm. Women's protests that the image impugned the manhood of Confederate soldiers fell on deaf ears.[92]

Functioning mostly in the South, where the racial clampdowns of Jim Crow made the maintenance of gender hierarchies among whites especially crucial, neo-Confederates took the most conservative stance of any group of female nationalists examined in this book on the question of women's progressive activism. Neo-Confederate women preferred relatively narrow definitions of female cultural authority. They focused on history and commemoration to the exclusion of most forms of reform work, showing that women as well as men reinforced gender orthodoxies. Even so, the women drew criticism for even their limited acceptance of white women's political activism.

DURING THE Progressive Era, Jim Crow clenched his hands around the country at large. In 1914 Mississippi senator James K. Vardaman flatly denied that "the negro" had ever built any monuments "to . . . perpetuate in the memory [of] posterity the virtues of his ancestors." It followed that he had never "created for himself any civilization."[93] Three years earlier, some African Americans had found that the act of remembrance endangered their persons, if not their lives. In the face of threats to burn down their meeting hall, WRC women in Marche, Arkansas, met in secret three miles into the woods. That same year, Julia Mason Layton, then a national officer of the WRC, found herself barred from railroad station waiting rooms and expressed her sense of menace at having to wait outside, all night, for her trains. She joined the NAACP early on.[94]

In 1913 Jim Crow arrived with a vengeance in Layton's hometown of Washington, with the inauguration of the Virginia-born Woodrow Wilson, the first native southern Democratic president since before the Civil War. As president, Wilson demonstrated a deep commitment to progressive reform. Under his leadership came the most ambitious federal reforms between Reconstruction and the New Deal: a permanent income tax, the direct popular election of U.S. senators, the creation of the Federal Reserve system, and the Owen-Keating child labor law of 1916 (struck down later by the Supreme Court).[95] Accompanying Wilson's progressivism was an equally heartfelt commitment to white supremacy. He spoke to the massive "Blue and Gray" reunion in Gettysburg on the battle's fiftieth anniversary in July 1913, flanked by a white Union veteran and by a white Confederate veteran—a forceful affirmation of race-based reconciliation. The Wilson administration also imposed racial segregation, to a new degree, on the federal government.[96]

Two winters later came the premiere of *The Birth of a Nation* (1915), the film based on the novel *The Clansman*. Wilson praised the film as "all so terribly true" and made it the first one ever shown in the White House. Such encomiums are understandable because the film's titles included multiple quotations from Wilson's own discussions of Reconstruction, published during his previous career as a political scientist. The film, much feted for the cinematic innovations of the Kentucky-born director David Wark Griffith (the son of a Confederate colonel), told a story of race-based reconciliation. Two well-to-do white families, one northern and one southern, were separated by the Civil War and reunited during Reconstruction. The film depicted blacks as too clownish to be true villains. They were pawns of nefarious white abolitionists. An exception was a man who menacingly trailed the innocent daughter of one of the white families. She plunged to her death from a cliff to avoid the inevitable rape. The story's avenging heroes were Ku Klux Klansmen on horseback. In the film's final frame, uniformed Klansmen milled around beside Jesus Christ in heaven.[97] The next year, a woman welcomed Thomas Dixon Jr. to a UDC state convention with the hope that neo-Confederates would record their debt to him "on a shaft reaching far up into the blue sky." She took her stand not in Dixieland but in New York.[98]

The Birth of a Nation's paean to the Ku Klux Klan energized civil rights activists around the country. The NAACP and the NACW both organized protests and pursued censorship efforts against the film, which, in Ohio, the UDC managed to reverse a few years later.[99] *The Birth of a Nation*'s popularity also demoralized some older African Americans who had consistently conflated their country with their nation, and who had assumed that virulent white supremacy would remain confined to the South. Fifty-nine-year-old Maria Louise Baldwin of Cambridge, Massachusetts, was a longtime teacher and principal of a school that catered mainly to the city's intelligentsia. In the 1890s she was a vice president of Boston's formidable Woman's Era Club; in 1910 she sat on the NAACP's first General Committee. A friend remembered that she "always made us believe more and more in the ideal America," except when *The Birth of a Nation* appeared. The friend invited "some of the colored race to meet with me one afternoon just for an expression of good-will" that included a singing of " 'My country, 'tis of thee.' " But the song's affirmations pained Baldwin that day. She asked the group not to sing it, " "for it would break my heart when I know of the feeling of so many in Boston and throughout the country, who do not recognize truly the fact that this is our country. I might sing it another time, but not now.' "[100]

It is impossible to extricate such excrescences as *The Birth of a Nation*, or to recount such histories separately, from those of reform and modernization. As Michael Rogin and others have shown, national mass culture developed simultaneously with the national spread of Jim Crow mores and the true emergence of Jim Crow America.[101] Within many individuals, notably Woodrow Wilson, there coexisted sincere support for both progressivism and white supremacy. Many clubwomen also lived contradictions that seem profound in our own time. In their multitudinous nationalisms, African American clubwomen continued to link the causes of women's political agency and racial justice, even as the male-led civil rights movement increasingly expressed its aims using idioms of manhood. DAR women intertwined civic nationalism, based on behavior, with blood-based nationalism, based on descent, in deriving from their own documented lineages the patriotic authority necessary to Americanize adults and children alike. Women-centered nationalism itself was profoundly contradictory. Even in its progressive incarnations, women-centered nationalism affirmed white supremacy (when articulated by white women) and gendered divisions of political labor as long as these divisions recognized women's organized activism outside the home as a legitimate and important form of service to the nation. In the meantime, Europe was burning. The war raging beyond most Americans' horizons in 1915 would eventually explode organized women's notions of how and why to bind themselves, and others, to their nations.

Chapter Four
The War

WORLD WAR I was the first in a half century to demand substantial sacrifices from U.S. civilians. Consequently, the U.S. government strove hard to produce prowar patriotism in the population once the country entered the war in April 1917. The resulting sense of national emergency—intensified by the Bolsheviks' takeover of Russia and their plans to spread communism worldwide—proved to be a crucible that left no variant of American nationalism untransformed. Especially significant, war and revolution masculinized women's nationalism to a new degree. With millions of American men going to war, and with the male-dominated state's new interest in fostering patriotism, women now conferred cultural and moral authority on living men—as distinguished from dead warriors and heroes—more than on women. The men-centered nationalism espoused by women did not entail the repudiation of female political activism as long as women allowed male-dominated entities, most notably the state, to shape those agenda.

The adoption of men-centered nationalism was especially apparent among the Daughters of the American Revolution and pro-Union women who had always conflated nation, country, and state. In wartime, the women increasingly placed themselves on the nation's sidelines, cheering the men on the field. Groups of women who were comparatively ambivalent about the state—African American and neo-Confederate—also masculinized their nationalisms to a new degree. To civil rights activists and Garveyites alike, citizenship and manhood were synonymous. Neo-Confederates newly embraced American, state-based nationalism in wartime. That change focused on one man, Woodrow Wilson. That the change ended with his presidency shows that neo-Confederates' support for male political supremacy within their nation remained consistent.

ALTHOUGH OVERSHADOWED in wartime, feminine, women-centered nationalism nevertheless endured. It presented women as cultural authorities, political activists, and—in its more ambitious incarnations—as shapers of civilization; it presented women as subjects and agents of history; and it targeted young and/or female audiences. Women-centered nationalism remained especially noticeable among those who found that Jim Crow–style white supremacy pervaded the country and the state. Black women's relationship with the male-dominated state was strained compared to that of white women who focused explicitly on patriotism. In 1917 Carrie Williams Clifford, now of Washington, announced the creation of the NAACP Juvenile Department. Straddling both sides of the double-consciousness controversy — whether African Americans should identify primarily as Americans or as "Negroes"—she described the department's aims to teach "the young people that all the races of mankind are one" and, at the same time, "to awaken in the children race consciousness and race pride." The latter entailed taking young people on a "pilgrimage" to the house in Washington where Frederick Douglass had lived and died.[1]

Opened to the public as a house museum in 1922, the Frederick Douglass Home, also known as Cedar Hill, was the first and only such museum administered by black women.[2] Moreover, the Frederick Douglass Home was the foremost artifact of women-centered nationalism during the war years and in the 1920s: it both addressed young people and positioned women as shapers of culture. After an initial flurry of interest in 1896, and then years of frustration in which the NACW had to let the Frederick Douglass Home project go and in which men connected to Booker T. Washington failed to raise sufficient funds to pay the house's mortgage, the NACW once again took over the project in 1916. By that time, unlike in the 1890s, the bulk of its members considered black history essential to a black child's education.[3] This time, the women reached their goal, spearheaded by NACW president Mary Burnett Talbert of Buffalo, New York. Between 1916 and 1918—in addition to their war-related fund-raising, and with crucial help from the beauty products entrepreneur Madame C. J. Walker—the clubwomen raised the $5,000 necessary to lift Cedar Hill's mortgage, as well as additional funds "to restore the home and its grounds."[4]

Talbert and others were well aware of the white historic preservation efforts that preceded their own "Black Mount Vernon."[5] Indeed, some parallels existed. Like the white DAR, the NACW raised some of the money through public subscriptions, by asking "schools and Sunday schools" to collect pennies from children.[6] Also like white women's house museums, Cedar Hill was intended by the NACW to contain and display historical "relics"—in this case, "pertaining to slavery." Among such artifacts were the table on which Senator Charles Sumner had composed "his" civil rights bill, and Douglass's two violins. Talbert announced plans to ask members to send in "battle flags, old bills of slave sale, free papers," likely manumission and emancipation documents, "and other things of historical nature."[7] Notwithstanding its commonalities with white commemorations, the Frederick Douglass Home constituted an autonomous black institution. At a time when many black-run entities were more tied to white philanthropy than they wanted to be, *The Crisis* reported in early 1918 that "[n]ot a dollar has come from white people."[8]

Further reinforcing women-centered nationalism, Cedar Hill was administered almost entirely by women, who acted within an all-female, self-consciously amateur institution, the NACW. Among the museum's trustees in 1919 was only one man, the black attorney Archibald Grimké.[9] Moreover, the NACW planned a compilation of articles for young readers on "our noted women," largely clubwomen (with the exception of the nineteenth-century writer and feminist Frances Ellen Watkins Harper), to be placed in the museum. One of those featured in the volume was Victoria Earle Matthews. Matthews, who had promoted the Cedar Hill project, and black history generally, early on, in the 1890s, had lost her life to tuberculosis in 1907.[10] Yet, as an institution run by female amateurs, Cedar Hill epitomized a fading breed. In the hands of Carter G. Woodson and the ASNLH, black history was gradually professionalizing. It was therefore becoming more male in its composition and more masculine in its content and methods, as was true generally of professionalization in the early twentieth century.[11] More fundamentally, the Cedar Hill project affirmed women-centered nationalism's conservative dimension in focusing primarily on a great man of history.

THROUGH WORLD WAR and distant revolution, white women who had organized as patriots continued to wrestle with themselves, and each other, over the appropriate relationship between women and nation. White women retained some elements of women-centered nationalism. An important characteristic of that nationalism was to infuse the most domestic, seemingly mundane objects and concerns with political significance. In calling on the state to compel immigrants to reject old cultures and allegiances, for example, a DAR president imparted national and nationalist meanings to food. "What kind of American consciousness can grow in the atmosphere of sauerkraut and Limburger cheese? Or, what can you expect of the Americanism of the man whose breath always reeks of garlic?" demanded Sarah Mitchell Guernsey, a bank president's wife and former high school principal from Independence, Kansas.[12] In a similar spirit, the Canton, Ohio, DAR reported teaching immigrant women "how to cook."[13]

The women also affirmed the necessity of female cultural authority in wartime. They harbored no doubts about the importance of civilian volunteers to the war effort. In making untold numbers of socks and pajamas with their own hands, and in conserving food and other supplies, white women, like black women, attached patriotic and therefore political significance to domestic, feminine labors. Raising patriotic children and proffering them to the nation—as distinguished from bearing children, the concern of men who anticipated "race suicide"—also constituted vital political work in the women's eyes. Over 7,000 women in the DAR lost sons or daughters to the war or to the subsequent influenza pandemic while still in uniform.[14]

Also in accordance with women-centered nationalism, white women continued in wartime to position women like themselves as civilizers and as shapers of culture, in the sense of everyday customs and attitudes. An Iowa DAR leader, Mabel Pratt Schoentgen, described her patriotic uplift of a Dresden native who had lived in the United States for three decades. Following what Schoentgen described as a "rousing, patriotic talk at the Y.W.C.A." in Council Bluffs by a "beloved" local colonel in 1918, the unnamed woman whispered to Schoentgen, "'You don't know how bad that makes me feel. My countrypeople were kind and good when I lived [in Germany] and it hurts me to hear such awful things about them.'" Schoentgen replied that the woman could no longer maintain what Schoentgen considered a dual identity: "'You have come to the parting of the way; you must be a good, loyal American or you will be classed among the pro-German.'" When the woman answered (in Schoentgen's recollection) that she wanted to "'do what is right, I want to be loyal, I want to do my duty,'" Schoentgen took her to a store and bought two small American flags. With the woman in tears, the two ritually reinforced each other's national identity. "I pinned [a] flag on her coat over her heart, and she pinned one on me," said Schoentgen, "and as she did so I felt as if I were repledging my love and devotion to my country."[15]

In one case, DAR women cast their own patriotism as superior to male patriotism—even to that of men in uniform. Delegates at the 1918 national convention passed a resolution pointedly condemning the interment of Central Powers dead with military honors in U.S. cemeteries. Denouncing the burial of enemy dead alongside one's own war dead was not unknown in the United States. Mothers of fallen Confederates had done the same.[16] Contemporaries in the military, however, found the women's fervor excessive. As was customary, the DAR forwarded the resolution to the White House, which in turn forwarded it to the War Department. A brigadier general puzzled over the resolution. "Inasmuch as death is look [sic] upon as the great leveler, it is not understood why the burial of enemy dead in our National Cemeteries can, in any wise, reflect upon the loyalty of those ordering such burial."[17]

In what was likely a result of their wartime self-validation as patriots, some white women overcame their longtime opposition to reforms that would increase women's political equality with men. In 1920 both the DAR and the WRC pressed for the independent naturalization of married women and for the restoration of U.S. citizenship to American women who were married to foreign nationals who were eligible for naturalization (that citizenship had been stripped in 1907).[18] At its national convention in April 1920, the DAR also finally endorsed votes for women—four years after the WRC had.[19] Helping to explain state-based nationalists' and national patriots' growing acceptance of women's exercise of political power are their changing perceptions of women's service to their country. American women did more than send male kin off to fight. In addition to drafting millions of young men, the government also recruited thousands of white, native-born, single women to be nurses, clerical workers, and canteen workers.[20] Among them were 250 DAR women. Two of them—one from Mississippi and one from Connecticut—"made the supreme sacrifice" in France.[21] Not only did the dyad reproduce the trope of North-South reconciliation; it challenged men's monopoly on dying for one's country.

At first glance, the DAR's and the WRC's new acceptance of woman suffrage and other forms of female political equality seems an especially bold form of women-centered nationalism and appears to present a sharp discontinuity. Yet these white women were acting consistently. By the late 1910s, support for women's political rights could and did express affinities for domesticity. As redefined by the suffrage movement's moderate and dominant wing, support for woman suffrage was now compatible with motherhood, with other prevailing definitions of middle-class femininity, and most fundamentally, with prowar patriotism. The suffrage movement's own "society turn" and its dominant wing's support for the war effort help explain the increase in support for suffrage among white women nationalists, though neo-Confederates for the most part still withheld their approval.[22]

Affirming women-centered nationalism's domestic leanings even more was its white adherents' increasingly fervent antiradicalism, which in turn increased their allegiance to monogamous marriage and motherhood. The DAR had long presented national unity as capitalism's protection and had long considered the private home a cornerstone of American national identity, as demonstrated by its hostility to Mormon polygamy. The Bolsheviks' triumph in Russia in late 1917 embodied the opposite of everything the women believed to be American—their political and social nightmares come true. Bolshevik conceptions of revolution included violent class struggle, the abolition of private property, and also, initially, the gradual disappearance of the family—not to mention of nations.[23] From the perspective of many Americans, the Bolsheviks were the enemy of both home and country, in that the Bolsheviks directly and deeply challenged American gender mores and loyalty to nation. White nationalists in turn sharpened their hostility to all forms of leftism, especially those that addressed gender relations. The DAR rejoiced at the deportation in late 1919 of Emma Goldman, the Russian-born anarchist and feminist iconoclast. Ascribing Goldman's radicalism to her incomplete Americanization, Sarah Mitchell Guernsey envisioned her boarding the ship to Finland still "wearing an American hat over her unaltered foreign head. A new shell but the same old nut!"[24]

DESPITE POSITIONING WOMEN as shapers of civilization and conferring on them rights of first-class citizenship, women-centered nationalists did not accept women's exercise of true political power within their nations. Women-centered nationalism's conservative tendencies were especially apparent during World War I, a war effort of a scale unseen since the Civil War and large enough to affect directly the lives of civilians who had no previous personal contact with the state.[25] Americans of all kinds, including organized women, were now much more likely than in peacetime, or during the comparably small-scale wars against Spain and the Filipino independence movement, to consider armed men the linchpin of their safety. Yet the First World War and communism's surge in Russia thoroughly transformed the relationship between gender and nationalism in the United States. Going beyond praising the patriotism of history's warriors and heroes, many women — more than ever — attributed cultural authority, the ability to reshape everyday life and custom, and moral authority within their nations to present-day men.

A major reason for the masculinization of white women's nationalism is that amateurs and volunteers were no longer pursuing their patriotic efforts alone. Joining them were the state and professionals who, at this time, were usually male. In 1918 the DAR spent $10,000 on buying and distributing American flags.[26] The federal government vastly outstripped voluntary organizations in its own herculean attempts to produce national, state-based patriotism in the population. Aided considerably by German submarine attacks, the government transformed the public image of a morally ambiguous struggle — originating in European scrambles for colonies and arms races — into a conflict between the moral absolutes of democracy and autocracy, freedom and unfreedom. The American state's efforts to foster patriotism took the forms of suasion—films, poster art, orations, and group singing—which were intended to win the allegiance of the people, and coercion, through the outlawing of antiwar and antigovernment speech.[27] That the government had come to share women's concerns about spreading patriotism lent additional legitimacy to the women's work. A DAR leader concluded later that from its inception, her organization had been "unconsciously preparing our country for 1914."[28] Such amateurs' initial farsightedness in fostering state-based patriotism, however, did not guarantee them credit or remembrance.

Adherents of men-centered nationalism shared a newly broad acceptance of present-day men's cultural authority. Dividing them still were disagreements on the relationship between nation and state. Even more than during the imperial wars, the DAR demanded unconditional, unquestioning allegiance to the government, including support for new federal laws that criminalized unpatriotic speech and for crackdowns on leftist radicals. As the U.S. commitment to the Allies escalated, state-based nationalists defined patriotism as militant support for the federal government and its policies, especially for military "preparedness." Military preparedness entailed guarding the United States from defeat and invasion through a large, well-armed military, universal military training for young men, and vigilance on the part of everyone else. Although some believers in preparedness also advocated weapons training for women, preparedness in general positioned decidedly masculine and male-dominated institutions, not least the military, as the country's saviors.[29]

The DAR was the largest independent women's organization to support military preparedness before the United States entered the war in 1917. Helping to explain the women's stance is, ironically, their own peace activism before the war. Starting in 1906, delegates at DAR meetings regularly made resolutions in favor of peace and international arbitration and promoted the "peace flag," the Stars and Stripes bordered in white.[30] In 1913— not anticipating the United States–Mexico strife and the conflagration in Europe that would dominate the next year's headlines—the DAR formed a national Peace and Arbitration Committee and resolved at that year's national convention that every chapter should devote at least one meeting a year to studying peace and arbitration.[31] On the local level, some hoped for "a federation of the world," fondly quoting Alfred Lord Tennyson to that effect, and lamented "the extravagance, absurdity and sinfulness of war."[32]

The DAR's support for international peace presents a startling contrast to the rightist, military-friendly reputation the organization acquired starting in the 1920s. However, these women's advocacy of peace never constituted pacifism. Unlike the female peace activists of the 1920s who aspired to purge everyday life—notably children's schooling—of anything vaunting violence, state-based nationalists' peace activism coexisted comfortably with their intense national loyalties, their commemorations of war, and their regard for men's political authority. The women focused on the possibility of male-run legal structures to settle quarrels among Western countries. Moreover, the women's peace rhetoric praised men who carried weapons. In 1910 DAR president Julia Green Scott justified the organization's participation in "the great modern crusade for arbitration of internation[a]l disputes" by pointing to the women's descent from "peace-loving" men "who took up arms . . . as true patriots always will—in defense of home and country, right or wrong."[33] As Charles DeBenedetti found of male peace activists, the women ultimately jettisoned their peace rhetoric when it no longer accommodated their allegiance to the state.[34]

When the First World War engulfed Europe in the summer of 1914, its spectacles of mass, industrialized killing among peoples who were considered the world's most highly civilized shocked Americans. Within the bastions of state-based nationalism, horrified women reaffirmed support for international peace and concurred with the Wilson administration's initial policy of neutrality. Remarkably, DAR president Daisy Allen Story, a New York mayor's daughter, and other leaders were present at the formation of the Woman's Peace Party (WPP) in Washington in January 1915. The DAR was the only self-identified patriotic organization to send representatives to that meeting, which had been inspired by a group of comparatively radical peace activists— among them Crystal Eastman of New York and the Hungarian-born Rosika Schwimmer—and convened by Jane Addams and the suffrage leader Carrie Chapman Catt.[35] The first all-female peace organization in U.S. history, the WPP initiated peace activism's feminine, militant turn following the war. The WPP became the U.S. Section of the Women's International League for Peace and Freedom (WILPF), headed by Addams, in 1919. By then, DAR representatives were long gone from such gatherings. Soon the DAR would consider the WILPF to be a prime enemy of patriotism—mirroring some peace activists' presentation of national patriotism, and of nationalism, as enemies of peace.[36]

Shortly after the WPP's initial meeting in 1915, the DAR began to move, as an organization, toward supporting military preparedness. A month before the *Lusitania* went down, the women had already raised more than $15,000 for the Red Cross. On May 7, a German submarine torpedoed the liner, a British passenger steamer out of New York that was later found to be carrying munitions. Nearly 1,200 civilians, among them 128 Americans, were killed.[37] This and subsequent events indicated a pattern of German aggression and caused many Americans, and not only stalwart statists, to change their minds about neutrality. Daisy Allen Story's own reversal was swift and complete. A mere six months after being present at the WPP's creation, Story helped establish the Woman's Section of the Navy League and in 1916 called on all DAR members to join—bending an internal rule against affiliating with other organizations.[38] After that, the contest within the DAR between advocates of peace and advocates of military preparedness became a rout by the latter.

When the United States entered the war in April 1917, the DAR continued fervently to advocate female political activism as vital to nationalism, and it threw both behind the state. This pattern exemplifies men-centered nationalism in that the women's regard for men's and male institutions' cultural authority was more intense than ever. In addition to local chapters' cooperation with the American Red Cross and with the Council of National Defense (the government agency overseeing civilian war work), the DAR raised on its own more than $3 million in cash and gifts for the war effort. DAR members also sold more than $51 million in government Liberty Loans.[39]

That women now elevated men (in this case, male lawmakers) as cultural authorities could also be seen in their cheering of the state's efforts to eliminate antiwar opinion from the American populace. The U.S. Congress passed the Sedition Act in March 1918. A major legal underpinning of the government raids, jailings, and deportations that were characteristic of the first Red Scare, the Sedition Act expanded the 1917 Espionage Act's definition of illegal speech (derogation of the war effort) to cover criticism of the American flag, the U.S. Constitution, government institutions, and the uniforms of the army and navy. Federal authorities enforced the Espionage and Sedition Acts selectively: neither against Woodrow Wilson's critics in Congress, nor against the dissident woman suffragists picketing the White House, but primarily against the left and against the foreign-born.[40] Shortly after the Sedition Act's passage, DAR president Sarah Mitchell Guernsey proclaimed to the national convention that up until the law's passage, "we have unwisely refrained from closing mouths that have too long and too loudly proclaimed treason."[41] The DAR and the national patriots of the WRC also applauded new legal constraints against immigrants' speaking their native languages in public or learning them in public schools, believing, with Woodrow Wilson himself, that immigrants' plural, "hyphenated" loyalties profoundly threatened the national unity that was so essential in wartime.[42]

DISPLAYING A considerably more complicated relationship with the state were neo-Confederates. The wartime masculinization of female nationalism was less obvious among neo-Confederates as they had always favored narrow definitions of women's authority. The pattern endured in the UDC's hostility to the Ku Klux Klan, revived in Georgia in 1915, on the grounds of both class and gender. In cultivating a truly mass membership among white Protestants nationwide, attracting millions in the early 1920s, the new Klan was not elitist enough to suit the UDC.[43] Pointedly, the women continued to celebrate lovingly the first, all-male Ku Klux Klan. In 1917, for example, the Pulaski, Tennessee, chapter unveiled a bronze tablet commemorating the formation of that Klan in 1866, on the outer wall of the law office where it had taken place. One thousand people attended the ceremony.[44] The Richmond, Virginia, chapter went so far as to protest the appropriation of the name "Ku Klux Klan" for the new group and to ask that the Virginia state government prohibit its use. With a woman prominent in its formation and with a sizable female auxiliary, the second Klan could not sufficiently emulate the first Klan, which had been intended primarily to "protect the white women," explained the Daughters.[45]

Regarding the relationship between nation and state, it is a fallacy to conflate all white southerners with neo-Confederates. White southerners led in developing the rigid state-based, national patriotism that undergirded the Red Scare. Prime examples were southerners within Woodrow Wilson's own administration, not to mention Wilson himself. Postmaster General Albert Burleson, a Texan, was a crucial enforcer of the Sedition and Espionage Acts and suppressed the circulation of many foreign-language newspapers.[46] Southerners who belonged to the DAR constitute another example.[47] In wartime even the Daughters of the Confederacy—more than ever, the principal keepers and enforcers of neo-Confederate mores—substantially reconceived relationships among country, state, and nation. The women showed unprecedented, unambiguous support for the state. Yet these patterns lasted only as long as Woodrow Wilson's presidency. Attributing cultural authority to men in the present more than ever, the patterns exemplified the men-centered nationalism newly regnant among women.

That many neo-Confederate women drew remarkably close to the federal government during World War I is evident from the UDC's fund-raising for the war effort, which was comparable to the DAR's despite neo-Confederates' concentration in the poorest region of the country and their past ambivalence toward the state. UDC women sold $46.6 million in war bonds, bought $24.6 million worth, and contributed more than $25 million "to Red Cross, other war relief, French and Belgian orphans, American military hospital, etc."[48] Immediately after the war, the UDC launched a fund-raising drive for a $50,000 Hero Fund dedicated to scholarships for "Southern boys in khaki," who were presumably white. All the money was raised by 1922.[49] In addition to money, some young, unmarried Daughters of the Confederacy contributed extensive time and labor to the war effort. Seventy-eight UDC women went overseas in government capacities.[50] Such commitment shows that many neo-Confederates in wartime denied any contradiction between their newly fervent allegiance to the present-day American state and their fealty to the bygone Confederacy. Disagreements occurred mainly over emphasis. Some UDC members felt more of a need than did others to continue to pay homage to the Confederacy as Americanism's main exemplar.

Before the United States joined the war in 1917, neo-Confederate women had traveled a long road. Up until 1916, they focused strictly on their usual peacetime objectives—the dissemination of pro-Confederate history among Confederates' white descendants and white Americans nationwide in the form of monuments, educational programs, and benevolence work among Confederate veterans and their relatives.[51] Questions of military preparedness proved polarizing, with many continuing to insist that American patriotism did not entail unquestioning loyalty to federal policies. In 1916 the UCV and the SCV passed strong pro-preparedness or pro-government resolutions, despite some objections. Disparaging the notion of "a large standing army," a Virginian considered the SCV's resolution an encroachment "upon the individual rights of members just as much as if the organization should undertake to say what religion or Church it favored."[52] The UDC, on the other hand, avoided any direct mention of the war at its own 1916 convention, and the women quietly bucked the new political orthodoxy. Holding the all-important post of historian general was Laura Martin Rose, who had made her name in the organization with her pamphlet on the first Ku Klux Klan. The Mississippian cannily appropriated a reigning buzzword of the day to reinforce neo-Confederate nationalism. When Rose told the convention to "[t]ake for your watchword this year 'Preparedness,'" she meant to "be prepared at all times to be an able exponent and defender of Southern history."[53]

The first gestures of state-based patriotism by neo-Confederate women came as U.S.-German relations deteriorated and then broke off altogether. The UDC's president was Cordelia Powell Odenheimer, a Marylander who socialized frequently with DAR leaders. In January 1917 Odenheimer represented the UDC at the annual meeting of the Navy League, a leading pro-preparedness organization, in which she held national office.[54] When the United States declared war in April, Odenheimer urged that all pledges and obligations to monument funds be "liquidated immediately." At the end of the year, the UDC at large resolved to abandon monument-building, its mainstay, temporarily.[55]

Odenheimer and her successor, a Vassar graduate and otherwise lifelong Charlestonian named Mary Poppenheim, earnestly promoted state-based nationalism to neo-Confederates. Odenheimer urged UDC members in 1917 to cooperate with war relief organizations, including the Red Cross and the Council of National Defense, to show as "indisputable fact" that "the patriotism of the South is second to that of no other section of the country." "To do less," she concluded, "would be an act of disloyalty to the nation in its hour of peril." Here, Odenheimer identified the contemporary American nation as neo-Confederates' own.[56] The 1917 national convention passed a resolution enjoining members to stand and to place their right hands over their hearts whenever the national anthem was played "and when the colors," meaning the American flag, "pass in review."[57] The next year, the president of the UDC's North Carolina Division reported that in raising war funds, "North Carolina . . . is never a slacker"—a derisive term for draft-dodgers and others who insufficiently supported the war. She also promoted the movement for state laws to punish the desecration of the American flag. That movement had achieved no success in the former Confederacy in peacetime.[58]

Aware of the novelty among many neo-Confederates of such notions, Odenheimer and Poppenheim sought to make state-based American nationalism palatable by syncretizing it with neo-Confederate beliefs. The women emphasized the white southern roots of national patriotic symbols or invented such roots where none were apparent. To the membership, for example, Poppenheim touted the "Southern" origins of the "national anthem"; Francis Scott Key had been a Marylander.[59] Odenheimer promoted the celebration of Flag Day (June 14). Marking the anniversary of the Continental Congress's adoption of the Stars and Stripes design in 1777, this holiday had been invented and disseminated in the 1880s and 1890s by northerners who were promoting national patriotism and/or Union commemoration. It had seldom been celebrated in the pre–World War I white South.[60] Odenheimer, on the other hand, told the UDC in 1917 that a southern newspaperwoman—even better, the daughter of a Confederate soldier—had invented Flag Day in the course of promoting Missouri's flag antidesecration law (1903).[61]

The blending of American state-based nationalism and Confederate patriotism could go only so far. Leaders were anxious, in wartime, to privilege American patriotism. The Tennessee DAR and the UDC's Tennessee Division announced plans to contribute flags to every Tennessean war funeral, with the DAR sending "a United States flag" and the UDC sending the "Confederate battle flag."[62] The UDC women quickly withdrew the proposal under fire from "certain parts of our country," in Poppenheim's words. However, Poppenheim did not, as prewar neo-Confederates might have, excoriate northern pressure (as she herself characterized it) not to flaunt Confederate flags at U.S. military funerals. Contending that such flags were best suited to the funerals of Civil War veterans, she suggested gently that the UDC honor "boys in khaki" instead with "the U.D.C. colors, red, white, and red, attached to . . . floral offerings."[63]

Some UDC women did not adapt as quickly as their national leaders to state-based nationalism's orthodoxies. A report from the Texas Division covering the spring and summer of 1917 made no mention of war work.[64] Some in the rank and file continued to fund and raise monuments. The war year of 1918 saw the dedication of a lavish Confederate soldier statue and fountain on the courthouse square in Denton, Texas.[65] Holding only local office in the UDC, an Upperville, Virginia, woman also dissented from the regnant Stars and Stripes patriotism. Writing in 1918, when criticism of the American flag became a federal crime, Mary D. Carter discussed the flag in remarkably relativist terms—"never better or worse, or other than the ideals of the nation who waves it." Carter linked "the orgy of militarism, known as the Reconstruction Era," when the flag was merely a "sectional" and partisan "symbol" and when "helpless women and children were martyred," with a later atrocity by U.S. forces, "the battle of Wounded Knee, where Indian women and children were mercilessly massacred." In the end, Carter supported the U.S. mission in Europe while affirming the American-ness of the Confederate cause—as neo-Confederates had always done. "We are fighting with England and the North now for exactly the same reason that we fought against the former in 1776 and the latter in the sixties . . . for constitutional liberty and against tyranny and invasion."[66]

With the war's end, neo-Confederate women loosened their embrace of national patriotic symbols and of the American state. Such women withheld support from the Red Scare crackdowns and deportations of 1919–1920. After the war, the UDC backed contemporary reforms regarding international cooperation for peace to an extent unprecedented in the organization's history.[67] Late in 1919, the UDC called on the U.S. Senate to ratify the Versailles Treaty without amendments or reservations, a stance that had much to do with the League of Nations' conception by a white southerner.[68] Susie S. Campbell of Virginia, historian general at the time, called Woodrow Wilson "the greatest since Washington, for he attempted to gain for the whole world through the League of Nations that freedom which Washington secured for his own country . . . . For the first time the United States sat at the council table of nations." Regarding the Senate's rejection of the treaty, which ultimately prevented the country from joining the league, Campbell wrote angrily that "We," meaning the United States, had "abdicated, ingloriously, ignominiously, at the mandate of those whose vindictive hatred was aroused by the preëminence of President Wilson."[69]

The First World War did leave some permanent marks on neo-Confederate nationalism. Campbell affirmed that neo-Confederates belonged to the United States, and vice versa, when she placed herself and her organization within the "We" that was the country. Moreover, many neo-Confederate women wanted white Americans outside the South to be able to incorporate Confederate symbols and heroes into their own definitions of Americanness, rather than awarding the Confederacy a monopoly on Americanness in the 1860s. The new thinking was illustrated by the comment of a Greenwood, Mississippi, woman during the dedication of a roadside boulder. The Jefferson Davis Highway project was "in no way designed to commemorate the fierce conflict between sovereign States comprising this great republic." It was intended solely to honor Davis as a "great American" and "national figure."[70]

Neo-Confederates' identification of their nation with the state ebbed, flowed, and ebbed again during the First World War and its aftermath. Yet the relative narrowness of neo-Confederates' women-centered nationalism before the war—treasuring a country, dead and gone, and its fighting force—enabled an easy transition to twentieth-century men-centered nationalism, in which the cultural as well as political authority of present-day men mattered most. The women's considerable war work, transmission of state-based patriotism, and focus on history's great men all upheld men's cultural and political supremacy within their nations—American and Confederate.

Unlike comparable women's organizations that were dedicated to nationalism, the UDC continued in wartime to avoid discussing or supporting child-centered reforms not directed at ex-Confederates and their kin in part because such reforms were often implemented by women. More fundamentally, while the DAR, the WRC, and the NACW all supported nationwide voting rights for women before their approval in August 1920, the UDC withheld endorsement of woman suffrage to the last. Daughters of the Confederacy likely believed, along with organized antisuffragists, that women's enfranchisement threatened white supremacy and current class hierarchies more than strengthening them.[71] Susie S. Campbell reflected glumly that the Nineteenth Amendment's ratification resulted from male politicians' partisan self-interest.[72] In overlooking the legions of women who had pressed for voting rights over the preceding seven decades, and in overlooking suffragism's twentieth-century compatibility with dominant notions of womanliness, Campbell implied a continued and pointed opposition to first-class citizenship for women.

DURING WORLD WAR I, black men and women conflated citizenship with manhood more than ever. Wartime and postwar indignities intensified the association of black civil rights with masculine self-assertiveness in the present. Against the backdrop of the postwar wave of white-on-black violence, Carita Owens Collins, writing in the black press in 1919, called on men, especially returning veterans, to "Be men, not cowards and demand your rights . . . . [T]hat same red blood so freely spent on Flanders' field, / Shall yet redeem your race." She concluded:

Demand what is right,
Not a weak suppliant demand;
But an eye for an eye, and a soul for a soul,
Strike back, black man, strike![73]

While many clubwomen would likely have recoiled from Collins's encouragement of violence, her affirmations of manhood were widespread.

In the war years, most strands of nationalism articulated by white Americans remained grounded in white supremacy and Jim Crow mores. In the heat of the wartime moment, one DAR officer enjoined members to learn the names of "the most influential Negro women in your community," to visit them in their homes, and to invite them "to take part in all patriotic demonstrations" — which she herself had done already in her hometown of Ann Arbor, Michigan. A major goal of this outreach to middle-class black women was to counteract German agents' "pernicious attempt to corrupt the patriotism of the Negro" in the South.[74] Another painful moment came at a food-conservation meeting in Washington attended by white and "nearly one hundred or so" black women. The first speaker, Mrs. Archibald Hopkins, opened her speech with a jibe in mock black dialect at her old mammy: "'Miss Hopkins, I'se got to have sugar.'" The second speaker, former DAR president Julia Green Scott, also sought to warm up the interracial audience with a "darkey" joke. To this meeting "called for the unity of all American women," a writer concluded anonymously in *The Crisis*, "we colored women were invited . . . for the specific purpose of being insulted."[75] White skepticism of black patriotism outlasted the war. In more than one southern town, women's war monuments segregated the names of doughboys even in death.[76]

Booker T. Washington's combination of racial self-help and lip service to Jim Crow preferences died with him, in and around 1915. The subsequent vigor of the movement for black civil rights, including the self-confident and militant trope of the "New Negro," stemmed in part from the extent to which the country at large and the national state adopted or tolerated Jim Crow practices in wartime.[77] Much of American military opinion accepted the canard that black men were racially unfit for combat—notwithstanding the importance of African American soldiers to the late nineteenth-century Indian wars in the American West, the Spanish-American War, and the Philippine-American War less than a generation before. Also demonstrating white Americans' objections to the sight of black men in military uniform were outbreaks of violence in 1906 and 1917 between white civilians and black troops stationed in Texas. These incidents followed civilians' "racial harassment" of the troops but resulted in swift, blanket punishments for the soldiers. Though black men ultimately served in the First World War in numbers exceeding African Americans' share of the U.S. population, they usually found themselves relegated to kitchen, stevedore, and burial duty.[78] After the American Legion, the powerful patriotic association of World War I veterans, formed in 1919, it admitted black veterans only on a segregated basis and barred them altogether from conventions.[79] Because white military leaders resisted putting weapons in black men's hands and insisted on their ineffectiveness as warriors, multiple black opinion-makers, most famously W. E. B. Du Bois, gloried in publicizing black men's military service and called the war "Our War."[80]

The denigration of black men's fighting ability and the treatment of black troops profoundly shaped black clubwomen's relationships with their country during the war years because, like Carita Owens Collins, they viewed present-day men as national redeemers. Many such women had always considered military service the very epitome of patriotism, as did many white women. Unlike white women, however, black women found many of their own wartime offers of patriotic service rejected or belittled—even as white women in their communities urged black women to conserve food and otherwise sought to tutor them in patriotism.[81] That clubwomen needed little such tutoring is evident from their war work. By the war's end, the NACW, though nearly half the DAR's size in 1916 (50,000 compared to 92,000) and raising funds among poorer populations than did any white "daughters," generated $5 million for the Third Liberty Loan drive alone and contributed $300,000 to the Red Cross.[82]

In 1917 black clubwomen little anticipated the disillusionments to come. Once the United States began its intervention, the women cooperated extensively with the Council of National Defense and with the Red Cross.[83] The women also exhorted each other, and those around them, to greater heights of state-based, prowar, American patriotism. Maria Louise Baldwin, the Massachusetts school principal who had despaired over *The Birth of a Nation*, reclaimed her country and proclaimed it her nation. She headed a Soldiers' Comfort Unit in Boston that provided black troops with "liberty sings," lectures, and garments.[84] Forty-two-year-old Mary McLeod Bethune of Daytona, Florida, whose declarations of allegiance to American democracy would pervade her civil rights activism throughout her career, addressed the Florida Federation of Colored Women's Clubs as its new president. "[S]he pledged anew the loyalty of the Negro to his race, his country, his God," a witness wrote, capturing Bethune's seamless combination of those loyalties.[85]

The next year, a Chicago physician demanded of other clubwomen, "If you are not in the [Red Cross] work is there a reason why?" Her exhortations were based on her beliefs that "We cannot afford to be slackers" and, moreover, that "Our men are in the war and we must back them up."[86] Making similar points about wartime patriotism was Alice Moore Dunbar-Nelson of Wilmington, Delaware. Best known to contemporaries as the widow of the poet Paul Laurence Dunbar, this writer and high school teacher had been active in the NACW and the WRC for two decades. In giving "love and tears" and money, Dunbar-Nelson wrote, black women had managed "to fan into a flame the sparks of patriotism in the breasts of those whom the country denied the privilege of bearing arms"—knowing well the importance of that privilege to American citizenship.[87]

The physician's demand that black clubwomen increase their involvement with the Red Cross alluded to another perception, which Dunbar-Nelson shared, that there had been a "loss of patriotic interest" among African Americans in 1918 as compared to the initial enthusiasm of the previous year. Dunbar-Nelson ascribed the falloff to white women's "indifference" toward "the well-meant efforts of the colored women in attempting to help in war relief; . . . the old, old stories of prejudice and growing bitterness in the labor situation; [and] rumors of increased lynching activities." More important here than the alleged ebb in African American civilians' support for the war is the patriotic disillusionment underlying that ebb.[88] Black clubwomen's wartime writings contain a litany of rejections by their country and demonstrate changes in the women's own perceptions. White-on-black insults and exclusions were nothing new or shocking in the 1910s—except when they occurred outside the South, and especially when they occurred in response to African Americans' renewed investment in their American identities.

For example, the federal government's and Red Cross's refusal for most of the war to register black women as nurses hurt because it frustrated the women's desires to serve the state, which was key to their own assertion of American citizenship. Expressing these desires is a contemporary photograph of a group of young women in Syracuse, New York, who called themselves the Women's War Relief Club. The NACW's published national records mention no such club. However, whether the Women's War Relief Club stood under the NACW's umbrella or whether its members were trained nurses matters less than the patriotism articulated by their white uniforms, their white caps, and their solemnity. The American state's repudiation of black nurses contrasted sharply with government practice only twenty years before. Because black troops had been more widely accepted as combatants in 1898, the War Department had made an effort, admittedly minimal, to recruit black women to care for those troops. The Secretary of War reversed the World War I ban on black nurses only in June 1918—fewer than six months before the war ended—under pressure from the NACW, the NAACP, the National Association of Colored Graduate Nurses, and the president of Tuskegee Institute. Even then, few orders came from Europe for African American nurses, and none ever went overseas in government capacities.[89] Some were thrilled at a rumor that three hundred light-skinned women had "passed," serving "the great cause at God's command" as white nurses. In the end, a Buffalo, New York, woman called on future "historians" to "[p]ut in a paragraph that the colored woman wanted to go, but the nation wouldn't let her."[90] This commentator's reference to "the nation" conflated state, country, and the American nation and placed African Americans outside them all.

Many black women responded by increasing their investment in their American identities, expressed in praise of history's fighting men. Adding injury to insult was a pogrom in Illinois—"the home state of Abraham Lincoln, who made the Negro free," noted a Pennsylvania club leader—only three months after the United States went to war.[91] A July 1917 "shooting incident" involving white police officers in a black neighborhood in East St. Louis burgeoned into a rampage by white mobs that left forty-eight people dead, thirty-nine of them black; 6,000 African Americans homeless; and "only a few whites" lightly punished.[92] Combined with violence in Waco, Texas, and in Memphis, Tennessee, the East St. Louis "race riot" inspired a silent parade of 15,000 in Harlem—fast becoming the cultural capital of African America. Eschewing music and chants, men, women, and children expressed their anger on signs. Many commented on American patriotism: "We have fought for the liberty of white Americans in 6 wars; our reward is East St. Louis"; "We helped plant the flag in every American Dominion"; "So treat us that we may love our country"; "Patriotism and loyalty presuppose protection and liberty."[93]

The next month saw a bloody confrontation in Houston, Texas. Protests from white locals when black troops were first stationed there, the subsequent enforcement of Jim Crow segregation against the troops, and (according to *The Crisis*) the disarmament of black soldiers by white officers all contributed to a mutiny. After black soldiers witnessed a white man's assault on a black woman, one hundred of them "marched on the city," killing nine white civilians, five white policemen, and two white soldiers and wounding "at least a dozen" more. The rampage resulted in the swift hanging of thirteen black soldiers, the subsequent execution of six more, and life sentences for more than sixty—in contrast to the light punishments or lack of pun-

Women's War Relief Club, Syracuse, New York, ca. 1917. Jesse Alexander Photograph Collection, Photographs and Prints Division, Schomburg Center for Research in Black Culture, New York Public Library, Astor, Lenox and Tilden Foundations.

ishment that greeted most white perpetrators of racial violence.[94] Selling buttons in Chicago commemorating the dead soldiers, fifty-six-year-old Ida B. Wells-Barnett believed it was "a terrible thing that our government would take the lives of men who had bared their breasts fighting for the defense of our country." Wells-Barnett saw no contradiction between patriotic support for U.S. troops—she had watched her own stepson enlist in February 1917 (before conscription began)—and protest against what she perceived as the state's unjust treatment of those troops. Her stance on Houston was a controversial one among middle-class African Americans. Wells-Barnett later excoriated black churches in Chicago for refusing to join the protests against the severe punishment of the soldiers. For her opinions, she narrowly escaped arrest for, as she put it, treason. She quickly showed the two "men from the secret service bureau" the candy boxes, cigarettes, and other goods that she and the Negro Fellowship League—the organization of young black men she supervised—were about to send to black soldiers at a local camp.[95]

Wells-Barnett was not the only civil rights activist on the receiving end of federal surveillance. The same government agencies cheered by many white women for protecting the country from leftist radicalism took an interest in other Americans who fused patriotism and protest.[96] Nannie Helen Burroughs, a leader in black Baptist organizations who was also important in the NACW, had long run a school for women workers in Washington. In the fall of 1918, the National Training School for Women and Girls offered a ten-week training camp for "colored women" in "home defense," ranging from car and truck repair to food conservation. Burroughs advertised her training camp by pointing to its location in Washington — "the Best Place in America to Understand . . . This Fight to Make Democracy Safe for the World." Her inversion of Woodrow Wilson's war cry to "make the world safe for democracy" no doubt alluded to Jim Crow. For more than a year before Burroughs advertised her "home defense" camp, the U.S. Military Intelligence Division (MID) — a branch of the U.S. Army and the Central Intelligence Agency's precursor — had been monitoring her activities and opening her mail. She had come under the MID's watch in 1917 for criticizing Wilson.[97] The MID also perceived that black history contained potentially anti-American messages. Starting in 1917, it monitored both the executive council of Carter G. Woodson's ASNLH and its *Journal of Negro History*.[98] In scrutinizing civil rights activists, clubwomen, and organizations dedicated to history, the federal government made an exception to its focus on the left and on foreign nationals. Here, the state targeted homegrown reformers. They included Americans who considered their country to be their nation, and who objected merely to the state's adoption of race-based nationalism.

Following the state's and the country's repudiation of their offers of patriotic service, black women drew new distinctions between patriotism and unconditional support for the state. The NACW did not, as a group, back the federal bans on antiwar and unpatriotic speech or the government's prosecutions of leftists. Dangers closer at hand than those presented by strikes, Bolshevik-friendly foreigners, or the sporadic bombings of 1919–1920 (blamed on anarchists) confronted black women and the men in their lives. The war "as it has presented itself on the battlefield is over," wrote a Louisville, Kentucky, club leader in 1920, but "[t]he battle has little more than commenced . . . . Many are only now beginning to catch the first glimpse of what freedom really means."[99] "Freedom" had been at the center of the federal government's presentation of the First World War as a struggle for democracy. To postwar African Americans, including those who identified primarily as Americans, freedom and democracy were the distant endpoints of ongoing struggles—not to be celebrated as if they had already arrived.

Also contrary to defining patriotism as unquestioning solidarity with the state, black clubwomen eyed coldly the extension of the American empire. That empire was now made up of protectorates—ostensibly independent countries—in addition to colonies. African Americans had long cherished Haiti, independent for more than a century, as a symbol of black agency. In 1915 the U.S. military began a twenty-year occupation of Haiti. Five years later, in the NACW's journal, an unnamed woman credited president Mary Burnett Talbert with inspiring the NAACP's ongoing investigations of conditions there. In 1919, the woman wrote, Talbert had contacted NAACP headquarters about a "Hun atrocity" in Haiti by the U.S. Marines (which excluded black men) after hearing "the marines, back in this country to spend a happy Xmas with their own families, tell on Xmas eve, one year ago, how they has [sic] slaughtered helpless and defenseless women and children."[100]

Separating their American nation from the state, some black women began espousing an internationalism compatible with American identity. This women-centered internationalism reached out to other women and to female entities. Black club leaders hoped that transatlantic publicity of racial discrimination in the United States would embarrass white Americans into changing their behavior. For African Americans to view progressive Europeans as counterweights to U.S. white supremacy was not new. Ida B. Wells-Barnett had made multiple trips to Britain in the 1890s in her efforts to foster indignation against lynching. After the First World War, after the American state disillusioned them to a new degree, black women placed heightened hopes in transatlantic contact. While white American women hailed international cooperation as a way to protect the world, and their country, from evils such as international war, African American women turned to international cooperation also to protect themselves from other Americans.[101] A good example was Mary Burnett Talbert's appearance at the 1920 International Council of Women meeting in Norway. "I shall go and plead for our rights, your rights," she declared in the course of raising traveling funds. "We are still riding Jim Crow; lynchings are still being staged, while we are wondering what to do." Once overseas, she predicted to European audiences that "mob law" (meaning lynchings) in the United States would fade away because "the spirit of the nations of the world, in its travail for a rebirth of freedom, will not countenance injustice in any nation."[102]

Other women turned to a black nationalism incompatible either with American nationalism or with state-based nationalism. Within the officially all-black, mixed-sex UNIA, men and women espoused a separatist nationalism that defined the "race" internationally—Africans and African-descended peoples worldwide—and aspired to create a national homeland in Africa for them all. The UNIA had been organized in Jamaica in 1914 by Marcus Garvey and Amy Ashwood, and it found fame after Garvey moved to the United States in 1916. Following the war, the UNIA—still dominated by Garvey and led, while he was in prison, by his second wife, Amy Jacques Garvey—gathered steam in Harlem and across the country, as well as in the Caribbean and in Central America.[103] The First World War's importance to the efflorescence of Garveyism in African America was obvious to a Coraopolis, Pennsylvania, woman. "[Black men and women] discovered during this debacle of the nations that they were all puffed up over a consciousness of their national self-sufficiency . . . . The war opened our eyes."[104] The UNIA's corps of African Black Cross Nurses, with their white and green uniforms and black armbands, presented a poignant contrast to the frustrations of those black women who had wanted to serve the red, white, and blue.[105] In locating cultural authority in present-day men—particularly in Marcus Garvey—the UNIA continued, in the 1920s, the masculinization of black nationalism. Its nemesis among African Americans, the U.S. civil rights movement, did the same.

DURING AND AFTER World War I, African American civic nationalists substituted confrontation for accommodationism and saw less reason to equate patriotism with obedience. In stark contrast, many white "daughters" concluded from the First World War and the Bolshevik Revolution that patriotism entailed supporting the state at all times. War and revolution truly radicalized these women. Thirty-six years old in 1917, Flora Bredes Walker of the DAR organized women in Washington State for the Council of National

Defense. She was also active in the National League for Women's Service, a preparedness organization that advocated "military service or instruction" for all American women. It is highly likely that Seattle's acrimonious general strike in 1919 helped drive Walker farther to the right, given her marriage to a Seattle factory owner.[106] In the 1920s, as chair of the new and powerful National Defense Committee of the DAR, Walker rallied white women at large to oppose reform in addition to radicalism. Motivated by perceptions of the nation's need for self-protection, Walker's and others' actions signaled a men-centered nationalism newly suspicious of female institutions. Notions of female cultural authority and women's solidarity would seem, to both sexes, increasingly quaint.

Chapter Five
The Security State

APPREHENSIONS AND disappointments resulting from the First World War further regendered women's nationalism. Especially influential among white women was the DAR's right wing. In the early 1920s it began shaping the organization's agenda. The women were rightists in that they attacked reformism and leftist radicalism simultaneously.[1] The women embraced the state — especially the surveillance agencies that comprised the new security state — more fervently and unconditionally than ever. Indeed, the women struggled against the female-dominated peace movement on the state's behalf. Their rubric of "national defense" elaborated on wartime beliefs in military preparedness and entailed preserving military readiness in the face of government retrenchments, international disarmament efforts, and peace activism. More broadly, national defense conflated the state's preservation with the nation's preservation. Foremost among external threats to the nation were Bolshevik hopes for worldwide communist revolution. The idea that Bolshevik infiltrators in the United States chose as their hosts credulous liberals and reformers caused state-based nationalists to oppose international peace initiatives and domestic reforms, especially those relating to women or children, and explains why the women applauded the government's permanent surveillance efforts, which were unprecedented in American peacetime. The development of the national defense ethos among state-based nationalists illustrates the masculinization of women's nationalism because of that ethos's relative skepticism of organized women and its characterization of present-day men — especially experts and men in uniform — as the country's ultimate protectors.

As during the First World War, African Americans in the 1920s found themselves on the receiving end of the same security apparatus welcomed by many white women. Garveyite leaders experienced hostile treatment from the American state in the form of surveillance by the MID and by the Justice Department's Bureau of Investigation starting in 1921, and later in the form of outright prosecution, in part because they urged African Americans to direct their primary allegiances away from their country and from the state. Financial and other shenanigans gave the state the opening it sought. Marcus Garvey was deported in 1927, Amy Jacques Garvey followed him out of the country, and the organization soon faded in the United States.[2] The MID also placed the NAACP under hostile surveillance, in spite of all the organization's pro-American rhetoric.[3] Yet African Americans' common experiences at the hands of the security state did not prevent tensions between integrationist American nationalists and "Negro" nationalists. The debate continued among women as well as among men. Among women, both sides of the debate viewed men as race leaders, both culturally and politically, more than ever.

In general, American women's disparate definitions of nation — conflating the nation with the state, the black race, the white race, and/or with representations of the erstwhile Confederacy as American — shared much in common after World War I. Adherents of each nationalism debated the forms that women's relationship with their nations should take. While most continued to support organized political activism on the part of women, some women — notably some Garveyites — reached back to the eighteenth century to argue that female patriotism should primarily consist of mothers' producing and grooming sons for citizenship. Except for neo-Confederates, who had always espoused a particularly male-centered nationalism, these female nationalists all helped bring about pronounced masculine turns within their respective ideologies. More than ever, they followed such male-led, all-male, or masculine entities as the U.S. military, federal surveillance agencies, the historical profession, the NAACP, and the charismatic Marcus Garvey. Especially in the case of the DAR's red-baiters, women helped diminish organized women's and amateurs' importance within nationalism and patriotism.

FOLLOWING THE First World War, women-centered nationalism endured in some quarters. It continued to emphasize the cultural authority of women. Black clubwomen, for example, affirmed the nationalist dimensions of mothering and of other labor done within the home. In 1930 NACW president Sallie Wyatt Stewart, a forty-seven-year-old real estate broker and teacher from Evansville, Indiana, praised the domestic prowess of black women in raising great men — "a [Paul Laurence] Dunbar, a [Booker T.] Washington, and a [W. E. B.] Dubois [sic]." She was countering the white supremacies that had long denied chastity and other prized forms of female distinctiveness to black women. Those forms of racism had helped inspire the NACW's own formation and had informed black middle-class women's emphasis on respectability.[4] In keeping with women-centered nationalism's affinities for domesticity, Stewart proposed a strict division of political labor between black men and black women. Intending to streamline the NACW's mission at a time of economic depression, she distinguished her organization from others that "[pooled] finance" or were "as watch dogs on the tower, remonstrating and demanding our rights. Each of these . . . has its place; but neither of these places is the work of the mothers and daughters of a race." Women's "first duty," in Stewart's mind, was instead to create "beautifully sweet and clean" homes "that shall teach the youth . . . to appreciate beauty" so that "our group shall not be repulsive, shall not be despised and evaded."[5]

A more politically ambitious women-centered nationalism was in evidence at the UNIA's helm. During her years in the United States, the Jamaican-born Amy Jacques Garvey articulated a nationalism that celebrated female agency. In her editorship of the "Our Women and What They Think" page of the *Negro World*, she combined blistering critiques of black men's failings, both as men and as patriots, with forceful advocacy of education and political prominence for black women, also in nationalism's name — to the point that her biographer, Ula Yvette Taylor, argues that Jacques Garvey combined nationalism and feminism. Indeed, Jacques Garvey's opposition to notions of women's intellectual inferiority soundly repudiated forms of nationalism that emphasized women's fertility at the expense of their public importance.[6]

Yet even in Jacques Garvey's confident hands, combining nationalism and feminism did not amount to reconciling them. The two sets of ideas waged a "tug-of-war," in Taylor's words. Jacques Garvey acknowledged no conflict between her own identities as political activist and helpmate to her husband; she took pride in her supportiveness as a wife of a great man.[7] Ultimately, Jacques Garvey did not go as far in her advocacy of women's authority within their nations as did those clubwomen of the 1890s who imagined women at the head of the race. In fact, Jacques Garvey's outrage at black men's failure to protect and to provide for black women communicated the opposite of what generations of clubwomen had believed. The latter had, especially before 1900, contended that the race could rise no higher than its women. A generation later, the old maxim was contested even within the NACW itself.[8] Jacques Garvey and many others believed that the race could rise no higher than its men. Racial empowerment entailed reinforcing men's leadership of families and of nations. In 1925 Jacques Garvey celebrated what history's "Pilgrim Fathers" had done for the white race and for white women ("They cast all fear aside and . . . they conquered both the red man and nature"), and she wondered "if there are any black Pilgrim Fathers in the world today."[9]

Also exemplifying women-centered nationalism, in its attribution of cultural authority to women, was the International Council of Women of Darker Races (ICWDR). It organized as an offshoot of the NACW in 1920 and began meeting in 1922.[10] The ICWDR was largely the brainchild of Margaret Murray Washington, who had long been interested in women around the world. However, the organization endured long after her death in 1925.[11] In keeping with its ideological roots in Tuskegee, the ICWDR combined black nationalisms old and new — notions of racial self-determination with a fully elaborated black transnationalism. Although considerably more socially exclusive than the UNIA — with steep dues and fees, and a membership initially limited to two hundred — the ICWDR shared ideas with Garveyites.[12] Both groups sought to foster international understanding and solidarity among African-descended peoples and, especially in the ICWDR's case, others of color. Yet the

ICWDR's women-centered nationalism helps distinguish it from Garveyism's organizational culture. The ICWDR stressed women's own self-education and the uplift of young people—promoting the study of "Negro" history (defined internationally) by both its own membership in local Committees of Seven and by black children at large in the United States. ICWDR members' lobbying of U.S. school boards and superintendents for more instruction in black history predated Carter G. Woodson's invention of Negro History Week in 1926. Placing emphasis on women within the international black nation, the ICWDR also sent women to study the lives of women and children in Haiti and the education of women and girls in Sierra Leone.[13]

Black women also expressed women-centered nationalism in continuing to support progressive reforms relating to women and children. In themselves, these reforms elevated female activism and all-female institutions, thus illustrating women-centered nationalism's simultaneous affirmations of women's cultural authority and women's political activism. In 1926 NACW president Mary McLeod Bethune urged members to send telegrams to their members of Congress in support of a raft of reformist legislation—"the educational bill, the World Court bill, the child labor bill, and the [Sheppard]-Towner Bill," which specified the renewal of federal pensions for maternal and infant health.[14] Black clubwomen also continued to act as reformers on the community level, in keeping with the NACW's own focus on aiding and culturally uplifting the black poor. They maintained their own "child welfare" departments all over the country in the late 1920s, from Pennsylvania to Virginia to Tennessee to Montana.[15] Such child-centered reforms and calls for government involvement were eschewed not only by Garveyites, who as a group considered such reforms irrelevant to their own missions, but also by white women nationalists following the DAR's rightward turn in 1923.

BEFORE 1923, white women, like black clubwomen, affirmed female cultural authority also in continuing—or in the WRC's case, starting—to support child-centered reforms. At the initiative of Illinois members, the WRC created its national Child Welfare Committee in 1919, which supported and lobbied for federal and state legislation, including child labor laws, compulsory education laws, age-of-consent laws, and in 1921, mothers' pensions. On one occasion in 1922, the WRC demonstrated a more solid commitment than the DAR's to child-centered reform. As a national body, it supported a federal constitutional amendment banning child labor.[16]

Among the DAR, reform work expressed members' stake in the United States: the belief that modifying capitalism would save it, and therefore save both state and country. State-based nationalism's progressive streak endured beyond the First World War and the first Red Scare in large part because of its compatibility with antiradicalism. In 1919 the DAR's national convention asserted that combating "Bolshevism" in the United States required Americanization campaigns: "[T]he apostles of that political and economic heresy . . . seem to find their most fertile ground for dangerous propaganda among the great foreign population."[17] On the community level, DAR women also continued to pursue the patriotic uplift of immigrants, notably Asians, while simultaneously favoring both the deportations of 1919–1920 and the 1920s immigration restrictions that discriminated in favor of northern and western Europeans and that banned Japanese.[18]

Regarding child- and women-centered reforms, the DAR joined a constellation of women's organizations in promoting the Sheppard-Towner Act of 1921.[19] Progressive Daughters continued their reform activism on state and local levels even after national leaders began opposing reform. In the spring of 1924, the Oklahoma state organization and the Rock Island, Illinois, chapter supported the ratification of the child labor amendment, an effort that ultimately failed.[20] The DAR in the early 1920s also favored a range of reforms relating to international peace or cooperation, such as supporting the United States's joining the League of Nations (before the U.S. Senate repudiated the Versailles Treaty), hosting part of the Washington Disarmament Conference of 1921–1922, and favoring in 1924 the United States's participation in the World Court.[21] The DAR belonged to such reformist umbrella organizations as the National Council of Women (NCW) and the Women's Joint Congressional Committee (WJCC).[22] The organization, however, abruptly terminated its support for progressive reform, apart from Americanization work, not as a direct result of the First World War and of Bolshevik victories, but as a result of a contingent radicalized by those events coming to power within the organization.

White women's occasional positioning of women as historical subjects, like the women's support for child-centered reform in patriotism's name, further demonstrated women-centered nationalism's endurance among white women. Such women's portrayals of women in history linked home and country ever more closely. Within the DAR, starting in 1923, newly dominant rightists opposed reform while retaining a belief in the political importance of organized women. While generally adhering to a men-centered nationalism that attributed cultural as well as political authority to men, some rightists also honored historic women's engagement in state-sanctioned violence. DAR president Grace Hall Lincoln Brosseau, married to the president of Mack Trucks, justified her opposition to disarmament in 1928 with a menacing vision of "750,000 women already mobilized for machine gun service in case of war" in the Soviet Union. Yet the Illinois native herself embraced military pageantry, calling her officers her "captains and lieutenants."[23] Moreover, during Brosseau's administration, the DAR funded twelve identical "Pioneer Mother of the Trail" statues along highways across the country in 1927. Designed by Arlene Nichols Moss of the St. Louis DAR and her son, the "Pioneer Mother" was proudly armed. Scanning the horizon for danger, the white woman stood ramrod straight in formidable boots, clutching a large rifle and sheltering a baby in her other arm. A small boy hid his face in her skirts.[24] Also celebrating armed women was the New York DAR. It arranged for the reburial of the bones of the Revolutionary soldier Margaret Corbin, discovered on land that had belonged to J. P. Morgan, in the U.S. Military Cemetery at West Point. The elaborate monument to "Captain Molly," showing a stern-faced woman behind a cannon, emphasized to viewers that the U.S. Congress had given Corbin— wounded in battle as she fought using her fallen husband's "field-piece"— "half the pay and allowances of 'A Soldier in Service.'"[25]

The "Pioneer Mother" statues and the monument to "Captain Molly" expressed women-centered nationalism's conservative tendencies—evident from the title of the "Pioneer Mothers" project. For her own part, Corbin had followed her husband into battle. Rightist women's celebrations of armed women —and, more broadly, of politically active women—assumed such women's defense of both home and country. As before the First World War, the private, capitalist home, in which women ideally functioned simultaneously as mothers and as political educators under the authority of individual men, stood at the center of white nationalists' vision. The DAR perceived no threat to the American home in consumer capitalism's rearranging of home life. Indeed, department store windows all over the country featured DAR exhibits on "American history"—with George and Martha Washington, Betsy Ross, and domestic life at its center. Dolls and flags joined home and country.[26]

In contrast, Bolsheviks' initially ambitious proposals for transforming family life, as understood by those hostile to Bolshevism, struck at the heart of these white women's notions of home and country. In the Russian Revolution's aftermath, Bolshevik feminists proposed communal nurseries, dining halls, and laundries and "companionate unions" in place of marriage. All were intended to end women's economic dependence on men, and all were part of a broader vision of the state's eventual fade. That these ideas eventually gave way in the Soviet Union to the Stalinist ideal of large socialist families, headed by strong socialist men, made them seem no less menacing to anticommunist Americans.[27] Rightist women believed that in the event of communism's triumph in the United States, the replacement of family functions by communal institutions and the discarding of marriage would result in women's "moral and physical enslavement." The enslavement constituted not only sexual exploitation, but motherhood leached of political importance. The home could no longer function as a governing institution in itself. "[W]ithout her home, without her social rights, what position has [the woman]? None," asserted Brosseau.[28] In 1932 one woman active in the DAR since its inception explicated the organization's motto of "Home and Country" in the language of the new rightist nationalism. She contended that DAR founders had composed the motto in 1890 "knowing that, unless the home is safe the nation cannot live."[29]

MEN-CENTERED nationalists also believed the reverse: unless the nation were safe, the home could not live. Some Garveyites and white rightists centered women's relationship to the nation on reproduction, as some men had always done. While occasional rightists celebrated history's women warriors, other rightists purged history of women. In 1925, the same year that the North Dakota DAR passed resolutions "attacking the pacifist organizations which are wedges of the 'Red Soviet' to foment revolution in this country," it opened a shrine to machismo on the capitol grounds in Bismarck. The women had bankrolled the moving and restoration of the cabin in which Theodore Roosevelt had lived alone and written his histories of the West while ranching in North Dakota in the 1880s. More than 5,000 visitors came in the first three months. The women's presentation of the Roosevelt Cabin—a home devoid of women—contrasted sharply with older DAR house museums that asserted the importance of women's domestic labors to the lives of great men, and to the nation's history at large. The contention of a North Dakotan that "No one could sit in that primitive cabin . . . without feeling a thrill of admiration of the 'Great American,' who will go down in history as an example of the finest type of American citizen," concerned Roosevelt himself, only.[30]

The DAR's sharp turn to the political right intensified the masculinization of white women's nationalism that had begun during the war. As many Daughters had always done, rightist nationalists of the 1920s defined patriotism as unquestioning support for the male-dominated state. To Flora Bredes Walker, patriotism was "such a loving sense of the unity and vitality of the national life as will lead one gladly to obey the law, to guard its dignity, to aid in its enforcement."[31] New in the 1920s, however, were rightist nationalists' rhetorical attacks on organized, propertied white women and on female institutions as threats to country, nation, and state. Rightist women joined Vice President Calvin Coolidge—whose breaking of the Boston police strike in 1919, as Massachusetts governor, gave him much credibility among antiradicals—in taking antiradicalism in a new direction that cast native-born white women as vectors of leftist radicalism. Coolidge's warnings in the women's magazine *The Delineator* in June 1921 regarding college women led astray by "reds" were preceded by a few months by similar statements from DAR president Anne Rogers Minor, a physician's wife from Connecticut.[32] She spoke to the membership in April of the inroads that "socialistic and radical teachings" had made into "our schools and colleges and even into our churches." Her statement anticipated many white nationalists' rejection of progressive reform. As long as leftist radicalism was thought to originate with the poor and foreign, the remedy lay in reforming them—uplifting them in the ways of Americanness and patriotism. To

Minor, however, not only "the radical" but "the radically minded reformer" threatened the country.[33]

In the next few years, the DAR put Minor's suspicion into practice, repudiating its own lengthy résumé of supporting reform. By the end of 1923, the DAR had withdrawn from the WJCC, which it had joined only two years before, and ended its affiliation of at least two decades with the NCW.[34] By 1924, DAR leaders generally rejected the progressive commonplace that the federal government should intervene in domestic affairs, although they still supported domestic surveillance and reforms relating to Native Americans.[35] By the end of the decade, the DAR leadership opposed even those peace initiatives originating from within the state. Shortly after President Herbert Hoover spoke at the 1930 DAR national convention in favor of U.S. participation in the World Court, delegates voted their opposition to "the commitment of our Country to entangling alliances which could operate to limit full liberty of decision in international affairs"—a position that not only defied Hoover's stance but reversed the DAR's own past support for the World Court.[36] Already bothered by the organization's ongoing red-baiting of the peace movement, some members perceived the vote as an insult to the U.S. president. Immediately following the incident, Palo Alto, California's first chapter, experienced the resignation of nearly one-third of its women (twelve of forty-two members) at once.[37] Rightists' isolationism, however, pertained only to Europe. The DAR steadfastly defended the United States's overseas empire. Leaders vowed to "refute the denunciations of the Monroe Doctrine," which had been interpreted to validate U.S. attempts to control the Western Hemisphere, "and deny the charges against our government of 'imperialism.'"[38]

Rightist, state-based nationalists also emphatically turned against reforms concerning women and children. DAR leaders rallied members to oppose the renewal of the Sheppard-Towner Act, a proposed federal department of education, and any other addition to the embryonic welfare state.[39] The Sheppard-Towner Act funded prenatal care and health information only for healthy married women and infant care only for healthy children, only in states consenting to raise matching funds, yet rightist women and others perceived a resemblance to Soviet-style compulsory, communal child care. "Collectivity and bureaucracy would snatch the child from the nursery and make of it an un-American citizen," Flora Bredes Walker asserted.[40] These stances against peace and against child-centered reforms illustrate the masculinization of women's nationalism in that they robbed women of authority, at a time when female peace activism and the female professionals who implemented child-centered reforms were both highly visible.

The DAR's collaboration with the new American security state—specifically, with male-run surveillance agencies that continued their operations in peacetime—also exemplifies men-centered nationalism. The women positioned men as authorities and eyed women and amateurs coldly, while still upholding the legitimacy of female activism dedicated to national defense. The MID directly surveilled women's organizations focusing on peace and informally enlisted other women as surrogate combatants against those organizations, both to garner public support for the cause of national defense and to conceal the "active counterespionage work" against those the MID considered "radical, pacifist and communist."[41] A January 1924 MID memorandum on "Enlisting the Aid of Women to Counteract Women's Pacifism" recommended that the DAR's "National Headquarters be approached with a view to dissemination . . . of the plans and purposes of the War Department."[42] The DAR was not the largest female organization supporting national defense. It counted 161,538 dues-paying members in 1929, while the WRC and the new American Legion Auxiliary together amounted to over 231,000.[43] The MID favored the DAR likely because of its social prestige, its nationwide membership, its consistent linking of nation and state, and its long history of fostering state-based patriotism. The MID gave the DAR materials it had collected on peace activism and radicalism, and it referred civilians who were inquiring about radical women or the peace movement to the DAR.[44] Undeniably, the men of the security state made considerable use of nationalist women.

For their part, nationalist women made considerable use of their friendly relations with such men, believing that connections with the security state enhanced their own patriotic authority. Both in their own perceptions and in practice, nationalist women did not function merely as military men's "cats-paws," as more than one contemporary alleged.[45] The DAR's comprehensive "national defense" program's development in 1923 predated any meaningful contact with the War Department and, more important, drew on a long history of female nationalists' lionizing men in uniform.[46] Imputing agency to rightist women—rather than reducing them to the dupes of men—does not require ignoring the effects of their red-baiting. In practice, the DAR's casting of native-born, white progressive women as threats to the country damaged the reputation, as well as the relative unity on reform, of organized white women at large. Reluctant to defy rightists because they feared having their organizations labeled unpatriotic, leaders of the GFWC, the NCW, and the WJCC gave the DAR free rein in driving out women from those three umbrellas that the DAR considered leftist—notably the WILPF. The tensions resulting from red-baiting culminated in the immense GFWC's withdrawal from the WJCC.[47] In theory, rightist women's characterization of patriotism as intrinsically "virile" further associated cultural, moral, and political authority within nations with masculinity.[48]

Yet men-centered nationalism accommodated and in fact required the political activism of right-thinking women (so to speak). Flora Bredes Walker viewed the state's operations against domestic radicalism as sadly limited. The government's hands were tied as long as "revolutionary groups" used only "legal methods" in seeking to overthrow the "capitalistic" form of government. Only "patriotic organizations" could protect the country from leftists who used peaceful methods.[49] She and other rightists treasured women volunteers in local communities far away from Washington, as is evident from their struggles to foster unanimity among those women.

Chaired by Walker, the National Defense Committee—created in 1925 and fully operational by the next year—marshaled the DAR's membership to lobby Congress for increased military appropriations and for civilian military training camps for young men. The committee asked Daughters to compel the cancellation of appearances by peace activists and other reformers where they themselves lived, or otherwise protest those appearances. Members' efforts to muzzle peace activists were successful in 1926 in Decatur, Georgia, where the DAR and American Legion succeeded in shutting down a speech at Agnes Scott College by Lucia Ames Mead of the National Council for the Prevention of War; in 1929 in Milwaukee, where wardens at an Episcopal church canceled a speech by Eleanor Brannan of the National Council for the Prevention of War following DAR and American Legion protests; and in 1928 in Des Moines, Iowa, where DAR leaders uninvited a GFWC leader on the day of her speech. In this last instance, the speaker had recently attended a meeting of the nonpacifist National Conference on the Cause and Cure of War.[50] The National Defense Committee also collected publications generated by "subversives" in order to exhibit them and to quote from them selectively in its reports. Furthermore, the women amassed materials generated by the anticommunist far right—one of which (Fred R. Marvin's pamphlet *The Common Enemy*) stated that liberals "differ[ed] only on the question of tactics" from communists, socialists, and "bolshevists"—and circulated them among the DAR's rank and file.[51]

In valuing women's political activism, DAR leaders used coercion as well as suasion to rally such women. The DAR's national defense projects were its best funded. A 1928 mandatory, per capita, national defense tax on the membership of ten cents a year (raised to fifteen cents in 1930), in addition to outsiders' generosity, swelled the National Defense Fund to more than $10,000 at a time.[52] No other female organization, not even the American Legion Auxiliary, required members to contribute specifically to the cause of national defense. In the late 1920s, leaders also sought to control the content of local chapter meetings by circulating lists of men, women, and organizations labeled "doubtful"—leftist radical or potentially so—in order to discourage members from inviting them to speak. Intended as internal, confidential documents, the "doubtful speakers" lists caused an uproar when disgruntled Daughters in Boston distributed them at a press conference in February 1928. Quickly dubbed "blacklists," the lists characterized many public figures and organizations with politically moderate and liberal reputations as "socialists," "pacifists," and "communists."[53]

Members' open disagreement with the National Defense Committee's agenda resulted in the expulsion of two women from the DAR in 1928 and 1929.[54] Other women left the DAR because they objected to leaders' attempts to shape local agenda, or because of differences regarding definitions of patriotism. "I do not believe in supporting the government of the United States indiscriminately," a young Quaker in Norristown, Pennsylvania, declared in her resignation; "Not my country right or wrong, but my country when she is right, that is aiding and not destroying human life."[55] Chapters in New Haven, Connecticut, Crawfordsville, Indiana, and Highland Park, Michigan, lost sizable chunks of their memberships following the revelations of the "doubtful speakers" lists.[56] Yet the rightists' triumph within the DAR cannot only be ascribed to the national leadership. The National Defense Committee appears to have operated with substantial support from members. In 1928, twenty-nine of the fifty-one active chapters (57 percent) in North Carolina reported studying a naval appropriations bill then before Congress and promoted heavily by Walker. The next year, forty-nine of fifty-nine Michigan chapters (83 percent) reported using National Defense Committee study outlines at their meetings. In 1931 only five of sixty chapters in Michigan, or 8.3 percent, reported no national defense activity. This pattern is also evident in states that lacked sizable industrial proletariats. In Vermont, twenty-nine of the thirty-three chapters (88 percent) reported having appointed national defense chairs by 1930.[57] Delegates at national conventions consistently elected leaders favored by rightist predecessors. Those delegates were in turn elected by the rank and file.[58]

Their adherence to men-centered nationalism and their new suspicion of some female institutions do not mean that rightist women ignored likeminded women. Kirsten Marie Delegard and others have situated the DAR within larger networks of rightist and antiradical women such as the Women's Patriotic Conference on National Defense, an umbrella organization formed in 1925. Yet while constituting a formidable political force as women, national defense activists placed particular emphasis on male expertise.[59] The new rightist nationalism among white women imputed ultimate authority to the men of the new security state and male contemporaries on the anticommunist right. Flora Bredes Walker's favorite sources of information all were men: Edward A. Hunter of the Industrial Defense Association, Harry A. Jung of the National Clay Products Industries Association (an open shop association in Chicago), and Fred R. Marvin of the Key Men of America. Walker counted the last two as personal friends. All controversial figures, the three men, who had simultaneous ties to munitions corporations and the military, were the subjects of multiple newspaper exposés.[60]

The derivativeness of much of rightist women's output also illustrates the masculinization of women's nationalism. The National Defense Committee disseminated considerably more than it composed. Many of its publications consisted largely of quotations from others on both the left and the right. Likely an effort to avoid libel suits, this ventriloquism also suggests a gendered division of labor, in which men and the occasional woman generated ideas and in which masses of women transmitted those ideas to socially respectable circles. DAR leaders were thrilled when they obtained confidential materials from MID officers.[61] The MID did not, in turn, distribute or recommend DAR leaders' writings to its agents, as it did the opuses of Marvin, Hunter, Jung, or of the War Department librarian Lucia Ramsey Maxwell (the compiler of "spider-web charts" purporting to connect American women's reform and peace organizations to Moscow), in part because many DAR writings relied on materials the MID had previously donated to the DAR, some otherwise destined for the "garbage man."[62]

Daughters displayed a similarly gendered reverence toward the members of Congress who inaugurated the investigations of domestic communism that would later become characteristic of McCarthyism. Repeatedly, in 1930 and 1931, Flora Bredes Walker publicized the work of the first enduring House committee on "communistic propaganda," headed by Representative Hamilton Fish Jr. of New York, to the DAR membership.[63] Fish acknowledged the importance of the DAR as an antiradical entity when he praised delegates at the New Jersey state conference in 1931 "for their stand." His and others' tributes to organized women show that some male nationalists did conceive of women's relationship to the nation as including political activism. Yet the DAR emphatically deferred to Fish; "[k]een interest centered around" him.[64] Later in the decade, at least one local chapter meeting—in Grand Rapids, Michigan—featured J. Edgar Hoover as a speaker. Chapters in Council Bluffs and Spencer, Iowa, hosted other Federal Bureau of Investigation men and boasted of their achievements.[65]

Rightists concerned with national defense remained convinced of organized women's political importance to nationalism. The DAR also now espoused a nationalism focused on female fertility, a nationalism that echoed the prewar tendency to place white women exclusively in the home to avoid "race suicide." Only after World War I did DAR women fund monuments to the first "white" or white "American" babies born in their communities, as in Monroe County, Iowa (1920s), Oakland, Michigan (1928), Moscow, Idaho (1923), and Minneapolis (1924).[66] Some rightist women denounced birth control on similarly racial and gendered grounds. The DAR's "doubtful speakers" lists of 1928 designated Margaret Sanger only as "Leader of Birth Control Movement"; no direct mention of her erstwhile socialism seemed necessary. A Connecticut leader feared that "birth control will not be practiced by the foreigner and the poor, whom it professes to benefit," but by women of her own background.[67]

THE FIRST WORLD WAR and the first Red Scare soothed North-South tensions among white women. Long-established understandings of race-based reconciliation muted sectionalism to the point of rendering remembrances of it relatively unthreatening. The DAR lifted its taboos against commemorating the Civil War (including Union military service), the sectional strife leading to it, and white abolitionism.[68] That eighty-four of Georgia's ninety-two DAR chapters (91 percent) gave money to the National Defense Committee in 1928 — the very first year members were required to contribute to the work — indicates that white southerners were not necessarily put off by the new, extremely state-based incarnation of women's nationalism.[69]

Commemorations regarding the Civil War still contained silences, however. Even in the South, DAR women stopped short of celebrating military service to the Confederacy. This omission resulted in part from an informal division of labor in southern locales that had DAR women studying and commemorating those areas' early American and antebellum history and the UDC doing the same for the Civil War and Reconstruction eras.[70] The absence of Confederate fighting men from DAR commemorations also reveals ideological differences that continued to distinguish one set of Daughters from the other, and state-based nationalism from neo-Confederate nationalism. No national leader of the DAR so emphatically reached out to the UDC as the Kentucky-born Julia Green Scott had in 1912.[71] The rightist leaders of the 1920s, generally northerners, placed Abraham Lincoln alongside George Washington in their patriotic pantheons without hesitation, while Lincoln remained a villain to many neo-Confederates.[72]

These ideological differences, along with rightist women's premium on political activism by organized women, help explain why the conservative UDC ultimately did not join the newly rightist DAR in fetishizing the security state. The masculinization of women's nationalism that accompanied the DAR's rightward turn in the 1920s is less noticeable among neo-Confederate nationalists. Alone among major women's organizations focusing on nation and patriotism, the UDC had never made the transition from supporting women's cultural authority—in the areas of commemoration and education—to supporting the notion of women's political prominence as reformers or the notion of women's political equality with men as voters. In postwar projects, whether focused on commemoration or scholarships, history's fighting men occupied center stage as they always had. Neo-Confederate women continued to assess women's historical significance by their proximity or allegiance to Confederate warriors.

Although many scholars end their discussions of the neo-Confederate movement before or with World War I, the UDC reached its numerical peak, to date, in the early 1920s.[73] Numbering 27,000 at the most in 1900—an important decade for Lost Cause activism—the UDC mushroomed to 63,479 in 1919 and exceeded 100,000 by 1924.[74] In South Carolina alone, 1,000 women joined the UDC in late 1923 and early 1924.[75] Commemorating the Confederacy apparently had a potent attraction for white women born well after the Civil War. Decades of outreach to white, Confederate-descended youngsters in Children of the Confederacy chapters were evidently bearing fruit. The UDC's celebration of the generation that had reached adulthood during the Civil War—the women's own parents and grandparents—resonated especially strongly at the time of that generation's passing.[76]

The rightist ethos newly regnant among state-based nationalists did not challenge Jim Crow or retrospective allegiances to the Confederacy, which helps to explain why the UDC joined in some projects that supported the state and the military establishment. Along with a host of other patriotic organizations, the UDC took part in and promoted the War Department's Defense Test Day mobilizations of September 1924.[77] The UDC also accepted the American Legion's invitation to help develop the U.S. Flag Code, also known as the Flag Etiquette Code—detailed rules redefining the Stars and Stripes as an object capable of being desecrated. The culmination of three decades of flag activism, the Flag Code was quickly adopted by state-level authorities for school instruction and became federal law during World War II. UDC president Leonora Rogers Schuyler, DAR president Lora Haines Cook, and the president of the National Congress of Mothers were the women chosen "to serve on the committee for the purpose of formulating the code" at the National Flag Conference in 1923, Schuyler proudly informed the UDC's membership.[78] To the others developing the Flag Code, there was little question that neo-Confederates were their allies in American patriotism, in part because of the UDC's extensive fund-raising and relief work during World War I, and fund-raising for white veterans' college scholarships following the war.[79]

Some neo-Confederates genuinely subscribed to the new rightism. Born in Florida to a Confederate colonel and his wife, Schuyler had lived in New York City for decades and was long active in the DAR.[80] In 1923 she defined antiradicalism in similar terms to those of her DAR contemporaries. Not only foreigners but some native-born white women threatened to aid Bolshevik plans for revolution in the United States, she thought. In a message to the UDC's membership, Schuyler reprinted a letter she had written to the U.S. secretary of state protesting the admission of three Soviet Russians to the country on the grounds that their "only reason for coming is a desire to subvert the government which we hold most precious." She also asked Daughters of the Confederacy to eschew membership or affiliation with the "un-American" WILPF.[81] In February 1925, the UDC sent representatives to the first Women's Patriotic Conference on National Defense. In 1926 Daughters of the Confederacy in and around Greenville, South Carolina, joined the DAR in trying to shut down the peace activist Lucia Ames Mead's appearance there.[82]

Yet the postwar rightist strand of American nationalism penetrated only shallowly into the UDC's membership and, indeed, its leadership. The organization at large remained overwhelmingly devoted to spreading pro-Confederate interpretations of U.S. history and to benevolence work among Confederate veterans and their descendants.[83] UDC members' apathy toward national patriotic orthodoxies was such that the president in 1925 felt compelled to remind the women of the 1917 resolution enjoining them to stand and salute whenever the national anthem was played or the American flag was raised.[84] Unlike the DAR, the WRC, or the American Legion Auxiliary, the UDC never dedicated a committee, or any funds, to national defense per se. Among national leaders, the new rightism was articulated by only one. Schuyler had long lived outside the South, and she pointed to Daughters of the Confederacy in Washington, D.C., as her inspiration.[85] Schuyler's successors, residing in the old Confederacy, did not take up her cry.

The starkest indication that the UDC did not follow its "sister organization" in espousing the new rightist nationalism came in 1927, when the leadership turned down the DAR's invitation to the second Women's Patriotic Conference on National Defense. Convened that year by DAR president Grace Hall Lincoln Brosseau and the president of the American Legion Auxiliary, that meeting strove in earnest to mobilize antiradical and rightist white women as a political force.[86] UDC leaders regularly declined invitations to join umbrella organizations on the grounds that its bylaws forbade the organization to affiliate, as a whole, with other organizations. Yet UDC president Ruth Jennings Lawton of Charleston, South Carolina, cited an additional reason for her decision regarding the second Women's Patriotic Conference: "Neither politics nor amalgamation being permissible."[87]

Here, the word "politics" evoked partisanship, excessive present-mindedness, undesirable controversy, and, most significant, a lack of femininity. In condemning a rightist cause—and not a leftist, reformist, or explicitly feminist one—as political, Lawton announced the arrival of the female right as a political movement. Her repeated defense of her decision indicates that the new rightism had some followers within the UDC.[88] Yet many neo-Confederates' definitions of antiradicalism adhered to older, race-based variants of nationalism. In 1925 a Morristown, Tennessee, woman associated disloyalty exclusively with foreigners—on racial grounds—and portrayed the South's "purest Anglo-Saxon blood" as the nation's safety.[89] Rightists' suspicion of white Anglo American reformers and peace activists had no place in that cosmology.

To be sure, Daughters of the Confederacy continued not to shy away from "politics" when the past was at stake. In 1922 the massive Lincoln Memorial was dedicated in Washington—a monument that evoked comparisons in DAR publications between the personal simplicity of "the Great Emancipator" and that of Jesus.[90] Neo-Confederates devised a rejoinder to the Lincoln Memorial, also in stone and also on Washington grass. One year after the memorial's dedication, the UDC's District of Columbia Division proposed a tribute to "the Faithful Colored Mammy of the Southland" to be planted on Massachusetts Avenue. Notwithstanding *The Birth of a Nation*, many in the UDC continued to prefer a softer white supremacy that eulogized "faithful slaves." The "mammy" statue came close to reality, with the U.S. Senate appropriating a generous $200,000 to the project in 1923. However, the bill died in the House "after extensive and bitter controversy." Criticism rained down on the proposal from outside as well as inside the Capitol, as the prospect of a "mammy" monument in the national capital helped rouse African Americans to new levels of engagement with their American pasts.[91]

WITHIN BLACK political life, Garveyite nationalists and American civic nationalists in the 1920s agreed on much: African Americans' political self-assertion at home, interest in the worldwide African diaspora, and opposition to European and U.S. imperialism in Africa and the Caribbean.[92] Yet the disagreement among African Americans between those stressing their Americanness and those identifying primarily with a worldwide race-based diaspora proved profound and, for the most part, estranging. With the exception of the ICWDR, which drew together leading NACW clubwomen with at least one woman, Theodora Holly of Haiti, active in the UNIA, little overlap in members or purposeful contact existed between the civil rights–minded NACW and Garveyite women, despite their leaders' similarly middle-class backgrounds and educations.[93]

African Americans belonging to or sympathizing with the UNIA did not renounce their Americanness completely. Instead they pledged allegiance to "the rebirth of Africa, at home and abroad," in the words of a Chicago woman.[94] A UNIA member who donated generously to the cause was, revealingly, commended as a "race patriot" or "Negro patriot," with "Negro" referring not specifically to African Americans but to the international black race.[95] Amy Jacques Garvey's clarion call for African Americans to identify, first and foremost, as "Negro" patriots came in 1925 in the *Negro World*. Addressing blacks in British colonies, French colonies, and the United States in turn, the twenty-nine-year-old explained in each case why their loyalty to country was both futile and foolish. Undoubtedly drawing on her own upbringing in British-ruled Jamaica, she castigated "Negroes" who joined white Britons in singing "Rule, Britannia" — " 'Britons never, never shall be slaves' " — as "parrots, imitating, without thinking . . . [that] their blood-brothers are being murdered and brutalized by the same English in Africa." Jacques Garvey reserved much of her discussion, however, for the notion of African Americans singing "'My country 'tis of thee, / sweet land of liberty.' But . . . [i]s it 'my country' that jim-crows, lynches and burns me?" She and other Garveyites made clear that they were not repudiating patriotic fetishes in themselves. Jacques Garvey pointed proudly to Garveyites' popularization of the red, black, and green flag and of her husband's "Ethiopian Anthem." These foretold "the day when the scattered members of our race shall be reunited in Mother Africa."[96]

Indeed, UNIA meetings in the United States and its territories usually paired the singing of the "Ethiopian Anthem" with the "American National Anthem" (the "Star-Spangled Banner"), omitting another patriotic song that was a staple at U.S. civil rights gatherings.[97] The 1926 biennial of the NACW had delegates sing the "Negro National Anthem" ("Lift Ev'ry Voice and Sing") on three separate occasions.[98] The NAACP leader James Weldon Johnson and his brother J. Rosamond Johnson had originally composed the song in 1900 for a schoolchildren's Lincoln's Birthday celebration in Jacksonville, Florida. James Weldon Johnson's lyrics expressed the joys and agonies of African-descended people who embraced their Americanness:

Stony the road we trod,
Bitter the chast'ning rod,
Felt in the days when hope unborn had died;
Yet with a steady beat,
Have not our weary feet
Come to the place for which our fathers sighed?
We have come over a way that with tears has been watered,
We have come, treading our path thro' the blood of the slaughtered.

The song closed with the lines:

Shadowed beneath Thy hand
May we forever stand,
True to our God
True to our native land.[99]

That these verses held both nationalist and patriotic significance for many is evident from a Georgia clubwoman's complaint that blacks did not stand for the "National Negro Anthem" as they customarily did for the "Star-Spangled Banner," "out of respect for that song and the spirit of patriotism which it creates."[100]

Women in the civil rights–oriented NACW—sharing members and ideals with the NAACP—considered their country's ideals an important motivation, as well as a language, for their fight against white supremacy.[101] Importantly, they still differentiated their loyalty to the American nation from state-based patriotism. The women continued to withhold unconditional support from the U.S. state, and not only because of wartime disillusionments. White-on-black pogroms of unprecedented scale killed hundreds in Tulsa, Oklahoma, in 1921 and Rosewood, Florida, in 1923. Lynchings continued, ranging as far north as Duluth, Minnesota. The revived Ku Klux Klan attracted millions, notably northerners, into its ranks. Especially galling to those who identified primarily as Americans was the federal government's continuing inaction against Jim Crow violence. Patriotism, then, became "loyalty that is based upon something stronger than sentiment," in the words of one president of the NACW.[102]

UNLIKE THOSE RIGHTISTS of the DAR who little doubted the importance of female political activism, black women often debated the extent to which black women should sustain the nation (American or "Negro") as political actors in their own right, or primarily as the mothers of male citizens. Many of their answers reveal nationalism's masculinization on both sides of the divide between American and "Negro" identity. Women from both schools of thought questioned the merits of female cultural authority and female political activism. The women focused their hopes for their nations on manhood and on motherhood.

The position of women within the civil rights movement and the UNIA in the 1920s expresses nationalism's masculine turn. In addition to Mary Burnett Talbert's Committee of Anti-Lynching Crusaders, in which 1,500 black women raised more than $10,000 for the NAACP in 1922 and 1923, "baby contests" held by black women within NAACP branches raised as much as $4,000 on one occasion, in Los Angeles.[103] In 1929 Memphis T. Garrison of West Virginia developed another important fund-raising and publicity device for the NAACP—annual Christmas seals. Contemporaries realized the importance of "the untiring work of colored women" within the branches to sustaining the early NAACP.[104] However, modern-day historians can acknowledge that such women were simultaneously "local heroines," in the words of one recent account—and, indeed, responsible for implanting the NAACP in local communities—and still, often on the subordinate end of a gendered division of labor.[105] Black women were now present in the national leadership, but Daisy Lampkin of Pittsburgh, a national field secretary of the NAACP as of 1930, and Jessie Redmon Fauset, literary editor of *The Crisis* from 1919 to 1926, nevertheless constituted exceptions.[106] Black and white men continued to hold most high offices and to serve as African American civil rights' standard-bearers. An even sharper division of labor characterized the UNIA. Marcus Garvey's masculine cult of personality was sustained by women—especially by his own widow, in later years—as well as by men. In his speeches, Garvey in turn addressed his audiences as "Fellow Men of the Negro Race." Moreover, UNIA women held a separate tier of offices such as "Lady President," all subordinate to their male counterparts.[107]

The masculinization of black women's nationalism occurred in the form of ideas as well as of institutional patterns. Black women continued to be important in fostering commemorations in the 1920s. Yet their remembrances centered on history's great men more than ever. In addition, female instigators of such commemorations often received little credit. Annie E. Oliver of Chicago decided in the late 1920s that her city needed to raise a permanent tribute to Jean Baptiste Pointe du Sable. The eighteenth-century Haitian had been the area's first nonindigenous settler and, in her words, "the first trader, pioneer and business man," and, indeed, the "FIRST CITIZEN of Chicago." Her appeals to the city council bore fruit, as it appropriated more than $20,000 to a du Sable monument in 1929. However, Oliver did not sit on the first, mayor-appointed committee on the monument. She was placed on it only after the black congressman Oscar De Priest dropped out.[108]

Other black clubwomen's discussions of history in the 1920s overlooked female amateurs' past importance in fostering regard for the past among

African Americans. A case in point was the praise Myrtle Foster Cook of Kansas City, then chair of the NACW's Negro History Department, gave to new, sweeping histories of African America by male scholars. "The recent interesting editions of Negro history by our Negro authors, DuBois [*sic*], [Benjamin] Brawley and [Carter G.] Woodson have discovered the Negro to himself and to the white man. We are all suddenly learning that we have a remarkable past," Cook wrote in 1928.[109] She was either unaware of or was intentionally marginalizing the pioneering studies and commemorations of the past generated within her own organization. Statements like Cook's privileged the work of professional historians — almost entirely male — before all. Although the interwar decades saw fruitful collaborations between middle-class black men and women within the ASNLH, that association's division of labor often resembled the NAACP's, with men as national leaders (except for Mary McLeod Bethune, elected ASNLH president in 1936) and women rooting the organization in local communities.[110]

Garveyite women made even deeper challenges to the nineteenth century's regard for female cultural and moral authority, and for female political activism. Within the UNIA, it was not only men who opposed Margaret Sanger's stance on birth control or worried about "race suicide" among black professionals, although men did both in the pages of the *Negro World*.[111] An Oakland, California, woman discussing what black parents should teach their children viewed women and girls solely as nationalism's muses. Fathers should make Marcus Garvey "your boys' ideal in life." Mothers should "instill in your daughter's heart the respect and honor due their father, brothers and the men of their race; that they must be their inspiration and that they are the noblest and bravest of all men."[112]

THE FIRST WORLD WAR did little to dislodge Jim Crow. On the contrary, the war years demonstrated the national triumph of race-based models of national unity. By then, such models were favored by the state. After the war, neo-Confederates lived surrounded by evidence of their movement's success. The UDC had so saturated southern ground with stone soldiers and obelisks that the organization generally funded monuments on the old Confederacy's margins (as in the Texas Panhandle), on roadsides, or outside the

South altogether.[113] In 1927 the UDC completed its marking of a nationwide chain of roads from Washington, D.C., to San Diego, California, as the Jefferson Davis Highway. Like the Daughters of the American Revolution, the Daughters of the Confederacy viewed paved roads and automobiles as aids to fostering historical and therefore patriotic consciousness.[114] The women also perceived new acceptance of neo-Confederate ideas by the country at large. The federal government's retrenchment in the early 1920s, with the exception of domestic surveillance, signified a "State Rights Renaissance."[115] Moreover, the neo-Confederate mission to reshape the telling of U.S. history achieved unprecedented national regard. The New York editor and leading Democrat Claude G. Bowers contacted UDC president Ruth Jennings Lawton in 1927. Through her, Bowers solicited Daughters of the Confederacy for family letters and diaries to help him "recreate the home atmosphere of the South during those dismal days" of Reconstruction.[116] The resulting best seller, *The Tragic Era* (1929), did so much to shape Americans' perception of Reconstruction as a nadir in U.S. history and to create retrospective sympathy for white southern Democrats that scholars of Reconstruction still found it necessary six decades later to confront the book by name.[117]

Alternatively, the DAR's rightists expressed civic nationalism rather than race-based nationalism in their premium on unanimous support for national defense and in their deep suspicion of even the most pedigreed Anglo Americans who disagreed. Some within the organization carried their civic nationalism to a logical conclusion in envisioning a truly interracial fight against communist infiltration. When a Michigander constructed "a solid wall of defense from East to West, from North to South, of the living, vibrant patriotism of our boys and girls," she included as "ours" "the colored girls and boys not in school, and in the schools for colored children in the South."[118] In practice and in theory, however, many in the DAR redoubled their commitment to national unity based on race, not only in their ideological affinities with neo-Confederates, but in outright clashes with civil rights activists and believers.

A number of organizations and individuals concerned with justice for African Americans appeared on the DAR's "doubtful speakers" lists of 1928 —W. E. B. Du Bois, the NAACP, and the UNIA's socialist rival in Harlem, the African Blood Brotherhood—because of real or alleged leftist affinities. Without explanation, the lists omitted the resolutely procapitalist UNIA, both Garveys, and the NACW, despite the black clubwomen's defiance three years earlier.[119] In 1925 clubwomen had protested racially segregated seating at the International Council of Women (ICW) convention in Washington by walking out numerous times. African Americans in the audience, and black musicians scheduled to perform, joined the women. The NACW had extracted promises from local ICW committees that seating would not be segregated and found that the promises had been violated more than once. No law required that the delegates sit separately. Determined by custom, segregation in the District of Columbia's theaters was far from universal. The historian Cynthia Neverdon-Morton attributes the convention's segregation to DAR pressure.[120]

The DAR's adherence to Jim Crow eventually exceeded Washington's and, indeed, southern custom. In 1929 the women dedicated a gleaming new auditorium. With its 4,000 seats and its sophisticated acoustics, Constitution Hall attracted the era's leading musicians.[121] In Washington as in the South, Jim Crow custom allowed artists of any color to perform onstage. The DAR's Executive Committee defied that practice; they eventually banned most nonwhite performers from Constitution Hall and, moreover, restricted the numbers of black ticket holders in addition to segregating them. In December 1930 the committee refused outright to allow the baritone Paul Robeson to perform. Three months later, the sale of seats to black patrons at a Hampton Institute Choir concert was restricted to 200 in a particular section of the auditorium, but after much pressure, the DAR relented and permitted African Americans to sit anywhere. This last confrontation led the DAR Executive Committee to devise a new requirement for artists' contracts, voted into existence in March 1932. The white artist–only clause was explained in retrospect to the membership as resulting from excessive numbers of applications for Constitution Hall's use "by colored groups and for the presentation of colored artists" and from performers' refusal to restrict the number of tickets sold to African Americans.[122] The white-artist clause later made the DAR infamous. Populated by race women, the organization's leadership inadvertently hammered a nail into Jim Crow's future coffin.

Epilogue

APRIL WAS EARLY in any year for an outdoor concert in
Washington, D.C. April 9, 1939, dawned especially blustery and cold. That
Sunday afternoon, the opera luminary Marian Anderson protected her
throat in fur. The Lincoln Memorial was her stage, with a lone accompanist
behind her. A massive, interracial crowd of 75,000 turned out in coats and
hats to listen. Surrounding microphones transmitted the music to millions
of household radios. The Philadelphia-born singer's fame, spanning the
Western world, and her performance of music that was congenial to white
tastes could not overcome the DAR's white-artist policy. The nearly unanimous vote by the DAR's National Board of Management not to allow Anderson to perform at Constitution Hall jarred with her experiences farther
south, where there was little question of allowing black artists to perform,
as long as audiences were racially segregated.[1]

For all its starkness, the DAR leadership's treatment of Marian Anderson
evoked complicated responses. Decrying the DAR did not amount to opposing Jim Crow. Likely realizing that the women's exaggeration of Jim Crow
endangered the very system, many white southern editorialists paired denunciations of the DAR with affirmations of the separation of the races.[2] Civil
rights activists found themselves in some disarray as they debated both the
form and the scope of their response. It was not only a women's voluntary
organization but also educational authorities in Washington (which were
overseen by the federal government) who had turned Anderson away on

Marian Anderson, Lincoln Memorial "Freedom Concert," Washington, D.C., April 9, 1939. Marian Anderson Collection, Rare Book and Manuscript Library, University of Pennsylvania.

racial grounds by denying her access to the large auditorium at the all-white Central High School. Whether to protest de jure segregation in addition to de facto segregation became a thorny question.[3] Civil rights activists also faced external criticism, and not only from those (including people within the DAR) who insinuated communist connections.[4] Nellie S. Davidson of Washington challenged integrationism head-on with a black nationalist response to the DAR's vote. "You," she told a NAACP leader, "will not be able to change those, our Pharisee neighbors, nor their decision." "[I]nstead of denouncing our brothers of another skin and trying to appeal to a so-called sense of justice that hardly ever exists," she suggested having Anderson perform at an African American venue, such as Howard University, with "HEADLINE publicity": "it is high time that we the Negro quit everlastingly trying to stick in where we are not welcome . . . . Indipendence [*sic*] creates Respect!"[5]

Yet civil rights activists saw ripe opportunities in the events surrounding the Anderson concert. The year 1939 was not the first time that the DAR had barred the performer from Constitution Hall's stage.[6] However, among propertied white Americans, the near-consensus on blacks' racial inferiority that had existed at the century's turn had begun to crack. Rightist women's portrayal of white reformers and radicals alike as menaces to America helped widen those cracks. Reformers struck back. Crucial in engineering Anderson's subsequent outdoor "freedom concert" at the Lincoln Memorial, with its powerful imagery, was Secretary of the Interior Harold L. Ickes. With the rest of Franklin D. Roosevelt's administration, he had been lavishly and repeatedly red-baited in publications endorsed and circulated by DAR leaders.[7]

For her part, First Lady Eleanor Roosevelt resigned from the DAR—an action supported by majorities in Gallup polls. Nearly simultaneously, she made public her opposition to Jim Crow by openly supporting a federal antilynching bill. That summer, she not only attended the NAACP's national convention, but she also stood before it to award Marian Anderson the organization's Spingarn Medal.[8] In her newspaper column and in other interactions with the public, Roosevelt repudiated the DAR with about as much fanfare as the DAR had given to her induction six years before. In 1933 the group had approached the first lady about joining, assembled her genealogical documentation, and paid all the fees for a life membership.[9] In that year of national emergency, those leaders had been eager to leave the confrontational tactics of the 1920s behind—to the point of withdrawing the DAR from the Women's Patriotic Conference on National Defense, and removing the fierce Flora Bredes Walker from the National Defense Committee's helm.[10] By mid-decade, however, as New Dealers increasingly focused on questions of social justice, DAR leaders renewed their opposition to reform and reformers.

The DAR's discrimination against Marian Anderson and her subsequent performance ultimately became iconic moments for the young movement for African American civil rights, with the power to rally believers in integration and in racial justice for generations. The enshrinement of those two events began immediately. "Through the Marian Anderson protest concert we made our triumphant entry into the democratic spirit of American life," Mary McLeod Bethune told a friend—on the following day.[11] In addition, the spectacle in Washington had profound symbolic ramifications for American nationalism and patriotism. Anderson's rendering of "America (My Country 'Tis of Thee)" had the effect of insisting that black fathers, too, had died—and lived—in the United States. With a ghostly Abraham Lincoln as her backdrop, Marian Anderson resuscitated ideas of Americanness from Lincoln's time that Jim Crow America had tried to bury. While compatible with white supremacy, Union patriotism had, in the hands of African Americans and white abolitionists, also privileged loyalty to the United States over race as the country's glue. The timing of Anderson's concert—on Easter Sunday—hinted at a resurrection to come. In a slow, violently contested process, the United States would rise again from tolerating the cruelties of Jim Crow.

MARIAN ANDERSON'S "freedom concert" and its unprecedented turnout show that the nation's and the state's commitments to Jim Crow were starting to weaken in the 1930s. That decade also marked the final decline and fall of women-centered forms of nationalism. Their adherents—black and white, working separately—had translated nationalism's abstractions into everyday objects and rituals. The opposite was also true. The women had infused seemingly mundane, domestic artifacts with profound historical and political significance. Practitioners of women-centered nationalism's boldest forms—most of them black and writing in the 1890s—had developed women-centered blueprints for leadership of the nation in question. Preferring women-centered nationalism's less ambitious forms, most white women had showed greater deference to male authority, past and present, in keeping with the tremendous amount of power commanded by white men relative to other men. Not for nothing did so many of those white women call themselves "daughters." Because they most valued women's relationships with illustrious, mostly male progenitors, these monikers in themselves— Daughters of the American Revolution, Daughters of the Confederacy— communicated female subordination, within and outside the home. Simultaneously, especially before the First World War, white Daughters and the white women who dominated the WRC also believed in the ability of female amateurs, grouped into all-female and female-led entities, to reshape American political cultures.

By the 1930s, the situations and perceptions that had originally inspired the development of women-centered nationalism were receding into history. Fiercely competing remembrances of the Civil War; propertied women's commitments to uplift the masses of their same race both culturally and politically; apprehensions about immigration; and, most of all, certitudes about propertied women's moral superiority to men, including men of their own race and class, were all redolent of Gilded Age and Progressive-Era America. In interwar America, white southerners and northerners bickered occasionally. Yet sectional disagreements did not truly threaten national unity among white Americans because nonsoutherners had accepted many (though not all) neo-Confederate agenda in the twentieth century's opening decades.

The Victorian didacticism underlying the women's attempts at patriotic uplift had also passed out of favor by the 1930s. With the exception of Mary McLeod Bethune, who denounced Jim Crow disfranchisement while voicing a deep affection for democracy, most female nationalists had not displayed either instincts or convictions that were democratic.[12] White Daughters in particular consistently proclaimed the country a "republic" instead of a democracy, consistently asserted the virtues of representative government, and denounced democratic reforms of the Progressive Era such as the popular referendum.[13] During the Great Depression, however, American national identity newly harnessed itself to democracy—and no longer only in the imaginations of African Americans who subscribed to civic nationalism. The New Deal contained democratic tendencies, even though its own commitment to democracy was uneven.[14] In radio "fireside chats" and in regular newspaper columns, Franklin and Eleanor Roosevelt spoke as companions, rather than as tutors, in representing the state and the country to the American people.

American national identity also incorporated pluralism—anticipated by Randolph Bourne's "Trans-National America" (1916), developed by the philosopher Horace Kallen and other intellectuals in the 1920s, and favored widely by liberals in the 1930s. Pluralists insisted on the acceptance of ethnic, religious, and cultural diversity at least among those of European stock, and they contended that there was no one way to live as an American.[15] The federal immigration restrictions that had sharply reduced European immigration starting in 1921 no doubt broadened pluralism's appeal and facilitated its linkage with Americanness, in addition to making Americanization work appear less urgent. Scholars have disagreed whether pluralism truly challenged Anglo-Saxon and other forms of racism; indeed, Walter Benn Michaels has argued that pluralism reinforced racism in its celebrations of difference.[16] Yet pluralism undeniably collided with the amalgam of hereditarianism, white Anglo-Saxon supremacy, and class elitism that informed white women's assumption of patriotic authority over those whom they wished to assimilate.

Between the world wars, female nationalists' age, sex, and gender—in themselves—and their own actions all announced the passing of women-centered nationalism. The literary scholar Ann Douglas has described "matricidal" convictions within mass culture in the 1920s, and she has detected them among both white and African American thinkers.[17] From all points of the political spectrum, men and women alike soundly repudiated Victorian notions of female cultural authority. According to those Victorian notions, propertied women derived such authority from personal sexual respectability, from their consequent moral superiority to men of their same race and class paired with their own political subordination to those men, and from their commitment to communing with respectable women of their same race and class—to the point that a singular noun, "woman," designated such women when grouped together. It was not only the woman suffragists who insisted that women should wield power in addition to influence, or the heterodoxy of Greenwich Village women who insisted on female individuality, that overturned these and other nineteenth-century strictures.[18] So, too, did an orthodoxy who shouted down those and other heterodoxies in the name of home and country. By no coincidence, Flora Bredes Walker of the DAR favored a decidedly modern self-presentation. Her knee-length, nearly sleeveless dresses spilled fringe over her otherwise bare arms. Walker's and other rightist women's defense of the American private home, conflated with nation, against leftism may sound old-fashioned. Yet the new-fashioned, consumer-capitalist home and marriage—redefined to mean every woman's natural destiny—comported with Walker's and others' antiradicalism.[19] At a time when world revolution seemed possible, and at a time when Bolshevik agents seemed to be working through unknowing women in the peace movement, a unified concept of "woman"—even one that included only white, pedigreed, propertied women—seemed antiquated at best and dangerous at worst.

At the twentieth century's turn, clubwomen in general had stirred apprehension in many men, both black and white, who feared that women's club involvements would undermine family life. After the First World War, more than ever, clubwomen were also objects of mockery. In their utter earnestness, some women aided that transition. The painter Grant Wood's *Daughters of Revolution* (1932) was inspired by a dispute with the Cedar Rapids, Iowa, DAR over his decision to have a stained-glass window for a World War I memorial manufactured in Germany. Wood gave the middle-aged women in his painting the same pinched lips as the farming couple in his more famous *American Gothic* (1930). Wood also created an ironic, derisive contrast among one woman's delicate teacup, another's dainty lace collar, and the rugged, brawny figures in Emanuel Leutze's *Washington Crossing the Delaware* (1851) on the background wall.[20] This decidedly counterrevolutionary women's nationalism, especially discreditable when juxtaposed with the braves of 1776, communicated how far patriotism had fallen. In their middle age, their intense femininity—and in their very femaleness—the women embodied a sharp declension from their warrior ancestors.

Ideas and debates familiar to American women's nationalism endured well beyond the 1930s. Apprehensions of "race suicide" proved to have a long shelf life. White Americans pondering national strength, including a Daughter of the American Revolution from California in 1921, continued throughout the interwar decades to treasure evidence of white Anglo American fecundity. In a resolution quashed by the national leadership, the Cali-

Grant Wood, *Daughters of Revolution*, 1932. Cincinnati Art Museum; © Estate of Grant Wood/Licensed by VAGA, New York, N.Y.

fornian proposed decorating any member of the organization who bore more than four children.[21] Admiring the American eugenics movement from a distance, German Nazis communicated a starkly masculine nationalism in awarding medals to German mothers of five or more, whom Hitler Youth were told to salute.[22] Another generation later in a very different America, black feminists confronted a black nationalism that also reduced the relationship between women and nation to making babies—as in 1968, when one group of men implored black women not to take oral contraceptives on those grounds: "When we produce children, we are aiding the REVOLUTION in the form of NATION building."[23] Whether women should also function as political activists in the course of serving their nations remained a painfully open question even during feminism's great reawakening.

The pattern of vast numbers of women coming together in all-female forums to promote patriotism also endured beyond the 1930s, although the organizations' meanings and significance changed, as Nancy F. Cott has contended of organized women in general.[24] All of the female groups discussed in this book survived the Cold War and the twentieth century, although the Depression hobbled some. Also bringing the WRC to its knees was its early insistence on admitting only those who had personally supported the Union cause.[25] After the generation died out that had served in the Civil

War, entities other than veterans' and women's organizations—not least the black civil rights movement and its supporters—shaped characterizations of Civil War history that favored the United States.

After the National Council of Negro Women (NCNW) split off from the NACW in 1935, with the NCNW the larger and more lively of the two, the African American women's movement underwent a democratic turn, shifting from attempting the uplift of the black masses to genuinely collaborating with them.[26] Kept alive by black clubwomen in particular in the early twentieth century, American civic nationalism has since become a commonplace in much of American political culture. Yet the post–World War II civil rights movement continued the division of labor begun at that movement's inception, with men as the movement's national standard-bearers, women as junior partners, and women as the nurturers of the movement in local communities. For the most part, men dominated both culturally and politically. Only recently have scholars fully realized the importance of black women, as individuals and in collectives, to civil rights victories.[27]

Though neo-Confederate women honored a defeat, their history in the early twentieth century was one of triumph. Outnumbering and out-energizing male neo-Confederates, the United Daughters of the Confederacy led other pro-Confederate white southerners in shaping how white America as a whole commemorated the Civil War. Having made its way in the late nineteenth century from southern cemeteries to the centers of southern towns, neo-Confederate statuary continued to shadow many a courthouse square even following a reversal of fortune among neo-Confederates themselves.[28] At the twenty-first century's turn, the Sons of Confederate Veterans operated in greater numbers, sought greater public visibility for their causes, and courted controversy more eagerly than Daughters of the Confederacy.[29] This situation suggests a new degree of nationalism's masculinization.

Race-based forms of nationalism have endured in forms in addition to stone monuments, even as the dismantling of Jim Crow's legal apparatuses put those nationalisms on the defensive. In response to the Second Reconstruction, white Americans defending Jim Crow revived ideas and symbols of the earlier Lost Cause, often placing those ideas and symbols in tension with explicitly national, state-based ones.[30] The South's "massive resistance" after 1954—led by governors and lawmakers, the top of the South's political elite, with substantial white popular support—was massive indeed. A major reason was organized women's production of pro-Confederate patriotism in the early twentieth century. No doubt the militant legions of the 1950s and 1960s contained both actual Children of the Confederacy, now grown, and spiritual ones.[31] More broadly, the UDC's monuments aspired to catechize anyone who viewed or stepped around them. Quite literally, the women's stone soldiers and obelisks naturalized the history on which Jim Crow's defense was based.

It would be inaccurate to recount the recent history of American race-based nationalism as a southern story. Following the DAR's own racial integration in the late 1970s, members and leaders nevertheless strove to minimize black membership, notably in the nation's capital.[32] Unknowingly, the DAR's late twentieth-century leaders duplicated the practices of national women's associations earlier in the century. When Jim Crow rode high, those organizations' white leaders had generally admitted but marginalized African Americans. For as long as the DAR promoted racial hierarchy and simultaneously stood for national, state-based patriotism, it remained a relic of Jim Crow America —of Jim Crow's national and state-based acceptance.

In the late twentieth century the DAR also sustained its commitment to state-based nationalism. Throughout the Cold War, the organization continued many traditions first developed in the 1920s. It remained an arbiter of antiradicalism and progovernment patriotism in U.S. communities.[33] Except when it sought to create support for the Franklin D. Roosevelt administration's emergency measures of 1933, the DAR's leadership consistently shared and advanced the views of the political right—largely alienating the ideological descendants of those moderate progressives who had felt at home in the organization before 1923. During the half century (the 1930s to the 1980s) when the state itself pursued progressive agenda, such as creating a full-fledged welfare state, supporting labor unions' existence, and eventually outlawing de jure segregation, the DAR's own allegiance to the state emphasized support for the military. The organization's loss of political diversity in the 1920s did not significantly hurt its growth. The DAR's membership continued to dwarf that of the SAR, and it shifted to the Sun Belt.[34] Within that membership were some who grafted together professional, volunteer, and family identities in novel ways. A generation after the organization first developed its potent National Defense Committee, a Harvard-trained attorney and mother of six from downstate Illinois nurtured her convictions as that committee's chair. Later, in the 1970s, Phyllis Schlafly and her female followers served a potent cocktail of antifeminism and anticommunism to policymakers, to stunned feminists, and to a country barely aware of the fact that there was more than one women's movement.[35]

Notably triumphant in recent times has been a particularly rigid form of the state-based nationalism in which the Daughters of the American Revolution has specialized, and in which the women have made their most significant innovations to date. September 11, 2001, radicalized large numbers of Americans—many of whom already identified as patriots—and propelled them toward the state. Produced especially by the mainstream media and by commercial enterprises, definitions of national patriotism as unquestioning support for government policies have since dominated. Yet throughout its history, American patriotism has assumed multiple incarnations, including some that are progressive, oppositionist, or compatible with attempts at international understanding. Therein lie reasons for hope.

Notes

Abbreviations

The following abbreviations are used throughout the notes.

AHC
   Atlanta History Center Library/Archives, Atlanta, Ga.
AMM
   American Monthly Magazine
CAM
   Colored American Magazine
CV
   Confederate Veteran
DAR
   Daughters of the American Revolution
DAR Americanization Reports
   National Society of the Daughters of the American Revolution, Americaniza-
   tion Committee Reports of Chapter Regents to State Regents, 1920 (1 folder),
   Western Reserve Historical Society, Cleveland, Ohio
DAR Chapter North Carolina
   Minutes of the Iredell County/Fort Dobbs Chapter DAR (Statesville, N.C.),
   microfilm reel X.29.1, North Carolina Division of Archives and History, Raleigh,
   N.C.
DAR Collection Atlanta
   Daughters of the American Revolution Collection, MSS 426, Atlanta History
   Center Library/Archives, Atlanta, Ga.
DAR Collection Chicago
   Chicago Chapter DAR application registers, Chicago Historical Society, Chi-
   cago, Ill.

DAR Collection Iowa
   Daughters of the American Revolution Collection, Library/Archives Bureau,
   State Historical Society of Iowa, Iowa City
DAR Collection Mississippi
   Daughters of the American Revolution Collection, University of Mississippi
   Special Collections, Oxford, Miss.
DAR Collection Missouri
   Missouri Society of the Daughters of the American Revolution Collection, West-
   ern Historical Manuscript Collection, University of Missouri/State Historical
   Society of Missouri, Columbia, Mo.
DAR Collection Nebraska
   Daughters of the American Revolution Collection, Manuscript Division, Ne-
   braska State Historical Society, Lincoln, Neb.
DAR Collection Stanford
   Daughters of the American Revolution "Blacklist" Controversy Collection, Stan-
   ford University Special Collections, Stanford, Calif.
DAR Collection Texas
   Daughters of the American Revolution, Texas Society Collection, Woman's Col-
   lection, Texas Woman's University, Denton, Tex.
DARM
   Daughters of the American Revolution Magazine
DAR Papers Cleveland
   Papers of the Western Reserve Chapter DAR (Cleveland), Western Reserve His-
   torical Society, Cleveland, Ohio
DAR Papers Litchfield
   Papers of Mary Floyd Tallmadge Chapter DAR (Litchfield, Conn.), Litchfield
   Historical Society, Litchfield, Conn.
DAR Papers Michigan
   Papers of the Daughters of the American Revolution, Michigan Society, Michi-
   gan Historical Collections, Bentley Library, University of Michigan, Ann Arbor,
   Mich.
DAR Papers Minnesota
   Papers of the Daughters of the American Revolution, Minnesota Society, Min-
   nesota Historical Society, Minnesota History Center, St. Paul, Minn.
DAR Papers Mississippi
   Daughters of the American Revolution Papers, Mississippi Department of Ar-
   chives and History, Jackson, Miss.
DAR Papers St. Paul
   Daughters of the American Revolution, St. Paul Chapter Papers, Minnesota
   Historical Society, Minnesota History Center, St. Paul, Minn.
DARPCC
   Daughters of the American Revolution, Proceedings of the Continental Congress

EHW Papers
   Papers of Ellen Hardin Walworth, Historical Society of Saratoga Springs, Saratoga Springs, N.Y.
LC
   Manuscript Division, Library of Congress, Washington, D.C.
LHS
   Litchfield Historical Society, Litchfield, Conn.
MA Collection
   Marian Anderson–DAR Controversy Collection, Moorland-Spingarn Research Center, Howard University, Washington, D.C.
MHC
   Michigan Historical Collections, Bentley Library, University of Michigan, Ann Arbor, Mich.
MIDC
   U.S. Department of War, Military Intelligence Division Correspondence, 1917–1941, Record Group 165, National Archives and Records Administration, Washington, D.C.
MNHS
   Minnesota Historical Society, Minnesota History Center, St. Paul, Minn.
MO
   Western Historical Manuscript Collection, University of Missouri/State Historical Society of Missouri, Columbia, Mo.
MSDAH
   Mississippi Department of Archives and History, Jackson, Miss.
NACW Records, Part 1
   Lillian Serece Williams and Randolph Boehm, eds., *Records of the National Association of Colored Women's Clubs, 1895–1992. Part 1: Minutes of National Conventions, Publications, and Presidents' Correspondence* (microfilm; Bethesda, Md.: University Publications of America, 1993)
NAN
   National Association Notes
NARA
   National Archives and Records Administration
NAW
   Edward T. James et al., eds., *Notable American Women, 1607–1950: A Biographical Dictionary*, 3 vols. (Cambridge, Mass.: Harvard University Press, 1971)
NCPW Papers
   Papers of the National Council for Prevention of War, Swarthmore College Peace Collection, Swarthmore, Pa.
NSDAR
   National Society Daughters of the American Revolution

NW
　Negro World
RG
　Record Group
SAR
　Sons of the American Revolution
SAR Papers Cleveland
　Papers of the Sons of the American Revolution, Western Reserve Society, West-
　ern Reserve Historical Society, Cleveland, Ohio
SAR Papers Nebraska
　Nebraska Society of the Sons of the American Revolution Collection, Manu-
　script Division, Nebraska State Historical Society, Lincoln
SCPC
　Swarthmore College Peace Collection, Swarthmore, Pa.
SHSI
　Library/Archives Bureau, State Historical Society of Iowa, Iowa City
SL
　Arthur and Elizabeth Schlesinger Library on the History of Women in America,
　Radcliffe Institute for Advanced Study, Cambridge, Mass.
UDC Scrapbook Missouri
　John S. Marmaduke Chapter (Columbia, Mo.), United Daughters of the Confed-
　eracy scrapbook, vol. 1, n.d. [1924–1925], Western Historical Manuscript Col-
　lection, University of Missouri/State Historical Society of Missouri, Columbia,
　Mo.
UKY
　University of Kentucky Special Collections, Lexington, Ky.
VN
　Voice of the Negro
WE
　Woman's Era
WRHS
　Western Reserve Historical Society, Cleveland, Ohio

Introduction

　　1. Anderson, *Imagined Communities*, 5–7; Hobsbawm, *Nations and Nationalism*,
8–13; Wiebe, *Who We Are*, 5–6.
　　2. Anderson, *Imagined Communities*, 141–47; Bodnar, "Attractions of Patriotism," 3–5; Zelinsky, *Nation into State*, 4–15; Bonner, *Colors and Blood*; Hansen,
Lost Promise of Patriotism.
　　3. I borrow this language from de Grazia, *How Fascism Ruled Women*. See also
Davin, "Imperialism and Motherhood"; and Bridenthal, Grossmann, and Kaplan,
When Biology Became Destiny.

4. Though truer to the early twentieth century than "women-centered" and "men-centered," the terms "womanly" and "manly" risk implying that certain behaviors are more becoming than others to the female or male sex. My treatment of gender and nationalism is especially indebted to Douglas, *Feminization of American Culture*, 8–13. Informing my terminology are Bederman, *Manliness and Civilization*, 18–20; Behling, *Masculine Woman in America*, 1–3; Hoganson, *Fighting for American Manhood*, 227 n. 8, 231–32 n. 12; Kimmel, *Manhood in America*, 2, 4–7, 119–21; Muncy, "Trustbusting and White Manhood in America"; Rotundo, *American Manhood*, 222–83; Summers, *Manliness and Its Discontents*, 8–9; and Townsend, *Manhood at Harvard*, 17, 25.

5. McClintock, "'No Longer in a Future Heaven,'" 374–75. Holidays and rituals that were invented by U.S. women include Confederate Memorial Day (1866), usually celebrated in late April. Whites, *Civil War as a Crisis in Gender*, 182–83, 187–88.

6. Brundage, "No Deed But Memory," 14; Brundage, "White Women and the Politics of Historical Memory," 115–16; Newman, *White Women's Rights*; Bederman, *Manliness and Civilization*.

7. See in particular Enloe, *Bananas, Beaches, and Bases*, 42–64. Contrasting assessments of the relationship between nationalism and feminism in U.S. contexts are Taylor, *Veiled Garvey*, esp. 69–70; White, *Too Heavy a Load*; Sneider, "Reconstruction, Expansion, and Empire"; and Higginbotham, *Righteous Discontent*, 47–87.

8. Douglas, *Feminization of American Culture*, 8–9; Kerber, *No Constitutional Right to Be Ladies*, 221–302; Attie, *Patriotic Toil*, 4–5, 30–33, 259–61.

9. Kaplan, *Anarchy of Empire*, 1.

10. Wexler, *Tender Violence*, 7, 21; Kerber, *Women of the Republic*, 283–88.

11. Axelrod, *Colonial Revival in America*; Hoganson, "Cosmopolitan Domesticity"; Marling, *George Washington Slept Here*; Rafael, "Colonial Domesticity"; Smith, *American Archives*; Ulrich, *Age of Homespun*; Wexler, *Tender Violence*.

12. Wiebe, *Search for Order*, 2–4.

13. O'Leary, *To Die For*, 157–71; Stewart and Ruffins, "Faithful Witness," 315–16; Goggin, *Carter G. Woodson*, 84–85, 87.

14. Blight, *Race and Reunion*, 140–210; Davies, *Patriotism on Parade*; Foster, *Ghosts of the Confederacy*; McConnell, *Glorious Contentment*, 206–38. On the ideals of manliness shared by men and women alike, see Edwards, *Angels in the Machinery*, 67–68, 122; Hoganson, *Fighting for American Manhood*, 24–29; and Rotundo, *American Manhood*, 232–35.

15. Hoganson, *Fighting for American Manhood*, 152–54 (on Henry Cabot Lodge, an example of one who distinguished between male patriotism and female domesticity); McConnell, *Glorious Contentment*, 218–19.

16. Though the Daughters of the American Revolution (DAR) was organized in 1890 in response to the SAR's exclusion of women, the two organizations later related as close siblings. Their members often belonged to the same families. Al-

though the early twentieth-century SAR was devoted largely to promoting members' socializing at smokers and banquets (with the exception of Americanization work and vigilante surveillance actions during World War I), it collaborated with and turned out for the much larger DAR's frequent monument dedications and celebrations of patriotic holidays. In 1900 the DAR numbered more than 30,000 women, compared to the Sons' fewer than 10,000 men. In the late 1920s, DAR membership was ten times the SAR's. Record book, vols. 1–2 (1892–1940), SAR Papers Cleveland; books of minutes (1890–1933), folders 1–2, box 8, Series 2: Records (1890–1935), SAR Papers Nebraska; SAR, California Society, flyer entitled "Confidential," July 12, 1918, file 171-2, item 3, box 190, MIDC; Davies, *Patriotism on Parade*, 77; *DARPCC* 36 (1927): 31, 47; *DARPCC* 38 (1929): 2–3, 42.

17. See chapter 2 of this work.

18. Waldstreicher, *In the Midst of Perpetual Fetes*; Smith, *American Archives*; Wexler, *Tender Violence*; Kaplan, *Anarchy of Empire*, 23–50; Nelson, *National Manhood*; Hoganson, "Cosmopolitan Domesticity"; Hoganson, *Fighting for American Manhood*; Gerstle, *American Crucible*; O'Leary, *To Die For*.

19. Davies, *Patriotism on Parade*, 77; Hosmer, *Presence of the Past*, 132–33; Foster, *Ghosts of the Confederacy*, 172. This pattern was less pronounced among African Americans. Frederick Douglass and male newspaper editors such as T. Thomas Fortune consistently urged commemoration efforts in the late nineteenth century. Kachun, *Festivals of Freedom*, 158–59, 165–67, 171–72, 203–4; Blight, *Race and Reunion*, 300–329.

20. Addams, *Twenty Years at Hull-House*, 92 (quotation). The literature on this point is enormous. See especially Baker, "Domestication of Politics"; Freedman, "Separatism as Strategy"; Ginzberg, *Women and the Work of Benevolence*; Hewitt and Lebsock, *Visible Women*; and Scott, *Natural Allies*. Strong presentations of clubwomen's self-education are Gere, *Intimate Practices*; and McHenry, *Forgotten Readers*, 187–250. Black women more frequently combined professional careers, club lives, and family obligations than white women in the early twentieth century. Shaw, *What a Woman Ought to Be and to Do*.

21. See especially Gordon, *Women, the State, and Welfare*; Sklar, "Historical Foundations of Women's Power in the Creation of the American Welfare State"; and Skocpol, *Protecting Soldiers and Mothers*.

22. Hobsbawm, "Introduction: Inventing Traditions"; Hobsbawm, "Mass-Producing Traditions"; Brundage, "'Woman's Heart and Hand and Deathless Love,'" 67–68; Hall, *Organization of American Culture*, 1–3. Capozzola, "Only Badge Needed Is Your Patriotic Fervor," emphasizes the importance of vigilantism from below to wartime American patriotism.

Recent scholarship has complicated the binary of "professional" and "amateur." Even as history's professionalization in the early twentieth century brought about history's regendering, amateurs and professionals collaborated and overlapped to a significant extent. The work of many outside the academy or on its margins, notably women, anticipated and sometimes directly influenced developments among professional historians. Des Jardins, *Women and the Historical Enterprise in America*; Fitzpatrick, *History's Memory*; Moses, *Afrotopia*; Dagbovie, "Black Women Historians"; West, *Domesticating History*; Brundage, "White Women and the Politics of Historical Memory," 124. Even so, I retain the concept of "amateur" in order to stress the distinctiveness of female associations' operations.

23. Higham, *Strangers in the Land*, 241, 246–47; Wallace, "Visiting the Past," 149–50; West, *Domesticating History*, 130–33.

24. Bodnar, *Remaking America*, 13–15, 257 n. 8 and n. 11 (distinguishing official from vernacular patriotisms); Morgan, "'Home and Country,'" 44–45, 52–53, 560; Bishir, "Landmarks of Power"; Brundage, "No Deed But Memory," 13.

25. The invitation-only National Society of the Colonial Dames of America (formed in 1891) also developed commemoration, historic preservation, Americanization, and other projects that sought to produce national patriotism. However, the Colonial Dames numbered only 4,000 nationwide in 1900. The organization screened prospective members' ancestors, as well as the applicants themselves, for social prominence. Important producers of regional patriotism and historical consciousness are the Daughters of the Republic of Texas (1891), the mixed-sex Association for the Preservation of Virginia Antiquities (1888), and the mixed-sex Society for the Preservation of New England Antiquities (1910). Davies, *Patriotism on Parade*, 77; Brundage, "White Women and the Politics of Historical Memory"; Des Jardins, *Women and the Historical Enterprise in America*, 20, 66–69; Lamar, *History of the National Society of the Colonial Dames of America*; Brear, *Inherit the Alamo*, 84–131; Flores, "Introduction: Adina de Zavala and the Politics of Restoration"; Turner, *Women, Culture, and Community*, 169–72; Lindgren, "'New Departure in Historic, Patriotic Work'"; Lindgren, *Preserving Historic New England*; Lindgren, *Preserving the Old Dominion*.

26. Brundage,"White Women and the Politics of Historical Memory"; Cox, *Dixie's Daughters*, 34; Simpson, *Edith D. Pope and Her Nashville Friends*, 131–32; Marshall, *Splintered Sisterhood*; Morgan, "'Home and Country,'" 286–347, 561–62.

27. There is some uncertainty about NACW membership figures in the 1920s. The organization revealed only 10,000 dues-paying members in 1928. *Minutes of the Fourteenth Biennial Convention of the National Association of Colored Women* (n.p., 1924), 24, in *NACW Records, Part 1*, reel 1, frame 00702 (figure of 100,000); *National Association of Colored Women (Incorporated), Sixteenth Biennial Session* (n.p., 1928), 57, in *NACW Records, Part 1*, reel 1, frame 00839; Cott, "Across the Great Divide," 364; McCluskey and Smith, eds., *Mary McLeod Bethune*, 138 n. 7.

28. This transition is most obvious in the shift in the NACW's official publications in 1897. The *Woman's Era*, based in Boston and edited by Josephine St. Pierre Ruffin, communicated a "talented tenth" mentality that blended society columns with condemnations of black inaction on civil rights and of white apologists for Jim Crow. The *National Association Notes*, edited by Margaret Murray Washington

(who was married to Booker T. Washington), usually eschewed society columns and overtly political discussions, especially before 1910. Instead, it emphasized kindergartens and other aspects of club work among the black poor. Linda Perkins, personal communication with the author, September 26, 2003; McHenry, *Forgotten Readers*, 216–24; "Miss Willard in Boston," *WE* 1 (July 1894): 7–8; "Miss Willard and the Colored People," *WE* 2 (July 1895): 12; "How Beautiful to Be with God," *NAN* 2 (April 1899), in *NACW Records, Part 1*, reel 23, frame 00286.

29. The literature on black clubwomen's social work is extensive. Emphasizing the political dimensions of black women's club life are White, *Too Heavy a Load*, 21–141; Johnson, "'Drill into Us . . . the Rebel Tradition,'" 531–32, 551–55; Salem, *To Better Our World;* Neverdon-Morton, *Afro-American Women of the South;* Hendricks, *Gender, Race, and Politics in the Midwest;* Wolcott, *Remaking Respectability*, 44–48, 149–57; and Knupfer, *Toward a Tenderer Humanity*, 46–64. On black clubwomen and club leaders who were also historians, see Des Jardins, *Women and the Historical Enterprise in America*, 118–31. On the ASNLH's formation, see Ruffins, "'Lifting as We Climb,'" 380; Stewart and Ruffins, "Faithful Witness," 318; and Goggin, *Carter G. Woodson*, 1.

30. Bederman, *Manliness and Civilization*, 18–20, attributes similar meanings to manliness.

31. Regarding U.S. women and class, also see Gaines, *Uplifting the Race*; Greenwood, *Bittersweet Legacy*, 4–5; Lerner, *Creation of Patriarchy*, 139–41, 215–16; Lerner, *Why History Matters*, 154, 172–81; White, *Too Heavy a Load*, 69–80, 91–97; Wolcott, *Remaking Respectability*, 5–7; and Ransby, *Ella Baker and the Black Freedom Movement*, 42–44. Deviating from the pattern of married women nationalists using their husbands' names is the WRC, which also prided itself on its socially diverse membership and nonhereditary admission requirements. Studies that parallel black women's uplift work and white reformers' Americanization work are Higginbotham, *Righteous Discontent*, 40, 112–13; and White, *Too Heavy a Load*, 78.

32. Margaret Murray Washington bemoaned "rag time music and vaudeville tendencies" and the "rhythm of [the] Turkey Trot," predicting that "the desire for music which not only sways the body but the soul in immoral emotion . . . will surely be less as the years come and go, and the race grows intellectually hungrier as it now seems to be." The DAR's Committee on the Welfare of Women and Children called the "objectionable dances . . . known as the Turkey Trot, the Bunny Hug, [and] the Bear . . . a serious menace to the morality of our Nation." "National Association of Colored Women's Clubs," *NAN* 16 (June 1913): 7, in *NACW Records, Part 1*, reel 23, frame 00523; Mary Anderson Orton in *DARPCC* 22 (1913): 831.

33. "Four Hundred Delegates Attend National Asso. of Colored Women," *Baltimore Afro-American*, August 12, 1916, 1, clipping in *NACW Records, Part 1*, reel 5, frame 00732. On white transnationalism, see in particular Kramer, "Empires, Exceptions, and Anglo-Saxons."

34. O'Leary, *To Die For*; Blight, *Race and Reunion*; Silber, *Romance of Reunion*.

35. Chapter 4 of this work elaborates on the latter point.

36. Scholars disagree on the extent to which late nineteenth-century and early twentieth-century forms of U.S. racism subordinated white women. See especially Bederman, *Manliness and Civilization*; Blee, *Women of the Klan*; Feimster, "'Ladies and Lynching'"; Hale, *Making Whiteness*, 85–120; Newman, *White Women's Rights*; Gilmore, *Gender and Jim Crow*, 95–99, 112–13; and Wexler, *Tender Violence*.

37. Sollors, *Beyond Ethnicity*, 6 (consent/descent formulation); Kedourie, "Nationalism and Self-Determination"; Connor, "Nation and its Myth"; Viroli, *For Love of Country*, 178–82; Greenfeld, *Nationalism*, 8, 13, 423, 484.

38. On Confederate nationalism, see Faust, *Creation of Confederate Nationalism*; Bonner, *Colors and Blood*; and Wiebe, *Who We Are*, 79–80. Neo- and ex-Confederates often called their nation "southern" or "the Southern people." "Not a Confederate!" *CV* 3 (December 1895): 353. However, I avoid that designation because it ignores white and black southerners who did not support the Confederacy and who, following the Civil War, did not share pro-Confederate views of history.

39. "From the President General," *CV* 32 (February 1924): 70. The UDC had grown steadily from over 20,000 members in 1900 to over 63,000 in 1919. "United Daughters of the Confederacy," *CV* 8 (April 1900): 150; "Twenty-Sixth Annual Convention, U.D.C.," *CV* 28 (January 1920): 33. These figures do not distinguish between active (currently dues-paying) members and others. The UDC was not entirely white because of its small Native American presence. "The Oklahoma Division," *CV* 26 (June 1918): 270; "The Monument [to] Gen. Stand Watie," *CV* 29 (September 1921): 326–27.

40. "From the President General," *CV* 32 (July 1924): 276 (monument statistic); Anna Carolina Benning, "Review of Histories Used in Southern Schools and Southern Homes," *CV* 10 (December 1902): 551 (quotation). Studies of women's neo-Confederate activism include Blight, *Race and Reunion*, 273, 277–91; Brundage, "White Women and the Politics of Historical Memory"; Brundage, "'Woman's Heart and Hand and Deathless Love'"; Case, "Historical Ideology of Mildred Lewis Rutherford"; Cox, *Dixie's Daughters*; Foster, *Ghosts of the Confederacy*; Gardner, *Blood and Irony*, 115–219; Hale, "'Some Women Have Never Been Reconstructed'"; Johnson, *Southern Ladies, New Women*, 14–59; Mills and Simpson, *Monuments to the Lost Cause*; Parrott, "'Love Makes Memory Eternal'"; Simpson, *Edith D. Pope and Her Nashville Friends*; and Stott, "From Lost Cause to Female Empowerment."

41. This treatment of neo-Confederate nationalism owes much to Daryl M. Scott, personal communication with the author, January 7, 2003.

42. Arguing that American nationalism in general contained both civic and blood-based elements are Gerstle, *American Crucible*; Gleason, "American Identity and Americanization"; Higham, *Send These to Me*, 175–97; Smith, *Civic Ideals*;

and Wiebe, *Who We Are*, 63–96. See also Singer, "Cultural versus Contractual Nations," on interrelationships between those two nationalisms.

43. *DARM* 65 (1931): 266–67; LaGanke, "National Society of the Daughters of the American Revolution," 377; West, *Domesticating History*, 45 (statistic on preservation). The DAR had grown without pause, even in wartime, since its formation in 1890. By 1912, chapters had formed in every state and in many territories. U.S. Senate, *Second Report of the National Society Daughters of the American Revolution* (1897), 214; *DARPCC* 21 (1912): 602–75. I refer to the DAR as mostly white because a few members drew attention to their Native American ancestry. Wood, *History and Register, Idaho State Society*, 52. Scholarly treatments of the DAR include Davies, *Patriotism on Parade*; Des Jardins, *Women and the Historical Enterprise in America*, 66–69, 202; LaGanke, "National Society of the Daughters of the American Revolution"; Morgan, "'Home and Country'"; McConnell, "Reading the Flag"; O'Leary, *To Die For*, 78–81; Silber, *Romance of Reunion*, 163–72; Smith, *American Archives*, 136–56; Truesdell, "Exalting U.S.ness"; Ulrich, *Age of Homespun*, 32–36; and West, *Domesticating History*, 43–46.

44. *Statutes of the National Society, Daughters of the American Revolution*, 7; Austin, "American Revolution." I have seen no direct evidence of women of African ancestry in the DAR before the late twentieth century. "DAR Accepts a Black Member," *Philadelphia Inquirer*, December 4, 1977, 22A.

45. The UDC apparently lacked any such policy. The Confederate military's own overwhelmingly white composition and proslavery mission, and most neo-Confederates' open support for white supremacy, likely made an explicit ban on African Americans superfluous. My argument about the DAR's uniqueness applies also to the General Federation of Women's Clubs' (GFWC) famous denial of admission to Boston's Woman's Era Club at the 1900 GFWC biennial, at the behest of white southerners. African Americans in Illinois, for example, subsequently continued to belong to local and county Federations of Women's Clubs despite their exclusion from national conventions. Gere, *Intimate Practices*, 165; Salem, *To Better Our World*, 42–43.

46. Bordin, *Woman and Temperance*, xviii, 82–83; Scott, *Natural Allies*, 102–3; Roydhouse, "Bridging Chasms," 275; Hill, *World Their Household*, 6, 8; Newman, *White Women's Rights*, 56–85; Terborg-Penn, *African American Women in the Struggle for the Vote*, 56, 116, 126, 130–31.

47. The WCTU counted a quarter of a million members. Among umbrella organizations, the GFWC claimed over a million women. Protestant women's mission organizations, together, attracted more than 3 million. Davies, *Patriotism on Parade*, 76; Bordin, *Woman and Temperance*, 140; Cott, *Grounding of Modern Feminism*, 87; Hill, *World Their Household*, 3.

48. O'Leary, *To Die For*, 91–107.

49. Of my own sample of southern Daughters of the American Revolution born before 1900, over two-thirds (forty-four out of sixty-four) were also Daughters of

the Confederacy according to their obituaries. These women lived in the former Confederacy (except Texas) and in Kentucky. Of my sample of similar women in the Southwest (Texas, Arizona, New Mexico, and Oklahoma), 45.4 percent (twenty-five of fifty-five) belonged also to the UDC. Morgan, "'Home and Country,'" 549–50, describes this sample further. Also see Davies, *Patriotism on Parade*, 104. Roth, *Matronage*, 96, finds an even larger overlap among Atlantans.

50. Du Bois, *Souls of Black Folk*, 155.

51. Saluting the American flag at the NACW's first convention, a Memphis woman vowed, "may we be united in demanding our heritage as American free-born citizens." Julia A. Hooks in *A History of the Club Movement among the Colored Women*, 68–69 (quotation), 112; Jones, *Quest for Equality*, 12; Terrell, *Colored Woman in a White World*, 99. An exception to the last point is an anti-immigration peroration by Josephine St. Pierre Ruffin. "Difficulties of Colonization," *WE* 1 (March 24, 1894): 9; Moses, *Golden Age of Black Nationalism*, 113.

52. Higginbotham, *Righteous Discontent*, 48 (quotation).

53. Stein, *World of Marcus Garvey*, 1. There is some disagreement regarding the UNIA's size. Many historians of Garveyism have accepted the UNIA's own reckoning that it attracted 6 million members and possessed around 900 branches worldwide. Most recently, Martin Summers follows Theodore Vincent in estimating UNIA membership, at its mid-1920s peak, at 400,000 dues-paying members, 750,000 "occasional" members, 2 to 3 million more "in and around the movement," and 700 branches within the United States. *NW* 15 (December 8, 1923): 10; Taylor, "'Negro Women Are Great Thinkers as Well as Doers,'" 122 n. 1; Summers, *Manliness and Its Discontents*, 296 n. 10. Also see Schneider, *"We Return Fighting,"* 140–41.

54. Exceptions are Moses, *Golden Age of Black Nationalism*; and O'Leary, *To Die For*. Silber, *Romance of Reunion*; Bederman, *Manliness and Civilization*; Hoganson, *Fighting for American Manhood*; and Nelson, *National Manhood* discuss American national identity explicitly in relation to men and gender.

55. Exceptions are Sneider, "Reconstruction, Expansion, and Empire"; and studies of southern milieus—Johnson, *Southern Ladies, New Women*; Roth, *Matronage*; Sims, *Power of Femininity in the New South*, 128–54; and Turner, *Women, Culture, and Community*, 165–83. The same scholarship on women's political activism features thriving literatures on internationalism and on imperialism. Alonso, *Peace as a Women's Issue*; Rupp, *Worlds of Women*; Foster, *Women and the Warriors*; Foster, *Women for All Seasons*; Schott, *Reconstructing Women's Thoughts*; Hoganson, "Cosmopolitan Domesticity"; Hoganson, "'As Badly Off as the Filipinos'"; Kaplan, *Anarchy of Empire*, 23–50; Rafael, "Colonial Domesticity"; Wexler, *Tender Violence*.

56. Chickering, "'Casting Their Gaze More Broadly'"; Koonz, *Mothers in the Fatherland*; Leck, "Conservative Empowerment and the Gender of Nazism"; Pugh, *Tories and the People*, 43–69.

57. Chatterjee, *Nation and Its Fragments*, 116–57; West, *Feminist Nationalism*;

Taylor, *Veiled Garvey*; Horne, *Race Woman*; Higginbotham, *Righteous Discontent*, 47–87; Colley, *Britons*, 237–73.

58. See, for example, Nussbaum et al., *For Love of Country*, 2–17.

59. Most female nationalists did not operate as feminists, in that most did not share feminism's attributes—presuming that most differences in treatment of men and women result from social constructions of the sexes; opposing those differences on that basis; or identifying with women as a whole. Most fundamentally, female nationalists did not consciously oppose sex hierarchy except when men sought to exclude them from political activism outside the home. I take this relatively strict definition of feminism from Cott, *Grounding of Modern Feminism*, 4–5. Scholars have demonstrated repeatedly that women could and did engage in organized political activity, and support such activity, while opposing feminism. Regarding the early twentieth-century United States, see Delegard, "Women Patriots"; Thurner, "'Better Citizens without the Ballot'"; Marshall, *Splintered Sisterhood*; Nielsen, *Un-American Womanhood*; and Benowitz, *Days of Discontent*. Black women more commonly combined nationalism with feminism, though not without difficulty. Taylor, *Veiled Garvey*.

60. Higginbotham, *Righteous Discontent*; Horne, *Race Woman*; Martin, *Race First*; Moses, *Afrotopia*; Moses, *Golden Age of Black Nationalism*; Bair, "True Women, Real Men"; Taylor, *Veiled Garvey*. Exceptions are Schneider, *"We Return Fighting"*; McHenry, *Forgotten Readers*, 18–19; Hansen, *Lost Promise of Patriotism*, 84–87, 104–5, 181–84, 186–87, 233 n. 18; and Samuel, *Pledging Allegiance*, 127–205 (regarding World War II).

61. See especially Murray, *Proud Shoes*; and Fields with Fields, *Lemon Swamp*.

62. My discussion of the contests over the shape of reconciliation owes much to Blight, *Race and Reunion*.

63. Peter Holquist and others argue that government surveillance's purpose was "to act on people, to change them," rather than merely gathering information on public opinion or simply keeping people under control. Holquist, "'Information Is the Alpha and Omega of Our Work,'" 417 (quotation), 419.

64. Hay, *Chapter Histories of the North Carolina Daughters of the American Revolution*, 99–101.

Chapter One

1. Earlier and later, Americans of both sexes engaged in sporadic peacetime patriotic activity in the form of public celebrations and rituals. Dennis, *Red, White, and Blue Letter Days*; Fabre, "African-American Commemorative Celebrations in the Nineteenth Century"; Litwicki, *America's Public Holidays*; Travers, *Celebrating the Fourth*; Waldstreicher, *In the Midst of Perpetual Fetes*.

2. Norton, *Liberty's Daughters*; Mayer, *Belonging to the Army*; Attie, *Patriotic*

Toil; Fahs, *Imagined Civil War*, 120–49; Faust, *Mothers of Invention*; Rable, *Civil Wars*; Whites, *Civil War as a Crisis in Gender.*

3. *NAW*, 3:227–28; Warren, *History of the Massachusetts Daughters of the American Revolution*, 210–11; Janet Elizabeth Richards, "Heroic Women of the American Revolution," *AMM* 1 (September 1892): 287–88; Victoria Earle Matthews, "Harriet Tubman," *WE* 3 (June 1896): 8; Davis, *Lifting as They Climb*, 261–62; Ulrich, *Good Wives*, 167–201; Lockwood and Ragan, *Story of the Records D.A.R.*, 156 (regarding a New Hampshire monument to Duston). Duston has also been spelled Dunston.

4. King, *Mount Vernon on the Potomac*; West, *Domesticating History*, 1–37; Varon, *We Mean to Be Counted*, 124–36.

5. Walworth's mother was herself a personal friend of Ann Pamela Cunningham, the founder of the MVLA. "Women of Saratoga," n.d. [March 1876], otherwise unidentified clipping, document 1, folder 5, file 23; Jean McGregor, "Chronicles of Saratoga: Mrs. Walworth Assisted in Restoring of Mt. Vernon," n.d. [August 1951], *Saratoga (N.Y.) Saratogian*, clipping, document 14, folder 9, file 22; both in EHW Papers.

6. Mary Burnett Talbert, "Concerning the Frederick Douglass Memorial," *Crisis* 14 (August 1917): 167.

7. Smith, *Gender of History*, esp. 147–84; Baym, *American Women Writers and the Work of History.*

8. Fabre, "African-American Commemorative Celebrations in the Nineteenth Century," 75–77; O'Leary, *To Die For*, 112–13.

9. Clark, "History Is No Fossil Remains," 62–63; Salem, *To Better Our World*, 9; quotation from folder 1, box 13G, Papers of American Negro Historical Society, Historical Society of Pennsylvania, Philadelphia, cited in Kachun, *Festivals of Freedom*, 156.

10. Kachun, *Festivals of Freedom*, 150–51, 156–58; Blight, *Race and Reunion*, 314–17.

11. Shaw, "Black Club Women"; Scott, *Natural Allies*, 1–78.

12. In 1897 the NACW's first president, Mary Church Terrell, linked black club-women's decision to organize nationally to the worsening racial climate. "From the Atlantic to the Pacific, . . . we wish to set in motion influences that shall stop the ravages made by practices that sap our strength, and preclude the possibility of advancement." Black clubwomen expanded their operations also for internal reasons, notably because they sought to recover the political power black women had possessed during the Civil War and Reconstruction. Jones, *Quest for Equality*, 133 (quotation); Brown, "Negotiating and Transforming the Public Sphere," 48–49, 63 n. 53.

13. Wells-Barnett, *Crusade for Justice*, 78–81; Moses, *Golden Age of Black Nationalism*, 107; "News from the Clubs," *WE* 1 (March 24, 1894): 3; Salem, *To Better Our World*, 18, 20; Higginbotham, *Righteous Discontent*, 152; Shaw, "Black Club

Women." Membership figures are from Victoria Earle Matthews, "An Open Appeal to Our Women for Organization," *WE* 3 (January 1897): 2; and Josephine Silone Yates, "The National Association of Colored Women," *VN* 1 (July 1904): 284.

14. I follow Kevin K. Gaines in labeling these women "middle class" not so much because of their personal or family wealth, but because of their own self-perceptions. Gaines, *Uplifting the Race*, 13–16; *Minutes of the Ninth Biennial Convention of the National Association of Colored Women* (n.p., 1914), 7–8 (mentioning state federations in South Dakota and Wyoming, where the black population was quite small), in *NACW Records, Part 1*, reel 1, frames 00410–11. While mostly African American, the NACW was not officially so. Boston's Woman's Era club, when it formed in 1893, possessed three or four white members. Total membership of black and white women reached 104 by the next year. Higginbotham, *Righteous Discontent*, 152; Moses, *Golden Age of Black Nationalism*, 107; Pauline E. Hopkins, "Famous Women of the Negro Race: Club Life among Colored Women," *CAM* 5 (August 1902): 273; "News from the Clubs," *WE* 1 (March 24, 1894): 4–5, 15.

15. Mrs. S. E. F. Rose (Laura Martin Rose), "Historical Work in Mississippi," *CV* 19 (May 1911): 209; "What We Are Doing and Chapter Work," *AMM* 14 (June 1899): 1239; Higginbotham, *Righteous Discontent*, 33, 55; Fields with Fields, *Lemon Swamp*, 212. The black women of Tuscaloosa, Alabama's Three Times Ten Club purchased a plot of land for a high school but were never able to fund a building. Du Bois, *Efforts for Social Betterment among Negro Americans*, 32.

16. Bailey, "Free Speech and the 'Lost Cause' in Texas," 461. Until 1906, no public library in the South served or even admitted black patrons. Shaw, *What a Woman Ought to Be and to Do*, 171; Du Bois, *Efforts for Social Betterment among Negro Americans*, 117–19; Winegarten, *Black Texas Women*, 195.

17. Mossell, *Work of the Afro-American Woman*, 164; "Social News," *WE* 1 (July 1894): 9 (on Mrs. J. E. Lynch departing Washington, D.C., for Germany); Terrell, *Colored Woman in a White World*, 98–99; Jones, *Quest for Equality*, 12.

18. Blight, *Race and Reunion*, 335–36; Ida B. Wells, *A Red Record* (1895), reprinted in Royster, *Southern Horrors and Other Writings*, 81–82.

19. Fields with Fields, *Lemon Swamp*, 126–27. See also Murray, *Proud Shoes*, 269–70, 272, 275–76.

20. Fabre, "African-American Commemorative Celebrations in the Nineteenth Century," 82–86.

21. Blight, *Race and Reunion*, 367; Kachun, *Festivals of Freedom*, 147–74.

22. Cooper, *Voice from the South*, xxxi–xxxii, 28–31, 139–45 (quotation on p. 139); Higginbotham, *Righteous Discontent*, 152; Gaines, *Uplifting the Race*, 132–35, 142; White, *Too Heavy a Load*, 36–43, 59–60; Shaw, "Black Club Women," 433; Des Jardins, *Women and the Historical Enterprise in America*, 128–29; Wolcott, *Remaking Respectability*, 14.

23. Brown, *Homespun Heroines*, 151–53; Wesley, *History of the National Association of Colored Women's Clubs*, 13–14; "Editorials," *WE* 1 (June 1894): 9 (quotation);

also see "Editorial," *WE* 2 (April 1895): 8. The white woman in question had, in the past, spoken before the Woman's Era Club (which directed a letter of protest at her). "An Open Letter to Mrs. Laura Ormiston Chant," *WE* 1 (June 1894): 6.

24. Victoria Earle Matthews, "Harriet Tubman," *WE* 3 (June 1896): 8.

25. Josephine B. Bruce, "The Ladies' Auxiliary," *WE* 3 (October–November 1896): 9; McHenry, *Forgotten Readers*, 243–44.

26. "News from the Clubs: New York Letter," *WE* 1 (March 24, 1894): 2; Du Bois, *Efforts for Social Betterment among Negro Americans*, 55–56. Biographical information on Matthews is in Moses, *Golden Age of Black Nationalism*, 111; and Harlan, *Booker T. Washington Papers*, 4:131–32 n. 2, 280.

27. S. Elizabeth Frazier, "Mrs. W. E. Matthews," *WE* 1 (May 1, 1894): 1.

28. Salem, *To Better Our World*, 44, 90–91; Brown, *Homespun Heroines*, 215.

29. In 1896 DAR historic preservation efforts had only barely begun, with an effort to renovate Independence Hall in Philadelphia. Only after 1905 did the Daughters of the Republic of Texas control the Alamo in San Antonio. "The Frederick Douglass Memorial and Pilgrimage Association," *WE* 3 (August 1896): 4; West, *Domesticating History*, 40; *Fifty Years of Achievement*, 189–90, 211.

30. Terrell, *Colored Woman in a White World*, 98–99; Jones, *Quest for Equality*, 12.

31. See the following articles by Pauline E. Hopkins: "Famous Men of the Negro Race: Charles Lenox Remond," *CAM* 3 (May 1901): 34–39; "William Wells Brown," *CAM* 2 (January 1901): 232–36; "Famous Men of the Negro Race: Lewis Hayden," *CAM* 2 (April 1901): 473–77; "Famous Men of the Negro Race: Sargeant [*sic*] William H. Carney," *CAM* 3 (June 1901): 84–89; and "Famous Men of the Negro Race: Robert Browne Elliott," *CAM* 2 (February 1901): 294–301. See also Blight, *Race and Reunion*, 367.

32. "Connecticut," *NAN* 7 (July 1904): 39, in *NACW Records, Part 1*, reel 23, frame 00437 (quotations); *Financial Report of the National Association of Colored Women for the Years 1896–1901* (n.p., n.d.), 19, in *NACW Records, Part 1*, reel 1, frame 00271.

33. Pauline E. Hopkins, "Famous Men of the Negro Race: Sargeant [*sic*] William H. Carney," *CAM* 3 (June 1901), 87; Bonner, *Colors and Blood*, 176.

34. "Honor to Whom Honor Is Due," *WE* 2 (May 1896): 7; *VN* 3 (September 1906): 618; J. Max Barber, "The Niagara Movement at Harpers Ferry," *VN* 3 (October 1906): 402–11; Reverdy C. Ransom, "The Spirit of John Brown," *VN* 3 (October 1906): 412–17; Gaines, *Uplifting the Race*, 63.

35. "Honor to Whom Honor Is Due," *WE* 2 (May 1896): 6–7. A lonely exception among white women was the journalist Isabel Worrell Ball of the WRC. This opponent of Jim Crow segregation paid tribute to Brown's bravery and the divinely ordained nature of his actions while conceding that he was a "fanatic" and a "lunatic" in the eyes of many. A DAR publication from upstate New York drew attention to Brown's local historical significance, celebrating the mournful militance of the

ceremonies following his death. *Journal of the Thirty-First National Convention of the Woman's Relief Corps* (1913), 397–98; Tuttle, *Three Centuries in Champlain Valley*, 151, 272–74, 403–5.

36. "The National Colored Woman's Convention," "Social Notes," and "Letter from the Governor of Minnesota Endorsing Mrs. T. H. Lyles," *WE* 2 (January 1896): 7, 13, 16, respectively; "Honor to Whom Honor Is Due," *WE* 2 (May 1896): 6–8.

37. Julia A. Hooks of Memphis (1896) in *History of the Club Movement among the Colored Women*, 110 (quotation); White, *Too Heavy a Load*, 83–84; Harlan, *The Booker T. Washington Papers*, 4:131–32 n. 2, 280. Conversely, advocates of black history promoted "rounded" education. Emma F. G. Merritt, "American Prejudice—Its Cause, Effect and Possibilities," *VN* 2 (July 1905): 469.

38. "The National Colored Woman's Convention," *WE* 2 (January 1896): 5, 7 (quotation); "Letter from the Governor of Minnesota Endorsing Mrs. T. H. Lyles," *WE* 2 (January 1896): 16; "Honor to Whom Honor Is Due," *WE* 2 (May 1896): 7; "Constitution of the National John Brown Memorial Association of Women," *WE* 3 (October–November 1896): 13. After the NACW went on to focus on other social welfare projects, Lyles shifted her own attention to temperance work and, later, civil rights work. She served on the executive committee of the St. Paul NAACP branch. Fannie Barrier Williams, "Work Attempted and Missed in Organized Club Work," *CAM* 14 (May 1908): 284; "News Concerning the W.C.T.U.," *NAN* 3 (May 1900), in *NACW Records, Part 1*, reel 23, frame 00357; "The Branches," *Crisis* 9 (April 1915): 305.

39. W. P. Barlow, "History of the Missouri Confederate Home," *CV* 1 (October 1893): 302; "Confederate Home of Missouri," *CV* 3 (April 1895): 111; Poppenheim et al., *History of the United Daughters of the Confederacy*, 1–6; Litwicki, *America's Public Holidays*, 12–13; Ada Ramp Walden, "Confederate Southern Memorial Association: C.S.M.A. Notes," *CV* 39 (April 1931): 157; Whites, *Civil War as a Crisis in Gender*, 182–98; Cox, *Dixie's Daughters*, 8–15; Simpson, *Edith D. Pope and Her Nashville Friends*, 71–72; Blair, *Cities of the Dead*.

40. Bishir, "'Strong Force of Ladies,'" 6–7; Mrs. R. L. Nesbitt, "Confederate Dead at Marietta, Ga.," *CV* 16 (August 1908): 373–74.

41. Foster, *Ghosts of the Confederacy*, 105, 108; *CV* 2 (October 1894): 306–7; Poppenheim et al., *History of the United Daughters of the Confederacy*, 10–11. Not all ladies' memorial associations joined the UDC. Some remained independent or gathered under another umbrella, the Confederate Southern Memorial Association (formed by 1900). "In Memoriam—Mrs. William J. Behan," *CV* 26 (September 1918): 414–15.

42. Cox, *Dixie's Daughters*, 22–23; "Synopsis of U.D.C. Convention Report," *CV* 20 (January 1912): 4; Foster, *Ghosts of the Confederacy*, 171; Simpson, *Edith D. Pope and Her Nashville Friends*, 74; Poppenheim et al., *History of the United Daughters of the Confederacy*, 27; "United Daughters of the South," *CV* 3 (December 1895): 374; Virginia Faulkner McSherry, "United Daughters of the Confederacy," *CV* 19

(January 1911): 3; Mrs. Roy W. McKinney (May M. Faris McKinney), "Proceedings in the U.D.C. Convention," *CV* 19 (January 1911): 5.

43. McCord also nursed Confederate soldiers during the war. *NAW*, 2:450–52; Rable, *Civil Wars*, 38–39; Clinton, *Tara Revisited*, 83.

44. The UDC soon dropped its ban on northern wives of Confederate veterans. Anne Bachman Hyde, "The United Daughters of the Confederacy," *CV* 23 (January 1915): 13.

45. "United Daughters of the Confederacy," *CV* 8 (April 1900): 150. Another UDC officer in 1899 claimed 27,000 members. *Minutes of the Sixth Annual Meeting of the United Daughters of the Confederacy*, 72.

46. On the presence of small numbers of Catholics and Jews in the UDC, see "Mrs. Isabella Kopperl," *CV* 10 (August 1902): 374; Turner, *Women, Culture, and Community*, 157; "Mr. Adolph S. Ochs, Newspaper Publisher," *CV* 13 (December 1905): 578–79; and "Loyalty That Defied an Army," *CV* 36 (May 1928): 164.

47. Simpson, *Edith D. Pope and Her Nashville Friends*, 122; Foster, *Ghosts of the Confederacy*, 171, 110.

48. Ruth Martin Phelps in "Fine Entertainment in Galveston," *CV* 4 (June 1896): 194.

49. "Southern Commercial Congress Commended," *CV* 19 (April 1911): 152; "Errors in Sketch of President M. H. Smith [of the Louisville & Nashville Railroad]," *CV* 19 (March 1911): 139; "About the Term 'New South,'" *CV* 15 (December 1907): 538; "Terms as to Who Was 'Right,' Etc.," *CV* 17 (July 1909): 313; Mrs. L. Eustace Williams, "Mission of the South's United Daughters," *CV* 20 (September 1912): 440. The *Confederate Veteran* also published a lengthy eulogy for the Atlanta editor and "New South" booster Henry Grady. "Henry W. Grady," *CV* 6 (March 1898): 98–105.

50. "United Daughters of the Confederacy," *CV* 8 (April 1900): 150.

51. Katie Alama Orgain in "Corsicana Convention of U.D.C.," *CV* 9 (February 1901): 75.

52. "Relics and records are symbols," a South Carolinian realized. "There is a subtle spirit in these, and if we do not . . . bind it to our uses we will have bread without salt." Mrs. Thomas Taylor in "South Carolina Daughters," *CV* 5 (January 1897): 14.

53. Ina Porter Ockenden, "To the Daughters of the Confederacy," *CV* 9 (September 1901): 407; "United Daughters of the Confederacy," *CV* 6 (October 1898): 460 (Ruth M. Phelps's eulogy for Varina "Winnie" Davis, daughter of Confederate president Jefferson Davis).

54. Fannie Eoline Selph, "Virginia Dyer," *CV* 15 (March 1907): 131.

55. Ruth Martin Phelps in "Fine Entertainment in Galveston," *CV* 4 (June 1896): 194.

56. Mrs. Augustine T. Smythe (Louisa Cheves McCord Smythe), "History of the United Daughters," *CV* 19 (February 1911): 61.

57. "Daughters, of the Confederacy," *CV* 3 (April 1895): 110.

58. She would drop out of the UDC almost entirely in 1903, however, in her grief at her brother's murder. She recovered her commitment to the cause later in the decade. "The Last Roll," *CV* 10 (September 1902): 422–23; Mrs. M. A. Zumwalt, "Miss Dunovant's Resignation," *CV* 11 (March 1903): 103–4.

59. Adelia Dunovant in *Minutes of the Seventh Annual Meeting of the United Daughters of the Confederacy*, 128–30; "The Term 'Nation,'" *CV* 9 (March 1901): 111; Cox, *Dixie's Daughters*, 145.

60. An unnamed correspondent protested from Hot Springs, Arkansas, that "Thomas Jefferson called us a nation, and we are known as a nation by all people." "History of the Term 'Nation,'" *CV* 9 (October 1901): 448.

61. Mrs. A. L. Lincecum, "Why Am I a U.D.C.?" *CV* 22 (August 1914): 349. General Bradley T. Johnston of Baltimore, who spoke at more than one UDC convention, called Emancipation "the great crime of the century." "Placing Principle Above Policy," *CV* 5 (October 1897): 509; "United Daughters in Baltimore," *CV* 5 (November 1897): 546; Blight, *Race and Reunion*, 256–58; Foster, *Ghosts of the Confederacy*, 55–62.

62. Adelia Dunovant, "Principles in Relation to Human Action," *CV* 10 (February 1902): 74–75. UDC discussions of the Confederate cause's Revolutionary lineage include "Tribute [to] the Carrolls, of Carrolton," *CV* 4 (June 1896): 181; Judith Gray, "Leave Us Our Dead," *CV* 7 (October 1899): 441; *Minutes of the Sixth Annual Meeting of the United Daughters of the Confederacy* (1900), 72–74. On Confederates' own views of the American Revolution, see Rubin, "Seventy-Six and Sixty-One."

63. Johnson, "'This Wonderful Dream Nation!'" 146. Examples of neo-Confederate women who were identified as Democratic "partisans" or spouses (as in the case of the first president of the Birmingham UDC chapter, married to Alabama governor Joseph F. Johnston) are in *CV* 5 (January 1897): 4; "The Last Roll," *CV* 8 (March 1900): 131–32; and "The Last Roll," *CV* 20 (October 1912): 486–87. Also see Foster, *Ghosts of the Confederacy*, 194–95; and Bishir, "Landmarks of Power."

64. Southern Railway advertisement showing rates for travel to that year's National Democratic Convention in *CV* 4 (June 1896): 198; "Honesty in the South," *CV* 4 (December 1896): 419–20; "Plea for Unity of Action in the South," *CV* 8 (November 1900): 480; "National Dignity and Confederate Honor," *CV* 6 (December 1898): 546 (on Reconstruction).

65. "Confederate Monument at Franklin," *CV* 8 (January 1900): 5–6; "Sumner Archibald Cunningham," *CV* 22 (January 1914): 6–9; *CV* 6 (November 1898): 512 (first quotation); Litwack, *Trouble in Mind*, 312–15; Gilmore, *Gender and Jim Crow*, 111–13; "M'Kinley, Roosevelt, and the Negro," *CV* 11 (January 1903): 4 (second quotation). Born into a slaveowning family, Cunningham had been a Confederate sergeant-major and later deserted the army. Simpson, *Edith D. Pope and Her Nashville Friends*, 25.

66. "Mrs. Lizzie George Henderson," *CV* 13 (December 1905): 533; Cox, *Dixie's Daughters*, 38; Litwack, *Trouble in Mind*, 224–25; "From the President General," *CV* 39 (August 1931): 309.

67. The UDC proposals had precedents. Independently of the neo-Confederate movement, a Fort Mill, South Carolina, man raised "faithful slave" monuments in 1895. "Monuments at Fort Mill, S.C.," *CV* 7 (May 1899): 210–11; "Monuments to Faithful Slaves," *CV* 13 (September 1905): 422; Savage, *Standing Soldiers, Kneeling Slaves*, 155–59.

68. Mrs. C. Gilliland Aston in "A Monument to the Faithful Old Slaves," *CV* 12 (September 1904): 443; Cox, *Dixie's Daughters*, 104–6. Some went so far as to portray slavery as roughest on the owners. Miss Winnie Davis, "The Ante-Bellam [*sic*] Southern Woman," *CV* 1 (March 1893): 74.

69. Mrs. W. Carleton Adams, "Slave Monument Question," *CV* 12 (November 1904): 525; Savage, *Standing Soldiers, Kneeling Slaves*, 161, 247 n. 92; McElya, "Commemorating the Color Line," 205–7.

70. Monuments to "faithful slaves," answered a woman from Adams's own UDC chapter, "will tell future generations that the white men of the South were the negro's best friends then and that the men of the South are the negro's best friends to-day." Mary M. Solari in "Monument to Faithful Slaves," *CV* 13 (March 1905): 123–24 (quotation on p. 124).

71. In 1914 no "faithful slave" monuments had yet been raised by the UDC or by its brother organizations. Kirk Savage has located a few such UDC monuments dating from the 1920s, such as in Natchitoches, Louisiana. In 1937 in West Virginia, the UDC dedicated a boulder to the memory of an enslaved man, Heywood Shepherd, who had refused to join John Brown's insurrection. Hugh B. Barclay, "A Monument to 'Uncle Ben' and 'Aunt Matilda,'" *CV* 22 (October 1914): 474; "Monument to Faithful Slaves," *CV* 22 (December 1914): 548; Savage, *Standing Soldiers, Kneeling Slaves*, 158; Dennis, *Red, White, and Blue Letter Days*, 230.

72. Mills, "Introduction," xix–xx. In 1900, "at the earnest request" of some UDC chapters, the Virginia state legislature closed public schools for the entire day on Jefferson Davis's birthday. "Resolution on Jefferson Davis's Birthday," *CV* 8 (March 1900): 116.

73. "Mrs. Norman V. Randolph: In Memoriam," *CV* 35 (December 1927): 446–47; Blight, *Race and Reunion*, 279 (quotation).

74. In 1906 Congress appropriated $100,000 for the project. "Confederate Graves in the North," *CV* 11 (February 1903): 54; Mary Wright Johnson, "Confederate Section Arlington Cemetery," *CV* 14 (May 1906): 206; Foster, *Ghosts of the Confederacy*, 153–54. In a move unconnected to the UDC, Congress also approved in 1905 the return of captured Confederate battle flags, then in the federal government's possession, to their states of origin. Foster, *Ghosts of the Confederacy*, 154; Blight, *Race and Reunion*, 356.

75. Gardner, *Blood and Irony*, 161–62. Between 1907 and 1914, the UDC raised

over $50,000 for that monument and for one for the site of the battle of Shiloh in Tennessee. "The Monument at Arlington," *CV* 22 (July 1914): 292; Mrs. A. A. Campbell (Susie S. Campbell), "Virginia Division Notes," *CV* 22 (July 1914): 301 (fund-raising figure); Cox, *Dixie's Daughters*, 52–56; Cox, "Confederate Monument at Arlington."

76. "Uncle Sam Erects Confederate Shaft," *CV* 20 (April 1912): 154–55.

77. The UDC developed its national Committee on History in 1897. "United Daughters Reunion," *CV* 5 (October 1897): 502; Mrs. St. John Alison Lawton (Ruth Jennings Lawton), "History Department of the U.D.C.," *CV* 31 (October 1923): 380; Cox, *Dixie's Daughters*, 124–33; Bailey, "Free Speech and the 'Lost Cause' in Texas"; Bailey, "Textbooks of the 'Lost Cause.'"

78. "Children of the Confederacy," *CV* 4 (May 1896): 141; Cox, *Dixie's Daughters*, 133–39.

79. "Heroines of the South," *CV* 4 (May 1896): 146–47; "Lucy Minor Otey Chapter," *CV* 5 (March 1897): 131; "Work of a Confederate Woman," *CV* 9 (July 1901): 321–25.

80. Mrs. J. Pinckney Smith (née Owen) in "Louisiana State Division, U.D.C.," *CV* 9 (June 1901): 255. Evidence in diaries and letters of white women's turning against the Confederate war effort, especially late in the war, found no place in these narratives. Faust, "Altars of Sacrifice"; Rable, *Civil Wars*, esp. 202–20.

81. Douglas, *Feminization of American Culture*, 8–13. Some argue that white southern women of the post–Civil War generation channeled their rage and disappointment at their male contemporaries into praise for the wartime bravery of their fathers. Whites, "Rebecca Latimer Felton and the Problem of 'Protection' in the New South"; Gilmore, *Gender and Jim Crow*, 95–96.

82. Examples of this presentation of women's patriotism are numerous. "Mrs. Gov. Northen's Plea for History," *CV* 1 (December 1893): 371; "Daughters of the Confederacy," *CV* 3 (October 1895): 302. The UDC awarded Crosses of Honor to Confederate veterans' widows and descendants, male and female, as well as to veterans themselves. Clinton, *Tara Revisited*, 183.

83. Mrs. A. A. Campbell (Susie S. Campbell), "The United Daughters of the Confederacy—Some of Their Aims and Accomplishments," *CV* 30 (March 1922): 86; Lizzie George Henderson, "United Daughters of the Confederacy," *CV* 15 (August 1907): 349, quoted in Foster, *Ghosts of the Confederacy*, 173. See also Hale, "'Some Women Have Never Been Reconstructed,'" 182.

84. "Confederate Monument at Franklin," *CV* 8 (January 1900): 5–6; "Daughters at Franklin: Address Made for Them at Monument Dedication," *CV* 8 (April 1900): 172.

85. Kerber, *Women of the Republic*, 227–31, 283–85; Mrs. Thomas Taylor in "South Carolina Daughters," *CV* 5 (January 1897): 14–15.

86. Nancy Lewis Greene, "United Daughters of the Confederacy," *CV* 9 (July 1901): 326; Adelia A. Dunovant, "That Columbia College Prize Essay," *CV* 20 (July 1912): 341.

87. Fields with Fields, *Lemon Swamp*, 44–45, 84 (quotation), 96; Lumpkin, *Making of a Southerner*, 109–47; Cox, *Dixie's Daughters*, 125.

88. Davies, *Patriotism on Parade*, 31, 38. On northern women's considerable patriotic activism during the Civil War, including history work, see West, *Domesticating History*, 39–42; Attie, *Patriotic Toil*, 198–219; and Lawson, *Patriot Fires*, 14–39.

89. *Synopsis of the Proceedings of the Department of Massachusetts Woman's Relief Corps*, 3, 5, 7; Davies, *Patriotism on Parade*, 35–36; O'Leary, *To Die For*, 77–78.

90. Before 1898, the WRC required that each local corps be affiliated with a GAR post. Davies, *Patriotism on Parade*, 38; O'Leary, *To Die For*, 76–78, 83; *Synopsis of the Proceedings of the Department of Massachusetts Woman's Relief Corps*, 6–7.

91. Emma B. Manchester in *Journal of the Eighth Annual Convention of the Woman's Relief Corps* (1890), 36; *Journal of the Twelfth Annual Convention of the Woman's Relief Corps* (1894), 154; Davies, *Patriotism on Parade*, 29, 38–39.

92. *Journal of the Sixteenth National Convention of the Woman's Relief Corps* (1898), 275; *Journal of the Thirteenth Annual Convention of the Woman's Relief Corps* (1895), 105.

93. *Journal of the Twelfth Annual Convention of the Woman's Relief Corps* (1894), 5–22, 151 (on southerners married to white Union veterans). On Native Americans in the WRC, in this case in Kashena, Wisconsin, see *Journal of the Thirty-Ninth National Convention of the Woman's Relief Corps* (1921), 190–91.

94. Layton was assistant national inspector in 1906. O'Leary, *To Die For*, 85–88; *Journal of the Fifteenth National Convention of the Woman's Relief Corps* (1897), 324–25, 330, 420; Alice Ruth Moore, "Louisiana," *WE* 2 (May 1896): 12.

95. O'Leary, *To Die For*, 100–107, 161–62, 172–93; Goldstein, *Saving "Old Glory,"* 16; Litwicki, *America's Public Holidays*, 20–26; *Journal of the Twelfth Annual Convention of the Woman's Relief Corps* (1894), 386; *Journal of the Eighth Annual Convention of the Woman's Relief Corps* (1890), 36, 87–102; *Journal of the Thirteenth Annual Convention of the Woman's Relief Corps* (1895), 37 (quotation); *Journal of Proceedings, Sixteenth National Convention, Department of Massachusetts, Woman's Relief Corps* (1895), 40, 47–48.

96. *Journal of the Eleventh National Convention of the Woman's Relief Corps* (1893), 152–53; O'Leary, *To Die For*, 180.

97. Black women did form corps in those states, but those corps remained "detached" from the departments. O'Leary, *To Die For*, 83–84, 87–88; *Journal of the Eighth Annual Convention of the Woman's Relief Corps* (1890), 262–63; *Journal of the Thirty-Ninth National Convention of the Woman's Relief Corps* (1921), 51; *Journal of the Fifteenth National Convention of the Woman's Relief Corps* (1897), 321–30, 409.

98. Black "detached" WRC corps raised tens of dollars in the depression year of 1894, in contrast to the thousands of dollars raised by nonsouthern statewide departments. *Journal of the Twelfth Annual Convention of the Woman's Relief Corps* (1894), 57.

99. Kate Brownlee Sherwood in *Journal of the Thirteenth Annual Convention of the Woman's Relief Corps* (1895), 249.

100. In 1895, for example, the WRC president focused her Memorial Day reflections on the proverbial "'vacant chair.'" Emma R. Wallace in *Journal of the Thirteenth Annual Convention of the Woman's Relief Corps* (1895), 37; Blight, *Race and Reunion*, 175–83.

101. WRC president Annie Wittenmyer in *Journal of the Eighth Annual Convention of the Woman's Relief Corps* (1890), 274. This sixty-three-year-old Ohioan had been prominent in Civil War relief work and postbellum temperance work. Davies, *Patriotism on Parade*, 89; *NAW*, 3:636–37.

102. *Journal of the Twelfth Annual Convention of the Woman's Relief Corps* (1894), 98–99, 130 (Hattie Loring).

103. The Bostonians in question were Harriette Wales Reed and Lizabeth A. Turner. Ibid., 45–46, 133, 135.

104. An example is Mamie Garvin Fields's account of African Americans' minor vandalism of a statue of John Calhoun in Charleston. "I believe white people were talking to us about Jim Crow through that statue," she recalled. Fields with Fields, *Lemon Swamp*, 57.

105. Hollen E. Day in *Journal of the Twelfth Annual Convention of the Woman's Relief Corps* (1894), 296–97.

106. Mary McCorkle Sims in *Journal of the Nineteenth National Convention of the Woman's Relief Corps* (1901), 118.

107. The pensions went to regular army nurses as distinguished from regimental ones. President Emma R. Wallace in *Journal of the Thirteenth Annual Convention of the Woman's Relief Corps* (1895), 34; Davies, *Patriotism on Parade*, 180–81; *Journal of the Twelfth Annual Convention of the Woman's Relief Corps* (1894), 35.

108. *Journal of the Twelfth Annual Convention of the Woman's Relief Corps* (1894), 98 (quotation); *Journal of Proceedings, Sixteenth National Convention, Department of Massachusetts* (1895), 43, 85.

109. *Journal of the Fifteenth National Convention of the Woman's Relief Corps* (1897), 229; *Journal of the Sixteenth National Convention of the Woman's Relief Corps* (1898), 159–61.

110. President Sarah C. Mink in *Journal of the Twelfth Annual Convention of the Woman's Relief Corps* (1894), 35.

111. The WRC's California Department turned down a GAR invitation in 1893 to join its parade because the women preferred to stand "on the sidewalks," as they had during the 1865 victory parades, to cheer "their fathers, brothers, sons and lovers." *Veteran* (Worcester, Mass.), April 1893, 4, quoted in McConnell, *Glorious Contentment*, 219.

112. *Journal of the Twentieth National Convention of the Woman's Relief Corps* (1902), 174; O'Leary, *To Die For*, 95–96.

113. National president Mary L. Carr of Colorado declared, "no organization

has greater responsibility laid upon it than ours, or more manifest an opportunity to pass on to the future the ideas which made this a distinctive nation . . . . [I]f in our thought it becomes displaced by literary study in clubs, we shall soon find it hard to hold our own." She characterized the WRC as "benevolent and educative, but not beneficiary." *Journal of the Nineteenth National Convention of the Woman's Relief Corps* (1901), 43.

114. Scott, *Natural Allies*, 111–40; and McHenry, *Forgotten Readers*, 224–27, 230–31, discuss the newness and sometimes controversial nature of clubwomen's literary work relative to charity work.

115. As in the UDC, applicants to the DAR demonstrated their personal acceptability by garnering signatures from current members. *Constitution and By-Laws of the Daughters of the American Revolution* (1890), 4; *Constitution and By-Laws of the Daughters of the American Revolution* (1894), 8. A president of the Order of First Families of Virginia made it especially clear that retrospective hereditary organizations valued much in addition to the fact of heredity. She urged members to propose for membership "only those who are representative of the best and finest in conservative society today—that our personnel may truly bespeak the Nation's social foundation. It is not enough that a casual acquaintance may have 1607–1620 ancestry." Minnie G. Cook to "the Members," March 28, 1928, folder 77, box 3, Helm-Davidson Family Papers, MO.

116. Also stressing the DAR's commitment to North-South reconciliation on racial terms are Davies, *Patriotism on Parade*, 277–79, 295; LaGanke, "National Society of the Daughters of the American Revolution," 66; Silber, *Romance of Reunion*, 163–72, 220 n. 9; O'Leary, *To Die For*, 79–81; and Smith, *American Archives*, 141–44.

117. Davenport, *Hereditary Society Blue Book*, 47, 66, 89, 143. I exclude from this discussion the all-male Society of the Cincinnati (formed in 1783), which was composed of Revolutionary officers and their eldest male descendants, as it originated the year the Revolution ended and therefore was not retrospective in its initial self-conception. Davies, *Patriotism on Parade*, 3–21; Waldstreicher, *In the Midst of Perpetual Fetes*, 67–73, 87–88; Myers, *Liberty without Anarchy*.

118. "Credential List," *DARPCC* 21 (1912): 602–75.

119. On the SAR's female members in its first year (including two vice presidents of the New Hampshire Society), see Hall, *Year Book of the Societies Composed of Descendants of the Men of the Revolution*, 9, 37–38, 336–37, 340, 342–46; and St. Paul, *History of the National Society of the Sons of the American Revolution*, 1–10, 156.

120. "Women Worthy of Honor: The Patriotic Spirit of '76," *Washington Post*, July 13, 1890, 12. Lockwood was later accused of having borrowed much of her account from the writings of another descendant of the same Revolutionary woman. Eugenia Washington to Ellen Hardin Walworth, April 19, 1897, document 14, folder 3, file 23, EHW Papers; Mary Moderwell DeBolt, "After Thirty-Five Years,"

DARM 59 (October 1925): 597–603. With the cooperation of many cofounders and charter members, the leadership drafted the first official history of the DAR's formation in November 1908. Boynton et al., "Early History." Also see LaGanke, "National Society of the Daughters of the American Revolution," 48–52. Though not present at the first organizing meeting in August, Lockwood was later, in 1897, designated the DAR's "pen-founder." Boynton et al., "Early History," 110.

121. Biographical sketch, "Mary Desha," n.d., folder "Miscellany: Biographical Material," box 827, Mary Desha Papers, LC; Davies, *Patriotism on Parade*, 102; *Minutes of the Thirteenth Annual Convention of the United Daughters of the Confederacy* (1907), 238; Virginia Frazer Boyle to Mary Desha, July 30, 1894, folder 4, box 1, Papers of Mary Desha, UKY.

122. "Proceedings of the Tenth Continental Congress," *AMM* 18 (April–May 1901): 731. This anecdote did not appear in accounts of Washington's life while she was still living, however. Ellen Hardin Walworth, "Eugenia Washington," *AMM* 1 (September 1892): 216–21.

123. *NAW*, 1:432–34; Willard and Livermore, *Woman of the Century*, 228–29.

124. Willard and Livermore, *Woman of the Century*, 144–45; Hunter, *Century of Service*, 45–46.

125. Typescript, annotated copy of letter, Brigadier General Martin D. Hardin to Myra C. Smith, April 5, 1880, folder 1, reel C1, Series I: Genealogical and Early Family Records, M-133, Somerville and Howorth Family Papers, SL; *NAW*, 3:537–38.

126. Mrs. Clifton R. Breckinridge of Arkansas in "Proceedings of the First Continental Congress," *AMM* 1 (July 1892): 29.

127. Georgia Moore de Fontaine, "A Monument to Southern Women," *CV* 2 (October 1894): 312.

128. Frances Fort Brown, "Georgia in the Revolution," *AMM* 23 (October 1903): 261.

129. D'Emilio and Freedman, *Intimate Matters*, 34–36, 93; Hodes, *White Women, Black Men*, 96, 144–45. The grandfather of Hallie Quinn Brown, NACW president in the 1920s, had been a white Revolutionary veteran in Virginia who emancipated his daughter, Brown's mother. Randall K. Burkett, "Introduction," in Brown, *Homespun Heroines*, xxvii.

130. For example, the great-grandfathers of Augusta Madge Hawley of Bridgeport, Connecticut, and of Anna J. Gilmore of Raynham, Massachusetts, had both fought in the Revolution. "Here and There," *CAM* 2 (March 1901): 378–79; "Social Uplift," *Crisis* 11 (November 1915): 8. The Massachusetts society of the SAR admitted Du Bois, but the national leadership turned him away, in its eagerness to promote the SAR's growth among white southerners. Lewis, *W. E. B. Du Bois: Biography of a Race*, 13, 374–75, 660 n. 66. Excluded African Americans with Revolutionary-era ancestry, including Du Bois, founded their own retrospective hereditary organization in 1930. On the Society of Descendants of Early New England Negroes, see

Des Jardins, *Women and the Historical Enterprise in America*, 125, 157; and "Along the Color Line," *Crisis* 37 (March 1930): 96.

131. The statute originated with a Cincinnatian's anxious query to the national DAR leadership as to whether the personal acceptability clause would allow "colored people" into the organization. *Statutes of the National Society, Daughters of the American Revolution*, 7; Mrs. Henry B. Moorehead in minutes of National Board of Management meeting, March 22, 1894, *AMM* 4 (April 1894): 404; *Chapter Directory, 1893*, 94.

132. Jacobson, *Whiteness of a Different Color*, 39–90; Dinnerstein, *Anti-Semitism in America*, 35–77.

133. Barrington, *Historical Restorations of the Daughters of the American Revolution*, 193 (Cherokee-descended members in Tahlequah, Oklahoma); Sarah Paine Hoffman, "Jewish Patriots in the American Revolution," December 3, 1936 (transcript of radio broadcast), folder 1, Papers of Sarah Paine Hoffman, SHSI; Turner, *Women, Culture, and Community*, 157. The Californian proposed inducting into the DAR descendants of eighteenth-century Spanish governors who had prevented British control of territory later conquered by the United States. Margaret B. Harvey, "California in the Revolution," *AMM* 21 (October 1902): 283.

134. O'Leary, "'Blood Brotherhood,'" 62; Cox, *Dixie's Daughters*, 146–49. Only in the South or in culturally southern areas did members of the DAR and UDC socialize before 1912, as in St. Louis, Missouri (1898), Richmond, Virginia (1899), and Statesville, North Carolina (1911). *Minutes of the Fifth Annual Meeting of the United Daughters of the Confederacy* (1899), 35; *Minutes of the Sixth Annual Meeting of the United Daughters of the Confederacy* (1900), 8, 86; minutes of meeting of November 20, 1911, vol. 2 (1915–1918), DAR Chapter North Carolina.

135. "United Daughters of the Confederacy," *CV* 21 (April 1913): 171; Leonard, *Woman's Who's Who of America*, 724; Davies, *Patriotism on Parade*, 98; "The Confederate Flag in Washington," *CV* 20 (December 1912): 548–49.

136. Clark, "History Is No Fossil Remains," 267–68; Neverdon-Morton, *Afro-American Women of the South*, 139–40; Gaines, *Uplifting the Race*, 49; *DARM* 53 (July 1919): 421.

137. Davies, *Patriotism on Parade*, 64.

138. *Lineage Book, National Society of the Daughters of the American Revolution*, v; *Chapter Histories: Daughters of the American Revolution in Georgia*, 117; Warren, *History of the Massachusetts Daughters of the American Revolution*, 210–11; *AMM* 19 (August 1901): 178–79.

139. The battle was that of Guilford Court House. Hay, *Chapter Histories of the North Carolina Daughters of the American Revolution*, 99–101. Especially famed for treating women's labors as subjects of history was the amateur historian Alice Morse Earle. Her works on childhood, family life, and material culture in colonial New England were still recognized as innovations a century later. She was active in the DAR in Brooklyn, New York. Kammen, *Mystic Chords of Memory*, 148;

Marling, *George Washington Slept Here*, 411–12 nn. 41–42; *NAW*, 1:541–42; Fitz-patrick, *History's Memory*, 32–33; Des Jardins, *Women and the Historical Enterprise in America*, 17–20, 23–24.

140. An example is Emily Nelson Ritchie McLean, "McKinley as Lover, Husband, and Father," *AMM* 31 (September 1907): 517–19.

141. Mrs. Charles Whittlesey Pickett (Marie Sperry Pickett) in Mouat, *Connecticut State History of the Daughters of the American Revolution*, 46–48; "Meeting of the D.A.R. at the Historic Cogswell Tavern in New Preston," *Litchfield (Conn.) Enquirer*, September 3, 1903 (quotation), and "She Dropped Dead Reading Paper to D.A.R.," *Hartford Courant*, November 11, 1904, both clippings in scrapbook "29 June 1903–29 May 1905," vol. 2, DAR Papers Litchfield.

142. "What We Are Doing and Chapter Work," *AMM* 16 (March 1900): 346.

143. "Response by Mrs. Wm. D. Cabell," *AMM* 3 (August 1893): 181.

144. Smith, *American Archives*, 140.

145. Among the UDC leaders who were single at the time they held their positions were Katie Daffan of Texas and Alice Baxter of Georgia, who headed the two largest state divisions in 1909–1910; Mildred Lewis Rutherford of Georgia, a national officer (historian general) and famed ideologue; and a president, Mary B. Poppenheim of South Carolina. "Officers Elected Texas Division, U.D.C.," *CV* 17 (January 1909): 9; "Confederate Monument at Monticello, Ga.," *CV* 18 (September 1910): 418; "Requests by U.D.C. Historian General," *CV* 20 (February 1912): 54; Mrs. Robert D. Wright, "South Carolina's Candidate for President General," *CV* 25 (June 1917): 282; Simpson, *Edith D. Pope and Her Nashville Friends*, 116–18.

146. Cott, *Public Vows*, 3–7.

147. The first lady's "personality would attract and be acceptible [*sic*] to eligible women from all sections of the country . . . . [A] woman with a sectional reputation was not to be thought of." Lockwood and Ragan, *Story of the Records D.A.R.*, 92; also see Washington, *History of the Organization*, 12.

148. Davies, *Patriotism on Parade*, 169–72.

149. "A Member of the Congress" (pseud.), "The Continental Congress, First and Second," typescript, document 12, folder 1, file 23, EHW Papers; see also *AMM* 2 (March 1893): 333–36. The founders' concurrence in recruiting wives as wives illustrates their own discomfort with manifestations of female political assertiveness. They found personal ambition repellent when manifested by women of their station. Eugenia Washington dismissed a New Yorker intent on rising within the organization as "nothing but a 'bulldozer.'" In retrospect, Walworth bemoaned the DAR's discarding of the "unwritten law" of the 1890s that the president "should always be a national woman" connected by marriage to "the United States Government"—a contrast to modern-day "women demagogues." Eugenia Washington to Ellen Hardin Walworth, April 9, 1897, document 13, folder 3, file 23, EHW Papers; Walworth, "The System of Government of the National Society of the Daughters of the American Revolution" (n.p., n.d. [1914]), 11, document 15, folder 2, file 23, EHW Papers.

150. The U.S. Congress governed the District of Columbia at the time. Incorporated by Congress in 1896, the DAR could hold up to $500,000 in real estate without paying property taxes; the amount rose to $1 million in 1915 and to $5 million in 1926. In 1926 the DAR's holdings were valued at $1.5 million. *Constitution and By-Laws of the Daughters of the American Revolution* (1931), 3–5; Flora A. Walker, "Supervising the Property of the National Society," *DARM* 60 (April 1926): 197.

151. Mary Beardsley Prince, married to the territorial governor of New Mexico, began her effort to organize DAR chapters there by mailing application blanks to women she already knew. She then made several visits to the public library in Denver, Colorado, "to ascertain the ancestry of several prospective members." This order of priorities became a major justification for the DAR's amassing of genealogical material. Kimmick, *History of the New Mexico State Organization*, 14–15, 20–21; Isabel Anderson, "The Growth and Development of Our Library," *DARM* 58 (April 1924): 212–13; Helen M. Prescott, "Beginning of D.A.R. in Atlanta" and "Origin of Joseph Habersham Chapter," n.d., Helen Prescott Collection, Joseph Habersham Chapter D.A.R. (Atlanta), folder 1, box 1, DAR Collection Atlanta.

152. The organization also attracted female entrepreneurs and professionals such as teachers, librarians, and faculty at women's colleges. Women who were married to wage earners or tenant farmers, or who earned wages as employees, were largely absent. I draw these conclusions from my collection of obituaries and other materials on 940 Daughters of the American Revolution born before 1900, from all over the United States. Morgan, "'Home and Country,'" 549–66.

153. For example, member Mary Custis Lee of Virginia was the daughter of the Confederate general Robert E. Lee, the granddaughter of Revolutionary general Henry "Light Horse Harry" Lee, and the great-granddaughter of Martha Custis Washington, wife of George Washington. *Remembrance Book of the Daughters of the American Revolution* (1919), 8; *Minutes of the Thirty-Second Annual Convention, United Daughters of the Confederacy* (1925), 6.

154. Harned, *Pennsylvania State History*, 212–13; Mrs. H. B. Tillotson, ed., "History of the D.A.R. Chapters of Minnesota," typescript, 1928, vol. 1, DAR Papers Minnesota; Leliah Gibson Kerr et al., comps., "Application register, Chicago Chapter D.A.R. (1897–1907)," DAR Collection Chicago; Scott, *Illinois State History*, 43; "Attack Made on Radicals Stirs D.A.R.," *Baltimore Sun*, March 20, 1930, clipping in folder "Lucia Ames Mead," box 496, NCPW Papers. The DAR leadership desired Jane Lathrop Stanford's involvement so much that, as late as 1895, her name appeared in a list of charter members with the notation "application not made out" beside it. The application of her sister was then complete. Lockwood, *Lineage Book of the Charter Members*, 217–18.

155. See, especially, Beckert, *Monied Metropolis*, 293–322.

156. Malvina S. Waring, "A Year's Spinning," *AMM* 13 (September 1898): 215 (quotation); Waring, "The Trance State of Woman," *AMM* 4 (February 1894): 163–72.

157. Unidentified clipping, July 11, 1896, Saratoga Chapter DAR scrapbook (September 1894–October 1912), EHW Papers.

158. Edwards, *Angels in the Machinery*, 119–22.

159. Goldstein, *Saving "Old Glory,"* 19–23; "Proceedings of the Eighth Continental Congress," *AMM* 14 (April 1899): 903–5 (quotation on p. 903); "Proceedings of the Eleventh Continental Congress," *AMM* 20 (June 1902): 1288. The DAR later focused on entrepreneurs' use of the flag in part because of concerns that broadly worded flag antidesecration laws would forbid legitimate Republican uses of the flag. "Proceedings of the Eighth Continental Congress," *AMM* 14 (April 1899): 909–10.

160. Harned, *Pennsylvania State History*, 211–12.

161. The architect commissioned by the DAR to perform the renovations, T. Mellon Rogers, came under fire from the American Institute of Architects for his relative lack of professional style and credentials. Hosmer, *Presence of the Past*, 86–88; West, *Domesticating History*, 40; Howe, "Women in Historic Preservation"; Kammen, *Mystic Chords of Memory*, 259.

162. Butler, "Another City upon a Hill"; "Loan Exhibition, Colonial Tea, DAR—(Mayflower)," poster, LHS; Ulrich, *Age of Homespun*, 34–35.

163. Elizabeth Butler Gentry, annual report of the chairman of the NSDAR National Old Trails Committee (1914), Committee on Historical Work, in State Chairmen Reports, vol. 2 (H–M), box 9, DAR Papers Michigan. Another vivid illustration of this point is Boston's Paul Revere House. Starting in 1896, the DAR joined other organizations in self-consciously reclaiming the house from the Italian immigrant neighborhood around it. A thorough renovation, including the removal of its Italian-language exterior signs (and businesses inside) and light-colored paint, was intended to transport the house and its beholders to the seventeenth century. *History of the Massachusetts Daughters of the American Revolution*; U.S. Senate, *Report of the Daughters of the American Revolution, 1890 to 1897*, 64, 67; Lindgren, *Preserving Historic New England*, 3, 37–41.

164. "What We Are Doing and Chapter Work," *AMM* 16 (March 1900): 325.

165. Julia Morgan Harding in *Fort Duquesne and Fort Pitt*, 47; "Work of the Chapters," *AMM* 20 (May 1902): 605–6; "The Open Letter," *AMM* 22 (March 1903): 273–74; *Chapter Directory, 1893*, 76. Wallace, "Visiting the Past," 138; and Lindgren, *Preserving the Old Dominion*, 25–36, 172–95, discuss other historic preservationists' denunciations of capitalist greed.

166. Mrs. Charles H. Smith, speech of February 19, 1917, folder 7; Louisa Johnson Smith, report on the 1906 Continental Congress, p. 3, folder 2; both in box 1, series II, DAR Papers Cleveland.

Chapter Two

1. One military camp in Georgia possessed few provisions for the sick, apart from five cots and five sets of sheets donated by the state of Ohio, before the DAR

began sending more. Painter, *Standing at Armageddon*, 157; McPherson, *Battle Cry of Freedom*, 485; Major and surgeon Frank E. Bunts to the Cavalry's commanding officer, May 29, 1898, and Bunts to Mrs. Andrew Squire (Eleanor Seymour Squire), June 18, 1898, folder 1, box 1, Papers of the War Emergency Relief Board, WRHS; Capt. J. H. Pond to Mrs. Orlando J. Hodge (Virginia Shedd Hodge), July 9, 1898, folder 2, box 1, Papers of the War Emergency Relief Board, WRHS. Also see *Journal of Proceedings, Twentieth Annual Convention, Department of Massachusetts, Woman's Relief Corps* (1899), 57, 118, 154–55; *Journal of the Sixteenth National Convention of the Woman's Relief Corps* (1898), 113, 318; *Minutes of the Fifth Annual Meeting of the United Daughters of the Confederacy* (1899), 35, 42; and "Proceedings of the Eighth Continental Congress," *AMM* 14 (April 1899): 495–96.

2. In addition to performing nursing and clerical work in Illinois for the war effort, Ida B. Wells-Barnett helped mobilize a black regiment for service. Gatewood, *Black Americans and the White Man's Burden*, 87, 98–100, 102 n. 1; Blight, *Race and Reunion*, 349.

3. The government chose the DAR over the Red Cross to select and assemble white nurses partly because of DAR leaders' personal and family connections to decision-makers. The wives of Secretary of War Russell Alger and of Army Surgeon General George M. Sternberg served prominently on DAR war relief committees. "Proceedings of the Eighth Continental Congress," *AMM* 14 (April 1899): 660–61; Hoganson, *Fighting for American Manhood*, 126; Shields, "History of the United States Army Nurse Corps (Female)," 4–5; "Official," *AMM* 13 (September 1898): 298; Mrs. Arturo Y. Casanova and Mrs. Z. Lewis Dalby, comps., "State History, District of Columbia Daughters of the American Revolution, in Three Volumes," typescript, 1934, 1:10, in Office of the Historian General, NSDAR Headquarters, Washington, D.C.; Gatewood, *Black Americans and the White Man's Burden*, 87, 98–100.

4. Roosevelt, *Strenuous Life*, 5–6 (quotation); "race suicide" in Roosevelt, *Presidential Addresses and State Papers*, 3:290; Roosevelt, "Race Decadence," *Outlook*, April 8, 1911, reprinted in Tone, *Controlling Reproduction*, 159–62; Bederman, *Manliness and Civilization*, 184–90, 192–95, 201–6; Gordon, *Woman's Body, Woman's Right*, 133–39, 150; Muncy, "Trustbusting and White Manhood in America," 33.

5. Thomas Baker in Jeanne L. Noble, *The Negro Woman's College Education* (New York: Bureau of Publications, Teachers College, Columbia University, 1956), 157, quoted in Gaines, *Uplifting the Race*, 140.

6. "The Successful Negro Mother," *CAM* 14 (July 1908): 396.

7. "Is the Negro Dying Out? (A Symposium)," *CAM* 15 (January 1909): 659–80. The physicians concurred that the race was not dying out largely because vital statistics were unreliable.

8. "Men of the Month," *Crisis* 5 (November 1912): 16; Josephine Silone Yates, "Parental Obligation," *CAM* 12 (April 1907): 289.

9. Mrs. A. Graves, "Motherhood," *CAM* 14 (September 1908): 495.

10. Mather, *Who's Who of the Colored Race*, 147–48; Addie W. Hunton, "A

Deeper Reverence for Home Ties," *CAM* 12 (January 1907): 59 (quotation); Mrs. Booker T. Washington (Margaret Murray Washington), "Club Work as a Factor in the Advance of Colored Women," *CAM* 11 (August 1906): 83–90; Josephine Silone Yates, "The Twentieth Century Negro—His Opportunities for Success," *CAM* 11 (October 1906): 237.

11. Yates, "The Twentieth Century Negro—His Opportunities for Success," 238.

12. "Woman's Part in the Uplift of the Negro Race," *CAM* 12 (January 1907): 53–59. Also see White, *Too Heavy a Load*, 44–45; and Satter, "Marcus Garvey, Father Divine, and the Gender Politics of Race Difference and Race Neutrality," 49.

13. "About Women," *NAN* 2 (September 1898), in *NACW Records, Part 1*, reel 23, frames 00261–62.

14. *NAN* 4 (February 1901), in *NACW Records, Part 1*, reel 23, frame 00387.

15. *NAN* 1 (June 15, 1897), in *NACW Records, Part 1*, reel 23, frame 00254; "Atlanta Woman's Club Notes," *NAN* 3 (April 1900), in *NACW Records, Part 1*, reel 23, frame 00350.

16. "Pauline E. Hopkins," *CAM* 2 (January 1901): 218.

17. Selena Sloan Butler, "Night Brings Out the Stars," *NAN* 4 (February 1901), in *NACW Records, Part 1*, reel 23, frame 00386; Pauline E. Hopkins, "Toussaint L'Ouverture," *CAM* 2 (November 1900): 24.

18. These numbers include children from all marriages, adopted children, foster children, children who died in infancy, and stepchildren whom the women appear to have raised. The fertility rate for white women nationwide in 1900 was 3.54 children. Perhaps demonstrating the attractions of club work for women who did not have children, over one-quarter (25.5 percent) of a larger group of married DAR members (698 women) were apparently childless, compared to a range of 8 to 19 percent for women nationwide who were born between 1840 and 1900. Morgan, "'Home and Country,'" 51, 556; Gordon, *Woman's Body, Woman's Right*, 150; U.S. Bureau of the Census, *Bicentennial Edition: Historical Statistics of the United States*, 53.

19. Miller, *"Benevolent Assimilation,"* 17–19, 117–18; Morgan, "'Home and Country,'" 50, 557; obituary of Mary Andrews Martin Gilman in *Remembrance Book of the Daughters of the American Revolution* (1918), 12; Russell, *Daughters Overseas*, 2; U.S. Senate, *Report of the Daughters of the American Revolution, 1890 to 1897*, 103. Mainline Protestant clergy were themselves among the most zealous imperialists.

20. Mary Smith Lockwood, "Editor's Note-Book," *AMM* 5 (August 1894): 185.

21. "Work of the Chapters," *AMM* 23 (July 1903): 24–25; *Eleventh Report of the National Society of the Daughters of the American Revolution*, 67–68; Russell, *Daughters Overseas*, x, 2; "Work of the Chapters," *DARM* 63 (October 1929): 624, 627. Cuba was a U.S. protectorate by 1901.

22. Mary Greene Montgomery Slocum in "Proceedings of the Eighth Continental Congress," *AMM* 14 (April 1899): 501–2.

23. Elizabeth C. Barney Buel, "Ninth Continental Congress, D.A.R.," *Litchfield (Conn.) Enquirer*, April 5, 1900, clipping in scrapbook "Volume I, Nov. 17th 1899 to June 27th 1903," DAR Papers Litchfield.

24. Lockwood and Ragan, *Story of the Records D.A.R.*, 102–3; Marian Longfellow O'Donoghue, "The D.A.R. Congress," *Patriotic Review* 1 (April 1901): 130–31; Davies, *Patriotism on Parade*, 98; *National Cyclopedia of American Biography*, 39:531–32; Leonard, *Woman's Who's Who of America*, 282; *AMM* 19 (July 1901): 1–2.

25. One example is a program for the Fourth of July in Saratoga Springs, New York. See "Saratoga Celebration of July the Fourth, 1896" and "Early Days of July," *Saratoga (N.Y.) Saratogian*, n.d. [July 1896], both in Saratoga Chapter DAR scrapbook (September 1894–October 1912), EHW Papers.

26. Howe, "Women in Historic Preservation," 36; Kaufman, *National Parks and the Woman's Voice*, 49–52, 251 nn. 77–79. At Valley Forge, the DAR was preceded by a group of women celebrating the site's centennial in the 1870s. The group eventually aborted its effort.

27. Ada Johnson McCleary in "Notes from the Twenty-Sixth Continental Congress," *DARM* 50 (1917): 300; Dunlap et al., *History and Register: Washington State Society*, 10.

28. Elizabeth Butler Gentry, annual report of the chairman of the NSDAR National Old Trails Committee (1914), Committee on Historical Work, in State Chairmen Reports, vol. 2 (H–M), box 9, DAR Papers Michigan.

29. In 1917 the Grand Rapids, Michigan, DAR placed a bronze plaque on the nearby site of an Ottawa village whose chief, Me-gis-o-me-me, "was among the first of his people to adopt the white man's ways and customs" and had been one of a group who went to Washington in 1836 to sell the territory. Less compliant Native American leaders, notably the Ottawa chief Pontiac, also had their graves marked by DAR monuments, if the leaders had also fought the British (as Pontiac had in the 1760s). Photograph of tablet, June 14, 1917, and "Marks Site of Big Indian Village," n.d. [1917], otherwise unidentified clipping, in Sophie de Marsac Campau Chapter DAR (Grand Rapids, Mich.) scrapbook of chapter activities, vol. 1 (1910–1929), p. 57, box 34, DAR Papers Michigan; "Work of the Chapters," *AMM* 19 (August 1901): 187–90 (Pontiac grave in St. Louis).

30. DAR cofounder Mary Desha spread interest in a monument to Pocahontas at the 1907 Jamestown (Virginia) Exposition. Daughters in Missouri, Oregon, and North Dakota funded statues of Sacagawea before the 1920s. A DAR plaque in Mesa, Colorado, contended that with Chief Ouray, Chipeta promoted "peace between the tribes and the white men." Her efforts had "turned free" a group of white prisoners following the "Meeker Massacre." Mary Desha to Mrs. Erwin, March 19, 1906, Desha to Edward Valentine, March 19, 1906, and Desha to Mary

M. A. Stevens, March 19, 1906, folder "Daughters of the American Revolution, March 11–20, 1906," box 826, Mary Desha Papers, LC; Dunlap et al., *History and Register: Washington State Society*, 79; Tarbell, *History of the Daughters of the American Revolution of Colorado*, 34, 37–38.

31. Harriet Farrand McLeod, "San Juan Capistrano Mission," *AMM* 22 (May 1903): 648; Morley, *History of California State Society*, 322–23 (quotation).

32. In the 1930s the Laredo DAR planned the preservation of the settlement known as "Dolores Borregueño" or "Dolores del Torreon" with the "wholehearted support" of descendants of Borrego who were still living on the same land. "A National Park Is Planned: Ancient Fort and Settlement Give Interesting History," clipping, n.d. [late 1930s], and Julia Bell Phelps, "Lucy Meriwether DAR Chapter Outlines Restoration Plan," clipping, n.d. [late 1930s], both in Mrs. George T. Spears, comp., "Scrapbook, Texas Chapters, N.S.D.A.R.," n.d. [1938], unpaginated (under Laredo), DAR Collection Texas.

33. Early twentieth-century DAR monuments having anything to say about Mexico focused entirely on its vanquishing by the United States in the United States–Mexican War in the late 1840s. Morley, *History of California State Society*, 113–16; Kimmick, *History of the New Mexico State Organization*, 77; "Work of the Chapters," *DARM* 66 (May 1932): 303 (San Benito, Tex.).

34. Margaret B. Harvey, "California in the Revolution," *AMM* 21 (October 1902): 273, 275–76, 283.

35. The mapping of old trails was sometimes made possible only by interviews with surviving "settlers." *Old Rail Fence Corners*, 3–4; Cordry, *Story of the Marking of the Santa Fe Trail*, 13, 18–20, 23–25, 35, 39, 102.

36. Among numerous examples are Tuttle, *Three Centuries in Champlain Valley*, 478; Grand Rapids Founders' Day program, June 23, 1910, in Sophie de Marsac Campau Chapter DAR (Grand Rapids, Mich.) scrapbook of chapter activities, vol. 1 (1910–1929), p. 44, box 34, DAR Papers Michigan; "Beginnings in Floyd County," typescript, n.d. [after 1921], and Mrs. George De Wald, "Sketch of the Early History of Black Hawk County," typescript, 1921, both in folder 2, box 1, DAR Collection Iowa; Marcaccini and Woytanowitz, "House Work"; and Tarbell, *History of the Daughters of the American Revolution of Colorado*, 31–39.

37. Hebard, *Marking the Oregon Trail*, 25. Later, in 1847, Narcissa Whitman was slaughtered with her husband by Cayuse in what became Washington State. The Tacoma DAR dedicated a fountain memorializing Whitman in 1899. "Work of the Chapters," *AMM* 20 (January 1902): 34. Des Jardins, *Women and the Historical Enterprise in America*, 104, 110–12, discusses Hebard herself.

38. Turner, "Significance of the Frontier in American History," 2–3; Des Jardins, *Women and the Historical Enterprise in America*, 102.

39. Mary Greene Montgomery Slocum in "Proceedings of the Eighth Continental Congress," *AMM* 14 (April 1899): 499–500 (quotation); Tarbell, *History of the Daughters of the American Revolution of Colorado*, 8.

40. Mrs. Cone Johnson in "United Daughters of the Confederacy," *CV* 11 (February 1903): 64.

41. Brundage, "'Woman's Heart and Hand and Deathless Love,'" 73. The UDC claimed 25,000 members in 1902 and burgeoned to 90,000 members by 1913. Although the UCV possessed 35,198 members in 1902, it later shrank. The SCV had attracted less than half that number, 16,000, in 1903. Nancy Lewis Greene, "Daughters of the Confederacy," *CV* 10 (January 1902): 9; Cox, *Dixie's Daughters*, 169–70 n. 1; Foster, *Ghosts of the Confederacy*, 172, 242 n. 9.

42. "A Model Appeal—What a Daughter Says," *CV* 19 (September 1911): 416. See also Cox, *Dixie's Daughters*, 44–48.

43. "What May Be Expected of Our Young Men," *CV* 20 (February 1912): 56. One modern-day scholar has similarly argued that the neo-Confederate movement's feminization after 1900 directly caused its decline in energy and influence. Foster, *Ghosts of the Confederacy*, 178–79, 196–98. On contemporary associations between notions of male supremacy and those of civilization, see especially Newman, *White Women's Rights*, 116–31.

44. Clara Hadley Wait in "In the Public Schools, Washington's Birthday Appropriately Celebrated," *Marshall (Mich.) Chronicle*, n.d. [February 1905], clipping in scrapbook, vol. 2 (1895–1914), p. 6, box 1, Papers of Clara Hadley Wait, MHC.

45. Terrell quoted in Jones, *Quest for Equality*, 159–60.

46. The National Monument Association gave up a few years later because of Hart's ill health and an overall "condition of quiescence" among African Americans. When the effort aborted in 1901, it had raised only $500 in pledges. "For the Monument Fund," *NAN* 2 (April 1899), in *NACW Records, Part 1*, reel 23, frames 00289–90; "Monument Association," *NAN* 4 (February 1901), in *NACW Records, Part 1*, reel 23, 00387; "Bright Outlook in the Southern Federation," *NAN* 7 (July 1904): 21, in *NACW Records, Part 1*, reel 23, frames 00428, 00434.

47. Both monuments honored local heroes who had participated in the naval battle of Manila in May 1898. "Work of the Chapters," *AMM* 21 (September 1902): 239–40; "Work of the Chapters," *AMM* 20 (May 1902): 591–92.

48. "Connecticut," *NAN* 7 (July 1904): 39, in *NACW Records, Part 1*, reel 23, frame 00437.

49. Miller, *"Benevolent Assimilation,"* 12, 80–81; Painter, *Standing at Armageddon*, 157; Mary Smith Lockwood, "Current Topics," *AMM* 13 (October 1898): 394–95.

50. Wiles in "What We Are Doing and Chapter Work," *AMM* 16 (February 1900): 136–37; "Annual Reports of State Regents," *AMM* 18 (June 1901): 1019–24. See also Mary Smith Lockwood, "The Policy of the United States," *AMM* 13 (November 1898): 417–18. Biographical information on Wiles is in Harlan et al., *Booker T. Washington Papers*, 5:679–80 (as a national official of the GFWC, Wiles sought Washington's approval for the GFWC's exclusion of black women from its 1900 biennial).

51. Frances M. Ingalls and Grace M. Wagman in Menges, *History of New York State Conference*, 381–82.

52. Malvina S. Waring, "A Year's Spinning," *AMM* 13 (September 1898): 215.

53. Miller, *"Benevolent Assimilation,"* 196–252; Grace Brown Salisbury quoted in "Rhea" (pseud.), "Norwalk Chapter Entertained," *New Haven Evening Leader*, April 20, 1901, clipping in scrapbook "Volume I, Nov. 17th 1899 to June 27th 1903," DAR Papers Litchfield.

54. Kammen, *Season of Youth*, 168–72, 340 n. 93; DeBenedetti, *Peace Reform in American History*, 59, 66, 68; Kramer, "Empires, Exceptions, and Anglo-Saxons," 1324–25, 1334.

55. Mary Smith Lockwood, "Parallels in History," *AMM* 13 (October 1898): 329.

56. "Current History," *AMM* 14 (June 1899): 1256.

57. Sara Thomson Kinney in "Annual Reports of State Regents," *AMM* 16 (May 1900): 1005. Such a chapter did develop after the First World War. As of 1926, thirty women belonged. "Local Woman Gave London D.A.R. Its Start," *Minneapolis Sunday Tribune*, January 3, 1926, clipping, and Margaret C. Moseley to Jennie A. H. Coolidge, February 25, 1926, both in folder 1925, box 3, Papers of Jennie Adelaide Holmes Coolidge, MNHS.

58. Josephine Burdick in *Journal of Proceedings, Twentieth Annual Convention, Department of Massachusetts, Woman's Relief Corps* (1899), 46; *Journal of the Seventeenth National Convention of the Woman's Relief Corps* (1899), 334.

59. *Journal of the Twentieth National Convention of the Woman's Relief Corps* (1902), 173–75; *Journal of the Twenty-First National Convention of the Woman's Relief Corps* (1903), 350, 453; *Journal of Proceedings, Twentieth Annual Convention, Department of Massachusetts, Woman's Relief Corps* (1899), 219.

60. "The U.D.C. of Texas to the President," *CV* 12 (February 1904): 84.

61. *CV* 6 (November 1898): 512; "National Dignity and Confederate Honor," *CV* 6 (December 1898): 546.

62. *Minutes of the Fifth Annual Meeting of the United Daughters of the Confederacy* (1899), 42.

63. Washington Gardner, "Vivid Account of the Panama Canal Work," *CV* 16 (April 1908): 170–72.

64. "Mrs. Robert Emory Park," *CV* 19 (October 1911): 481–83; "Proceedings of the Ninth Continental Congress," *AMM* 16 (April 1900): 393–94 (quotations). On similar critiques of British imperialism, see Painter, *Standing at Armageddon*, 158; and Kramer, "Empires, Exceptions, and Anglo-Saxons," 1339–42.

65. Mrs. Edwin H. O'Brien quoted in Poppenheim et al., *History of the United Daughters of the Confederacy*, 40. Also see Bonner, *Colors and Blood*, 163.

66. Blight, *Race and Reunion*, 348–49; William Loren Katz, "Preface," in Marks, *Black Press Views American Imperialism*, viii.

67. She answered in the negative. "Report of the Woman's New Century Club of

Providence," *NAN* 2 (September 1898), in *NACW Records, Part 1*, reel 23, frames 00261–62.

68. Marks, *Black Press Views American Imperialism*, 12, 14–15, 17, 29.

69. Hoganson, "'As Badly Off as the Filipinos,'" 20; Moses, *Afrotopia*, 26–27, 64–65, 91, 131–33, 188–89, 199–202.

70. Higginbotham, *Righteous Discontent*, 157–58; S. Willie Layton [*sic*], "California," *WE* 2 (April 1895): 9–10; Sarah Willie Layten, "A Glimpse at California Missions," *WE* 2 (May 1895): 12.

71. Cora L. Smith, "Texas," *WE* 2 (July 1895): 16.

72. Royster, *Southern Horrors and Other Writings*, 87, 152.

73. Elizabeth Piper Ensley, "Colorado: Election Day," *WE* 1 (December 1894): 17–18 (quotation); Ensley, "Colorado: Club Land," *WE* 2 (May 1895): 9.

74. "Club Gossip," *WE* 1 (March 24, 1894): 15; "Queen Lilioukulani [*sic*] Now Lives in Brookline, Mass.," "Social Notes," and "Some 'Off-Color' Happenings at the Hub," *WE* 3 (January 1897): 7, 10–11.

75. Gaines, *Uplifting the Race*, 29–30; Blight, *Race and Reunion*, 335–36; Ida B. Wells, *A Red Record* (1895), reprinted in Royster, *Southern Horrors and Other Writings*, 81–82.

76. Salem, *To Better Our World*, 32–33; Mary Church Terrell, "Service Which Should Be Rendered the South" (1905), in Jones, *Quest for Equality*, 206–7 (quotation). Also see Carrie W. Clifford, "Which Shall It Be?" *CAM* 12 (January 1907): 34, in which she contended that the "American people are not yet civilized or Christianized enough to recognize God's image through the veil of race or color."

77. Kaplan, *Anarchy of Empire*, 12–17.

78. Alternative lyrics to the tune of "America (My Country, 'Tis of Thee)," written in opposition to lynching, asked, "How long will this base wrong / Pollute thy freedom's song?" Charles Fred White, "Afro-American," *CAM* 1 (September 1900): 245; Salem, *To Better Our World*, 154. Biographical information on Merritt is found in "Along the Color Line," *Crisis* 37 (September 1930): 310.

79. Emma F. G. Merritt, "American Prejudice—Its Cause, Effect and Possibilities," *VN* 2 (July 1905): 466–67, 469; Merritt, "Douglas [*sic*] Day: Why Not Make it National," *VN* 3 (April 1906): 279–81.

80. Higginbotham, *Righteous Discontent*, 67.

81. Gaines, *Uplifting the Race*, 132; Moses, *Golden Age of Black Nationalism*, 19; S. E. F. C. C. Hamedoe, "The First Pan-African Conference of the World," *CAM* 1 (September 1900): 226–27. Rief, "Thinking Globally, Acting Locally," 206–8, describes individual clubwomen's participation starting in 1899 in meetings of the International Congress of Women.

82. Moses, *Afrotopia*, 26–27, 64–65.

83. Selena Sloan Butler, "Heredity," *Spelman Messenger*, June 1897, quoted in Neverdon-Morton, *Afro-American Women of the South*, 4. Butler had drawn applause at the 1896 NACW convention when she said that "the twentieth-century

woman will be the woman of color . . . as proud of the Negro blood that courses through her veins as her white sister is proud of the Anglo-Saxon blood that courses through hers." *History of the Club Movement among the Colored Women,* 57.

84. Gaines, *Uplifting the Race,* 109–10; Moses, *Afrotopia,* 39–40, 83–84 (quotation).

85. Pauline E. Hopkins, "Toussaint L'Ouverture," *CAM* 2 (November 1900): 24. Hopkins's career as a historian is further described in Dagbovie, "Black Women Historians," 245–46.

86. *Minutes of the Fourth Biennial Meeting or Fifth Convention of the National Association of Colored Women* (n.p., 1906), 18, in *NACW Records, Part 1,* reel 1, frame 00309; "Light Color Bar to Office," *Baltimore Afro-American Ledger* 14 (July 21, 1906), 1, in *NACW Records, Part 1,* reel 5, frame 00695; Rouse, "Out of the Shadow of Tuskegee," 40.

87. *Minutes of the Fifth Biennial Meeting or Sixth Convention of the National Association of Colored Women* (New Bedford, Mass.: New Bedford Printers, 1909), 30, in *NACW Records, Part 1,* reel 1, frame 00344.

88. Here I draw on Paul A. Kramer's useful distinction between racial Anglo-Saxon exceptionalism and national (American) Anglo-Saxon exceptionalism in "Empires, Exceptions, and Anglo-Saxons."

Chapter Three

1. Edna K. Bigelow, historian's report, 1900–1901, folder 6 (papers 1891–1905), box 1, DAR Papers St. Paul.

2. On similar tendencies among white reformers in general, see especially Ginzberg, "Pernicious Heresies"; Kunzel, *Fallen Women, Problem Girls*; and Ladd-Taylor, *Mother-Work,* 43–73.

3. *NAN* 17 (November–December 1914): 5–6 (quotations on p. 6), in *NACW Records, Part 1,* reel 23, frames 00551–52.

4. Some of the black press, notably T. Thomas Fortune's *New York Age,* criticized the women for not erecting a monument in a more public place where more black children, and African Americans in general, would see it. Preceding this monument was a plaque to Tubman funded by the Cayuga County Historical Society and dedicated in June 1914 in a public building in Auburn. Charlotte Bell, "Personals," *NAN* 17 (November–December 1914): 15, in *NACW Records, Part 1,* reel 23, frame 00566; "Report of the Empire State Federation of Women's Clubs Made at Wilberforce, Ohio," *NAN* 17 (March–April 1915): 2, in *NACW Records, Part 1,* reel 23, frame 00576; Davis, *Lifting as They Climb,* 261–62; Kachun, *Festivals of Freedom,* 288 n. 30; Brown, *Homespun Heroines,* 65; "Social Uplift," *Crisis* 8 (August 1914): 166.

5. "Daughters in Summerville, S.C.," *CV* 6 (April 1898): 154. The leader of the Waco, Texas, DAR chapter was presented with a gavel made from "the Spanish

flagship at the battle of Manila" in 1898. "Work of the Chapters," *AMM* 20 (May 1902): 591–92.

6. *Minutes of the Eighth Biennial Convention of the National Association of Colored Women, July Twenty-Third to Twenty-Seventh, 1912* (n.p., 1912), 22 (quotation), in *NACW Records, Part 1*, reel 1, frame 00373; "Women Hold Big Convention," *New York Age* 25 (August 1, 1912): 1, clipping in *NACW Records, Part 1*, reel 5, frame 00720.

7. "[H]umane teaching," meaning "love and care for all helpless creatures," pervaded the WRC's patriotic instruction work in the 1900s. The 1896 convention first endorsed the Humane Society's concept of Bands of Mercy. In 1902 members around the country reported forming a total of 234 Bands of Mercy in local public schools. Mary L. Carr in *Journal of the Nineteenth National Convention of the Woman's Relief Corps* (1901), 51 (quotations); *Journal of the Fifteenth National Convention of the Woman's Relief Corps* (1897), 233; *Journal of the Twentieth National Convention of the Woman's Relief Corps* (1902), 167, 175.

8. Gordon, *Pitied But Not Entitled*; Gordon, *Women, the State, and Welfare*; Ladd-Taylor, *Mother-Work*; Lindenmeyer, *"A Right to Childhood"*; Muncy, *Creating a Female Dominion in American Reform*; Sklar,"Historical Foundations of Women's Power in the Creation of the American Welfare State"; Skocpol, *Protecting Soldiers and Mothers*, 311–524.

9. "From Oklahoma," *NAN* 16 (May 1913): 5, in *NACW Records, Part 1*, reel 23, frame 00511. Clubwomen in Alabama and in Missouri also successfully approached the state for assistance in funding projects, especially reform schools, aimed at poor black children. Josephine Turpin Washington, "Child Saving in Alabama," *CAM* 14 (January 1908): 48–51; Addie W. Hunton, "Women's Clubs," *Crisis* 2 (May 1911): 18; "Social Uplift," *Crisis* 11 (November 1915): 9; "Social Uplift," *Crisis* 9 (April 1915): 270; Salem, *To Better Our World*, 110–11.

10. "Declaration of Principles Adopted at the Baltimore Convention," *NAN* 19 (October 1916): 11, in *NACW Records, Part 1*, reel 23, frame 00674; "Personals," *NAN* 19 (January 1917): 10, in *NACW Records, Part 1*, reel 23, frame 00693; *NAN* 20 (April 1918): 3, in *NACW Records, Part 1*, reel 23, 00746; "Men of the Month," *Crisis* 15 (April 1918): 279.

11. Davis, *American Heroine*, 267. On reports of members creating or aiding settlement houses, see Menges, *History of New York State Conference*, 162 (in Fredonia); Morley, *History of California State Society*, 123–25, 132–33, 252, 326 (in Berkeley, Pasadena, and San Francisco); Mrs. John A. Shellman, chapter paper, February 28, 1928, folder 2 (papers 1927–1938), box 2, DAR Papers St. Paul; and Mrs. Clyde E. Lewis, *History of Oregon Society*, 50–52 (Portland).

12. Wood, *History of the General Federation of Women's Clubs*, esp. 303–12.

13. Alice Day Marston to Julia C. Lathrop, November 27, 1914, Central File 4-0-1 (1914–1920), box 23, RG 102, U.S. Department of Labor, Records of the Children's Bureau, NARA, College Park, Md. (quotation). Of my own sample of

661 DAR members born before 1900 with other known club affiliations, only 89 (13.5 percent) expressed support for progressive reforms in those additional affiliations. These women were suffragists, settlement house volunteers or benefactors, state and national leaders in the GFWC, WCTU members, advocates of the social purity movement ("rescuing" unwed mothers or promoting reforms in marriage and divorce laws), or workers in the Americanization of immigrants in capacities other than within the DAR. Morgan, " 'Home and Country,' " 549–66. Also commenting on the presence of less activist women in the DAR are Lockwood and Ragan, *Story of the Records D.A.R.*, 34–35; and Malvina S. Waring, "A Year's Spinning," *AMM* 13 (September 1898): 216.

14. Deutsch, *Women and the City*, 136–218; Payne, *Reform, Labor, and Feminism*; Sklar, *Florence Kelley and the Nation's Work*. The Indiana Federation of Women's Clubs' Committee on Industrial and Child Labor was, as of 1906, enjoining local clubs to study the conditions of wage-earning women "and then assist in improving them." Courtney and Balz, *History: Indiana Federation of Clubs*, 163. Regarding the DAR's antiradicalism, see "Editor's Note-Book," *AMM* 1 (August 1892): 188–89 (on the Homestead, Pennsylvania, steelworkers' strike); Cornelia Grey Lunt, "Address," *AMM* 5 (September 1894): 237–40 (on the railroad workers' strike based in Pullman, Illinois); *DARPCC* 23 (1914): 1168–69 (regarding attacks on strikebreakers during a copper workers' strike in Calumet, Michigan). One exception to this pattern was a DAR chapter leader named Alice Skillman Boswell Morrison. In 1908 she married Frank Morrison, a Washington lawyer and a national secretary of the American Federation of Labor. Mrs. Arturo Y. Casanova and Mrs. Z. Lewis Dalby, comps., "State History, District of Columbia Daughters of the American Revolution, in Three Volumes," typescript, 1934, 1:5, in Office of the Historian General, NSDAR Headquarters, Washington, D.C.

15. These publications were translated into common immigrant languages. The 1910 *Guide* was a collaboration between Buel and the lecturer John Foster Carr. "President McKinley," *AMM* 19 (October 1901): 445; Mouat, *Connecticut State History*, 38–41; Carr, *Guide for the Immigrant Italian*, 40–41; Carr, *Guide to the United States for the Jewish Immigrant*, 41–43; *Manual of the United States for the Information of Immigrants*.

16. *DARPCC* 23 (1914): 1168–69; Gerstle, *American Crucible*, 65–72. A woman performing Americanization work in Cleveland lamented immigrant boys' "closed minds on the open shop and other industrial problems. They had heard only one side as their fathers all belong to the unions." Duff, *Making of Americans*, 15–16, copy in WRHS.

17. Charlotte Emerson Main, "Patriotism in Civil Service Reform," *AMM* 33 (August 1908): 428–30.

18. U.S. Senate, *Report of the Daughters of the American Revolution, 1890 to 1897*, 60–61 (Americanization projects in Evanston, Bloomington, and Highland Park, Ill.); *History of the Massachusetts Daughters of the American Revolution*, 134–36; Morley, *History of California State Society*, 108.

19. From the 1850s to 1922, married women were ineligible for independent naturalization; they became citizens when their husbands did. DAR Americanizers also funded patriotic lectures on U.S. history, often having them translated into common European languages. Bredbenner, *Nationality of Her Own*, 45–112; "Proceedings of the Seventh Continental Congress," *AMM* 12 (April 1898): 425; "Proceedings of the Seventh Continental Congress," *AMM* 12 (May 1898): 963–65; Warren, *History of the Massachusetts Daughters of the American Revolution*, 344–45; Canton (Ohio) Chapter DAR, DAR Americanization Reports; *Iowa Daughters of the American Revolution, Annual Conference* 26 (1925): 44–45; "Work of the Chapters," *DARM* 63 (April 1929): 228. On WRC Americanization work (justified on the grounds of the participation of "foreign-born citizens" in the "War of the Rebellion" and, in the West, extended to non-Europeans), see *Journal of the Thirty-Eighth National Convention of the Woman's Relief Corps* (1920), 290 (quotations), 291–305; and *Journal of the Fortieth National Convention of the Woman's Relief Corps* (1922), 175, 200.

20. The Boston-based, all-male Immigration Restriction League (formed in 1894) stated to Congress in 1911 that "[t]here is no reason to suppose that a change of location will result in a change of inborn tendencies" toward crime and illiteracy. U.S. Immigration Commission, *Statements and Recommendations Submitted by Societies and Organizations Interested in the Subject of Immigration*, 107 (quotation); Solomon, *Ancestors and Immigrants*; Jacobson, *Whiteness of a Different Color*, 39–90.

21. Sánchez, *Becoming Mexican American*, 95, 100; Rex et al., *History of the Kansas State Daughters of the American Revolution*, 62, 81; Wood, *History and Register, Idaho State Society*, 44, 58, 61; Morley, *History of California State Society*, 332–33, 339, 350–52; Clark, *Arizona State History*, 49–50, 82; *Report of the Twenty-Fourth Annual State Conference, Texas Daughters of the American Revolution* (1924), 115; *DARPCC* 23 (1914): 930. I have found no mention of DAR work among African or African-descended immigrants.

22. Newman, *White Women's Rights*, esp. 7–8, 11–14.

23. Carrie Peables Cushman, "The Girl Home-Makers," *DARM* 61 (February 1927): 131. Especially insightful on the racial dimensions of Europeans' Americanization is Rogin, *Blackface, White Noise*.

24. See especially Sallee, "Inventing 'the Forgotten Child.'"

25. Thomas, *New Woman in Alabama*, 99; "Notes of the Sixteenth Congress," *AMM* 30 (May 1907): 456; "Proceedings of the Sixteenth Continental Congress," *AMM* 31 (August 1907): 443–45; "Proceedings of the Seventeenth Continental Congress," *AMM* 32 (May 1908): 543–44; Edwards, *Angels in the Machinery*; Gustafson, *Women and the Republican Party*, 61–89.

26. *DARPCC* 21 (1912): 869–72; "Work of the Chapters," *AMM* 32 (April 1908): 481–82; Estelle Mockey Head, report of the tenth annual state conference, November 10–11, 1909, secretary's book, 1906–1910 (vol. 2), p. 48, DAR Collection Missouri.

27. "State Conferences," *AMM* 30 (February 1907): 116; "Compulsory Education," *Atlanta Constitution Woman's Edition*, 1914, clipping in Mrs. Howard McCall, comp., scrapbook, vol. 1 (1902–1903), and McCall, state regent's letter to chapter regents, September 1, 1916, in McCall, comp., scrapbook, vol. 4 (1916–1950), Papers of Mrs. D. Miller Cox, AHC; "Newspaper articles and other activities of Emma Garrett Boyd," scrapbook (1900s–1910s), box 13, Garrett/Boyd Papers, AHC; *Proceedings of the Twelfth State Conference of the Daughters of the American Revolution in Mississippi* (1917), 43, 70; Muncy, *Creating a Female Dominion*, 59; Lindenmeyer, *"A Right to Childhood,"* 18, 33, 41, 61; Skocpol, *Protecting Soldiers and Mothers*, 488–90; *Iowa Daughters of the American Revolution, Annual Conference* 10 (1909): 28–29; "Muskegon D.A.R. Takes Up Fight on Behalf of Anti Child Labor Bill," n.d. [1916], unidentified clipping in Muskegon (Mich.) Chapter DAR scrapbook of chapter activities, vol. 1 (1910–1929), p. 159, box 34, DAR Papers Michigan; *DARM* 48 (1916): 187–88.

28. *DARPCC* 21 (1912): 15.

29. *DARPCC* 22 (1913): 692, 776; Hall et al., *Like a Family*, 9–10, 52, 56; Edmonds, *Historical Perspective*, 1, 47.

30. Mrs. Edward L. Harris in *DARPCC* 23 (1914): 245–46.

31. Della Graeme Smallwood in ibid., 251; "D.A.R. in the District of Columbia," *AMM* 32 (March 1908): 214–15.

32. Martha S. Gielow, "Southern Industrial Education," *CV* 14 (March 1906): 114; Mrs. D. A. S. Vaught (née Bayme), "Annual Convention of Louisiana Division," *CV* 14 (October 1906): 438. One of many examples of the UDC's specifying scholarships for "lineal" Confederate descendants (in this case, at Buford College in Nashville) is in "Daughters of the Confederacy at Monteagle," *CV* 16 (September 1908): 474. The UDC directed its scholarships and prizes to white Confederate descendants in part because of a 1908 controversy at Columbia University's Teachers College in New York. A panel of professors awarded a UDC essay prize to a Minnesotan critical of Robert E. Lee. Cox, *Dixie's Daughters*, 112–16; "Mrs. Livingston Rowe Schuyler, President General U.D.C.," *CV* 30 (January 1922): 4.

33. "To the United Daughters of the Confederacy: Replying to Mrs. Lizzie George Henderson's Letter of May 1906," circular, n.d., quoted in Cox, *Dixie's Daughters*, 88. The UDC's Georgia Division was exceptional in giving money to the Rabun Gap Industrial School in that state. Foster, *Ghosts of the Confederacy*, 173.

34. The WRC began its work among mountain people in 1912 by funding scholarships at Lincoln Memorial University in Tennessee and at Berea College in Kentucky (which had recently restricted admission to whites only). The project continued throughout the 1920s. Gaines, *Uplifting the Race*, 73–74; *Journal of the Thirtieth National Convention of the Woman's Relief Corps* (1912), 80–82, 355; *Journal of the Forty-Second National Convention of the National Woman's Relief Corps* (1924), 347; *Journal of the Forty-Fourth Convention of the National Woman's Relief Corps* (1926), 224.

35. The NACW had first created its Suffrage Department in 1904. *Fourth Convention of the National Association of Colored Women* (n.p., 1904), 29, in *NACW Records, Part 1*, reel 1, frame 00293; Salem, *To Better Our World*, 105.

36. Mary Church Terrell, "The Justice of Woman Suffrage," and Adella Hunt Logan, "Colored Women as Voters," *Crisis* 4 (September 1912): 243–45; Coralie Franklin Cook and Carrie W. Clifford, "Votes for Women," *Crisis* 10 (August 1915): 184–85 (quotations); Hendricks, *Gender, Race, and Politics in the Midwest*, 72–74; White, *Too Heavy a Load*, 48–49; Addams, "Why Women Should Vote."

37. "Wifehood and Motherhood: Woman's Greatest Profession," *NAN* 15 (February 1912): 4–5, in *NACW Records, Part 1*, reel 23, frames 00497–98.

38. Margaret Washington, "National Association of Colored Women's Clubs," *NAN* 16 (June 1913): 7 (quotation), in *NACW Records, Part 1*, reel 23, frame 00523; "Personals," *NAN* 19 (January 1917): 11, in *NACW Records, Part 1*, reel 23, frame 00694; White, *Too Heavy a Load*, 83; McHenry, *Forgotten Readers*, 366–67 n. 64.

39. The gag rule covered controversial topics relating to "religion, politics and prohibition." On the April 18, 1914, rule see *DARM* 64 (June 1930): 360.

40. *NAW*, 3:537–538; Elizabeth Cady Stanton, "Christmas on the Mayflower," *AMM* 5 (December 1894): 584–86; Graham, *Woman Suffrage and the New Democracy*, 44.

41. "Address by Mrs. Julia Ward Howe," *AMM* 4 (January 1894): 1–5; "Proceedings of the Seventh Continental Congress," *AMM* 12 (April 1898): 349; "Proceedings of the Eighth Continental Congress," *AMM* 14 (April 1899): 601.

42. Marshall, *Splintered Sisterhood*, 47–49 (quotation on p. 49), 199, 252 n. 123.

43. Lebsock, "Woman Suffrage and White Supremacy," 69–76; Green, *Southern Strategies*, 87–98; Simpson, *Edith D. Pope and Her Nashville Friends*, 131.

44. Alexander, *Mormonism in Transition*, 60–68, 71–72; "Mormon Effrontery," *VN* 1 (April 1904): 129; *VN* 1 (May 1904): 176; Josephine B. Bruce, "The Afterglow of the Women's Convention," *VN* 1 (November 1904): 543; Davies, *Patriotism on Parade*, 307–8; "The Utah Delegate Wanted to Unseat Senator Smoot," *CV* 13 (December 1905): 535–36.

45. Davies, *Patriotism on Parade*, 308; LaGanke, "National Society of the Daughters of the American Revolution," 123; "Notes on the Congress," *AMM* 24 (May 1904): 471; Alexander, *Mormonism in Transition*, x–xi, 16–18, 241; "Proceedings of the Fifteenth Continental Congress," *AMM* 28 (June 1906): 706.

46. "Resolutions Passed by the St. Paul Chapter Daughters of the American Revolution," typescript, September 20, 1899, folder 6, box 1, DAR Papers St. Paul.

47. Clarissa S. Williams was president in the 1920s of the Relief Society, the principal women's auxiliary of the Latter-Day Saints church. By then she also belonged to the DAR. Alexander, *Mormonism in Transition*, 72, 128–34, 340 n. 6; Derr, "'Strength in Our Union,'" 181.

48. Newman, *White Women's Rights*, 36–42.

49. Caroline Menzies Murphy in Cincinnati Chapter DAR, DAR Americanization Reports. In 1900 Murphy organized in Cincinnati the first of numerous, DAR-supervised clubs of immigrant and poor native-born children (in contrast to the hereditary Children of the American Revolution, formed in 1895). The clubs were known variously as Children of the Republic, Sons of the Republic, and Daughters of the Republic clubs. See also Mary P. Jenney, "Children of the Republic," *AMM* 19 (December 1901): 586–88.

50. "D.A.R. Doing Much to Aid Boys, Youths; Unique Club at Menominee Virtually Puts Juvenile Court Out of Business," October 1, 1924, unidentified clipping in scrapbook of Menominee Chapter DAR activities, vol. 1 (1910–1929), p. 143, box 34, DAR Papers Michigan; Mrs. James H. McDonald, "Michigan," DAR National Publicity Committee Bulletin, April 1934, clipping in scrapbook of state and chapter activities, vol. 2 (1933–1936), box 34, DAR Papers Michigan. For instructive contrasts, see Hoxie, *Final Promise*; and Wexler, *Tender Violence*, 106–26.

51. Duff, *Making of Americans*, 23.

52. Katzman, *Seven Days a Week*, 53, 228, 241–43; Tax, *Rising of the Women*, 234–36; *Proceedings of the Thirteenth Ohio State Conference of the Daughters of the American Revolution* (1911), 78–80 (Neff quotation).

53. Carrie Peables Cushman, "The Girl Home-Makers," *DARM* 61 (February 1927): 130–31.

54. "As women and patriots, I think our greatest care should be our foreign-born sisters . . . to realize our standards of living, and to know and love the best in America. For the women, of course, in their homes determine the ideals of our (potential) citizens." Alice Louise McDuffee, "Report of Chairman of the Americanization of Foreign-Born Men and Women" (1916), p. 3, in State Chairmen Reports, vol. 1 (A–G), box 8, DAR Papers Michigan. For DAR Americanization projects among women in general, see also Menges, *History of New York State Conference*, 330; Gullett, "Women Progressives and the Politics of Americanization in California," 79–82, 86, 89; Raftery, "Progressivism Moves into the Schools," 100; and Seller, "Education of the Immigrant Woman," 309–10.

55. *History of the Massachusetts Daughters of the American Revolution*, 133; "Work of the Chapters," *AMM* 29 (July 1906): 22. A southern exception was the chapter in San Antonio, Texas, headed by the Indiana-born suffrage leader Mary Eleanor Brackenridge. In 1907 the women reported contributing to the San Antonio Industrial School for Colored Girls. "Work of the Chapters," *AMM* 30 (February 1907): 127–28; Baker, *Texas State History*, 216; Hall, *Revolt against Chivalry*, 24.

56. Abbie Williams R. Boyle in *Proceedings of the Fifteenth Ohio State Conference of the Daughters of the American Revolution* (1913), 65–66.

57. The black club leaders and educators Mary Church Terrell, Anna Julia Cooper, Frances Jackson Coppin, Mary Burnett Talbert, Judith Horton Carter, and Nettie Langston Napier all attended or graduated from Oberlin, as did the NAACP organizer and later communist Shirley Graham Du Bois. Jones, *Quest for Equality*, 12; Mary Helen Washington, "Introduction," in Cooper, *Voice from the South*,

xxxiii; Brown, *Homespun Heroines*, 119–26; *WE* 3 (October–November 1896): 8; Harlan et al., *Booker T. Washington Papers*, 8:321; "Men of the Month," *Crisis* 15 (April 1918): 279; Davis, *Lifting as They Climb*, 222–24; Horne, *Race Woman*.

58. White, *Too Heavy a Load*, 36–43, 64–66, 110–41; Wolcott, *Remaking Respectability*, 8–9. Also see Schechter, *Ida B. Wells-Barnett and American Reform*, 121–68, 247–53; and Brown, "Negotiating and Transforming the Public Sphere," 48–49.

59. Salem, *To Better Our World*, 146–47; Gaines, *Uplifting the Race*, 63.

60. Hendricks, *Gender, Race, and Politics in the Midwest*, 63–70; Wells-Barnett, *Crusade for Justice*, 321–28; "The N.A.A.C.P.," *Crisis* 1 (November 1910): 12; Mary White Ovington, "How the National Association for the Advancement of Colored People Began," *Crisis* 8 (August 1914): 184.

61. "National Association for the Advancement of Colored People: Sixth Annual Report, 1915," *Crisis* 11 (March 1916): 245; Salem, *To Better Our World*, 151–52, 155, 158–59; Hine and Thompson, *Shining Thread of Hope*, 199–200.

62. "National Association for the Advancement of Colored People," *Crisis* 7 (January 1914): 139 (an announcement of the creation of the NAACP's Legal Bureau).

63. Salem, *To Better Our World*, 147; Carrie W. Clifford, "The Great American Question," *CAM* 12 (May 1907): 364–73 (quotation on p. 371); "A Founder Dies," *Crisis* 42 (January 1935): 26.

64. "The Women's Committee," *Crisis* 5 (March 1913): 238.

65. Salem, *To Better Our World*, 128.

66. "The Nominating Committee," *Crisis* 19 (December 1919): 73. On Talbert's early prominence in the NAACP, see Salem, *To Better Our World*, 155, 159. The NAACP's first General Committee in 1910 included such important black women as Mary Church Terrell and Ida B. Wells-Barnett. Yet in the organization's first years, the top women in the NAACP were white. The four women on the board of directors in March 1916 were the white reformers Jane Addams, Mary White Ovington, Florence Kelley, and Lillian Wald. The other twenty-six directors were men. Salem, *To Better Our World*, 148–49; "Board of Directors," *Crisis* 11 (March 1916): 264.

67. "How to Keep Women at Home," *CAM* 14 (January 1908): 7–8; Cleveland, "Woman's Mission and Woman's Clubs."

68. Du Bois, *Efforts for Social Betterment among Negro Americans*; Hendricks, *Gender, Race, and Politics in the Midwest*, 71–74; "Votes for Women," *Crisis* 4 (September 1912): 236; "A Woman's Suffrage Symposium," *Crisis* 4 (September 1912): 240–47; "Votes for Women," *Crisis* 10 (August 1915): 184–85.

69. Carby, *Race Men*, 30–41.

70. Many black clubwomen, including Ida B. Wells-Barnett, lavishly praised *Souls of Black Folk*. Salem, *To Better Our World*, 150; Thompson, *Ida B. Wells-Barnett*, 255–60; Josephine Silone Yates, "The Twentieth Century Negro—His Opportunities for Success," *CAM* 11 (October 1906): 239.

71. Lyons quoted in Brown, *Homespun Heroines*, 61; Mather, *Who's Who of the Colored Race*, 182.

72. Cromwell fought in the battles of Trenton, Princeton, and Monmouth. This

account does not name the women's club that proposed the monument. "Social Uplift," *Crisis* 8 (July 1914): 113; W. T. Freeman, "Oliver Cromwell," *Crisis* 10 (May 1915): 42–43.

73. "Social Uplift," *Crisis* 8 (September 1914): 216.

74. NSDAR Committee on Patriotic Education circular, November 10, 1909, miscellaneous correspondence (1899–1939), box 10, David Reese Chapter DAR (Oxford, Miss.) materials, DAR Collection Mississippi; Mrs. Charles F. Starr, "An Opportunity for the Daughters of the American Revolution," *AMM* 24 (June 1904): 505; *Proceedings of the Twelfth State Conference of the Daughters of the American Revolution in Mississippi* (1917), 44–45.

75. Cox, *Dixie's Daughters*, 73–83.

76. Ibid., 35. See also Simpson, *Edith D. Pope and Her Nashville Friends*, 138–42. Best known as a pioneering legislator, Rebecca Latimer Felton of Georgia meshed identities as an outspoken progressive and as a white Daughter, of both the Confederacy and the American Revolution. Whites, "Rebecca Latimer Felton and the Problem of 'Protection' in the New South"; Cox, *Dixie's Daughters*, 37; Dolores Boisfeuillet Colquitt, "America's First Woman Senator a Member of the D.A.R.," *DARM* 56 (December 1922): 723–24.

77. Mrs. T. J. Latham, "Evolution of the Women of the South," *CV* 11 (May 1903): 217–18 (quotation on p. 218).

78. Nellie Nugent Somerville, presidential address at the First Mississippi Woman's Suffrage Convention, March 28, 1898, folder 36, and Lucy Somerville Howorth, "Nellie Nugent Somerville," n.d. [1952], folder 19, both reel C4, series II, M-133, Somerville and Howorth Family Papers, SL. Having cofounded the DAR, Mary Desha also combined ardent woman suffragism with neo-Confederate work: she helped to organize a UDC chapter in Washington, D.C. *Minutes of the Thirteenth Annual Convention of the United Daughters of the Confederacy* (1907), 238; "Organized New Chapter," *Washington Post*, May 20, 1905, clipping in folder "Daughters of the American Revolution, 1894–1899," box 822, Mary Desha Papers, LC. On differences over woman suffrage within the UDC, see Parrott, "'Love Makes Memory Eternal,'" 230–31; Hale, "'Some Women Have Never Been Reconstructed,'" 179–80; Brundage, "White Women and the Politics of Historical Memory," 129–30; and Simpson, *Edith D. Pope and Her Nashville Friends*, 131–32. Green, *Southern Strategies*, 71–72, argues that UDC members stood mostly against female suffrage.

79. "Important Meeting of Legislative Committee, U.D.C.," *Our Heritage* 6 (March 1913): 7; Clinton, *Tara Revisited*, 184–85.

80. Maggie Stone, "Memorial to Women of the Confederacy," *CV* 22 (August 1914): 348–49; Tomes, *Gospel of Germs*, 180–81.

81. "The Utah Delegate Wanted to Unseat Senator Smoot," *CV* 13 (December 1905): 535–36.

82. "The Heart of the South," *CV* 23 (February 1915): 56.

83. Mrs. Thomas M. Long in *Minutes of the Thirteenth Annual Convention of the United Daughters of the Confederacy* (1907), 209.

84. Miss A. E. Caruthers and Mrs. John W. Tench (quotation) in "Convention Florida Division, U.D.C.," *CV* 14 (July 1906): 314.

85. Mrs. N. D. Goodwin, "The Ku Klux Klan," *Our Heritage* 8 (November 1917): 6; Cox, *Dixie's Daughters*, 107–10. On the pamphlet's fund-raising success, see *CV* 17 (September 1909): 476; "The Ku-Klux Klan," *CV* 22 (August 1914): 380; *CV* 19 (March 1911): 108; and "Worthy U.D.C. Worker in Mississippi," *CV* 21 (November 1913): 518.

86. Virginia Redditt Price, "President's Letter for February," *Our Heritage* 7 (February 1917): 1.

87. "Daughters of the Confederacy Criticised [*sic*]," *CV* 10 (January 1902): 3–4; Cox, *Dixie's Daughters*, 144. Similarly, a Missouri native reported that when she was organizing a UDC chapter in Minnesota, she was asked, "What are you—a lot of organized anarchists?" Mrs. Joseph Johnson (née Shaw), "Confederate Daughters in Minnesota," *CV* 17 (April 1909): 161.

88. Mildred Lewis Rutherford of Georgia, national historian of the UDC in the 1910s, located white southern women's comparatively deeper dedication to commemorating the Confederate cause in the history of Reconstruction, when men had to take loyalty oaths and women did not. Mildred Lewis Rutherford, "Confederate Monuments and Cemeteries," *CV* 11 (January 1903): 17–18; Hale, "'Some Women Have Never Been Reconstructed,'" 183.

89. Anna Carolina Benning, "Review of Histories Used in Southern Schools and Southern Homes," *CV* 10 (December 1902): 550.

90. Silber, *Romance of Reunion*, esp. 9, 13–38, 196; Mills, "Gratitude and Gender Wars," 184–85.

91. Obituary of Louisa Cresap Patterson in "The Last Roll," *CV* 8 (March 1900): 131–32 (a Marylander whose Congressman father had been close friends with John C. Calhoun); "The Last Roll," *CV* 20 (October 1912): 486–87.

92. The monument was finally unveiled in Nashville in 1926, with a different design. Cunningham in "Monument to Confederate Women," *CV* 17 (April 1909): 152; *CV* 17 (July 1909): 316; Foster, *Ghosts of the Confederacy*, 177–78; Mills, "Gratitude and Gender Wars"; Simpson, *Edith D. Pope and Her Nashville Friends*, 100–101. After Cunningham died in 1913, his longtime secretary, Edith Drake Pope of Nashville, became the editor of the *Confederate Veteran*. The periodical then accepted women's pro-Confederate activism to the point of resembling "an associational newsletter" for the UDC. Simpson, *Edith D. Pope and Her Nashville Friends*, 57 (quotation), 62–63.

93. Vardaman quoted in Kachun, "Faith That the Dark Past Has Taught Us," 234.

94. O'Leary, *To Die For*, 89; "The Branches," *Crisis* 9 (April 1915): 300, 302.

95. Muncy, *Creating a Female Dominion*, 90.

96. O'Leary, *To Die For*, 205; Blight, *Race and Reunion*, 383–87; "Gettysburg, Gettysburg," *CV* 21 (August 1913): 377–86. For black clubwomen's reactions to segregation in the federal government, see *Minutes of the Ninth Biennial Convention of the National Association of Colored Women* (n.p., 1914), 39, 41, 43, in *NACW Records, Part 1*, reel 1, frames 00426–00428.

97. Wilson, *History of the American People*, vols. 4–5; Litwack, "Birth of a Nation."

98. Mrs. Jesse Drew Beale in "The New York Division," *CV* 25 (January 1917): 38. The feelings were mutual: Dixon told the North Carolina Division in 1910 that the UDC was "the guardian of the breed of men who showed the world how to die for what is right." Quoted in Johnson, "'This Wonderful Dream Nation!'" 113.

99. "Fighting Race Calumny," *Crisis* 10 (May 1915): 40–42; "Four Hundred Delegates Attend National Asso. of Colored Women," *Baltimore Afro-American*, August 12, 1916, clipping in *NACW Records, Part 1*, reel 5, frame 00731; *Minutes of the Eleventh Biennial Convention of the National Association of Colored Women* (n.p., 1918), 41, in *NACW Records, Part 1*, reel 1, frame 00522; "The Ohio Division," *CV* 25 (April 1917): 179; McHenry, *Forgotten Readers*, 178–79.

100. Pauline E. Hopkins, "Famous Women of the Negro Race. VII. Educators (Continued)," *CAM* 5 (June 1902): 127; Salem, *To Better Our World*, 153; *WE* 1 (May 1, 1894): 4; "The N.A.A.C.P.," *Crisis* 1 (November 1910): 12; Brown, *Homespun Heroines*, 186–87 (quotations).

101. Rogin, *Blackface, White Noise*; Hale, *Making Whiteness*, 121–97.

Chapter Four

1. Carrie W. Clifford, "National Association for the Advancement of Colored People: Our Children," *Crisis* 14 (October 1917): 306 (quotations); "A Founder Dies," *Crisis* 42 (January 1935): 26.

2. *Minutes of the Thirteenth Biennial Convention of the National Association of Colored Women* (n.p., 1922), 46–47, 85–86, in *NACW Records, Part 1*, reel 1, frames 00656, 00674–75. The home was administered by the NACW's offshoot, the National Council of Negro Women, after 1935. In 1963 control transferred to the U.S. National Park Service.

3. Neverdon-Morton, *Afro-American Women of the South*, 133–34; *Minutes of the Twelfth Biennial of the National Association of Colored Women* (n.p., 1920), 55, in *NACW Records, Part 1*, reel 1, frame 00620. Some black women did continue to value social service work over commemoration, dichotomizing the two. A Raynham, Massachusetts, woman recommended that her family's "old homestead, built about 1800 . . . be bought by the town for a home for the aged," instead of being set aside as a historically significant property. Anna J. Gilmore in "Social Uplift," *Crisis* 11 (November 1915): 8.

4. Giddings, *When and Where I Enter*, 138–39 (quotation); Ruffins, "'Lifting as We Climb,'" 376–77; Davis, *Lifting as They Climb*, 58–59, 78–82; Mary B. Tal-

bert, "Letter from Our National President," *NAN* 19 (January 1917): 5, in *NACW Records, Part 1*, reel 23, frame 00688. Giddings gives the total figure of $30,000 raised to restore the house and grounds, but two other sources tell of a total of $15,000: Neverdon-Morton, *Afro-American Women of the South*, 195; and Mary B. Talbert, "The Frederick Douglass Home," *Crisis* 13 (February 1917), 175.

5. Davis, *Lifting as They Climb*, 80–81.

6. "Confederate Dead at Fredericksburg," *CV* 4 (July 1896): 230; folder "Columbian Liberty Bell Committee, 1892–1893," box 821, Mary Desha Papers, LC; Savage, *Standing Soldiers, Kneeling Slaves*, 6–7, 210; Neverdon-Morton, *Afro-American Women of the South*, 195.

7. U.S. Senate, *Third Report of the National Society of the Daughters of the American Revolution*, 300–305; Mary B. Talbert, "Concerning the Frederick Douglass Memorial," *Crisis* 14 (August 1917): 167–68 (first quotation); Talbert, "State Presidents—Take Notice," *NAN* 24 (January–March 1922): 3 (second quotation), in *NACW Records, Part 1*, reel 23, frames 00825–27.

8. "The Douglass Home," *Crisis* 15 (February 1918): 164; Goggin, *Carter G. Woodson*, 83.

9. The rest were NACW stalwarts. *NAN* 21 (February–May 1919): 8, in *NACW Records, Part 1*, reel 23, frame 00788.

10. "Club Notes," *NAN* 24 (January–March 1922): 5, in *NACW Records, Part 1*, reel 23, frame 00827; "Necrology," *CAM* 12 (April 1907): 250.

11. See especially Smith, *Gender of History*, 103–56; and Des Jardins, *Women and the Historical Enterprise in America*, 30–51, 145–76. Anne Ruggles Gere describes a similarly gendered form of professionalization (replete with attacks on clubwomen) regarding literary studies in *Intimate Practices*, 208–47.

12. *DARPCC* 28 (1919): 11–13; Rex et al., *History of the Kansas State Daughters of the American Revolution*, 7–9; "New Head of D.A.R. is 'Born Leader,'" n.d. [April 1917], and "Our President General," n.d. [April 1917], unidentified clippings in Mrs. Howard McCall, comp., scrapbook, vol. 4 (1916–1918), Papers of Mrs. D. Miller Cox, AHC.

13. Canton (Ohio) Chapter DAR, DAR Americanization Reports.

14. *DARPCC* 27 (1918): 100–102; *Report of the Publicity Director of the War Relief Service Committee*, 13.

15. *Iowa Daughters of the American Revolution, Annual Conference* 20 (1919): 64.

16. Blair, "Reburying Caesar, with Plenty of Praise."

17. Copy of memorandum, Brig. Gen. Lytle Brown to the Chief of Staff, "Resolutions adopted by the Daughters of the American Revolution," May 16, 1918, War College Division file 8580-95, box 320, RG 165, U.S. Department of War, War College Division General Correspondence (1903–1919), NARA, Washington, D.C.

18. These reforms became law in 1922. *DARPCC* 29 (1920): 69; *Journal of the Thirty-Eighth National Convention of the Woman's Relief Corps* (1920), 291, 322.

19. *DARPCC* 29 (1920): 69; O'Leary, *To Die For*, 79.

20. Susan Zeiger counts at least 16,500 women who served overseas under U.S.

military auspices, both as members of the army and as civilian employees. Twelve thousand more served within the United States. Zeiger, *In Uncle Sam's Service*, 2, 27, 31–32, 36.

21. *DARPCC* 27 (1918): 100–102; *Report of the Publicity Director of the War Relief Service Committee*, 13 (quotation).

22. See especially Graham, *Woman Suffrage and the New Democracy*, 33–127; and Fowler, "Carrie Chapman Catt, Strategist."

23. Goldman, *Women, the State, and Revolution*. DAR chapters in the Philippines and China sent reading materials, garments, and hospital supplies to U.S. troops in Siberia who were covertly assisting anti-Bolshevik forces in the Russian Civil War. Russell, *Daughters Overseas*, 11.

24. Kennedy, *Disloyal Mothers and Scurrilous Citizens*; *DARPCC* 29 (1920): 11–12.

25. Hickel, "Entitling Citizens," esp. 10–56.

26. *DARPCC* 27 (1918): 43.

27. Kennedy, *Over Here*, 45–92; Vaughn, *Holding Fast the Inner Lines*.

28. Anne Rogers Minor, "A Message from the President General," *DARM* 57 (January 1923): 16.

29. DeBenedetti, *Peace Reform in American History*, 108–16; Steinson, *American Women's Activism in World War I*, 1–2; Jensen, "Minerva on the Field of Mars," and Jensen, "Women, Citizenship, and Civic Sacrifice."

30. "Proceedings of the Fifteenth Continental Congress," *AMM* 28 (May 1906): 416; "Proceedings of the Sixteenth Continental Congress," *AMM* 30 (June 1907): 694–95. Cox, *Dixie's Daughters*, 149–50, shows similar activities by the UDC. On the WRC's peace activism, see *Journal of the Twenty-First National Convention of the Woman's Relief Corps* (1903), 185, 426, 434; and O'Leary, *To Die For*, 97.

31. *DARPCC* 22 (1913): 234.

32. "The Open Letter," *AMM* 19 (December 1901): 623 (first quotation); "Work of the Chapters," *AMM* 34 (June 1909): 616 (second quotation). An unnamed reader sent in the Tennyson excerpt to the DAR's magazine; I thank Denis Paz for identifying it. "For I dipt into the future, far as human eye could see, / Saw the vision of the world and all the wonder that would be; / Till the war drums throbb'd no longer and the battle flags were furl'd / In the Parliament of man, the Federation of the world."

33. "Proceedings of the Nineteenth Continental Congress," *AMM* 36 (May 1910): 499.

34. DeBenedetti, *Peace Reform in American History*, 82–83.

35. Menges, *History of New York State Conference*, 264; Leonard, *Woman's Who's Who of America*, 788; Alonso, *Peace as a Women's Issue*, 58–63; Steinson, *American Women's Activism in World War I*, 32–34.

36. Not all peace activists, not even all those in self-consciously international entities, repudiated nationalism. On the complicated relationship between nationalism and internationalism in this connection, see Rupp, *Worlds of Women*, 107–29.

37. "Ready Reference D.A.R. Chronology: Arranged from the Records," *DARM* 59 (October 1925): 622; Gilbert, *First World War*, 157.

38. The DAR also sent a large delegation to the first Women's National Defense Conference, held in Washington in November 1915. Steinson, *American Women's Activism in World War I*, 175–76, 182, 185.

39. Projects included contributing over $42,000 to rebuilding a French village and almost $138,000 to support French war orphans. *DARPCC* 27 (1918): 94–96; *Report of the Publicity Director of the War Relief Service Committee*, 7–8.

40. For his utterances against the draft in 1917, for example, the Indiana-born socialist leader Eugene V. Debs spent nearly five years in federal prison for violating the Espionage Act. The suffragists of the National Woman's Party were arrested instead for obstructing traffic and received sentences of a few months, with the exception of Alice Paul who was jailed longer. Kennedy, *Over Here*, 26, 80, 85–86; Ford, "Alice Paul and the Triumph of Militancy," 284–86, 288.

41. *DARPCC* 27 (1918): 9–10.

42. Kennedy, *Over Here*, 82–84, 87; Higham, *Strangers in the Land*, 247–48; Capozzola, "Only Badge Needed Is Your Patriotic Fervor"; Wall, *Iowa*, 173. The 1918 Oregon state conference of the DAR was one of many that endorsed the banning of German instruction in public schools and "strict regulations . . . on the conduct and speech of enemy aliens." *DARPCC* 27 (1918): 493 (quotation); "Work of the Chapters," *DARM* 55 (November 1921): 658; *Journal of the Thirty-Eighth National Convention of the Woman's Relief Corps* (1920), 90, 94.

43. MacLean, *Behind the Mask of Chivalry*, 5; Cox, *Dixie's Daughters*, 171 n. 19. The DAR chapter in Port Gibson, Mississippi, also denounced the second Klan — "a menace to the peace and order of our political and social life" — on class grounds. Harriette A. Person in *Proceedings of the Eighteenth State Conference of the Mississippi Daughters of the American Revolution* (1923), 62.

44. Grace Meredith Newbill, "Birthplace of the Ku-Klux Klan," *CV* 25 (July 1917): 335–36.

45. MacLean, *Behind the Mask of Chivalry*, 5; Blee, *Women of the Klan*; "Division Notes," *CV* 29 (February 1921): 73 (quotation).

46. Kennedy, *Over Here*, 26–27, 75–78.

47. Amid the deportations of 1919, the wife of a former governor of Mississippi called on DAR women in the state to "use our influence to have the law so amended that it will not be difficult to . . . expel from our homes all who preach and teach seditious and anarchists [*sic*] doctrine, and disloyalty to the Government." This pattern is not absolute, however. At the 1920 national convention, it was an Alabamian who tried unsuccessfully to insert the word "voluntary" into a resolution endorsing universal military training for young men. *Proceedings of the Fifteenth State Conference of the Daughters of the American Revolution in Mississippi* (1920), 13; Mary Capers Enochs, meeting minutes of Ralph Humphreys Chapter (Jackson, Miss.) DAR, October 12, 1910, vol. 2 (1908–1911), pp. 63–65, box 2, DAR Papers Mississippi; *DARPCC* 29 (1920): 226–27.

48. With $42,000 of the $25 million in contributions, the UDC endowed a total of seventy hospital beds at a military hospital in France, each named "for a Confederate hero." "Twenty-Sixth Annual Convention, U.D.C.," *CV* 28 (January 1920): 34; Mary D. Carter, "The South as a National Asset," *CV* 26 (November 1918): 499; "From the President General," *CV* 27 (February 1919): 66; "Convention Notes," *CV* 27 (May 1919): 191; Cox, *Dixie's Daughters*, 155–57; Gardner, *Blood and Irony*, 214–19.

49. Mrs. A. A. Campbell (Susie S. Campbell), "The United Daughters of the Confederacy—Some of Their Aims and Accomplishments," *CV* 30 (March 1922): 87; "Hero Fund Scholarships," *CV* 30 (June 1922): 333.

50. "Twenty-Sixth Annual Convention, U.D.C.," *CV* 28 (January 1920): 34.

51. I draw this conclusion from the 1915 and 1916 issues of the *Confederate Veteran*. See in particular *CV* 24 (March 1916).

52. "Patriotic Action by Confederate Veterans," *CV* 24 (June 1916): 243; "Report of Birmingham Reunion, S.C.V.," *CV* 24 (July 1916): 324; Lloyd T. Everett, "S.C.V.—'Strictly Historical and Benevolent,'" *CV* 24 (September 1916): 426 (quotation).

53. "U.D.C. Convention in Dallas," *CV* 24 (December 1916): 532–33; Mrs. S. E. F. Rose, "Historian General's Page," *CV* 24 (December 1916): 535 (quotation). The suffix "general" in Rose's job title denotes her standing as a national leader in the organization and does not refer to military rank, real or emulated. The DAR also used "general" to denote its national officers.

54. Also in early 1917, Odenheimer was active in the Navy League's Woman's Committee, the same entity that Daisy Allen Story had helped organize and wanted all DAR members to join. "From the President General," *CV* 25 (March 1917): 122; "From the President General," *CV* 25 (April 1917): 178; "Maryland Division, U.D.C.," *CV* 17 (January 1909): 10; "From the President General," *CV* 24 (July 1916): 300.

55. The delegates vowed to pursue only war work, educational work, and benevolent work "for the needy men and women of the sixties." "From the President General," *CV* 25 (April 1917): 178–79; "Twenty-Fourth Annual Convention," *CV* 25 (December 1917): 568.

56. "From the President General," *CV* 25 (May 1917): 230 (first quotation); "From the President General," *CV* 25 (August 1917): 376–77 (second quotation on p. 377).

57. "From the President General," *CV* 26 (April 1918): 174.

58. Mrs. E. B. Burkheimer in "The North Carolina Division," *CV* 26 (May 1918): 224. The first state in the old Confederacy to pass a flag antidesecration law was Alabama in 1915—the thirty-fourth state to do so since the spate of such legislation began in 1897. Most other southern states passed flag protection laws during and after World War I, with Virginia's 1932 law as the country's last. The culturally southern states of Maryland and Missouri passed flag laws in 1902 and 1903, respectively. Neither had joined the Confederacy. Goldstein, *Saving "Old Glory,"* 41.

59. "From the President General," *CV* 26 (July 1918): 317.

60. In 1907 a DAR leader in Greenville, South Carolina, boasted that the chapter's celebration of Flag Day was "the first observance . . . so far as we know in the state." Litwicki, *America's Public Holidays*, 179–80; Mary Montague White, "Flag Day in Greenville, South Carolina," *AMM* 31 (November 1907): 721–25.

61. This story's veracity is doubtful because Louise Dalton of St. Louis reportedly belonged to the DAR, and the DAR would almost certainly have publicized the invention of Flag Day by one of its own. Instead, the DAR credited the SAR's Connecticut branch in 1890. "From the President General," *CV* 25 (May 1917): 230; L. Byrd Mock, "Founder of National Flag Day," *CV* 25 (May 1917): 237; "Honoring the Flag," *AMM* 20 (January 1902): 15.

62. It is unclear whether the women included black Tennesseans in their plan. Mrs. Thomas Polk and Birdie Askew Owen in "A Tribute to Our Boys," *CV* 26 (February 1918): 53.

63. "From the President General," *CV* 26 (April 1918): 175.

64. Edith E. T. Lessing, "The Texas Division," *CV* 25 (August 1917): 380.

65. Photograph in author's collection. The monument was still standing in 2004.

66. Carter was her chapter's historian. Mary D. Carter, "The South and the Flag," *Our Heritage* 8 (May 1918): 4 (quotations); Carter, "The South as a National Asset," *CV* 26 (November 1918): 499.

67. For example, the UDC's Washington State Division expressed enthusiastic support, in a 1921 resolution, for the disarmament conference that year in Washington, D.C. "Division Notes," *CV* 30 (March 1922): 114.

68. "The Reunion in Atlanta," *CV* 27 (November 1919): 406; "Twenty-Sixth Annual Convention, U.D.C.," *CV* 28 (January 1920): 34.

69. Mrs. A. A. Campbell, "Comparison and Appraisal," *CV* 31 (January 1923): 11.

70. Mary Hunter Southworth Kimbrough in "Marking the Jefferson Davis Highway," *CV* 35 (August 1927): 312. Kimbrough's full name and hometown are given in *CV* 38 (June 1930): 213.

71. Lebsock, "Woman Suffrage and White Supremacy," 75; Green, *Southern Strategies*, 78–100; Marshall, *Splintered Sisterhood*.

72. Mrs. A. A. Campbell, "A Chosen People," *CV* 29 (January 1921): 12.

73. Carita Owens Collins, "Be a Man!" quoted in Kerlin, *Voice of the Negro, 1919*, 185. The publication that originally featured Collins's poem is not identified.

74. Throughout the country, and throughout the war, the white press (such as the *New York Tribune* and Associated Press in April 1917) aired similar rumors. Mrs. William Henry Wait (Clara Hadley Wait), "The Enemy Within Our Gates," NSDAR War Relief Service Committee Bulletin no. 29, May 23, 1918, in Wait, "Appeals and War Bulletins" (typescript), 341–42, box 1, Papers of Clara Hadley Wait, MHC; Wait, "Report of State Regent, State Conference in 1918," in "Reports and Data of Sixth State Regent, Daughters of the American Revolution of Michigan" (typescript volume), 191, box 1, Papers of Clara Hadley Wait, MHC; Ellis, *Race, War, and Surveillance*, 5–9.

75. "Unconscious Insult," *Crisis* 16 (May 1918): 9–10.

76. A DAR woman boasted that the tablet "[proclaiming] the patriotism of the colored race" in Wadesboro, North Carolina, was "one of the very few memorials to the negro in the South." Elizabeth Divine Horn in "Work of the Chapters," *DARM* 61 (February 1927): 144; see also "Work of the Chapters," *DARM* 56 (August 1922): 465. The DAR was not the only entity to segregate names by race on World War I monuments. The U.S. Treasury Department initially did the same on a plaque listing employees "killed in the Great War." "The Horizon," *Crisis* 29 (January 1925): 124.

77. Locke, *New Negro*.

78. Thirty-six of every one hundred black men and twenty-five of every one hundred white men registered for the draft. Salem, *To Better Our World*, 223; Neverdon-Morton, *Afro-American Women of the South*, 218; Hunton and Johnson, *Two Colored Women with the American Expeditionary Forces*, 41–133.

79. Black men were organized into "sub-posts in each county under authority of local posts" as of 1919, and they were excluded from conventions as late as 1927. *Hot Springs (Ark.) Echo*, 1919, quoted in Kerlin, *Voice of the Negro, 1919*, 72; Pencak, *For God and Country*, 99; "The American Legion, Again," *Crisis* 19 (January 1920): 108; "Social Progress," *Crisis* 22 (August 1921): 182–93. The American Legion eventually developed a "states' rights policy" in which southerners maintained all-white departments and in which black northerners joined both integrated and all-black posts. Pencak, *For God and Country*, 68–69.

80. "Save," *Crisis* 16 (May 1918): 7; Moses, *Golden Age of Black Nationalism*, 227–28. On the controversy created by Du Bois's stance, see Jordan, " 'Damnable Dilemma' "; and Ellis, "W. E. B. Du Bois and the Formation of Black Opinion."

81. UDC leaders in Maryland and in Tennessee reported teaching home canning techniques and "thrift" to "colored" women. "From the President General," *CV* 25 (September 1917): 424–25.

82. Nellie Y. McKay, "Introduction," in Terrell, *Colored Woman in a White World*, xxv; *DARPCC* 25 (1916): 28; "Meetings," *Crisis* 16 (September 1918), 240; Dunbar-Nelson, "Negro Women in War Work," 391; Salem, *To Better Our World*, 214.

83. "Meetings," *Crisis* 14 (August 1917): 195; Hull, *Give Us Each Day*, 16; "Personal," *Crisis* 16 (October 1918): 296; Breen, "Black Women and the Great War"; "Club Reports," *NAN* 19 (April–May 1917): 11, in *NACW Records, Part 1*, reel 23, frame 00714; Hettie B. Tilghman, "California Notes," *NAN* 20 (October 1917): 7, in *NACW Records, Part 1*, reel 23, frame 00731.

84. Dunbar-Nelson, "Negro Women in War Work," 389.

85. McCluskey and Smith, *Mary McLeod Bethune*, 4; Mrs. M. F. Days, "Florida Federation of Colored Women's Clubs," *NAN* 20 (October 1917): 4, in *NACW Records, Part 1*, reel 23, frame 00728 (quotation). On a similar "patriotic address" by Bessie C. Jones of West Baden, Indiana, entitled "The Call of the Flag," see Elizabeth Lamar in "Club Reports," *NAN* 19 (April–May 1917): 13 (quotation), in *NACW Records, Part 1*, reel 23, frame 00716; and "Report of Indiana State Federation," *NAN* 20 (October 1917): 5 in *NACW Records, Part 1*, reel 23, frame 00729.

86. Mary Fitzbutler Waring in *NAN* 20 (April 1918): 5, in *NACW Records, Part 1*, reel 23, frame 00748.

87. Dunbar-Nelson, "Negro Women in War Work," 375.

88. Ibid., 394. Ellis, *Race, War, and Surveillance*, 16–17, 228–29, finds a range of opinions, including apathy and disillusionment, among African Americans at large throughout the war years.

89. Black women went overseas in capacities other than as nurses. Yet only three black women served in France, with the Young Men's Christian Association (YMCA), until April 1919, "when they were joined by a dozen or so others." Two dozen black nurses served at military installations within the United States, caring mostly for influenza victims. Hunton and Johnson, *Two Colored Women with the American Expeditionary Forces*; Salem, *To Better Our World*, 206; Zeiger, *In Uncle Sam's Service*, 28; Neverdon-Morton, *Afro-American Women of the South*, 64; Rief, "Thinking Globally, Acting Locally," 209–11.

90. Nettie Jackson in "The War," *Crisis* 17 (April 1919): 295.

91. Ruth L. Bennett in Mrs. S. L. Jackson, "Report of Pennsylvania State Federation of Negro Women's Clubs," *NAN* 20 (October 1917): 2, in *NACW Records, Part 1*, reel 23, frame 00726.

92. Moses, *Golden Age of Black Nationalism*, 227; Hendricks, *Gender, Race, and Politics in the Midwest*, 121–22; Salem, *To Better Our World*, 223 (quotations).

93. Other silent parades were held in Providence, Rhode Island, and Newark, New Jersey. "The Negro Silent Parade," *Crisis* 14 (September 1917): 241–44 (quotations on 241, 244); "Social Progress," *Crisis* 15 (December 1917): 88.

94. Pitre, *In Struggle against Jim Crow*, 17; Schneider, *"We Return Fighting,"* 218–20; "The Houston Horror," *Crisis* 15 (February 1918): 187; "National Association for the Advancement of Colored People," *Crisis* 27 (December 1923): 72–74; Salem, *To Better Our World*, 223. The NAACP later managed to reduce the life sentences; the last man was freed in 1938. "The Men of the 24th Infantry," *Crisis* 28 (July 1924): 133; Walter Wilson, "Old Jim Crow in Uniform," *Crisis* 46 (February 1939): 44.

95. Wells-Barnett, *Crusade for Justice*, 368–71 (quotations); McMurry, *To Keep the Waters Troubled*, 317–20; Schechter, *Ida B. Wells-Barnett and American Reform*, 157–58; Hendricks, *Gender, Race, and Politics in the Midwest*, 124.

96. On the centrality of the First World War to governments' adoption of surveillance in Europe, see Holquist, "'Information Is the Alpha and Omega of Our Work,'" 438–46.

97. "A Training Camp for Colored Women," *Crisis* 16 (September 1918): 245; Higginbotham, *Righteous Discontent*, 12, 225–26, 235 n. 33.

98. Goggin, *Carter G. Woodson*, 172–73. For further discussion of government surveillance of African American activists, see Kornweibel, *"Seeing Red"*; and Ellis, *Race, War, and Surveillance*.

99. Georgia A. Nugent in *Minutes of the Twelfth Biennial of the National Association of Colored Women* (n.p., 1920), 40, in *NACW Records, Part 1*, reel 1, frame 00613.

100. "Hon. Mrs. Talbert Returns from Abroad," *NAN* 23 (October–December 1920): 12, in *NACW Records, Part 1*, reel 23, frame 00805. NAACP national secretary James Weldon Johnson alleged later that more than 3,000 Haitians had been killed during the first years of the U.S. occupation. Later reports by the marines agreed, estimating 3,250 Haitian deaths. "The Truth about Haiti," *Crisis* 20 (September 1920): 217–24; "The Battle of 1920 and Before," *Crisis* 21 (March 1921): 206; Schneider, *"We Return Fighting,"* 79–89.

101. Regarding white women's internationalism in this period, see in particular Rupp, *Worlds of Women*.

102. "Reports from State Clubs," *NAN* 21 (February–May 1919): 5, in *NACW Records, Part 1*, reel 23, frame 00785; "Hon. Mrs. Talbert Returns from Abroad," *NAN* 23 (October–December 1920): 12, in *NACW Records, Part 1*, reel 23, frame 00805.

103. Bair, "True Women, Real Men," 154, 164–65; Stein, *World of Marcus Garvey*, 32; Moses, *Golden Age of Black Nationalism*, 197.

104. Louise J. Edwards, "The New Day Appears," *NW* 20 (June 12, 1926): 7.

105. "The African Black Cross Nurse," *NW* 14 (April 21, 1923): 3; "Notice: To All Divisions and Members of the Universal African Black Cross Nurses," *NW* 14 (April 28, 1923): 9.

106. William Sherman Walker owned Pantorium Dye Works. Harned, *Pennsylvania State History*, 15; Dunlap et al., *History and Register: Washington State Society*, 7, 41–42, 193; Mrs. William Sherman Walker, proclamation of candidacy, April 1923, April 1923 folder, box 3, Papers of Jennie Adelaide Holmes Coolidge, MNHS; "National Officers of the Daughters of the American Revolution Elected at the Thirty-Second Continental Congress," *DARM* 57 (May 1923): 280–82; Mary Anderson Orton in *DARPCC* 26 (1917): 13 (quotation); *Polk's Seattle City Directory*, 44:1317, 1758; Delegard, "Women Patriots," 150–52.

Chapter Five

1. I prefer the term "rightist" over "conservative" to describe these women because conservatism's essence recoils from disruption and, most of all, from revolution. The women, in contrast, committed disruptive actions because they believed that the United States was in imminent danger of Bolshevik takeover. The term "antiradical" does not capture their opposition to reform. The term "reactionary" speaks more of gestures than of ideas, and the term "super-patriot," favored especially by some contemporaries, ignores patriotism's multivalent meanings. Other scholars use the terms "conservatism" and "rightism" interchangeably, or distinguish conservatives only from far rightists. Kirk, *Portable Conservative Reader*, xi–xxviii; Brinkley, Yohn, and Ribuffo, *"AHR* Forum: American Conservatism"; McGirr, *Suburban Warriors*; Delegard, "Women Patriots," 18–23; Cott, *Grounding of Modern Feminism*, 256, 259–60.

2. Stein, *World of Marcus Garvey*, 186–95; Kornweibel, *"Seeing Red,"* 100–131. Beryl Satter ascribes Garveyism's fade in the United States not only to its leaders' departure but to the Great Depression's undercutting of the patriarchy it advocated. Satter, "Marcus Garvey, Father Divine, and the Gender Politics of Race Difference and Race Neutrality," 51–52.

3. Kornweibel, *"Seeing Red,"* 54–75; Lt. Col. Edmund A. Buchanan to Capt. Snow, memorandum, "Negro Radicalism in Louisiana," April 8, 1920, file 10110-1909, items 1–2, box 2826, MIDC.

4. "Mrs. Sallie W. Stewart, Our National President, Heads Woman's Auxiliary of National Negro Business League," *National Notes* 31 (March 1929): 5, in *NACW Records, Part 1*, reel 24, frame 00413; biographical information in Davis, *Lifting as They Climb*, 179–82. The 1895 assertion by James W. Jacks, a white newspaper editor in Missouri, that all black women were liars, prostitutes, and thieves was widely cited by those forming the NACW the next year. *WE* 2 (August 1895): 11; White, *Too Heavy a Load*, 60, 70. On respectability, see also Higginbotham, *Righteous Discontent*, 185–229; Giddings, *When and Where I Enter*, 85–94; and Wolcott, *Remaking Respectability*, 22–27.

5. *Minutes of the National Association of Colored Women (Incorporated) Held at Hot Springs, Ark.* (n.p., 1930), 72, in *NACW Records, Part 1*, reel 1, frame 00909.

6. Taylor, *Veiled Garvey*, 1–2, 74, 82–84; Summers, *Manliness and Its Discontents*, 139–40.

7. Taylor, *Veiled Garvey*, 86 (quotation), 75–76.

8. "The National Association of Colored Women," *National Notes* 29 (May 1927): 4, in *NACW Records, Part 1*, reel 24, frame 00191; "Southern Federation of Colored Women's Clubs Held 4th Biennial Session at Birmingham, Alabama," *National Notes* 29 (September 1927): 6, in *NACW Records, Part 1*, reel 24, frame 00214.

9. "Will the Entrance of Woman in Politics Affect Home Life?" *NW* 16 (June 14, 1924), 12; Amy Jacques Garvey, "Women as Leaders Nationally and Racially," *NW* 19 (October 24, 1925): 7; Jacques Garvey, "A Dearth of Husbands," *NW* 22 (July 9, 1927): 4; Jacques Garvey, "'They Conquer Who Believe They Can,'" *NW* 19 (September 26, 1925): 7 (quotations); White, *Too Heavy a Load*, 120–24, 130–31.

10. Rouse, "Out of the Shadow of Tuskegee," 40.

11. While married to Booker T. Washington (who died ten years before she did), Margaret Murray Washington was the organizer and longtime leader of the Tuskegee Woman's Club, made up of Tuskegee Institute female faculty and faculty wives. Among the club's international studies was a series of programs in 1915 on women in "The Warring Countries." Neverdon-Morton, *Afro-American Women of the South*, 133–34; Hoytt, "International Council of Women of the Darker Races," 55; "Reports from State Clubs: Alabama," *NAN* 18 (November 1915): 3, in *NACW Records, Part 1*, reel 23, frame 00625; *Minutes of the Twenty-First Biennial Convention of the National Association of Colored Women, Inc.* (n.p., 1939), 33, in *NACW Records, Part 1*, reel 2, frame 00168.

12. As of November 1924, each ICWDR member was required to pay twenty dollars down and a "yearly gift" of twenty-five dollars. Washington intended that the membership consist of "one hundred fifty American women of color and fifty foreign women of color." Margaret Murray Washington circular, November 10, 1924, reprinted in Hoytt, "International Council of Women of the Darker Races," 54.

13. Neverdon-Morton, *Afro-American Women of the South*, 200–201; Rief, "Thinking Globally, Acting Locally," 214–18; Johnson, "'Drill into Us . . . the Rebel Tradition,'" 558–59; Hoytt, "International Council of Women of the Darker Races," 55; Des Jardins, *Women and the Historical Enterprise in America*, 157; Rouse, "Out of the Shadow of Tuskegee," 40–42.

14. Members living outside the South were able to vote at this time. "Telegraphic Message from National President Bethune," *National Notes* 28 (February 1926): 10, in *NACW Records, Part 1*, reel 24, frame 00050 (quotation); "A Department of Education Should Be Created," *National Notes* 31 (September–October 1928): 7, in *NACW Records, Part 1*, reel 24, frame 00367; Hanson, *Mary McLeod Bethune and Black Women's Political Activism*, 113–14.

15. *National Association of Colored Women (Incorporated), Sixteenth Biennial Session* (n.p., 1928), 55, in *NACW Records, Part 1*, reel 1, frame 00838.

16. *Journal of the Thirty-Eighth National Convention of the Woman's Relief Corps* (1920), 164; *Journal of the Fortieth National Convention of the Woman's Relief Corps* (1922), 320–21, 345.

17. *DARPCC* 28 (1919): 199. See also *Journal of the Thirty-Ninth National Convention of the Woman's Relief Corps* (1921), 195–96.

18. In 1922 the DAR's national convention affirmed the 1921 law that originally created the national origins quota system (in the form of a resolution praising "restricted immigration"). After 1923, the DAR newly funded, on a national basis, work among Chinese and other women detained on San Francisco's Angel Island, and it sponsored the translation of the *Manual of the United States for the Information of Immigrants* (later the *D.A.R. Manual for Citizenship*) into Chinese and Japanese in addition to European languages. Nearly simultaneously, the DAR called for the extension of the 1924 "national origins" quotas to "unassimilable" Mexican and other Latin immigrants. Lora Haines Cook, "A Message from the President General," *DARM* 58 (March 1924): 140–41; Morley, *History of California State Society*, 132–34, 261; Margaret Hart Strong, "Angel Island—Keeper of the Western Door," *DARM* 63 (June 1929): 355. *Resolutions Adopted by the Thirty-Third Congress* (1924), 17; *DARPCC* 36 (1927): 131; *DARPCC* 38 (1929): 684 (quotation); "41st Continental Congress, N.S., D.A.R.," *DARM* 66 (June 1932): 331.

19. *DARM* 54 (1920): 356; *DARPCC* 29 (1920): 82, 278.

20. "State Conferences," *DARM* 58 (December 1924): 755; Grace R. Sweeney to Grace Abbott, March 24, 1924, Central File 1-9-1 (1) (1921–1924), box 235, U.S. Department of Labor, Records of the Children's Bureau, RG 102, NARA, College Park, Md. On the child labor amendment, see Nielsen, *Un-American Womanhood*, 89–111; and Trattner, *Crusade for the Children*, 167–78.

21. The WRC also endorsed the Washington Disarmament Conference with a rare telegram to the White House. "Proceedings of the Twenty-Eighth Continental Congress, 1919," *DARM* (May 1919): 7; *DARPCC* 28 (1919): 315; Anne Rogers Minor, "A Message from the President General," *DARM* 56 (January 1922): 20–21; "The Peace Hymn of the Republic," *DARM* 56 (January 1922): 21; *DARPCC* 31 (1922): 8; *Resolutions Adopted by the Thirty-Third Congress* (1924), 12; *Journal of the Thirty-Ninth National Convention of the Woman's Relief Corps* (1921), 109, 312.

22. Lemons, *Woman Citizen*, 61–62 n. 48, 213; Jensen, "All Pink Sisters," 208.

23. Brosseau may well have been influenced by reports of an all-female Russian "Battalion of Death" engaging in combat during World War I. Mouat, *Connecticut State History*, 15–19; Grace Hall Lincoln Brosseau to Col. Stanley H. Ford, August 24, 1928, file 2037-1909, item 2, box 707, MIDC; Gibbs, *DAR*, 113, 115; Jensen, "Minerva on the Field of Mars," 110–55.

24. The statue was executed by professional sculptor August Leimbach. Bauer, *Historic Treasure Chest of the Madonna of the Trail Monuments*, 6–7, 17. Thanks to Pamela H. Simpson for directing me to this source. Some DAR contemporaries preferred the title "Pioneer Mother" to "Madonna" because the latter sounded too "European." "National Board of Management: Regular Meeting of April 25, 1927," *DARM* 61 (June 1927): 480; "The Madonna of the Trail," *DARM* 63 (July 1929): 399–404. Proposed by the DAR for Santa Fe, New Mexico, the statue was rebuffed on the grounds that it slighted "Spanish people," the area's "real pioneers." The statue was instead erected in Albuquerque. Wilson, *Myth of Santa Fe*, 315.

25. Amelia Campbell Parker, "Revolutionary Heroine Interred in West Point Cemetery," *DARM* 60 (June 1926): 346–52 (quotation on p. 352).

26. Nielsen, *Un-American Womanhood*, 1–2; Flora Myers Gillentine in "American History Depicted in Shop Windows," *DARM* 64 (April 1930): 237–39 (gives examples from Colorado Springs, Ann Arbor, Mich., North Plainfield, N.J., Caldwell, Idaho, and Punxsutawney, Pa.). "Work of the Chapters," *DARM* 66 (July 1932): 436–38, furnishes additional examples, including a Woodward and Lothrop Christmas display in Washington, D.C.

27. Goldman, *Women, the State, and Revolution*, 1–58, 337–43.

28. "State Conferences," *DARM* 62 (January 1928): 39.

29. "Proceedings of the Tenth Continental Congress," *AMM* 18 (April–May 1901): 731; Ella Loraine Dorsey, "The D.A.R. Magazine and D.A.R. History," *DARM* 66 (July 1932): 409 (quotation).

30. Jessie S. MacKenzie in "State Conferences," *DARM* 59 (December 1925): 760; Barrington, *Historical Restorations of the Daughters of the American Revolution*, 179. Roosevelt had died in 1919.

31. Mrs. William Sherman Walker, "National Defense Committee," *DARM* 62 (September 1928): 558.

32. This notion did not originate with either Coolidge or the DAR, but with the antisuffragist Massachusetts Public Interests League in 1920. Nielsen, *Un-American Womanhood*, 33; Mouat, *Connecticut State History*, 21–24.

33. Anne Rogers Minor, "A Message from the President General," *DARM* 55 (April 1921): 183.

34. Delegard, "Women Patriots," 144, 267. Also withdrawing from the NCW was the WRC, which believed that the NCW's domination by peace activists kept it from "[standing] for loyalty to the Government and patriotic service to our own people." Flo Jamison Miller in *Journal of the Forty-Fifth Convention of the National Woman's Relief Corps* (1927), 349, 381.

35. Reports of Native American men's exemplary performances as soldiers during World War I created support in the DAR for reforming the federal government's administration of reservations, and for having Native Americans at large designated U.S. citizens. In 1934 the national DAR convention supported the repeal of the Dawes Act of 1887, to end government policies that had divided and privatized reservation lands and had compelled assimilation. *DARPCC* 26 (1917): 208–15; Anne Rogers Minor, "A Message from the President General," *DARM* 55 (July 1921): 368; *DARPCC* 43 (1934): 625.

36. Edith Irwin Hobart, "The President General's Message," *DARM* 64 (June 1930): 351; Mrs. William Sherman Walker, "Department of National Defense Committee," *DARM* 64 (June 1930): 381 (quotation).

37. Inspired partly by the president and first lady's own connections to Stanford University, and by the DAR's red-baiting of former Stanford president David Starr Jordan in 1928, the exodus was led by his wife, Jessie Knight Jordan. Cott, *Grounding of Modern Feminism*, 359 n. 26; Gibbs, *DAR*, 141; clippings in folder 7, box 1, DAR Collection Stanford; Palo Alto Chapter DAR Resolution, November 11, 1929, folder 3, box 1, DAR Collection Stanford; Helen E. Crumpton to David Starr Jordan, n.d. [May 1930], folder 4, box 1, DAR Collection Stanford.

38. Flora Bredes Walker in Elisabeth Ellicott Poe, "Patriotic Women Once More Rally for National Defense," *DARM* 63 (March 1929): 148. See also Walker, "Department of National Defense Committee," *DARM* 63 (December 1929): 723–25; and DAR president Edith Irwin Hobart's defense of the U.S. occupation of Nicaragua in *DARPCC* 40 (1931): 11.

39. *DARPCC* 36 (1927): 12–13; minutes of meeting of November 15, 1927, vol. 5 (1926–1931), p. 32, DAR Chapter North Carolina; *Proceedings of the Twenty-Eighth Ohio State Conference of the Daughters of the American Revolution* (1927), 92–93; Nielsen, *Un-American Womanhood*, 104.

40. Ladd-Taylor, *Mother-Work*, 168–69; Lemons, *Woman Citizen*, 158–59; Mrs. William Sherman Walker, "National Defense Committee," *DARM* 62 (July 1928): 434–35 (quotation). On the opposition to the Sheppard-Towner Act, which in 1929 was not renewed, see especially Nielsen, *Un-American Womanhood*, 104–11.

41. Copy of memorandum, Col. J. H. Reeves to the "Secretary, General Staff," "Subject: Report on Meetings of Ultra-Pacifist and Patriotic Organizations," July 17, 1924, file 10314-547, item 2, box 3025, MIDC.

42. Col. William K. Naylor, copy of "Memorandum for the Adjutant General of

the Army" (written originally by Col. Arthur C. Rogers), January 17, 1924; Maj. Gen. J. H. McRae, excerpt of memorandum to the Adjutant General of the Army, January 9, 1924 (quotation), file 10314-526, item 93, box 3024, MIDC.

43. *DARPCC* 38 (1929): 42; *DARPCC* 39 (1930): 28, 36, 38; *DARM* 65 (1931): 266–67; *Journal of the Forty-Seventh Convention of the National Woman's Corps* (1929), 127; "The Thirty-Eighth Continental Congress," *DARM* 63 (May 1929): 268.

44. Mrs. M. R. Schatz (Birmingham, Mich.) to the "United States Government, Intelligence Dept.," October 21, 1926, item 61; Lieut. Col. Walter O. Boswell to Schatz, October 26, 1926, item 61; Elizabeth P. Ryder (Lancaster, Pa.) to the Intelligence Bureau, War Department, n.d. [stamped April 4, 1931], item 77; copy of letter, Col. William H. Wilson to Ryder, April 6, 1931, item 78; all in file 10110-1935, box 2826, MIDC; Nielsen, *Un-American Womanhood*, 1.

45. "Americanism Run Riot," Lieut. Lansdale Post No. 67 (American Legion) *Bulletin* (San Francisco), n.d. [1928], clipping in folder "D.A.R. (Mostly Clippings)," Attacks, box 494, NCPW Papers (quotation); " 'Dear, Sweet Girls' of the D.A.R. Sassed," *Detroit News*, May 10, 1928, clipping in scrapbook of Continental Congress and NSDAR activities (1893–1931), box 34, DAR Papers Michigan; "White Voices Ridicule of D.A.R. Blacklist," *Washington Post*, April 3, 1928; Elaine Goodale Eastman, "Are D.A.R. Women Exploited?" *Christian Century* (September 11, 1929), 1114–17.

46. The MID proposed approaching the DAR in January 1924. In the previous year, DAR leaders had begun an extensive study of "national defense"—initially kept confidential from the membership—that culminated in the creation of the National Defense Committee in 1925. Also in 1923, following her election to the DAR presidency, Lora Haines Cook wrote to the MID with her change of address; a clerk puzzled over whether the MID had had any previous contact with her. No prior contact between Cook and the War Department survives in the MID's correspondence files. Col. William K. Naylor, copy of "Memorandum for the Adjutant General of the Army" (written originally by Col. Arthur C. Rogers), January 17, 1924; Maj. Gen. J. H. McRae, excerpt of memorandum to the Adjutant General of the Army, January 9, 1924; file 10314-526, item 93, box 3024, MIDC; Mrs. Alfred J. Brosseau to Nellie Nugent Somerville, June 15, 1926, folder 51, reel C5, Series II: Nellie Nugent Somerville—Organizations, M-133, Somerville and Howorth Family Papers, SL; "National Board of Management: Regular Meeting, June 28, 1924," *DARM* 58 (August 1924): 505; Lora Haines Cook to "War Dept. Executive Division," November 26, [1923], item 1; Lieut. Col. M. E. Locke to Cook, November 30, 1923, item 2; routing slip, November 28, 1923, item 2; all in file 10319-655, box 3050, MIDC.

47. Cott, *Grounding of Modern Feminism*, 248–49, 256–58; Jensen, "All Pink Sisters," 213, 215–17; Nielsen, *Un-American Womanhood*, 117–20; Delegard, "Women Patriots," 134–44, 305–6, 357–58.

48. "Patriotism is virile. If people fail to align themselves with us" on the ques-

tion of loyalty oaths for public school teachers, "perhaps it may be due to a lapse on our part." Edith Irwin Hobart, "The President General's Message," *DARM* 65 (September 1931): 527.

49. Mrs. William Sherman Walker, "National Defense Committee," *DARM* 63 (April 1929): 238.

50. In Decatur, Mead later spoke at a meeting of the local League of Women Voters. Mrs. William Sherman Walker, "D.A.R. Congressional Report of the National Defense Committee," *DARM* 61 (August 1927): 592; May Erwin Talmadge to Dr. J. R. McCain, November 15, 1926, folder "Lucia Ames Mead," box 496, Attacks, NCPW Papers; "City Heads Prohibit Woman from Giving Speech to Students," *Everett (Wash.) Herald*, December 4, 1926, clipping in folder "Lucia Ames Mead," box 496, Attacks, NCPW Papers; "D.A.R. Legion Protest Bans Peace Speaker," *New York World*, November 11, 1929, clipping in folder "Attackers: Daughters of the American Revolution—Clippings about the D.A.R. (1924–1929)," box "Daughters of the American Revolution," Special Collections: Attackers, SCPC; William Allen White, "Lady Sheep," *Emporia (Kans.) Weekly Gazette*, May 3, 1928, 1. Also see Delegard, "Women Patriots," 315–31, 340–44.

51. Quoted in Nielsen, *Un-American Womanhood*, 120–21.

52. Prominent in contributing to the National Defense Fund was Colonel Walter Scott, father of DAR president Edith Scott Magna of Massachusetts. "National Board of Management: Regular Meeting, April 16, 1927," *DARM* 61 (May 1927): 387–89, 402; Mrs. William Sherman Walker, "D.A.R. Congressional Report of the National Defense Committee," *DARM* 61 (August 1927): 590–92; "National Officers Elected at the Thirty-Eighth Continental Congress," *DARM* 63 (May 1929): 280; "National Board of Management: Regular Meeting, April 13, 1929," *DARM* 63 (May 1929): 303; "National Board of Management: Regular Meeting, October 5, 1930," *DARM* 64 (December 1930): 763; "National Board of Management: Regular Meeting, April 18, 1931," *DARM* 65 (May 1931): 307.

53. Scholars have not established exactly who composed these lists. The possibilities are numerous. What matters most is that DAR leaders gave the lists broad distribution among hundreds of thousands of influential others, who were able to shape the opinions of additional political and social elites. The lists appear in full in Nielsen, *Un-American Womanhood*, 143–57.

54. Helen Matilda Tufts Bailie of Cambridge, Massachusetts, belonged also to the WILPF and was the ringleader of the Boston group who had first made the lists public. The other, Mary Perley MacFarland of Mountain Lakes, New Jersey, was married to the national secretary of the liberal Federal Council of Churches and was herself active in a number of other blacklisted organizations. Nielsen, *Un-American Womanhood*, 124–25; Delegard, "Women Patriots," 336–39; Morgan, "'Home and Country,'" 436–39, 441.

55. Virginia Walker had recently graduated from Swarthmore College. Virginia Walker to the Valley Forge Chapter DAR, n.d. [1928], folder "Attackers: Daughters

of the American Revolution—Virginia Walker Papers," box "Daughters of the American Revolution," Special Collections: Attackers, SCPC.

56. Eleven resigned at once from New Haven's two chapters; fourteen simultaneously departed the much smaller Crawfordsville chapter; and twenty-three women, including five former officers, left the Highland Park chapter (which numbered over one hundred) between 1928 and 1931. "Women Censure D.A.R. as Tyrant," *New York Times*, May 4, 1928; "Mrs. Winchester Bennett Quits D.A.R. in New Haven," *New York Herald-Tribune*, May 4, 1928; "14 Quit D.A.R. in Protest Against 'Blacklist' Policy," *New York World*, May 29, 1928; clippings in folder "D.A.R. (Mostly Clippings)," Attacks, box 494, NCPW Papers; "Anti-Blacklist Vote Lost in Detroit D.A.R.," *Pontiac (Mich.) Daily Press*, June 5, 1928; "D.A.R. Protest Is Unofficial," *Detroit Free Press*, June 8, 1928; clippings in scrapbook of state and chapter activities, vol. 1 (1903–1936), box 34, DAR Papers Michigan; Ferne F. Savage, "Fifteen Years' History, 1916–1931, of Fort Pontchartrain Chapter," "Chapter Statistics," and "Chapter Officers," in notebook (1931), Fort Pontchartrain Chapter DAR (Highland Park, Mich.), box 20, DAR Papers Michigan.

57. *Report of the Twenty-Eighth Annual State Conference of the Daughters of the American Revolution* (1928), 67–68; *Report of the Twenty-Ninth Annual State Conference of the Daughters of the American Revolution* (1929), 155; Christine J. McDonald, report of the state chairman on National Defense, October 1929, p. 1, and report of the state chairman on National Defense, April 1931, in "State Chairmen Reports, vol. II (H–M)," box 9, DAR Papers Michigan; Hinman, *Vermont State Conference*, 262.

58. "Mrs. W. S. Walker Wins Biggest D.A.R. Vote in Election," n.d. [April 1927], clipping in 1917–1928 scrapbook, p. 15, folder 1, box 4, Series 4: District Records, DAR Collection Nebraska; "The 35th Continental Congress of the Daughters of the American Revolution," *DARM* 60 (June 1926): 343; "Georgian Beaten in Race to Head D.A.R.," April 19, 1929, clipping in Mrs. Howard McCall, comp., scrapbook, vol. 6 (1929–1934), Papers of Mrs. D. Miller Cox, MSS 340, AHC; *DAR-PCC* 39 (1930): 19.

59. Delegard, "Women Patriots," 146–76; Nielsen, *Un-American Womanhood*, 58–61.

60. Marvin also lost a libel suit brought by the peace activist Rosika Schwimmer. Flora Bredes Walker to Mabel Thorpe Smith, July 28, 1928, in scrapbook of Continental Congress and NSDAR activities (1893–1931), box 34, DAR Papers Michigan; Key Men of America appeal, 1928, folder 13, box 1, Papers of Henry Bourne Joy, MHC; Hapgood, *Professional Patriots*; McCausland, *"Blue Menace"*; Wenger, "Radical Politics in a Reactionary Age."

61. Among these materials were a far-right pamphlet entitled "The German-Bolshevik Conspiracy," "statistics" pertaining to "South American revolutions," and a copy of a report on the Chekha, Stalin's secret police. Flora Bredes Walker to Maj. W. H. Simpson, February 3, 1931, and Simpson to Walker, February 11, 1931,

file 10322-1038, items 1–2, box 3059, MIDC; Walker to Gen. Hersey, January 2, 1931, item 1; Col. Alfred T. Smith to Maj.-Gen. Mark L. Hersey, January 12, 1931, item 2; Simpson to Walker, January 12, 1931, item 3; Walker to Simpson, January 19, 1931, item 3; all in file 2657-155, box 1619, MIDC.

62. Lieut. Col. Walter O. Boswell to Assistant Chiefs of Staff, April 10, 1926; Boswell to Maj. Robert G. Kirkwood, April 27, 1926; Lieut. Col. William A. Graham to Boswell, May 8, 1926; Boswell to Graham, May 10, 1926; all in file 10110-2520, items 6, 9–11, box 2837, MIDC; Boswell, "Memorandum for Chief M.I.4," May 13, 1924, file 10110-1935, item 39, box 2826, MIDC; Graham to Boswell, n.d. [received May 29, 1927] (quotation), file 10110-2590, box 2838, MIDC.

Mainly because of its membership in the WJCC, and generally because of its past support for progressive reforms and for international peace, the DAR appeared on the first of multiple spider-web charts composed by Maxwell, who reportedly belonged to the DAR. She worked in the Chemical Warfare Service branch, a nemesis of peace activists. She omitted the DAR from future charts and annotated her first chart of May 1923 once the DAR withdrew from the WJCC. Cott, *Grounding of Modern Feminism*, 242, 249–50; Delegard, "Women Patriots," 1–6; Lemons, *Woman Citizen*, 209–27; Nielsen, *Un-American Womanhood*, 76–78; Gibbs, *DAR*, 109. A copy of the first chart listing the DAR survives in MID files. "L. R. M.," comp., "The Socialist-Pacifist Movement in America Is an Absolutely Fundamental and Integral Part of International Socialism," May 1923, file 10110-1935, item 24, box 2826, MIDC.

63. Mrs. William Sherman Walker, "Department of National Defense Committee," *DARM* 64 (August 1930): 496; Walker, "Department of National Defense Committee," *DARM* 64 (November 1930): 701–2; Walker, "Department of National Defense Committee," *DARM* 65 (August 1931): 488.

64. Grace L. C. Ward in "State Conferences," *DARM* 65 (December 1931): 744 (quotation); Elisabeth Ellicott Poe, "Sixth Women's Patriotic Conference on National Defense," *DARM* 65 (March 1931): 147–48.

65. "G-Man Here, Warns Against Return of Public Apathy in War on Crime," *Grand Rapids (Mich.) Herald*, March 19, 1937, clipping in scrapbook of state and chapter activities, vol. 3 (1936–1940), box 34, DAR Papers Michigan; "John Flynn of the F.B.I. Speaks at D.A.R. Meeting Thursday," *Council Bluffs (Iowa) Nonpareil*, November 6, 1942, and "Patriotic Tea Held by Lydia Alden Chapter Here on Monday," *Spencer (Iowa) Reporter*, February 9, 1943, both clippings in Iowa Society DAR scrapbook (Historian's Book), 1942–1943 (vol. III), box 2, DAR Collection Iowa.

66. Typescript lists of "Iowa historic spots," n.d. [1920s and after], folder 3, box 1, DAR Collection Iowa; Mrs. S. W. Clarkson, report of state historian, October 8, 1929, in book of state executive board minutes, vol. 4 (1928–1931), box 1, DAR Papers Michigan; Wood, *History and Register, Idaho State Society*, 85; "D.A.R. Pays Honor to Harriet Godfrey," *Minneapolis Sunday Tribune*, May 4, 1924, clipping in 1924 folder, box 3, Papers of Jennie Adelaide Holmes Coolidge, MNHS.

67. Nielsen, *Un-American Womanhood*, 148; Anne Rogers Minor in *DARPCC* 32 (1923): 15–16.

68. The Illinois DAR blanketed the state with monuments to Abraham Lincoln—there were thirteen by 1923. A 1923 plaque in St. Paul, Minnesota's Union Station honored the first man in the country to volunteer "in defense of the Union" in 1861. Daughters in Brunswick, Maine, marked the church pew that Harriet Beecher Stowe had occupied in the early 1850s as she was writing *Uncle Tom's Cabin*. "Work of the Chapters," *DARM* 57 (May 1923): 315–16 (Springfield, Ill.); "Work of the Chapters," *DARM* 59 (August 1925): 518 (Lincoln, Ill.); "D.A.R. Unveils Tablet to First 1861 Volunteer," *Minneapolis Journal*, n.d. [1923], clipping in 1923 folder, box 3, Papers of Jennie Adelaide Holmes Coolidge, MNHS; "Work of the Chapters," *DARM* 62 (September 1928): 579–81 (Springfield, Ill.); "Work of the Chapters," *DARM* 64 (April 1930): 246 (Brunswick, Maine).

69. DeLamar and Ward, *History of the Georgia State Society*, 7–8, 180–81, 359–80; *Chapter Histories: Daughters of the American Revolution in Georgia*, 3.

70. Prologue, "Some Early History of Lafayette County, Mississippi, Compiled by David Reese Chapter, D.A.R." (typescript), 1930, box 2, Papers of Mrs. Calvin S. Brown (Maud Morrow Brown), MSDAH.

71. The second time a DAR president appeared at a national UDC convention, in 1923, was also the second time the UDC met in Washington. Lora Haines Cook delivered brief greetings. "Notes on the Washington Convention," *CV* 32 (January 1924): 30.

72. Grace H. Brosseau, "A Message from the President General," *DARM* 61 (February 1927): 99. Shortly after World War I, the UDC's Virginia Division held an essay contest for U.S. history teachers on Charles Landon Carter Minor's anti-Lincoln pamphlet *The Real Lincoln*. Sallie Bruce Dickinson, " 'The Real Lincoln' Reviewed," *CV* 28 (April 1920): 157; Davis, *Image of Lincoln in the South*, 123–26. Also see "Should Lincoln's Image Be in Southern Schools?" *CV* 33 (October 1925): 364; and Simpson, *Edith D. Pope and Her Nashville Friends*, 52.

73. Exceptions are Gardner, *Blood and Irony*, 209–50; Parrott, " 'Love Makes Memory Eternal' "; Roth, *Matronage*; and Simpson, *Edith D. Pope and Her Nashville Friends*.

74. *Minutes of the Sixth Annual Meeting of the United Daughters of the Confederacy* (1900), 72 (27,000 members); "United Daughters of the Confederacy," *CV* 8 (April 1900): 150 (20,000 members); "Twenty-Sixth Annual Convention, U.D.C.," *CV* 28 (January 1920): 33; "From the President General," *CV* 32 (February 1924): 70; Parrott, " 'Love Makes Memory Eternal,' " 235 n. 9; Roth, *Matronage*, 54–55. Likely due to the Depression, nationwide UDC membership dropped back to 70,000 by 1934. Cott, *Grounding of Modern Feminism*, 85.

75. "Division Notes," *CV* 33 (February 1925): 70.

76. Neo-Confederate publications regularly expressed condolences to activists who had lost parents. Simpson, *Edith D. Pope and Her Nashville Friends*, 119; *CV* 35 (February 1927): 71.

77. Lora Haines Cook, circular on Defense Test, June 30, 1924, folder 4 (papers 1923–1924), box 1, DAR Papers St. Paul; Arthur H. Jennings, "Sons of Confederate Veterans: News and Comment," *CV* 32 (September 1924): 362. The War Department intended Defense Test Day as a rehearsal in American communities for the possible invasion of the United States. Civilians were asked to demonstrate support for the military.

78. Guenter, *American Flag*, 178. Schuyler and Cook served intermittently as the conference's chairs. The WRC and the U.S. Daughters of 1812 also sent representatives. "From the President General," *CV* 31 (August 1923): 310 (quotation); "United States Flag Code," *DARM* 57 (September 1923): 546–48.

79. When the UDC's president spoke at the American Legion and American Legion Auxiliary conventions in 1930, "[b]oth audiences seemed deeply interested in the activities of the [UDC] in its relation to the Soldiers of the World War." Elizabeth Burford Bashinsky in "From the President General," *CV* 38 (September 1930): 358. The American Legion's interactions with the UDC did draw criticism from some Legionnaires. "The Tempering of Time," *CV* 31 (August 1923): 316.

80. Leonard, *Woman's Who's Who of America*, 722.

81. The Russians in question were Ludwig C. A. K. Martens, Gregory Weinstein, and Madame Kalenina. "From the President General," *CV* 31 (May 1923): 192.

82. Delegard, "Women Patriots," 127 n. 67; "Oppose Plans to Allow Woman to Make Talk Here," *Greenville (S.C.) News*, December 11, 1926, clipping in folder "Lucia Ames Mead," Attacks, box 496, NCPW Papers.

83. I draw this conclusion from the "U.D.C. Notes" published in the *Confederate Veteran* between 1926 and 1930 (volumes 34 to 38). Though brief, these reports emphasized the projects the women considered important. If national defense activism had mattered much to them, it would have appeared in these reports.

84. Allene Walker Harrold in "From the President General," *CV* 33 (August 1925): 309.

85. "From the President General," *CV* 31 (May 1923): 192.

86. At the first conference, in 1925, women more passively took in the speeches of male experts. Delegard, "Women Patriots," 129.

87. "From the President General," *CV* 35 (April 1927): 148; Lawton's hometown is found in S. Cary Beckwith, "The Church of the Three Presidents General," *CV* 35 (November 1927): 411.

88. "From the President General," *CV* 35 (May 1927): 188; "From the President General," *CV* 35 (November 1927): 430.

89. Mrs. H. M. Branson in "To Keep Green Southern Valor," *CV* 33 (July 1925): 259.

90. Georgia V. Chubbuck, "Beauty in Markers," *DARM* 62 (January 1928): 23–24; *DARM* 65 (January 1931): 61.

91. Mrs. J. Blackburn Moran, circular and photograph, n.d., UDC Scrapbook Missouri; McElya, "Commemorating the Color Line"; Johnson, "'Ye Gave Them a

Stone'"; Blight, *Race and Reunion*, 288–89; Thurber, "Development of the Mammy Image and Mythology," 99 (quotation); White, *Too Heavy a Load*, 134–35.

92. Wells-Barnett, *Crusade for Justice*, 381; Hendricks, *Gender, Race, and Politics in the Midwest*, 127; *Minutes of the Fourteenth Biennial Convention of the National Association of Colored Women* (n.p., 1924), 39, in *NACW Records, Part 1*, reel 1, frame 00709; "Questions and Answers in Negro History," *National Notes* 27 (September 1925): 7, in *NACW Records, Part 1*, reel 24, frame 00017; "Questions and Answers in Negro History," *National Notes* 28 (October 1925): 11 in *NACW Records, Part 1*, reel 24, frame 00029; "The Women Protest," *NW* 18 (July 25, 1925): 7.

93. The daughter of the "first missionary bishop of the Protestant Episcopal Church" in Haiti, Holly, a journalist and teacher, came to the United States in 1923 at the invitation of Margaret Murray Washington. She spoke at the ICWDR's "first public meeting" in Chicago in 1924. As of 1925, she edited the French language section of the *Negro World*. Hoytt, "International Council of Women of the Darker Races," 54; "The New and Brilliant French Editor of the Negro World," *NW* 17 (February 7, 1925): 4. Another exception was Lizzie Branch, the "lady president" of the UNIA's Cincinnati division, who belonged also to the NAACP, the Young Women's Christian Association (YWCA), and a "Colored Woman's Club." Stein, *World of Marcus Garvey*, 236. On the overall estrangement between the NACW and UNIA, see Hendricks, *Gender, Race, and Politics in the Midwest*, 127–28; and Wolcott, *Remaking Respectability*, 95, 127. As of 1925, the UNIA forbade its members to belong also to the NAACP. Reed, *Chicago NAACP and the Rise of Black Professional Leadership*, 74. On the UNIA's dominant "bourgeois" contingent, see Stein, *World of Marcus Garvey*, 225, 235, 246.

94. "Back to Africa and How to Go Back," *NW* 19 (February 6, 1926): 4; Eunice Lewis in "Our Letter Box," *NW* 16 (April 19, 1924): 10 (quotation).

95. "Contribution to African Redemption Fund," *NW* 15 (December 22, 1923): 2; "Roll of Negro Patriots," *NW* 18 (August 1, 1925): 5; "Contributors to Black Cross Reserve and Operating Fund," *NW* 19 (December 26, 1925): 5.

96. Amy Jacques Garvey, "Wherefore a National Urge?" *NW* 18 (June 6, 1925): 7. On the Garveyite flag, see also Leona L. Ellis, "A Toast to Our Flag," *NW* 16 (May 10, 1924): 10.

97. "Woman's Day Celebrated by U.N.I.A., Div. No. 16, in Gatun, Canal Zone," *NW* 14 (May 12, 1923): 7; Stein, *World of Marcus Garvey*, 223; Summers, *Manliness and Its Discontents*, 98.

98. *National Association of Colored Women, Fifteenth Biennial Session* (n.p., 1926), 17, 20, 33, in *NACW Records, Part 1*, reel 1, frames 00761, 00763, 00769.

99. Lyrics reprinted in *Souvenir Program, 14th Biennial Session, National Association of Colored Women* (Chicago: Charles S. Hunter, 1924), in *NACW Records, Part 1*, reel 1, frame 00731; Wayne Francis, "'Lift Every Voice and Sing,'" *Crisis* 32 (September 1926): 234, 236.

100. Rosa P. King, "Southeastern Region," *National Notes* 30 (December 1927): 10, in *NACW Records, Part 1*, reel 24, frame 00262.

101. On the closeness of the NACW and the NAACP, see "N.A.A.C.P. Sees Segregation as Biggest Issue for Negro," *National Notes* 28 (October 1925): 5, in *NACW Records, Part 1*, reel 24, frame 00023; and "Greetings from the N.A.C.W. to the N.A.A.C.P. in its Denver Meeting," *National Notes* 28 (October 1925): 9, in *NACW Records, Part 1*, reel 24, frame 00027. One of many NACW women who was also important in the NAACP was Sue Wilson Brown (Mrs. S. Joe Brown) of Des Moines, Iowa; she was one of only five women on the NAACP Resolutions Committee in 1926. *Minutes of the Fourteenth Biennial Convention of the National Association of Colored Women* (n.p., 1924), 4, in *NACW Records, Part 1*, reel 1, frame 00692; "National Association for the Advancement of Colored People," *Crisis* 32 (August 1926): 181; Davis, *Lifting as They Climb*, 198. Daisy Lampkin of Pittsburgh, a national field secretary of the NAACP as of 1930, simultaneously chaired the NACW's executive board. "N.A.A.C.P.," *Crisis* 37 (January 1930): 31; *National Notes* 32 (July 1930): 13, in *NACW Records, Part 1*, reel 24, frame 00530.

102. Hallie Q. Brown, "Club Women Greetings," *NAN* 23 (October–December 1920): 4, in *NACW Records, Part 1*, reel 23, frame 00797.

103. Hine and Thompson, *Shining Thread of Hope*, 200; Neverdon-Morton, *Afro-American Women of the South*, 226. The historian Mark Robert Schneider states that the Crusaders raised only $7,000. *The Crisis* reported in September 1923 that the women had raised $13,000, although $2,000 remained outstanding (withheld by "selfish if not dishonest agents"). Schneider, *"We Return Fighting,"* 188; "The Crusaders," *Crisis* 26 (September 1923): 201. On baby contest fundraisers, see "N.A.A.C.P. Notes," *Crisis* 34 (March 1927): 10; "The Horizon," *Crisis* 31 (February 1926): 179 (St. Louis, Mo.); "The Horizon," *Crisis* 32 (October 1926): 310 (Little Rock, Ark.).

104. "N.A.A.C.P.," *Crisis* 37 (January 1930): 31.

105. Schneider, *"We Return Fighting,"* 49 (quotation); Salem, *To Better Our World*, 158–59. See also Pitre, *In Struggle against Jim Crow*; Cumberbatch, "Working for the Race," 146–92; Sullivan, *Days of Hope*, 142–43; Reed, *Chicago NAACP and the Rise of Black Professional Leadership*, 69; and Ransby, *Ella Baker and the Black Freedom Movement*, 105–47.

Another example of a gendered division of labor is the Fourth Pan-African Congress, convened by W. E. B. Du Bois in 1927 in New York and intended to connect leading African Americans and leading Africans. This gathering was the first, and only, of the four Pan-African Congresses chaired by Du Bois between 1919 and 1927 to meet in the United States (the Great Depression prevented a fifth Congress). The fourth Congress drew a total of 5,000 delegates from the United States, the West and East Indies, and British West Africa; over 200 were paid delegates. Du Bois chaired the meeting, as he had the previous three. The NACW's Peace and Foreign Relations Circle, headed by Addie Waites Hunton, raised "nearly Three Thousand Dollars to finance the Congress and made all the arrangements." W. E. Burghardt Du Bois, "The Pan-African Congress," *Crisis* 17 (April 1919): 271–74; Schneider,

"We Return Fighting," 166–67, 170; "Pan-Africa," *Crisis* 32 (October 1926): 284; "Postscript," *Crisis* 34 (August 1927): 203; "The Pan-African Congresses," *Crisis* 34 (October 1927): 263–64 (quotation on p. 263).

106. "N.A.A.C.P.," *Crisis* 37 (January 1930): 31; Schneider, *"We Return Fighting,"* 391; "Miss Fauset," *Crisis* 32 (May 1926): 7.

107. Amy Jacques Garvey's 1968 retrospective of the movement barely mentions her own or other women's significance within it. Jacques Garvey, *Garvey and Garveyism*; "Negro Race Going Forward to the Point of Destiny," *NW* 14 (March 24, 1923): 1 (quotation); Bair, "True Women, Real Men," 155, 157. A group of women within the UNIA (not including Jacques Garvey) fought unsuccessfully in 1922 for a more egalitarian structure. Taylor, *Veiled Garvey*, 44–46.

108. "A De Saible [*sic*] Memorial," *National Notes* 31 (February 1929): 7 (quotations; figure of $20,000), in *NACW Records, Part 1*, reel 24, frame 00401; "Mayor Names Woman for De Saible Board," *National Notes* 32 (November 1929): 10, in *NACW Records, Part 1*, reel 24, frame 00478. The second account calls Oliver "the originator of the plan" and gives $25,000 as the amount appropriated.

109. "Departmental Reports," *National Notes* 30 (July 1928): 28, in *NACW Records, Part 1*, reel 24, frame 00359.

110. Des Jardins, *Women and the Historical Enterprise in America*, 147–60; Ruffins, "'Lifting as We Climb,'" 379; *National Notes* 31 (September–October 1928): 5, 21, in *NACW Records, Part 1*, reel 24, frames 00366, 00374; *National Association of Colored Women (Incorporated), Sixteenth Biennial Session* (n.p., 1928), 22, 35, in *NACW Records, Part 1*, reel 1, frames 00822, 00828; McCluskey and Smith, *Mary McLeod Bethune*, 6; Dagbovie, "Black Women," 30–31, 33–34 (who argues alternatively that Carter G. Woodson attributed considerable importance to black women, both as historians and as historical figures, relative to male contemporaries).

111. Benito Thomas in "The People's Forum," *NW* 18 (April 4, 1925): 10; Kelly Miller, "Educated Negroes Said Not to Marry and Raise Large Families," *NW* 17 (February 7, 1925): 7. Miller briefly addressed male selfishness but devoted most of his discussion to women's behavior, notably their overly lengthy educations. On birth control, also see Amy Jacques Garvey, "A Dearth of Husbands," *NW* 22 (July 9, 1927): 4.

112. Frances Jackson, "Home Building for the Negro Youth," *NW* 18 (May 23, 1925): 7. Also see Taylor, *Veiled Garvey*, 79–81; Satter, "Marcus Garvey, Father Divine, and the Gender Politics of Race Difference and Race Neutrality," 47–52; and Summers, *Manliness and Its Discontents*, 66–114, 121–26, 133–38.

113. "Confederate Monument at Amarillo, Tex.," *CV* 39 (July 1931): 263. An exception is Gutzon Borglum's relief of Confederate generals and leaders on the side of Stone Mountain, outside Atlanta. A number of UDC chapters raised funds for the monument. Stone Mountain Confederate Memorial Founders Roll circular, n.d. [1924], UDC Scrapbook Missouri.

114. "From the President General," *CV* 35 (July 1927): 270; "From the Presi-

dent General," *CV* 36 (May 1928): 190; Simpson, *Edith D. Pope and Her Nashville Friends*, 110–11; Ruby E. Livingston, "Confederate Mothers' Park," *CV* 31 (November 1923): 435 (discussion of a "skyline drive" leading to a planned Confederate Mothers' park in Russellville, Arkansas).

115. Mary D. Carter, "The State Rights Renaissance," *CV* 30 (September 1922): 325.

116. Ruth Jennings Lawton, "From the President General," *CV* 35 (March 1927): 110 (quotation); Lawton, "From the President General," *CV* 35 (April 1927): 148.

117. Foner, *Reconstruction*, 609–10. Like many African Americans, Anna Julia Cooper (who by then held a doctorate in history) was horrified by *The Tragic Era*. In imploring W. E. B. Du Bois to answer it, she encouraged his *Black Reconstruction* (1935), a milestone in historiography. "The Browsing Reader," *Crisis* 37 (January 1930): 19; Gaines, *Uplifting the Race*, 132.

118. Grace Upton Bathrick to "State Regents and State Chairmen," September 1, 1925, circular of the NSDAR Committee on Children, Sons and Daughters of the Republic, folder 1 (papers 1925–1926), box 2, DAR Papers St. Paul.

119. Nielsen, *Un-American Womanhood*, 144, 151–52. On the African Blood Brotherhood, see Gaines, *Uplifting the Race*, 236–37; and Schneider, *"We Return Fighting,"* 386. In labeling Du Bois a "Negro socialist," the DAR may well have been taking note of his trip to the Soviet Union in 1926, which turned out to be an early step in his eventual conversion to Marxism. Schneider, *"We Return Fighting,"* 387–88; "Russia, 1926," *Crisis* 33 (November 1926): 8; Lewis, *W. E. B. Du Bois: The Fight for Equality and the American Century*, 199–203.

120. Hine and Thompson, *Shining Thread of Hope*, 251; "'Do Unto Others As You Would They Should do Unto [*sic*],'" *National Notes* 27 (June 1925): 11, in *NACW Records, Part 1*, reel 24, frame 00010; "The Battle of Washington," *Crisis* 30 (July 1925): 114–15; Delegard, "Women Patriots," 135–36; Keiler, *Marian Anderson*, 188–89; Anderson, *Daughters*, 127–29; Black, "Championing a Champion," 721; Neverdon-Morton, *Afro-American Women of the South*, 201.

121. Keiler, *Marian Anderson*, 185.

122. Fred E. Hand, "Facts Concerning the Management of Constitution Hall," n.d. [1940], folder 2: General Correspondence, box 1, Series 1: State Regent, DAR Collection Nebraska; LaGanke, "National Society of the Daughters of the American Revolution," 391–400; Sandage, "Marble House Divided," 143–44. The institution of the white-artist policy was kept secret from the membership, in that published notes of meetings of the National Board of Management contained no mention of the change. However, delegates to the national convention elected by the membership voted to retain the policy in 1947. *DARM* 66 (March–May 1932): 129–320; "Constitution Hall Race Policy Indorsed by DAR Congress," *Washington Post*, April 21, 1947, 1.

Epilogue

1. The vote's margin was thirty-nine to one. "Minutes, National Board of Management, Regular Meeting, February 1, 1939," cited in LaGanke, "National Society of the Daughters of the American Revolution," 394. Although the leadership's action was explained to members as the result of the white-artist rule, Constitution Hall's manager added falsely that Anderson's bookers at Howard University had been inflexible about the date of her performance—insisting only on a Sunday night, April 9, when the National Symphony Orchestra had already booked. Sixty years later, this canard still endured among some Daughters. In reality, Anderson's bookers had asked also for April 8 or April 10. On those nights, Constitution Hall stood empty. Fred E. Hand, "Facts Concerning the Management of Constitution Hall," n.d. [1940], folder 2: General Correspondence, box 1, Series 1: State Regent, DAR Collection Nebraska; Charles C. Cohen to Fred Hand, February 8, 1939, and Hand to Cohen, February 10, 1939, both in folder 27, box 1, MA Collection; Charles H. Houston and John Lovell Jr. to Mrs. Henry M. Robert Jr. (Sarah Corbin Robert), April 20, 1939, folder 9, box 1, MA Collection; Black, "Championing a Champion," 722–23.

2. As one example, see "Much Ado About Nothing," *Charleston (S.C.) News and Courier*, March 1, 1939 (typescript copy), folder 44, box 2, MA Collection.

3. Walter White to Charles H. Houston, March 6, 1939, and White to Houston, March 13, 1939, folder 11, box 1, MA Collection; Black, "Championing a Champion," 723.

4. John Lovell Jr. to Charles H. Houston, June 1, 1939, folder 7, box 1, MA Collection.

5. Nellie S. Davidson to Charles H. Houston, February 26, 1939, folder 5, box 1, MA Collection.

6. Keiler, *Marian Anderson*, 189–90.

7. *The Red Network* (1934) and *The Roosevelt Red Record and Its Background* (1936) were the work of the far-rightist Elizabeth Kirkpatrick Dilling. The Chicagoan did not belong to the DAR but, by some accounts, wanted badly to join. Florence Hague Becker of Connecticut, then the National Defense Committee chair, won the DAR's presidency in 1935 by a landslide (70 percent of the vote), despite controversy over her endorsement of *The Red Network*. Even scholars who are sympathetic to anticommunism consider Dilling's work "bizarre." She was later indicted during World War II for disseminating profascist propaganda. "Mrs. Becker Wins D.A.R. Presidency: 'Conservative' Candidate Turns Back Insurgent Rival," *Grand Rapids (Mich.) Press*, n.d. [April 1935], clipping in Marie Therese Cadillac Chapter DAR (Cadillac, Mich.) scrapbook (1931–1949), box 18, DAR Papers Michigan; Amy Cresswell Dunne to Mabel Thorpe Smith, April 1, 1935, in scrapbook of state and chapter activities, vol. 2 (1933–1936), box 34, DAR Papers Michigan; Benowitz, *Days of Discontent*; Jeansonne, *Women of the Far Right*, esp. 10–28; Powers,

Not Without Honor, 129 (quotation), 130–32, 183–87; Ribuffo, *Old Christian Right*, 196–215.

8. Black, "Championing a Champion," 730–31; "Mrs. F.D.R. Supports Anti-Lynch Bill," *Crisis* 46 (February 1939): 54; "Mrs. Roosevelt Awards Medal," *Crisis* 46 (September 1939): 265, 285.

9. "A Distinguished D.A.R.," *DARM* 67 (May 1933): 270–71; Kearney, *Anna Eleanor Roosevelt*, 89; Lash, *Love, Eleanor*, 189–90; Beasley, *White House Press Conferences of Eleanor Roosevelt*, 21, 93.

10. "D.A.R. Withdraws from Membership in Defense Group," n.d. [1933], unidentified clipping, in folder "DAR, 1924–1928," Attacks, box 494, NCPW Papers; "National Board of Management: Regular Meeting, April 14, 1934," *DARM* 68 (May 1934): 316.

11. Sandage, "Marble House Divided"; Mary McLeod Bethune to Charles H. Houston, April 10, 1939, folder 4, box 1, MA Collection.

12. "Great Designs: President's Address to the Fifteenth Biennial Convention of the National Association of Colored Women" (1926) and "Certain Unalienable Rights" (1944), both in McCluskey and Smith, *Mary McLeod Bethune*, 159–61, 20–27.

13. Flora Bredes Walker, "Confidential Memorandum for D.A.R. Members Only" (1928), 10, State Committee on National Defense, in State Chairmen Reports, vol. II (H–M), box 9, DAR Papers Michigan. Exceptions to white women's labeling of the United States as a "republic" came from southerners. An Arkansas DAR leader, for example, insisted that "We are a *Democracy*, with Bunker Hill and Washington Monuments for our signal towers." Ellen Harrell Cantrell, "What Genealogy Is," *AMM* 7 (November 1895): 394. Black clubwomen also often preferred to designate the United States a "republic" or, alternatively, "the nation." Brown, *Homespun Heroines*, 63; Julia A. Hooks, "In Union There is Strength," in *History of the Club Movement among the Colored Women*, 69; Ida B. Wells, "Preface: To the Seeker after Truth," in Wells, Douglass, Penn, and Barnett, *Reason Why the Colored American Is Not in the World's Columbian Exposition*, 3.

14. See especially Sullivan, *Days of Hope*.

15. Higham, *Send These to Me*, 58–60, 198–232; Gleason, "American Identity and Americanization," 41–45; Vaughan, "Cosmopolitanism, Ethnicity, and American Identity."

16. Michaels, *Our America*.

17. Douglas, *Terrible Honesty*, 6–8 (quotation on p. 7 and elsewhere), 217–99.

18. Cott, *Grounding of Modern Feminism*, esp. 13–50.

19. Dunlap et al., *History and Register: Washington State Society*, 193; Cott, *Grounding of Modern Feminism*, 145–74. Ironies abound when Walker's public pronouncements on home and country are juxtaposed with her personal life at the time. She inhabited a "female world of love and ritual" that echoed those of many bourgeois Victorians. Living across the country from each other, Walker and her hus-

band, who were childless, divorced by 1930. She lived in close companionship and vacationed with onetime DAR president Grace Brosseau. An equally heartfelt rightist, Brosseau was also divorced by the early 1930s, and childless. Smith-Rosenberg, "Female World of Love and Ritual"; Delegard, "Women Patriots," 152.

20. Marling, *George Washington Slept Here*, 335–37, 345–46; Dennis, *Grant Wood*, 110–12. Another example of declining respect for clubwomen in the mid-twentieth century is Frazier, *Black Bourgeoisie*, 222–23; see also White, *Too Heavy a Load*, 188–89.

21. Mrs. Johnson in *DARPCC* 30 (1921): 100. Scholars point to ideological affinities between the hereditarian DAR and the contemporary eugenics movement. In practice, the DAR promoted eugenics only sporadically. Its national publications do not mention supporting laws, passed in twenty-six states between 1907 and 1932, allowing the involuntary sterilization of institutionalized people judged unfit to reproduce—a staple of contemporary eugenics. Smith, *American Archives*, 137, 139; David Fairchild, "A Genetic Portrait Chart, According to Sir Francis Galton," *DARM* 56 (June 1922): 354–360 (reprinted from the Washington-based *Journal of Heredity*).

22. Koonz, *Mothers in the Fatherland*, 186.

23. Black Unity Party (Peekskill, N.Y.), "Birth Control Pills and Black Children," in Patricia Robinson, "Poor Black Women" (Boston: New England Free Press, n.d. [1968?]), available online in *Documents from the Women's Liberation Movement*, Rare Book, Manuscript, and Special Collections Library, Duke University, Durham, N.C., ‹http://scriptorium.lib.duke.edu/wlm/poor/› (accessed November 10, 2004); White, *Too Heavy a Load*, 212–56.

24. Cott, "Across the Great Divide"; Cott, *Grounding of Modern Feminism*, 85–114.

25. The WRC survived into the twenty-first century as an ambition to "perpetuate the memory of the Grand Army of the Republic," and as an auxiliary to the Sons of Union Veterans of the Civil War. The WRC counted 2,360 members nationwide in 2001. "Auxiliary to the Grand Army of the Republic, Woman's Relief Corps," June 3, 2001, ‹http://suvcw.org/wrc.htm› (accessed November 10, 2004).

26. Ruffins, "'Lifting as We Climb,'" 384–85; Hine and Thompson, *Shining Thread of Hope*, 252; Hanson, *Mary McLeod Bethune and Black Women's Political Activism*, 116–19, 164–205; White, *Too Heavy a Load*, 142–211.

27. See especially Robinson, *Montgomery Bus Boycott and the Women Who Started It*; Ransby, *Ella Baker and the Black Freedom Movement*; Standley, "Role of Black Women in the Civil Rights Movement."

28. Bishir, "Landmarks of Power," 143.

29. Cox, *Dixie's Daughters*, 163. With 35,000 members as of 2002, the SCV was roughly two-thirds bigger than the UDC, numbering 21,000 in 2003. Joe DePriest, "Black Leader of Confederate Gray," *Charlotte (N.C.) Observer*, November 24, 2002, ‹www.charlotte.com/mld/observer/news/local/4593152.htm?1c› (accessed

March 24, 2004); "Controversy Surrounds Christmas Parade," December 4, 2003, ‹www.cnn.com/2003/US/South/12/04/parade.controversy.ap/› (accessed March 24, 2004). A guided news search of the "LexisNexis Academic" database for "Daughters of the Confederacy" and "Sons of Confederate Veterans" for the year preceding November 2004 yielded 292 hits for the men and 177 hits for the women. These numbers represent the sum of hits for each organization in southeastern, midwestern, northeastern, and western news sources. LexisNexis Academic, ‹http://web.lexis-nexis.com/universe/› (accessed November 10, 2004).

30. See especially Horwitz, *Confederates in the Attic*.

31. Jacoway and Williams, *Understanding the Little Rock Crisis*; Kellar, *Make Haste Slowly*; Leidholdt, *Standing before the Shouting Mob*; Pride, *Political Use of Racial Narratives*; Cox, *Dixie's Daughters*, 160–62. Of course, not all white southerners who had, as children, been steeped in neo-Confederate assumptions retained them in adulthood. Lumpkin, *Making of a Southerner*, esp. 109–47; Hall, "'You Must Remember This'"; Durr, *Outside the Magic Circle*, 44–45.

32. The first known African American in the DAR, Karen Batchelor Farmer, joined a Detroit chapter in 1977. In 1983, after three years of effort, Lena Santos Ferguson of Washington, D.C., joined the DAR as a nonvoting, at-large member (unaffiliated with any chapter) after a chapter refused her admission. Ferguson had documented her Revolutionary descent—from a white fighter—and had produced two sponsors, as required. She tried again without success to join a Washington chapter. At around the same time, in 1984, some national leaders proposed amending a DAR bylaw to restrict membership to those "legitimately descended" from Revolutionaries. This amendment failed to pass. That year, the DAR estimated its black membership nationwide at five. Ferguson later joined another Washington chapter. When she died in 2004, no other black Daughters in the District of Columbia survived her. Starting in the mid-1980s, as part of the legal settlement relating to Ferguson's efforts to become a member, the DAR amassed and published documents regarding Native American and black Revolutionary fighters in order to aid their descendants in joining. Donnie Radcliffe, "The DAR's Changing Image," *Washington Post*, April 21, 1978, C1; Jacqueline Trescott, "National DAR Admits Black," *Washington Post*, May 10, 1983, B3; Ronald Kessler, "Sponsors Claim Race Is Stumbling Block; Black Unable to Join Local DAR," *Washington Post*, March 12, 1984, A1; Ruth Marcus, "DAR Reprimands, Then Suspends Punishment of Two Members," *Washington Post*, October 11, 1985, C1; Jeff Jacoby, "Revolutionary Daughters in Racial Time Warp," *Wall Street Journal*, January 6, 1986, 1; Elisabeth Hickey, "The DAR's Patriot Game," *Washington Times*, October 26, 1990, E1; "D.A.R. Continues to Integrate Its Chapters," *Los Angeles Sentinel*, November 20, 1997, C2; Robert Knox, "DAR Uses Research to Attract Minority Members," *Boston Globe*, February 14, 2002, "Globe South" section, 1; Bart Barnes, "Lena Ferguson Dies at 75; Challenged the DAR on Race," *Washington Post*, March 14, 2004, C10. I thank Maurice Barboza for directing me to this material.

33. Examples may be found in Lynd and Lynd, *Middletown*, 200–201, 489–91, 496.

34. The DAR counted 170,000 active members in 2004. Texas overtook New York in 1973 as the state containing the largest number of DAR members. "About DAR," ⟨http://www.dar.org/natsociety/whoweare.cfm⟩ (accessed November 10, 2004); Anderson, *Daughters*, 43. On the congruence between the DAR and the postwar right, see Mathews and De Hart, *Sex, Gender, and the Politics of ERA*, 153–54.

35. Schlafly is best known for rallying conservatives and rightists to defeat the Equal Rights Amendment (ERA). Zimmerman, *Centennial History of the Illinois State Organization*, 63, 110; Felsenthal, *Sweetheart of the Silent Majority*, 20, 167; Mathews and De Hart, *Sex, Gender, and the Politics of ERA*, esp. 68–69.

Bibliography

Archival Collections

Atlanta History Center Library/Archives, Atlanta, Ga.
    Papers of Mrs. D. Miller Cox
    Daughters of the American Revolution Collection
    Garrett/Boyd Papers
Chicago Historical Society, Chicago, Ill.
    Chicago Chapter DAR application registers
Duke University, Rare Book, Manuscript, and Special Collections Library,
    Durham, N.C.
    *Documents from the Women's Liberation Movement: An On-Line Archival
    Collection*, ‹http://scriptorium.lib.duke.edu/wlm/› (last accessed November 10, 2004)
Georgia Department of Archives and History, Atlanta, Ga.
    Papers of Zillah Lee Bostick Redd Agerton
    Daughters of the American Revolution, Georgia Society Scrapbooks
    Papers of Rowena Hanes Ford
Historical Society of Saratoga Springs, Saratoga Springs, N.Y.
    Papers of Ellen Hardin Walworth
Howard University, Moorland-Spingarn Research Center, Washington, D.C.
    Marian Anderson–DAR Controversy Collection
Library of Congress, Manuscript Division, Washington, D.C.
    Papers of Kate Waller Barrett
    Papers of the Daniel Newcomb Chapter (Yankton, S.D.), Daughters of the
    American Revolution
    Papers of Mary Desha, Breckinridge Family Papers
    Papers of Mrs. Daniel Manning
    Papers of Horace Porter
Litchfield Historical Society, Litchfield, Conn.

Papers of Mary Floyd Tallmadge Chapter DAR

Michigan Historical Collections, Bentley Library, University of Michigan, Ann Arbor, Mich.

Papers of Sarah Caswell Angell

Papers of the Daughters of the American Revolution, Michigan Society

Papers of Henry Bourne Joy

Papers of Clara Hadley Wait

Minnesota Historical Society, Minnesota History Center, St. Paul, Minn.

Papers of Jennie Adelaide Holmes Coolidge

Papers of the Daughters of the American Revolution, Minnesota Society

Daughters of the American Revolution, St. Paul Chapter Papers

Papers of the Sibley House Association

Mississippi Department of Archives and History, Jackson, Miss.

Papers of Mrs. Calvin S. Brown (Maud Morrow Brown)

Daughters of the American Revolution Papers

National Archives and Records Administration, College Park, Md.

RG 102: U.S. Department of Labor, Records of the Children's Bureau

RG 165: U.S. Department of War, Military Intelligence Division Correspondence, 1917–1941, Personnel Files

National Archives and Records Administration, Washington, D.C.

RG 94: U.S. Department of War, Adjutant General's Office Files, Correspondence of the Adjutant General

RG 165: U.S. Department of War, Military Intelligence Division Correspondence, 1917–1941

RG 165: U.S. Department of War, War College Division General Correspondence, 1903–1919

National Society Daughters of the American Revolution Headquarters, Office of the Historian General, Washington, D.C.

Mrs. Arturo Y. Casanova and Mrs. Z. Lewis Dalby, comps., "State History, District of Columbia Daughters of the American Revolution, in Three Volumes," 3 vols., typescript, 1934

Nebraska State Historical Society, Manuscript Division, Lincoln, Neb.

Daughters of the American Revolution Collection

Nebraska Society of the Sons of the American Revolution Collection

New York Public Library, Manuscripts and Archives Section, New York, N.Y.

Baldwin-McDowell Papers

North Carolina Division of Archives and History, Raleigh, N.C.

Papers of the Caswell-Nash Chapter DAR (Raleigh, N.C.)

Papers of Toccoa Page Cozart

Papers of the Daughters of the American Revolution, North Carolina Society

Minutes of Iredell County/Fort Dobbs Chapter DAR (Statesville, N.C.), microform

Papers of Lida Rodman, Rodman Family Papers
Papers of Jessica Randolph Smith
Arthur and Elizabeth Schlesinger Library on the History of Women in America, Radcliffe Institute for Advanced Study, Cambridge, Mass.
Corinne Marie Tuckerman Allen Papers
Mary Anderson Papers, Papers of the Women's Trade Union League and Its Principal Leaders, microform
Elizabeth Porter Gould Papers
Emma Guffey Miller Papers, Women in National Politics Collection, microform
Edith Nourse Rogers Papers
Nellie Nugent Somerville Papers, Somerville and Howorth Family Papers
Anna Wiley Papers
Sophia Smith Collection, Smith College, Northampton, Mass.
Papers of Helen Tufts Bailie
Stanford University Special Collections, Stanford, Calif.
DAR "Blacklist" Controversy Collection
State Historical Society of Iowa, Library/Archives Bureau, Iowa City
Daughters of the American Revolution Collection
Papers of Sarah Paine Hoffman
Swarthmore College Peace Collection, Swarthmore, Pa.
Papers of Ellen Starr Brinton
Papers of Dorothy Detzer
Papers of Hannah Clothier Hull
Papers of Lucia Ames Mead, Scholarly Resources microfilm edition
Papers of the National Council for Prevention of War
Special Collections: Attackers
University of Kentucky Special Collections, Lexington, Ky.
Papers of Mary Desha
University of Mississippi Special Collections, Oxford, Miss.
Daughters of the American Revolution Collection
Western Historical Manuscript Collection, University of Missouri/State Historical Society of Missouri, Columbia, Mo.
Helm-Davidson Family Papers
John S. Marmaduke Chapter (Columbia, Mo.), United Daughters of the Confederacy scrapbook
Missouri Society of the Daughters of the American Revolution Collection
Western Reserve Historical Society, Cleveland, Ohio
Daughters of the American Revolution, Americanization Committee Reports of Chapter Regents to State Regents, 1920
Papers of the Daughters of the American Revolution, vertical file
Papers of the Western Reserve Chapter DAR (Cleveland, Ohio)

Papers of Orlando John Hodge
Papers of the Sons of the American Revolution, Western Reserve Society
Papers of the War Emergency Relief Board
Woman's Collection, Texas Woman's University, Denton, Tex.
Daughters of the American Revolution, Texas Society Collection

Periodicals

American Monthly Magazine
Boston Globe
Colored American Magazine
Confederate Veteran
Crisis
Daughters of the American Revolution Magazine
Daughters of the American Revolution, Proceedings of the Continental Congress
Iowa Daughters of the American Revolution, Annual Conference
Los Angeles Sentinel
Negro World
Our Heritage: Official Organ U.D.C. of Mississippi
Patriotic Review
Philadelphia Inquirer
Voice of the Negro
Wall Street Journal
Washington Post
Washington Times
Woman's Era

Published Works

Addams, Jane. *Twenty Years at Hull-House, with Autobiographical Notes.* Edited
    with an introduction by Victoria Bissell Brown. Boston: Bedford/
    St. Martin's, 1999.
———. "Why Women Should Vote." In *One Woman, One Vote: Rediscovering
    the Woman Suffrage Movement,* edited by Marjorie Spruill Wheeler, 179–202.
    Troutdale, Ore.: NewSage Press, 1995.
Alexander, Thomas G. *Mormonism in Transition: A History of the Latter-Day
    Saints, 1890–1930.* Urbana and Chicago: University of Illinois Press, 1986.
Alonso, Harriet Hyman. *Peace as a Women's Issue: A History of the U.S. Move-
    ment for World Peace and Women's Rights.* Syracuse, N.Y.: Syracuse University
    Press, 1993.
Anderson, Benedict. *Imagined Communities: Reflections on the Origin and Spread
    of Nationalism.* Rev. ed. London and New York: Verso, 1991.

Anderson, Peggy. *The Daughters: An Unconventional Look at America's Fan Club—The DAR*. New York: St. Martin's Press, 1974.

Attie, Jeanie. *Patriotic Toil: Northern Women and the American Civil War*. Ithaca, N.Y.: Cornell University Press, 1998.

Austin, Allan D. "American Revolution." In Vol. 1 of *Encyclopedia of African-American History*, edited by Jack Salzman, David Lionel Smith, and Cornel West, 121–22. New York: Simon and Schuster, 1996.

Axelrod, Alan, ed. *The Colonial Revival in America*. New York: W. W. Norton, 1985.

Bailey, Fred Arthur. "Free Speech and the 'Lost Cause' in Texas: A Study of Social Control in the New South." *Southwestern Historical Quarterly* 97 (January 1994): 453–78.

————. "Mildred Lewis Rutherford and the Patrician Cult of the Old South." *Georgia Historical Quarterly* 78 (Fall 1994): 509–35.

————. "The Textbooks of the 'Lost Cause': Censorship and the Creation of Southern State Histories." *Georgia Historical Quarterly* 75 (Fall 1991): 507–33.

Bair, Barbara. "True Women, Real Men: Gender, Ideology, and Social Roles in the Garvey Movement." In *Gendered Domains: Rethinking Public and Private in Women's History*, edited by Dorothy O. Helly and Susan M. Reverby, 154–66. Ithaca, N.Y.: Cornell University Press, 1992.

Baker, Helen Dow, comp. and ed. *Texas State History of the Daughters of the American Revolution*. Abilene, Tex.: Abilene Printing and Stationery Co., 1929.

Baker, Paula. "The Domestication of Politics: Women and American Political Society, 1780–1920." *American Historical Review* 89 (June 1984): 620–47.

Barrington, Lewis. *Historical Restorations of the Daughters of the American Revolution*. New York: Richard R. Smith, 1941.

Bauer, Fern Ioula. *The Historic Treasure Chest of the Madonna of the Trail Monuments*. 1986; reprint, Springfield, Ohio: Process Printing, 1993.

Baym, Nina. *American Women Writers and the Work of History, 1790–1860*. New Brunswick, N.J.: Rutgers University Press, 1995.

Beard, Mary Ritter. *Woman's Work in Municipalities*. New York: Appleton, 1915.

Beasley, Maurine, ed. *The White House Press Conferences of Eleanor Roosevelt*. New York: Garland Publishing, 1983.

Beckert, Sven. *The Monied Metropolis: New York City and the Consolidation of the American Bourgeoisie, 1850–1896*. New York: Cambridge University Press, 2001.

Bederman, Gail. *Manliness and Civilization: A Cultural History of Gender and Race in the United States, 1880–1917*. Chicago: University of Chicago Press, 1995.

Behling, Laura L. *The Masculine Woman in America, 1890–1935*. Urbana and Chicago: University of Illinois Press, 2001.

Benowitz, June Melby. *Days of Discontent: American Women and Right-Wing Politics, 1933–1945*. DeKalb: Northern Illinois University Press, 2002.

Bishir, Catherine W. "Landmarks of Power: Building a Southern Past in Raleigh and Wilmington, North Carolina, 1885–1915." In *Where These Memories Grow: History, Memory, and Southern Identity*, edited by W. Fitzhugh Brundage, 139–68. Chapel Hill: University of North Carolina Press, 2000.

―――. " 'A Strong Force of Ladies': Women, Politics, and Confederate Memorial Associations in Nineteenth-Century Raleigh." In *Monuments to the Lost Cause: Women, Art, and the Landscapes of Southern Memory*, edited by Cynthia Mills and Pamela H. Simpson, 3–26. Knoxville: University of Tennessee Press, 2003.

Black, Allida M. "Championing a Champion: Eleanor Roosevelt and the Marian Anderson 'Freedom Concert.' " *Presidential Studies Quarterly* 20 (Fall 1990): 719–36.

Blair, William. *Cities of the Dead: Contesting the Memory of the Civil War in the South, 1865–1914*. Chapel Hill: University of North Carolina Press, 2004.

Blee, Kathleen M. *Women of the Klan: Racism and Gender in the 1920s*. Berkeley and Los Angeles: University of California Press, 1991.

Blight, David W. *Race and Reunion: The Civil War in American Memory*. Cambridge, Mass.: Harvard University Press, 2001.

Bodnar, John. "The Attractions of Patriotism." In *Bonds of Affection: Americans Define Their Patriotism*, edited by John Bodnar, 3–18. Princeton, N.J.: Princeton University Press, 1996.

―――. *Remaking America: Public Memory, Commemoration, and Patriotism in the Twentieth Century*. Princeton, N.J.: Princeton University Press, 1992.

Boehm, Randolph, ed. *Papers of the NAACP, Part 2: 1919–1939, Personal Correspondence of Selected NAACP Officials*. Bethesda, Md.: University Publications of America, 1982.

Bonner, Robert E. *Colors and Blood: Flag Passions of the Confederate South*. Princeton, N.J.: Princeton University Press, 2002.

Bordin, Ruth. *Woman and Temperance: The Quest for Power and Liberty, 1873–1900*. 1981; reprint, New Brunswick, N.J.: Rutgers University Press, 1990.

Bowers, Claude G. *The Tragic Era: The Revolution after Lincoln*. New York: Blue Ribbon Books, 1929.

Boynton, Helen M., et al. "Early History: Daughters of the American Revolution." In *History of the Kansas State Daughters of the American Revolution, 1894–1938*, by Leda Ferrell Rex et al., 109–26. N.p.: Kansas Daughters of the American Revolution, 1938.

Brear, Holly Beachley. *Inherit the Alamo: Myth and Ritual at an American Shrine*. Austin: University of Texas Press, 1995.

Bredbenner, Candice Lewis. *A Nationality of Her Own: Women, Marriage, and the Law of Citizenship*. Berkeley and Los Angeles: University of California Press, 1998.

Breen, William J. "Black Women and the Great War: Mobilization and Reform in the South." *Journal of Southern History* 44 (August 1978): 421–40.

Bridenthal, Renate, Atina Grossmann, and Marion Kaplan, eds. *When Biology Became Destiny: Women in Weimar and Nazi Germany*. New York: Monthly Review Press, 1984.

Brinkley, Alan, Susan M. Yohn, and Leo Ribuffo. "*AHR* Forum: American Conservatism." *American Historical Review* 99 (April 1994): 409–52.

Brown, Elsa Barkley. "Negotiating and Transforming the Public Sphere: African American Political Life in the Transition from Slavery to Freedom." In *Jumpin' Jim Crow: Southern Politics from Civil War to Civil Rights*, edited by Jane Dailey, Glenda Elizabeth Gilmore, and Bryant Simon, 28–66. Princeton, N.J.: Princeton University Press, 2000.

Brown, Hallie Q. *Homespun Heroines and Other Women of Distinction*. 1926; reprint, with an introduction by Randall K. Burkett, New York: Oxford University Press, 1988.

Brundage, W. Fitzhugh. "No Deed But Memory." In *Where These Memories Grow: History, Memory, and Southern Identity*, edited by W. Fitzhugh Brundage, 1–28. Chapel Hill: University of North Carolina Press, 2000.

————. "White Women and the Politics of Historical Memory in the New South, 1880–1920." In *Jumpin' Jim Crow: Southern Politics from Civil War to Civil Rights*, edited by Jane Dailey, Glenda Elizabeth Gilmore, and Bryant Simon, 115–39. Princeton, N.J.: Princeton University Press, 2000.

————. "'Woman's Heart and Hand and Deathless Love': White Women and the Commemorative Impulse in the New South." In *Monuments to the Lost Cause: Women, Art, and the Landscapes of Southern Memory*, edited by Cynthia Mills and Pamela H. Simpson, 64–82. Knoxville: University of Tennessee Press, 2003.

Butler, William. "Another City upon a Hill: Litchfield, Connecticut, and the Colonial Revival." In *The Colonial Revival in America*, edited by Alan Axelrod, 15–51. New York: W. W. Norton, 1985.

Capozzola, Christopher. "The Only Badge Needed Is Your Patriotic Fervor: Vigilance, Coercion, and the Law in World War I America." *Journal of American History* 88 (March 2002): 1354–82.

Carby, Hazel V. *Race Men*. Cambridge, Mass.: Harvard University Press, 1998.

Carr, John Foster. *Guide for the Immigrant Italian in the United States of America, Published under the Auspices of the Connecticut Daughters of the American Revolution*. New York: Doubleday, Page and Co., 1911.

————. *Guide to the United States for the Jewish Immigrant: A Nearly Literal Translation of the Second Yiddish Edition*. N.p.: Connecticut Daughters of the American Revolution, 1912.

Case, Sarah H. "The Historical Ideology of Mildred Lewis Rutherford: A Confederate Historian's New South Creed." *Journal of Southern History* 68 (August 2002): 599–628.

Chapter Directory, 1893, Daughters of the American Revolution. N.p., 1893.

Chapter Histories: Daughters of the American Revolution in Georgia, 1891–1931. Augusta, Ga.: Ridgely-Tidwell Co., n.d. [1931].

Chatterjee, Partha. *The Nation and Its Fragments: Colonial and Postcolonial Histories.* Princeton, N.J.: Princeton University Press, 1993.

Chickering, Roger. " 'Casting Their Gaze More Broadly': Women's Patriotic Activism in Imperial Germany." *Past and Present* 118 (February 1988): 156–85.

Clark, Ethel Maddock, comp. and ed. *Arizona State History of the Daughters of the American Revolution.* Greenfield, Ohio: Greenfield Printing and Publishing, n.d. [1930].

Cleveland, Grover. "Woman's Mission and Woman's Clubs." *Ladies' Home Journal* 22 (May 1905): 3–4.

Clinton, Catherine. *Tara Revisited: Women, War, and the Plantation Legend.* New York: Abbeville Press, 1995.

Colley, Linda. *Britons: Forging the Nation, 1707–1837.* New Haven, Conn.: Yale University Press, 1992.

Collier-Thomas, Bettye, and V. P. Franklin, eds. *Sisters in the Struggle: African American Women in the Civil Rights–Black Power Movement.* New York: New York University Press, 2001.

Connor, Walker. "The Nation and Its Myth." *International Journal of Comparative Sociology* 33 (January–April 1992): 48–57.

Constitution and By-Laws of the Daughters of the American Revolution. Washington, D.C.: Press of Gedney and Roberts, 1890.

Constitution and By-Laws of the Daughters of the American Revolution. Washington, D.C.: Press of W. F. Roberts, 1894.

Constitution and By-Laws of the Daughters of the American Revolution. Washington, D.C.: National Society Daughters of the American Revolution, 1931.

Cook, Blanche Wiesen. *Eleanor Roosevelt.* 2 vols. New York: Penguin Books, 1992–99.

Cooper, Anna Julia. *A Voice from the South.* 1892; reprint, with an introduction by Mary Helen Washington, New York: Oxford University Press, 1988.

Cordry, Mrs. T. A. *The Story of the Marking of the Santa Fe Trail by the Daughters of the American Revolution in Kansas and the State of Kansas.* Topeka, Kans.: Crane and Co., Printers, 1915.

Cott, Nancy F. "Across the Great Divide: Women in Politics Before and After 1920." In *One Woman, One Vote: Rediscovering the Woman Suffrage Movement,* edited by Marjorie Spruill Wheeler, 353–73. Troutdale, Ore.: NewSage Press, 1995.

―――. *The Grounding of Modern Feminism.* New Haven, Conn.: Yale University Press, 1987.

―――. *Public Vows: A History of Marriage and the Nation.* Cambridge, Mass.: Harvard University Press, 2000.

Courtney, Grace Gates, comp., and Arcada Stark Balz, ed. *History: Indiana Federation of Clubs*. Fort Wayne, Ind.: Fort Wayne Printing Company, 1939.

Cox, Karen L. "The Confederate Monument at Arlington: A Token of Reconciliation." In *Monuments to the Lost Cause: Women, Art, and the Landscapes of Southern Memory*, edited by Cynthia Mills and Pamela H. Simpson, 149–62. Knoxville: University of Tennessee Press, 2003.

———. *Dixie's Daughters: The United Daughters of the Confederacy and the Preservation of Confederate Culture*. Gainesville: University Press of Florida, 2003.

Dagbovie, Pero Daglo. "Black Women, Carter G. Woodson, and the Association for the Study of African American Life and History, 1915–1950." *Journal of African American History* 88 (Winter 2003): 21–41.

———. "Black Women Historians from the Late Nineteenth Century to the Dawning of the Civil Rights Movement." *Journal of African American History* 89 (Summer 2004): 241–61.

Davenport, Robert R., ed. *Hereditary Society Blue Book*. Baltimore, Md.: Genealogical Publishing Co., 1994.

Davies, Wallace Evan. *Patriotism on Parade: The Story of Veterans' Organizations and Hereditary Organizations in America, 1783–1900*. Cambridge, Mass.: Harvard University Press, 1955.

Davin, Anna. "Imperialism and Motherhood." In *History and Politics*. Vol. 1 of *Patriotism: The Making and Unmaking of British National Identity*, edited by Raphael Samuel, 203–35. London and New York: Routledge, 1989.

Davis, Allen F. *American Heroine: The Life and Legend of Jane Addams*. New York: Oxford University Press, 1973.

Davis, Elizabeth Lindsay. *Lifting as They Climb*. 1933; reprint, New York: G. K. Hall and Co., 1996.

Davis, Michael. *The Image of Lincoln in the South*. Knoxville: University of Tennessee Press, 1971.

DeBenedetti, Charles. *The Peace Reform in American History*. 1980; reprint, Bloomington: Indiana University Press, 1984.

de Grazia, Victoria. *How Fascism Ruled Women: Italy, 1922–1945*. Berkeley and Los Angeles: University of California Press, 1992.

DeLamar, Mrs. Leonard G., and Mrs. Jerido Ward, comps. and eds. *History of the Georgia State Society of the National Society of the Daughters of the American Revolution, 1899–1981*. Roswell, Ga.: W. H. Wolfe Associates, 1981.

D'Emilio, John, and Estelle Freedman. *Intimate Matters: A History of Sexuality in America*. 2d ed. Chicago: University of Chicago Press, 1997.

Dennis, James M. *Grant Wood: A Study in American Art and Culture*. Columbia: University of Missouri Press, 1986.

Dennis, Matthew. *Red, White, and Blue Letter Days: An American Calendar*. Ithaca, N.Y.: Cornell University Press, 2002.

Derr, Jill Mulvay. "'Strength in Our Union': The Making of Mormon Sisterhood." In *Sisters in Spirit: Mormon Women in Historical and Cultural Perspective*, edited by Maureen Ursenbach Beecher and Lavinia Fielding Anderson, 153–207. Urbana and Chicago: University of Illinois Press, 1987.

Des Jardins, Julie. *Women and the Historical Enterprise in America: Gender, Race, and the Politics of Memory, 1880–1945*. Chapel Hill: University of North Carolina Press, 2003.

Deutsch, Sarah. *Women and the City: Gender, Space, and Power in Boston, 1870–1940*. New York: Oxford University Press, 2000.

Dinnerstein, Leonard. *Anti-Semitism in America*. New York: Oxford University Press, 1994.

Douglas, Ann. *The Feminization of American Culture*. 1977; reprint, New York: Anchor Books, 1988.

———. *Terrible Honesty: Mongrel Manhattan in the 1920s*. New York: Farrar, Straus, and Giroux, 1995.

Du Bois, W. E. B. *Black Reconstruction: An Essay toward a History of the Part Which Black Folk Played in the Attempt to Reconstruct Democracy in America, 1860–1880*. New York: Harcourt, Brace and Company, 1935.

———. *The Souls of Black Folk*. Edited with an introduction by David W. Blight. Boston: Bedford Books, 1997.

———, ed. *Efforts for Social Betterment among Negro Americans*. Atlanta, Ga.: Atlanta University Press, 1909.

Duff, Jessie. *The Making of Americans: Five Years with the Roosevelt Club, Sons of the Republic*. Cleveland, Ohio: Western Reserve Chapter DAR, 1923.

Dunbar-Nelson, Alice. "Negro Women in War Work." In *Scott's Official History of the American Negro in the World War*, edited by Emmett J. Scott, 374–97. 1919; reprint, New York: Arno Press, 1969.

Dunlap, Mrs. William Finley, et al. *History and Register: Washington State Society of the American Revolution*. Seattle, Wash.: Lowman and Hanford, n.d. [ca. 1924].

Durr, Virginia Foster. *Outside the Magic Circle: The Autobiography of Virginia Foster Durr*. Edited by Hollinger F. Barnard. Tuscaloosa: University of Alabama Press, 1985.

Edmonds, Charles Hugh. *An Historical Perspective: The History of the Kate Duncan Smith, Daughters of the American Revolution School, Grant, Alabama*. Grant, Ala.: privately published, 1977.

Edwards, Rebecca. *Angels in the Machinery: Gender in American Party Politics from the Civil War to the Progressive Era*. New York: Oxford University Press, 1998.

Eleventh Report of the National Society of the Daughters of the American Revolution, October 11, 1907–October 11, 1908. Washington, D.C.: Government Printing Office, 1909.

Ellis, Mark. *Race, War, and Surveillance: African Americans and the United*

States Government during World War I. Bloomington and Indianapolis: Indiana University Press, 2001.

————. "W. E. B. Du Bois and the Formation of Black Opinion in World War I." *Journal of American History* 81 (March 1995): 1584–90.

Enloe, Cynthia. *Bananas, Beaches, and Bases: Making Feminist Sense of International Politics*. Rev. ed. Berkeley and Los Angeles: University of California Press, 2000.

Fabre, Geneviève. "African-American Commemorative Celebrations in the Nineteenth Century." In *History and Memory in African-American Culture*, edited by Geneviève Fabre and Robert O'Meally, 72–91. New York: Oxford University Press, 1994.

Fahs, Alice. *The Imagined Civil War: Popular Literature of the North and South, 1861–1865*. Chapel Hill: University of North Carolina Press, 2001.

Fahs, Alice, and Joan Waugh, eds. *The Memory of the Civil War in American Culture*. Chapel Hill: University of North Carolina Press, 2004.

Faust, Drew Gilpin. "Altars of Sacrifice: Confederate Women and the Narratives of War." In *Divided Houses: Gender and the Civil War*, edited by Catherine Clinton and Nina Silber, 171–99. New York: Oxford University Press, 1992.

————. *The Creation of Confederate Nationalism: Ideology and Identity in the Civil War South*. Baton Rouge: Louisiana State University Press, 1988.

————. *Mothers of Invention: Women of the Slaveholding South in the American Civil War*. Chapel Hill: University of North Carolina Press, 1996.

Felsenthal, Carol. *The Sweetheart of the Silent Majority: The Biography of Phyllis Schlafly*. Garden City, N.Y.: Doubleday and Co., 1981.

Fields, Mamie Garvin, with Karen Fields. *Lemon Swamp and Other Places: A Carolina Memoir*. 1983; reprint, New York: Free Press, 1985.

Fifty Years of Achievement: History of the Daughters of the Republic of Texas, Together with the Charter, By-Laws, Constitution and List of Members. Dallas, Tex.: Banks Upshaw and Co., 1942.

Fitzpatrick, Ellen. *History's Memory: Writing America's Past, 1880–1980*. Cambridge, Mass.: Harvard University Press, 2002.

Flores, Richard. "Introduction: Adina de Zavala and the Politics of Restoration." In *History and Legends of the Alamo and Other Missions in and around San Antonio*, by Adina de Zavala, edited by Richard Flores, v–lvii. Houston, Tex.: Arte Público Press, 1996.

Foner, Eric. *Reconstruction: America's Unfinished Revolution, 1863–1877*. New York: Harper and Row, 1988.

Ford, Linda G. "Alice Paul and the Triumph of Militancy." In *One Woman, One Vote: Rediscovering the Woman Suffrage Movement*, edited by Marjorie Spruill Wheeler, 277–94. Troutdale, Ore.: NewSage Press, 1995.

Fort Duquesne and Fort Pitt: Early Names of Pittsburgh Streets, Fourth Edition,

Published by Daughters of the American Revolution of Allegheny County, Penn-sylvania. Pittsburgh, Pa.: Reed and Witting, 1914.

Foster, Carrie A. *The Women and the Warriors: The U.S. Section of the Women's International League for Peace and Freedom, 1915–1946*. Syracuse, N.Y.: Syracuse University Press, 1995.

Foster, Catherine. *Women for All Seasons: The Story of the Women's International League for Peace and Freedom*. Athens: University of Georgia Press, 1989.

Foster, Gaines M. *Ghosts of the Confederacy: Defeat, the Lost Cause, and the Emergence of the New South, 1865 to 1913*. New York: Oxford University Press, 1987.

Fowler, Robert Booth. "Carrie Chapman Catt, Strategist." In *One Woman, One Vote: Rediscovering the Woman Suffrage Movement*, edited by Marjorie Spruill Wheeler, 295–314. Troutdale, Ore.: NewSage Press, 1995.

Frazier, E. Franklin. *Black Bourgeoisie*. 1957; reprint, New York: Free Press, 1965.

Freedman, Estelle B. "Separatism as Strategy: Female Institution-Building and American Feminism, 1870–1930." *Feminist Studies* 5 (1979): 512–29.

Gaines, Kevin K. *Uplifting the Race: Black Leadership, Politics, and Culture in the Twentieth Century*. Chapel Hill: University of North Carolina Press, 1996.

Gardner, Sarah E. *Blood and Irony: Southern White Women's Narratives of the Civil War, 1861–1937*. Chapel Hill: University of North Carolina Press, 2004.

Gatewood, Willard B., Jr. *Black Americans and the White Man's Burden, 1898–1903*. Urbana and Chicago: University of Illinois Press, 1975.

Gere, Anne Ruggles. *Intimate Practices: Literacy and Cultural Work in U.S. Women's Clubs, 1880–1920*. Urbana and Chicago: University of Illinois Press, 1997.

Gerstle, Gary. *American Crucible: Race and Nation in the Twentieth Century*. Princeton, N.J.: Princeton University Press, 2001.

Gibbs, Margaret. *The DAR*. New York: Holt, Rinehart, and Winston, 1969.

Giddings, Paula. *When and Where I Enter: The Impact of Black Women on Race and Sex in America*. New York: William Morrow, 1984.

Gilbert, Martin. *The First World War: A Complete History*. New York: Henry Holt and Co., 1994.

Gilmore, Glenda Elizabeth. *Gender and Jim Crow: Women and the Politics of White Supremacy in North Carolina, 1896–1920*. Chapel Hill: University of North Carolina Press, 1996.

Ginzberg, Lori D. "Pernicious Heresies: Female Citizenship and Sexual Respectability in the Nineteenth Century." In *Women and the Unstable State in Nineteenth-Century America*, edited by Alison M. Parker and Stephanie Cole, 139–61. College Station: Texas A&M University Press, 2000.

———. *Women and the Work of Benevolence: Morality, Politics, and Class in the Nineteenth-Century United States*. New Haven, Conn.: Yale University Press, 1990.

Gleason, Philip. "American Identity and Americanization." In *Harvard Encyclopedia of American Ethnic Groups*, edited by Stephan Thernstrom, Ann Orlov, and Oscar Handlin, 31–58. Cambridge, Mass.: Harvard University Press, 1980.

Goggin, Jacqueline A. *Carter G. Woodson: A Life in Black History*. Baton Rouge: Louisiana State University Press, 1993.

Goldman, Wendy Z. *Women, the State, and Revolution: Soviet Family Policy and Social Life, 1917–1936*. Cambridge, U.K.: Cambridge University Press, 1993.

Goldstein, Robert Justin. *Saving "Old Glory": The History of the American Flag Desecration Controversy*. Boulder, Colo.: Westview Press, 1995.

Gordon, Linda. *Pitied But Not Entitled: Single Mothers and the History of Welfare, 1890–1935*. Cambridge, Mass.: Harvard University Press, 1994.

———. *Woman's Body, Woman's Right: Birth Control in America*. Rev. ed. New York: Penguin Books, 1990.

———, ed. *Women, the State, and Welfare*. Madison: University of Wisconsin Press, 1990.

Gordon-Reed, Annette. *Thomas Jefferson and Sally Hemings: An American Controversy*. Charlottesville: University Press of Virginia, 1997.

Graham, Sara Hunter. *Woman Suffrage and the New Democracy*. New Haven, Conn.: Yale University Press, 1996.

Green, Elna C. *Southern Strategies: Southern Women and the Woman Suffrage Question*. Chapel Hill: University of North Carolina Press, 1997.

Greenfeld, Liah. *Nationalism: Five Roads to Modernity*. Cambridge, Mass.: Harvard University Press, 1992.

Greenwood, Janette Thomas. *Bittersweet Legacy: The Black and White "Better Classes" in Charlotte, 1850–1910*. Chapel Hill: University of North Carolina Press, 1994.

Guenter, Scot M. *The American Flag, 1777–1924: Cultural Shifts from Creation to Codification*. Cranbury, N.J.: Associated University Presses, 1990.

Gullett, Gayle. "Women Progressives and the Politics of Americanization in California, 1915–1920." *Pacific Historical Review* 64 (February 1995): 71–94.

Gustafson, Melanie Susan. *Women and the Republican Party, 1854–1924*. Urbana and Chicago: University of Illinois Press, 2001.

Hale, Grace Elizabeth. *Making Whiteness: The Culture of Segregation in the South, 1890–1940*. New York: Pantheon Books, 1998.

———. "'Some Women Have Never Been Reconstructed': Mildred Lewis Rutherford, Lucy M. Stanton, and the Racial Politics of Southern White Womanhood, 1900–1930." In *Georgia in Black and White: Explorations in the Race Relations of a Southern State, 1865–1950*, edited by John C. Inscoe, 173–201. Athens: University of Georgia Press, 1994.

Hall, Henry. *Year Book of the Societies Composed of Descendants of the Men of the Revolution*. New York: Republic Press, 1890.

Hall, Jacquelyn Dowd. *Revolt against Chivalry: Jessie Daniel Ames and the Women's Campaign against Lynching.* Rev. ed. New York: Columbia University Press, 1993.

―――. "'You Must Remember This': Autobiography as Social Critique." *Journal of American History* 85 (September 1998): 439–65.

Hall, Jacquelyn Dowd, James Leloudis, Robert Korstad, Mary Murphy, Lu Ann Jones, and Christopher B. Daly. *Like a Family: The Making of a Southern Cotton Mill World.* Chapel Hill: University of North Carolina Press, 1987.

Hall, Peter Dobkin. *The Organization of American Culture, 1700–1900: Private Institutions, Elites, and the Origins of American Nationality.* New York: New York University Press, 1982.

Hansen, Jonathan M. *The Lost Promise of Patriotism: Debating American Identity, 1890–1920.* Chicago: University of Chicago Press, 2003.

Hanson, Joyce A. *Mary McLeod Bethune and Black Women's Political Activism.* Columbia: University of Missouri Press, 2003.

Hapgood, Norman, ed. *Professional Patriots.* New York: Albert and Charles Boni, 1927.

Harlan, Louis R., et al., eds. *The Booker T. Washington Papers.* 13 vols. Urbana: University of Illinois Press, 1972–84.

Harned, Miriam Kern, comp. and ed. *Pennsylvania State History of the Daughters of the American Revolution.* Lititz, Pa.: Wagaman Brothers, 1947.

Hay, Gertrude Sloan, comp. *Chapter Histories of the North Carolina Daughters of the American Revolution (Vol. I).* Durham, N.C.: North Carolina Society, Daughters of the American Revolution, and the Seeman Press, 1930.

Hebard, Grace Raymond. *Marking the Oregon Trail, the Bozeman Road, and Historic Places in Wyoming, 1908–1920: Presented by the Daughters of the American Revolution in Wyoming.* N.p., 1921.

Hendricks, Wanda A. *Gender, Race, and Politics in the Midwest: Black Club Women in Illinois.* Bloomington and Indianapolis: Indiana University Press, 1998.

Hewitt, Nancy, and Suzanne Lebsock, eds. *Visible Women: New Essays on American Activism.* Urbana and Chicago: University of Illinois Press, 1993.

Higginbotham, Evelyn Brooks. "Clubwomen and Electoral Politics in the 1920s." In *African American Women and the Vote, 1837–1965*, edited by Ann Gordon, 134–55. Amherst: University of Massachusetts Press, 1997.

―――. *Righteous Discontent: The Women's Movement in the Black Baptist Church, 1880–1920.* Cambridge, Mass.: Harvard University Press, 1993.

Higham, John. *Send These to Me: Immigrants in Urban America.* Rev. ed. 1975; reprint, Baltimore, Md.: Johns Hopkins University Press, 1984.

―――. *Strangers in the Land: Patterns of American Nativism, 1860–1925.* Rev. ed. New York: Atheneum, 1963.

Hill, Patricia R. *The World Their Household: The American Woman's Foreign*

Mission Movement and Cultural Transformation, 1870–1920. Ann Arbor: University of Michigan Press, 1985.

Hine, Darlene Clark, and Kathleen Thompson. *A Shining Thread of Hope: The History of Black Women in America*. New York: Broadway Books, 1999.

Hinman, Alice A., comp. *Vermont State Conference, Daughters of the American Revolution, 1892–1930*. Rutland, Vt.: Tuttle Co., 1931.

A History of the Club Movement among the Colored Women of the United States of America as Contained in the Minutes of the Conventions, Held in Boston, July 29, 30, 31, 1895, and of the National Federation of Afro-American Women, Held in Washington, D.C., July 20, 21, 22, 1896. 1902; reprint, Washington, D.C.: National Association of Colored Women's Clubs, 1978.

History of the Massachusetts Daughters of the American Revolution: December, 1891–December, 1905. Boston: Massachusetts Daughters of the American Revolution, n.d. [1906].

Hobsbawm, Eric J. "Introduction: Inventing Traditions." In *The Invention of Tradition*, edited by Eric J. Hobsbawm and Terence Ranger, 1–14. Cambridge, U.K.: Cambridge University Press, 1983.

———. "Mass-Producing Traditions: Europe, 1870–1914." In *The Invention of Tradition*, edited by Eric J. Hobsbawm and Terence Ranger, 263–307. Cambridge, U.K.: Cambridge University Press, 1983.

———. *Nations and Nationalism since 1780: Programme, Myth, Reality*. 2d ed. Cambridge, U.K.: Cambridge University Press, 1992.

Hodes, Martha Elizabeth. *White Women, Black Men: Illicit Sex in the Nineteenth-Century South*. New Haven, Conn.: Yale University Press, 1997.

Hoganson, Kristin. "'As Badly Off as the Filipinos': U.S. Women's Suffragists and the Imperial Issue at the Turn of the Twentieth Century." *Journal of Women's History* 13 (Summer 2001): 9–33.

———. "Cosmopolitan Domesticity: Importing the American Dream, 1865–1920." *American Historical Review* 107 (February 2002): 55–83.

———. *Fighting for American Manhood: How Gender Politics Provoked the Spanish-American and Philippine-American Wars*. New Haven, Conn.: Yale University Press, 1998.

Holquist, Peter. "'Information Is the Alpha and Omega of Our Work': Bolshevik Surveillance in Its Pan-European Context." *Journal of Modern History* 69 (September 1997): 415–50.

Horne, Gerald. *Race Woman: The Lives of Shirley Graham Du Bois*. New York: New York University Press, 2000.

Horwitz, Tony. *Confederates in the Attic: Dispatches from the Unfinished Civil War*. New York: Vintage Books, 1998.

Hosmer, Charles B., Jr. *Presence of the Past: A History of the Preservation Movement in the United States before Williamsburg*. New York: G. P. Putnam's Sons, 1965.

Howe, Barbara. "Women in Historic Preservation: The Legacy of Ann Pamela Cunningham." *Public Historian* 12 (Winter 1990): 31–61.

Hoxie, Frederick E. *A Final Promise: The Campaign to Assimilate the Indians, 1880–1920*. Lincoln: University of Nebraska Press, 1984.

Hoytt, Eleanor Hinton. "International Council of Women of the Darker Races: Historical Notes." *Sage: A Scholarly Journal on Black Women* 3 (Fall 1986): 54–55.

Hull, Gloria T., ed. *Give Us Each Day: The Diary of Alice Dunbar-Nelson*. New York: W. W. Norton, 1984.

Hunter, Ann Arnold. *A Century of Service: The Story of the DAR*. Washington, D.C.: National Society of the Daughters of the American Revolution, 1991.

Hunton, Addie W., and Kathryn M. Johnson. *Two Colored Women with the American Expeditionary Forces*. 1920; reprint, New York: AMS Press, 1971.

Jacobson, Matthew Frye. *Whiteness of a Different Color: European Immigrants and the Alchemy of Race*. Cambridge, Mass.: Harvard University Press, 1998.

Jacoway, Elizabeth, and C. Fred Williams, eds. *Understanding the Little Rock Crisis: An Exercise in Remembrance and Reconciliation*. Fayetteville: University of Arkansas Press, 1999.

Jacques Garvey, Amy. *Garvey and Garveyism*. 1968; reprint, New York: Collier Books, 1970.

James, Edward T., et al., eds. *Notable American Women, 1607–1950: A Biographical Dictionary*. 3 vols. Cambridge, Mass.: Harvard University Press, 1971.

Jeansonne, Glen. *Women of the Far Right: The Mothers' Movement and World War II*. Chicago: University of Chicago Press, 1996.

Jensen, Joan M. "All Pink Sisters: The War Department and the Feminist Movement in the 1920s." In *Decades of Discontent: The Women's Movement, 1920–1940*, edited by Lois Scharf and Joan M. Jensen, 199–222. Boston: Northeastern University Press, 1987.

Jensen, Kimberly. "Women, Citizenship, and Civic Sacrifice: Engendering Patriotism in the First World War." In *Bonds of Affection: Americans Define Their Patriotism*, edited by John Bodnar, 139–59. Princeton, N.J.: Princeton University Press, 1996.

Johnson, Joan Marie. "'Drill into Us . . . the Rebel Tradition': The Contest over Southern Identity in Black and White Women's Clubs, South Carolina, 1898–1930." *Journal of Southern History* 66 (August 2000): 525–62.

———. *Southern Ladies, New Women: Race, Region, and Clubwomen in South Carolina, 1890–1930*. Gainesville: University Press of Florida, 2004.

———. "'Ye Gave Them a Stone': African American Women's Clubs, the Frederick Douglass Home, and the Black Mammy Monument." *Journal of Women's History* 17 (Spring 2005): forthcoming.

Jones, Beverly Washington. *Quest for Equality: The Life and Writings of Mary Eliza Church Terrell, 1863–1954*. Brooklyn, N.Y.: Carlson Publishing, 1990.

Jordan, William. "'The Damnable Dilemma': African-American Accommodation and Protest during World War I." *Journal of American History* 81 (March 1995): 1562–83.

Journal of the Eighth Annual Convention of the Woman's Relief Corps, Auxiliary to the Grand Army of the Republic. Boston: E. B. Stillings and Co., 1890.

Journal of the Eleventh National Convention of the Woman's Relief Corps. Boston: E. B. Stillings and Co., 1893.

Journal of the Fifteenth National Convention of the Woman's Relief Corps, Auxiliary to the Grand Army of the Republic. Boston: E. B. Stillings and Co., 1897.

Journal of the Fortieth National Convention of the Woman's Relief Corps, Auxiliary to the Grand Army of the Republic. Washington, D.C.: National Tribune Co., 1922.

Journal of the Forty-Fifth Convention of the National Woman's Relief Corps, Auxiliary to the Grand Army of the Republic. Washington, D.C.: National Tribune Co., 1927.

Journal of the Forty-Fourth Convention of the National Woman's Relief Corps, Auxiliary to the Grand Army of the Republic. Washington, D.C.: National Tribune Co., 1926.

Journal of the Forty-Second National Convention of the National Woman's Relief Corps, Auxiliary to the Grand Army of the Republic. Washington, D.C.: National Tribune Co., 1924.

Journal of the Forty-Seventh Convention of the National Woman's Corps, Auxiliary to the Grand Army of the Republic. Minneapolis, Minn.: Japs-Olson Co., 1929.

Journal of the Nineteenth National Convention of the Woman's Relief Corps, Auxiliary to the Grand Army of the Republic. Boston: E. B. Stillings and Co., 1901.

Journal of Proceedings, Sixteenth National Convention, Department of Massachusetts, Woman's Relief Corps. Boston: E. B. Stillings and Co., 1895.

Journal of Proceedings, Twentieth Annual Convention, Department of Massachusetts, Woman's Relief Corps. Boston, Mass.: E. B. Stillings and Co., 1899.

Journal of the Seventeenth National Convention of the Woman's Relief Corps, Auxiliary to the Grand Army of the Republic. Boston: E. B. Stillings and Co., 1899.

Journal of the Sixteenth National Convention of the Woman's Relief Corps, Auxiliary to the Grand Army of the Republic. Boston: E. B. Stillings and Co., 1898.

Journal of the Thirteenth Annual Convention of the Woman's Relief Corps, Auxiliary to the Grand Army of the Republic. Boston: E. B. Stillings and Co., 1895.

Journal of the Thirtieth National Convention of the Woman's Relief Corps, Auxiliary to the Grand Army of the Republic. Boston: Griffith-Stillings Press, 1912.

Journal of the Thirty-Eighth National Convention of the Woman's Relief Corps, Auxiliary to the Grand Army of the Republic. Washington, D.C.: National Tribune Co., 1920.

Journal of the Thirty-First National Convention of the Woman's Relief Corps,

Auxiliary to the Grand Army of the Republic. Boston: Griffith-Stillings Press, 1913.

Journal of the Thirty-Ninth National Convention of the Woman's Relief Corps, Auxiliary to the Grand Army of the Republic. Washington, D.C.: National Tribune Co., 1921.

Journal of the Twelfth Annual Convention of the Woman's Relief Corps, Auxiliary to the Grand Army of the Republic. Boston: E. B. Stillings and Co., 1894.

Journal of the Twentieth National Convention of the Woman's Relief Corps, Auxiliary to the Grand Army of the Republic. Boston, Mass.: Griffith-Stillings Press, 1902.

Journal of the Twenty-First National Convention of the Woman's Relief Corps, Auxiliary to the Grand Army of the Republic. Boston: Griffith-Stillings Press, 1903.

Kachun, Mitch. *Festivals of Freedom: Memory and Meaning in African American Emancipation Celebrations, 1808–1915*. Amherst: University of Massachusetts Press, 2003.

Kammen, Michael. *Mystic Chords of Memory: The Transformation of Tradition in American Culture*. 1991; reprint, New York: Vintage Books, 1993.

———. *A Season of Youth: The American Revolution and the Historical Imagination*. 1978; reprint, Ithaca, N.Y.: Cornell University Press, 1988.

Kaplan, Amy. *The Anarchy of Empire in the Making of U.S. Culture*. Cambridge, Mass.: Harvard University Press, 2002.

Katzman, David M. *Seven Days a Week: Women and Domestic Service in Industrializing America*. 1978; reprint, Urbana and Chicago: University of Illinois Press, 1981.

Kaufman, Polly Welts. *National Parks and the Woman's Voice: A History*. Albuquerque: University of New Mexico Press, 1996.

Kearney, James R. *Anna Eleanor Roosevelt: The Evolution of a Reformer*. Boston: Houghton Mifflin Co., 1968.

Kedourie, Elie. "Nationalism and Self-Determination." In *Nationalism*, edited by John Hutchinson and Anthony D. Smith, 49–51. New York: Oxford University Press, 1994.

Keiler, Allan. *Marian Anderson: A Singer's Journey*. New York: Scribner, 2000.

Kellar, William Henry. *Make Haste Slowly: Moderates, Conservatives, and School Desegregation in Houston*. College Station: Texas A&M University Press, 1999.

Kennedy, David M. *Over Here: The First World War and American Society*. New York: Oxford University Press, 1980.

Kennedy, Kathleen. *Disloyal Mothers and Scurrilous Citizens: Women and Subversion during World War I*. Bloomington and Indianapolis: Indiana University Press, 1999.

Kerber, Linda K. *No Constitutional Right to Be Ladies: Women and the Obligations of Citizenship*. New York: Hill and Wang, 1998.

————. *Women of the Republic: Intellect and Ideology in Revolutionary America.* 1980; reprint, New York: W. W. Norton, 1986.

Kerlin, Robert T. *The Voice of the Negro, 1919.* 1920; reprint, New York: Arno Press, 1968.

Kimmel, Michael. *Manhood in America: A Cultural History.* New York: Free Press, 1996.

Kimmick, Elizabeth, comp. and ed. *History of the New Mexico State Organization of the National Society, Daughters of the American Revolution.* Vol. 1: *1894–1957.* N.p., 1957.

King, Grace. *Mount Vernon on the Potomac: History of the Mount Vernon Ladies' Association of the Union.* New York: Macmillan, 1929.

Kirk, Russell, ed. *The Portable Conservative Reader.* New York: Viking Press, 1982.

Knupfer, Anne Meis. *Toward a Tenderer Humanity and a Nobler Womanhood: African American Women's Clubs in Turn-of-the-Century Chicago.* New York: New York University Press, 1996.

Koonz, Claudia. *Mothers in the Fatherland: Women, the Family, and Nazi Politics.* New York: St. Martin's Press, 1987.

Kornweibel, Theodore, Jr. *"Seeing Red": Federal Campaigns against Black Militancy, 1919–1925.* Bloomington and Indianapolis: Indiana University Press, 1998.

Kramer, Paul A. "Empires, Exceptions, and Anglo-Saxons: Race and Rule between the British and United States Empires, 1880–1910." *Journal of American History* 88 (March 2002): 1315–53.

Kunzel, Regina G. *Fallen Women, Problem Girls: Unmarried Mothers and the Professionalization of Social Work, 1890–1945.* New Haven, Conn.: Yale University Press, 1993.

Ladd-Taylor, Molly. *Mother-Work: Women, Child Welfare, and the State, 1890–1930.* Urbana and Chicago: University of Illinois Press, 1994.

Lamar, Mrs. Joseph Rucker. *A History of the National Society of the Colonial Dames of America from 1891 to 1933.* Atlanta, Ga.: Walter W. Brown Publishing Co., 1934.

Lash, Joseph P. *Love, Eleanor: Eleanor Roosevelt and Her Friends.* Garden City, N.Y.: Doubleday and Co., 1982.

Lawson, Melinda. *Patriot Fires: Forging a New American Nationalism in the Civil War North.* Lawrence: University Press of Kansas, 2002.

Lebsock, Suzanne. "Woman Suffrage and White Supremacy: A Virginia Case Study." In *Visible Women: New Essays on American Activism*, edited by Nancy A. Hewitt and Suzanne Lebsock, 62–100. Urbana and Chicago: University of Illinois Press, 1993.

Leck, Ralph M. "Conservative Empowerment and the Gender of Nazism: Paradigms of Power and Complicity in German Women's History." *Journal of Women's History* 12 (Summer 2000): 147–69.

Leidholdt, Alexander. *Standing before the Shouting Mob: Lenoir Chambers and Virginia's Massive Resistance to Public-School Integration*. Tuscaloosa: University of Alabama Press, 1997.

Lemons, J. Stanley. *The Woman Citizen: Social Feminism in the 1920s*. 1973; reprint, Charlottesville: University Press of Virginia, 1990.

Leonard, John William, ed. *Woman's Who's Who of America, 1914–1915*. New York: American Commonwealth Co., 1914.

Lerner, Gerda. *The Creation of Patriarchy*. New York: Oxford University Press, 1986.

————. *Why History Matters: Life and Thought*. New York: Oxford University Press, 1997.

Lewis, Mrs. Clyde E., comp. and ed. *History of Oregon Society, Daughters of the American Revolution*. Portland, Ore.: Columban Press, n.d. [1931].

Lewis, David Levering. *W. E. B. Du Bois: Biography of a Race, 1868–1919*. New York: Henry Holt and Co., 1993.

————. *W. E. B. Du Bois: The Fight for Equality and the American Century, 1919–1963*. New York: Henry Holt and Co., 2000.

Lindenmeyer, Kriste A. *"A Right to Childhood": The U.S. Children's Bureau and Child Welfare, 1912–46*. Urbana and Chicago: University of Illinois Press, 1997.

Lindgren, James M. "'A New Departure in Historic, Patriotic Work': Personalism, Professionalism, and Conflicting Concepts of Material Culture in the Late Nineteenth and Early Twentieth Centuries." *Public Historian* 18 (Spring 1996): 41–60.

————. *Preserving Historic New England: Preservation, Progressivism, and the Remaking of Memory*. New York: Oxford University Press, 1995.

————. *Preserving the Old Dominion: Historic Preservation and Virginia Traditionalism*. Charlottesville: University Press of Virginia, 1993.

Lineage Book, National Society of the Daughters of the American Revolution, Volume II, 1892. Harrisburg, Pa.: Harrisburg Publishing Co., n.d. [1892].

Litwack, Leon F. "The Birth of a Nation." In *Past Imperfect: History According to the Movies*, edited by Mark C. Carnes with Ted Mico, John Miller-Monzon, and David Rubel, 136–41. New York: Henry Holt and Co., 1996.

————. *Trouble in Mind: Black Southerners in the Age of Jim Crow*. 1998; reprint, New York: Vintage Books, 1999.

Litwicki, Ellen M. *America's Public Holidays, 1865–1920*. Washington, D.C.: Smithsonian Institution Press, 2000.

Locke, Alain, ed. *The New Negro: An Interpretation*. New York: Albert and Charles Boni, 1925.

Lockwood, Mary S. *Lineage Book of the Charter Members of the Daughters of the American Revolution (Revised), 1890–1891*. Harrisburg, Pa.: Harrisburg Publishing Co., 1895.

Lockwood, Mary S., and Emily Lee Sherwood Ragan. *Story of the Records D.A.R.* Washington, D.C.: George E. Howard, 1906.

Lumpkin, Katharine Du Pre. *The Making of a Southerner.* 1946; reprint, Athens: University of Georgia Press, 1991.

Lynd, Robert S., and Helen Merrell Lynd. *Middletown: A Study in Modern American Culture.* New York: Harcourt Brace Jovanovich, 1929.

MacLean, Nancy. *Behind the Mask of Chivalry: The Making of the Second Ku Klux Klan.* New York: Oxford University Press, 1994.

Manual of the United States for the Information of Immigrants. Washington, D.C.: National Society, Daughters of the American Revolution; Press of Judd and Detweiler, Inc., 1921.

Marcaccini, Ann and George Woytanowitz. "House Work: The DAR at the Sibley House." *Minnesota History* 57 (Spring 1997): 187–201.

Marks, George P., III, comp. and ed. *The Black Press Views American Imperialism (1898–1900).* New York: Arno Press, 1971.

Marling, Karal Ann. *George Washington Slept Here: Colonial Revivals and American Culture, 1876–1986.* Cambridge, Mass.: Harvard University Press, 1988.

Marshall, Susan E. *Splintered Sisterhood: Gender and Class in the Campaign against Woman Suffrage.* Madison: University of Wisconsin Press, 1997.

Martin, Tony. *Race First: The Ideological and Organizational Struggles of Marcus Garvey and the Universal Negro Improvement Association.* Westport, Conn.: Greenwood Press, 1976.

Mather, Frank Lincoln, ed. *Who's Who of the Colored Race: A General Bibliographical Dictionary of Men and Women of African Descent, Volume One: 1915.* 1915; reprint, Detroit, Mich.: Gale Research Co., 1976.

Mathews, Donald G., and Jane Sherron De Hart. *Sex, Gender, and the Politics of ERA: A State and the Nation.* New York: Oxford University Press, 1990.

Mayer, Holly. *Belonging to the Army: Camp Followers and Community during the American Revolution.* Columbia: University of South Carolina Press, 1996.

McCausland, Elizabeth. *"The Blue Menace": A Series of Articles Originally Printed under the Nom-de-Plume of "Libertas" in the* Springfield Republican, *March 19–27, 1928.* Springfield, Mass.: Springfield Republican, 1928.

McClintock, Anne. "'No Longer in a Future Heaven': Nationalism, Gender, and Race." In *Imperial Leather: Race, Gender, and Sexuality in the Colonial Contest,* 352–90. New York: Routledge, 1995.

McCluskey, Audrey Thomas, and Elaine M. Smith, eds. *Mary McLeod Bethune: Building a Better World: Essays and Selected Documents.* Bloomington and Indianapolis: Indiana University Press, 1999.

McConnell, Stuart. *Glorious Contentment: The Grand Army of the Republic, 1865–1900.* Chapel Hill: University of North Carolina Press, 1992.

———. "Reading the Flag: A Reconsideration of the Patriotic Cults of the

1890s." In *Bonds of Affection: Americans Define Their Patriotism*, edited by John Bodnar, 102–19. Princeton, N.J.: Princeton University Press, 1996.

McElya, Micki. "Commemorating the Color Line: The National Mammy Monument Controversy of the 1920s." In *Monuments to the Lost Cause: Women, Art, and the Landscapes of Southern Memory*, edited by Cynthia Mills and Pamela H. Simpson, 203–18. Knoxville: University of Tennessee Press, 2003.

McGirr, Lisa. *Suburban Warriors: The Origins of the New American Right*. Princeton, N.J.: Princeton University Press, 2001.

McHenry, Elizabeth. *Forgotten Readers: Recovering the Lost History of African American Literary Societies*. Durham, N.C.: Duke University Press, 2002.

McMurry, Linda O. *To Keep the Waters Troubled: The Life of Ida B. Wells*. New York: Oxford University Press, 1998.

McPherson, James M. *Battle Cry of Freedom: The Civil War Era*. New York: Ballantine Books, 1988.

Menges, Florence Skidmore Brown, comp. *History of New York State Conference, Daughters of the American Revolution, Its Officers and Chapters*. Saratoga Springs, N.Y.: Saratogian Printing Service, n.d. [1923].

Michaels, Walter Benn. *Our America: Nativism, Modernism, and Pluralism*. Durham, N.C.: Duke University Press, 1995.

Miller, Stuart Creighton. *"Benevolent Assimilation": The American Conquest of the Philippines, 1899–1903*. New Haven, Conn.: Yale University Press, 1982.

Mills, Cynthia. "Gratitude and Gender Wars: Monuments to the Women of the Sixties." In *Monuments to the Lost Cause: Women, Art, and the Landscapes of Southern Memory*, edited by Cynthia Mills and Pamela H. Simpson, 183–200. Knoxville: University of Tennessee Press, 2003.

———. "Introduction." In *Monuments to the Lost Cause: Women, Art, and the Landscapes of Southern Memory*, edited by Cynthia Mills and Pamela H. Simpson, xv–xxx. Knoxville: University of Tennessee Press, 2003.

Mills, Cynthia, and Pamela H. Simpson, eds. *Monuments to the Lost Cause: Women, Art, and the Landscapes of Southern Memory*. Knoxville: University of Tennessee Press, 2003.

Minutes of the Fifth Annual Meeting of the United Daughters of the Confederacy. Nashville, Tenn.: Foster and Webb, 1899.

Minutes of the Seventh Annual Meeting of the United Daughters of the Confederacy. Nashville, Tenn.: Foster and Webb, 1901.

Minutes of the Sixth Annual Meeting of the United Daughters of the Confederacy. Nashville, Tenn.: Foster and Webb, 1900.

Minutes of the Thirteenth Annual Convention of the United Daughters of the Confederacy. Opelika, Ala.: Post Publishing Co., 1907.

Minutes of the Thirty-Second Annual Convention, United Daughters of the Confederacy. Jackson, Tenn.: McCowat-Mercer Printing, 1925.

Montgomery, Rebecca. "Lost Cause Mythology in New South Reform: Gender, Class, Race, and the Politics of Patriotic Citizenship." In *Negotiating the Boundaries of Southern Womanhood: Dealing with the Powers That Be*, edited by Janet L. Coryell et al., 174–98. Columbia: University of Missouri Press, 2000.

Morley, Mrs. Walter S., comp. *History of California State Society, Daughters of the American Revolution, 1891–1938*. Berkeley, Calif.: Lederer, Street, and Zeus Co., 1938.

Moses, Wilson Jeremiah. *Afrotopia: The Roots of African American Popular History*. Cambridge, U.K.: Cambridge University Press, 1998.

———. *The Golden Age of Black Nationalism, 1850–1925*. Hampden, Conn.: Archon Books, 1978.

Mossell, Mrs. N. F. *The Work of the Afro-American Woman*. 1894; reprint, New York: Oxford University Press, 1988.

Mouat, Emilie M., comp. and ed. *Connecticut State History of the Daughters of the American Revolution*. Hartford, Conn.: Finlay Brothers, Inc., 1929.

Muncy, Robyn. *Creating a Female Dominion in American Reform, 1890–1935*. New York: Oxford University Press, 1991.

———. "Trustbusting and White Manhood in America, 1898–1914." *American Studies* 38 (Fall 1997): 21–42.

Murray, Pauli. *Proud Shoes: The Story of an American Family*. 1956; reprint, New York: Harper and Row, 1987.

Myers, Minor, Jr. *Liberty without Anarchy: A History of the Society of the Cincinnati*. Charlottesville: University Press of Virginia, 1983.

The National Cyclopedia of American Biography. Vol. 39. New York: James T. White and Co., 1954.

Nelson, Dana D. *National Manhood: Capitalist Citizenship and the Imagined Fraternity of White Men*. Durham, N.C.: Duke University Press, 1998.

Neverdon-Morton, Cynthia. *Afro-American Women of the South and the Advancement of the Race, 1895–1925*. Knoxville: University of Tennessee Press, 1989.

Newman, Louise Michele. *White Women's Rights: The Racial Origins of Feminism in the United States*. New York: Oxford University Press, 1999.

Nielsen, Kim E. *Un-American Womanhood: Antiradicalism, Antifeminism, and the First Red Scare*. Columbus: Ohio State University Press, 2001.

Norton, Mary Beth. *Liberty's Daughters: The Revolutionary Experience of American Women, 1750–1800*. 1980; reprint, Ithaca, N.Y.: Cornell University Press, 1996.

Nussbaum, Martha C., et al. *For Love of Country: Debating the Limits of Patriotism*. Edited by Joshua Cohen. Boston: Beacon Press, 1996.

Old Rail Fence Corners: The A.B.C.'s of Minnesota History: Authentic Incidents Gleaned from the Old Settlers by the Book Committee. Austin, Minn.: F. H. McCulloch, 1914.

O'Leary, Cecilia Elizabeth. "'Blood Brotherhood': The Racialization of Patriotism, 1865–1918." In *Bonds of Affection: Americans Define Their Patriotism*, edited by John Bodnar, 53–81. Princeton, N.J.: Princeton University Press, 1996.

———. *To Die For: The Paradox of American Patriotism*. Princeton, N.J.: Princeton University Press, 1999.

Painter, Nell Irvin. *Standing at Armageddon: The United States, 1877–1919*. New York: W. W. Norton, 1987.

Parrott, Angie. "'Love Makes Memory Eternal': The United Daughters of the Confederacy in Richmond, Virginia." In *The Edge of the South: Life in Nineteenth-Century Virginia*, edited by Edward L. Ayers and John C. Willis, 219–38. Charlottesville: University Press of Virginia, 1991.

Pascoe, Peggy. *Relations of Rescue: The Search for Female Moral Authority in the American West, 1874–1939*. New York: Oxford University Press, 1990.

Payne, Elizabeth. *Reform, Labor, and Feminism: Margaret Dreier Robins and the Women's Trade Union League*. Urbana: University of Illinois Press, 1988.

Pencak, William. *For God and Country: The American Legion, 1919–1941*. Boston: Northeastern University Press, 1989.

Pitre, Merline. *In Struggle against Jim Crow: Lulu B. White and the NAACP, 1900–1957*. College Station: Texas A&M University Press, 1999.

Polk's Seattle City Directory. Vol. 44. Seattle, Wash.: R. L. Polk, 1930. In *City Directories of the United States, Segment IV, 1902–1935*. Microform; Woodbridge, Conn.: Research Publications, n.d.

Poppenheim, Mary, et al. *The History of the United Daughters of the Confederacy*. Raleigh, N.C.: Edwards and Broughton, 1925.

Powers, Richard Gid. *Not Without Honor: The History of American Anticommunism*. New York: Free Press, 1995.

Pride, Richard A. *The Political Use of Racial Narratives: School Desegregation in Mobile, Alabama, 1954–97*. Urbana and Chicago: University of Illinois Press, 2002.

Proceedings of the Eighteenth State Conference of the Mississippi Daughters of the American Revolution. N.p.: Mississippi Daughters of the American Revolution, 1923.

Proceedings of the Fifteenth Ohio State Conference of the Daughters of the American Revolution. N.p., 1913.

Proceedings of the Fifteenth State Conference of the Daughters of the American Revolution in Mississippi. West Point, Miss.: West Point Leader Print, 1920.

Proceedings of the Thirteenth Ohio State Conference of the Daughters of the American Revolution. N.p., 1911.

Proceedings of the Twelfth State Conference of the Daughters of the American Revolution in Mississippi. West Point, Miss: West Point Leader Print, 1917.

Proceedings of the Twenty-Eighth Ohio State Conference of the Daughters of the American Revolution. N.p., 1927.

Pugh, Martin. *The Tories and the People, 1880–1935.* New York: Basil Blackwell, 1985.

Putney, Clifford. *Muscular Christianity: Manhood and Sports in Protestant America, 1880–1920.* Cambridge, Mass.: Harvard University Press, 2001.

Pyron, Darden Asbury. *Southern Daughter: The Life of Margaret Mitchell.* New York: Oxford University Press, 1991.

Rable, George C. *Civil Wars: Women and the Crisis of Southern Nationalism.* 1989; reprint, Urbana and Chicago: University of Illinois Press, 1991.

Rafael, Vicente L. "Colonial Domesticity: Engendering Race at the Edge of Empire, 1899–1912." In *White Love and Other Events in Filipino History,* 52–75. Durham, N.C.: Duke University Press, 2000.

Raftery, Judith. "Progressivism Moves into the Schools: Los Angeles, 1905–1918." *California History* 66 (June 1987): 94–103.

Ransby, Barbara. *Ella Baker and the Black Freedom Movement: A Radical Democratic Vision.* Chapel Hill: University of North Carolina Press, 2003.

Reed, Christopher Robert. *The Chicago NAACP and the Rise of Black Professional Leadership, 1910–1966.* Bloomington and Indianapolis: Indiana University Press, 1997.

Remembrance Book of the Daughters of the American Revolution. Washington, D.C.: National Society Daughters of the American Revolution, July 1918.

Remembrance Book of the Daughters of the American Revolution. Washington, D.C.: National Society Daughters of the American Revolution, January 1919.

Report of the Publicity Director of the War Relief Service Committee of the National Society of the Daughters of the American Revolution to the Twenty-Eighth Continental Congress. Washington, D.C.: National Society Daughters of the American Revolution, 1919.

Report of the Twenty-Eighth Annual State Conference of the Daughters of the American Revolution. Raleigh, N.C.: Edwards and Broughton Co., n.d. [1928].

Report of the Twenty-Fourth Annual State Conference, Texas Daughters of the American Revolution. Temple, Tex.: American Printing Co., n.d. [1924].

Report of the Twenty-Ninth Annual State Conference of the Daughters of the American Revolution. Durham, N.C.: Seeman Printery, n.d. [1929].

Resolutions Adopted by the Thirty-Third Congress, National Society Daughters of the American Revolution, April 14–19, 1924. Washington, D.C.: National Society Daughters of the American Revolution, 1924.

Rex, Leda Ferrell, et al. *History of the Kansas State Daughters of the American Revolution, 1894–1938.* N.p.: Kansas Daughters of the American Revolution, 1938.

Ribuffo, Leo P. *The Old Christian Right: The Protestant Far Right from the Great Depression to the Cold War.* Philadelphia: Temple University Press, 1983.

Rief, Michelle. "Thinking Globally, Acting Locally: The International Agenda of African American Clubwomen, 1880–1940." *Journal of African American History* 89 (Summer 2004): 203–22.

Robinson, Jo Ann Gibson. *The Montgomery Bus Boycott and the Women Who Started It: The Memoir of Jo Ann Gibson Robinson.* Edited by David J. Garrow. Knoxville: University of Tennessee Press, 1987.

Rogin, Michael. *Blackface, White Noise: Jewish Immigrants in the Hollywood Melting Pot.* Berkeley and Los Angeles: University of California Press, 1996.

Roosevelt, Theodore. *Presidential Addresses and State Papers.* 4 vols. New York: Review of Reviews Co., 1905.

————. *The Strenuous Life.* New York: Review of Reviews Co., 1910.

Roth, Darlene Rebecca. *Matronage: Patterns in Women's Organizations, Atlanta, Georgia, 1890–1940.* Brooklyn, N.Y.: Carlson Publishing, 1994.

Rotundo, E. Anthony. *American Manhood: Transformations in Masculinity from the Revolution to the Modern Era.* New York: Basic Books, 1993.

Rouse, Jacqueline Anne. *Lugenia Burns Hope: Black Southern Reformer.* Athens: University of Georgia Press, 1989.

————. "Out of the Shadow of Tuskegee: Margaret Murray Washington, Social Activism, and Race Vindication." *Journal of Negro History* 81 (Winter 1996): 31–46.

Roydhouse, Marion W. "Bridging Chasms: Community and the Southern YWCA." In *Visible Women: New Essays on American Activism,* edited by Nancy A. Hewitt and Suzanne Lebsock, 270–95. Urbana and Chicago: University of Illinois Press, 1993.

Royster, Jacqueline Jones, ed. *Southern Horrors and Other Writings: The Anti-Lynching Campaign of Ida B. Wells, 1892–1900.* Boston and New York: Bedford Books, 1997.

Rubin, Anne Sarah. "Seventy-Six and Sixty-One: Confederates Remember the American Revolution." In *Where These Memories Grow: History, Memory, and Southern Identity,* edited by W. Fitzhugh Brundage, 85–105. Chapel Hill: University of North Carolina Press, 2000.

Ruffins, Faith Davis. "'Lifting as We Climb': Black Women and the Preservation of African American History and Culture." *Gender and History* 6 (November 1994): 376–96.

Rupp, Leila J. *Worlds of Women: The Making of an International Women's Movement.* Princeton, N.J.: Princeton University Press, 1997.

Russell, Virginia C. *Daughters Overseas: A History of Units Overseas.* Washington, D.C.: National Society Daughters of the American Revolution, 1990.

St. Paul, John, Jr. *The History of the National Society of the Sons of the American Revolution.* New Orleans, La.: Pelican Publishing Co., 1962.

Salem, Dorothy. *To Better Our World: Black Women in Organized Reform, 1890–1920.* Brooklyn, N.Y.: Carlson Publishing, 1990.

Samuel, Lawrence R. *Pledging Allegiance: American Identity and the Bond Drive of World War II.* Washington, D.C.: Smithsonian Institution Press, 1997.

Sánchez, George C. *Becoming Mexican American: Ethnicity, Culture, and Iden-*

tity in Chicano Los Angeles, 1900–1945. New York: Oxford University Press, 1993.

Sandage, Scott A. "A Marble House Divided: The Lincoln Memorial, the Civil Rights Movement, and the Politics of Memory, 1939–1963." *Journal of American History* 80 (June 1993): 135–67.

Satter, Beryl. "Marcus Garvey, Father Divine, and the Gender Politics of Race Difference and Race Neutrality." *American Quarterly* 48 (March 1996): 43–76.

Savage, Kirk. *Standing Soldiers, Kneeling Slaves: Race, War, and Monument in Nineteenth-Century America*. Princeton, N.J.: Princeton University Press, 1997.

Schechter, Patricia A. *Ida B. Wells-Barnett and American Reform, 1880–1930*. Chapel Hill: University of North Carolina Press, 2001.

Schneider, Mark Robert. *"We Return Fighting": The Civil Rights Movement in the Jazz Age*. Boston: Northeastern University Press, 2002.

Schott, Linda K. *Reconstructing Women's Thoughts: The Women's International League for Peace and Freedom before World War II*. Stanford, Calif.: Stanford University Press, 1997.

Scott, Anne Firor. *Natural Allies: Women's Associations in American History*. Urbana and Chicago: University of Illinois Press, 1992.

Scott, Rose Moss, comp. and ed. *Illinois State History, Daughters of the American Revolution*. Danville, Ill.: Illinois Printing Co., 1929.

Seller, Maxine. "The Education of the Immigrant Woman, 1900–1935." *Journal of Urban History* 4 (May 1978): 307–30.

Shaw, Stephanie J. "Black Club Women and the Creation of the National Association of Colored Women." In *"We Specialize in the Wholly Impossible": A Reader in Black Women's History*, edited by Darlene Clark Hine, Wilma King, and Linda Reed, 433–48. Brooklyn, N.Y.: Carlson Publishing, 1995.

———. *What a Woman Ought to Be and to Do: Black Professional Women Workers during the Jim Crow Era*. Chicago: University of Chicago Press, 1996.

Silber, Nina. *The Romance of Reunion: Northerners and the South, 1865–1900*. Chapel Hill: University of North Carolina Press, 1993.

Simpson, John A. *Edith D. Pope and Her Nashville Friends: Guardians of the Lost Cause in the* Confederate Veteran. Knoxville: University of Tennessee Press, 2003.

Sims, Anastatia. *The Power of Femininity in the New South: Women's Organizations and Politics in North Carolina, 1883–1930*. Columbia: University of South Carolina Press, 1997.

Singer, Brian C. J. "Cultural versus Contractual Nations: Rethinking Their Opposition." *History and Theory* 35 (October 1996): 309–37.

Sklar, Kathryn Kish. *Florence Kelley and the Nation's Work: The Rise of Women's Political Culture*. New Haven, Conn.: Yale University Press, 1995.

———. "The Historical Foundations of Women's Power in the Creation of the

American Welfare State, 1830–1930." In *Mothers of a New World: Maternalist Politics and the Origins of Welfare States*, edited by Seth Koven and Sonya Michel, 43–93. New York: Routledge, 1993.

Skocpol, Theda. *Protecting Soldiers and Mothers: The Political Origins of Social Policy in the United States.* Cambridge, Mass.: Harvard University Press, 1992.

Smith, Bonnie G. *The Gender of History: Men, Women, and Historical Practice.* Cambridge, Mass.: Harvard University Press, 1998.

Smith, Rogers M. *Civic Ideals: Conflicting Visions of Citizenship in U.S. History.* New Haven, Conn.: Yale University Press, 1997.

Smith, Shawn Michelle. *American Archives: Gender, Race, and Class in Visual Culture.* Princeton, N.J.: Princeton University Press, 1999.

Smith-Rosenberg, Carroll. "The Female World of Love and Ritual: Relations between Women in Nineteenth-Century America." In *Disorderly Conduct: Visions of Gender in Victorian America*, 53–76. New York: Oxford University Press, 1985.

Sollors, Werner. *Beyond Ethnicity: Consent and Descent in American Culture.* New York: Oxford University Press, 1986.

Solomon, Barbara Miller. *Ancestors and Immigrants: A Changing New England Tradition.* 1956; reprint, Boston: Northeastern University Press, 1989.

Spain, Daphne. *How Women Saved the City.* Minneapolis: University of Minnesota Press, 2001.

Standley, Anne. "The Role of Black Women in the Civil Rights Movement." In *Black Women's History: Theory and Practice*, edited by Darlene Clark Hine, 183–201. Brooklyn, N.Y.: Carlson Publishing, 1990.

Statutes of the National Society, Daughters of the American Revolution, 1890 to 1897. Washington, D.C.: National Society Daughters of the American Revolution, n.d. [1897].

Stein, Judith. *The World of Marcus Garvey: Race and Class in Modern Society.* Baton Rouge: Louisiana State University Press, 1986.

Steinson, Barbara J. *American Women's Activism in World War I.* New York: Garland Publishing, 1982.

Stewart, Jeffrey C. and Fath Davis Ruffins. "A Faithful Witness: Afro-American Public History in Historical Perspective, 1828–1984." In *Presenting the Past: Essays on History and the Public*, edited by Susan Porter Benson, Stephen Brier, and Roy Rosenzweig, 307–36. Philadelphia: Temple University Press, 1986.

Sullivan, Patricia. *Days of Hope: Race and Democracy in the New Deal Era.* Chapel Hill: University of North Carolina Press, 1996.

Summers, Martin. *Manliness and Its Discontents: The Black Middle Class and the Transformation of Masculinity, 1900–1930.* Chapel Hill: University of North Carolina Press, 2004.

Synopsis of the Proceedings of the Department of Massachusetts Woman's Relief

Corps, Auxiliary to the Grand Army of the Republic, From Its Institution in 1879 Until the Close of the Year 1886, First to Seventh Department Conventions. Boston: E. B. Stillings and Co., 1889.

Tarbell, Grace Butler. *History of the Daughters of the American Revolution of Colorado, 1894–1941*. N.p., 1941.

Tax, Meredith. *The Rising of the Women: Feminist Solidarity and Class Conflict, 1880–1917*. New York: Monthly Review Press, 1980.

Taylor, Ula Yvette. "'Negro Women Are Great Thinkers as Well as Doers': Amy Jacques-Garvey and Community Feminism, 1914–1927." *Journal of Women's History* 12 (Summer 2000): 104–26.

———. *The Veiled Garvey: The Life and Times of Amy Jacques Garvey*. Chapel Hill: University of North Carolina Press, 2002.

Terborg-Penn, Rosalyn. *African American Women in the Struggle for the Vote, 1850–1920*. Bloomington and Indianapolis: Indiana University Press, 1998.

———. "Discontented Black Feminists: Prelude and Postscript to the Passage of the Nineteenth Amendment." In *"We Specialize in the Wholly Impossible": A Reader in Black Women's History*, edited by Darlene Clark Hine, Wilma King, and Linda Reed, 487–504. Brooklyn, N.Y.: Carlson Publishing, 1995.

Terrell, Mary Church. *A Colored Woman in a White World*. 1940; reprint, with an introduction by Nellie Y. McKay, New York: G. K. Hall and Co., 1996.

Thomas, Mary Martha. *The New Woman in Alabama: Social Reforms and Suffrage, 1890–1920*. Tuscaloosa: University of Alabama Press, 1992.

Thompson, Mildred I. *Ida B. Wells-Barnett: An Exploratory Study of an American Black Woman, 1893–1930*. Brooklyn, N.Y. Carlson Publishing, 1990.

Thurber, Cheryl. "The Development of the Mammy Image and Mythology." In *Southern Women: Histories and Identities*, edited by Virginia Bernhard, Betty Brandon, Elizabeth Fox-Genovese, and Theda Perdue, 87–108. Columbia: University of Missouri Press, 1992.

Thurner, Manuela. "'Better Citizens without the Ballot': American Anti-Suffrage Women and Their Rationale during the Progressive Era." In *One Woman, One Vote: Rediscovering the Woman Suffrage Movement*, edited by Marjorie Spruill Wheeler, 203–20. Troutdale, Ore.: NewSage Press, 1995.

Tomes, Nancy. *The Gospel of Germs: Men, Women, and the Microbe in American Life*. Cambridge, Mass.: Harvard University Press, 1997.

Tone, Andrea, ed. *Controlling Reproduction: An American History*. Wilmington, Del.: Scholarly Resources, 1997.

Townsend, Kim. *Manhood at Harvard: William James and Others*. New York: W. W. Norton, 1996.

Trattner, Walter I. *Crusade for the Children: A History of the National Child Labor Committee and Child Labor Reform in America*. Chicago: Quadrangle Books, 1970.

Travers, Len. *Celebrating the Fourth: Independence Day and the Rites of Nation-*

alism in the Early Republic. Amherst: University of Massachusetts Press, 1997.

Truesdell, Barbara. "Exalting U.S.ness: Patriotic Rituals of the Daughters of the American Revolution." In *Bonds of Affection: Americans Define Their Patriotism*, edited by John Bodnar, 273–89. Princeton, N.J.: Princeton University Press, 1996.

Turner, Elizabeth Hayes. *Women, Culture, and Community: Religion and Reform in Galveston, 1880–1920*. New York: Oxford University Press, 1997.

Turner, Frederick Jackson. "The Significance of the Frontier in American History." In *The Frontier in American History*, 1–38. 1920; reprint, Tucson: University of Arizona Press, 1994.

Tuttle, Mrs. George Fuller, comp. and ed. *Three Centuries in Champlain Valley: A Collection of Historical Facts and Incidents*. Albany, N.Y.: Brandow Press Printing, 1909.

Ulrich, Laurel Thatcher. *The Age of Homespun: Objects and Stories in the Creation of an American Myth*. New York: Alfred A. Knopf, 2001.

———. *Good Wives: Image and Reality in the Lives of Women in Northern New England, 1650–1750*. New York: Vintage, 1982.

U.S. Bureau of the Census. *Bicentennial Edition: Historical Statistics of the United States, Colonial Times to 1970, Part 1*. Washington, D.C.: Government Printing Office, 1975.

U.S. Immigration Commission. *Statements and Recommendations Submitted by Societies and Organizations Interested in the Subject of Immigration*. Vol. 41 of *Reports of the Immigration Commission*. 61st Cong., 3d sess., no. 764. Washington, D.C.: Government Printing Office, 1911.

U.S. Senate. *Report of the Daughters of the American Revolution, 1890 to 1897*. 55th Cong., 3rd sess., no. 164. Washington, D.C.: Government Printing Office, 1899.

———. *Second Report of the National Society Daughters of the American Revolution, October 11, 1897–October 11, 1898*. 56th Cong., 1st sess., no. 425. Washington, D.C.: Government Printing Office, 1900.

———. *Third Report of the National Society of the Daughters of the American Revolution, October 11, 1898–October 11, 1900*. 56th Cong., 2d sess., no. 219. Washington, D.C.: Government Printing Office, 1901.

Varon, Elizabeth R. *We Mean to Be Counted: White Women and Politics in Antebellum Virginia*. Chapel Hill: University of North Carolina Press, 1998.

Vaughan, Leslie J. "Cosmopolitanism, Ethnicity, and American Identity: Randolph Bourne's 'Trans-National America.'" *Journal of American Studies* 25 (December 1991): 443–59.

Vaughn, Stephen. *Holding Fast the Inner Lines: Democracy, Nationalism, and the Committee on Public Information*. Chapel Hill: University of North Carolina Press, 1980.

Viroli, Maurizio. *For Love of Country: An Essay on Patriotism and Nationalism.* New York: Oxford University Press, 1995.

Waldstreicher, David. *In the Midst of Perpetual Fetes: The Making of American Nationalism, 1776–1820.* Chapel Hill: University of North Carolina Press, 1997.

Wall, Joseph Frazier. *Iowa: A Bicentennial History.* New York: W. W. Norton, 1978.

Wallace, Michael. "Visiting the Past: History Museums in the United States." In *Presenting the Past: Essays on History and the Public,* edited by Susan Porter Benson, Stephen Brier, and Roy Rosenzweig, 137–64. Philadelphia: Temple University Press, 1986.

Warren, Catherine M., comp. and ed. *History of the Massachusetts Daughters of the American Revolution.* Somerville, Mass.: Somerville Printing Co., 1932.

Washington, Eugenia. *History of the Organization of the Society of the Daughters of the American Revolution.* Washington, D.C.: National Society of the Daughters of the American Revolution, 1895.

Wells, Ida B., Frederick Douglass, Irvine Garland Penn, and Ferdinand L. Barnett. *The Reason Why the Colored American Is Not in the World's Columbian Exposition: The Afro-American's Contribution to Columbian Literature.* Edited by Robert Rydell. 1893; reprint, Urbana and Chicago: University of Illinois Press, 1999.

Wells-Barnett, Ida B. *Crusade for Justice: The Autobiography of Ida B. Wells.* Edited by Alfreda M. Duster. Chicago: University of Chicago Press, 1970.

Wenger, Beth S. "Radical Politics in a Reactionary Age: The Unmaking of Rosika Schwimmer, 1914–1930." *Journal of Women's History* 2 (Fall 1990): 66–99.

Wesley, Charles Harris. *The History of the National Association of Colored Women's Clubs: A Legacy of Service.* Washington, D.C.: National Association of Colored Women's Clubs, Inc., 1984.

West, Lois A., ed. *Feminist Nationalism.* New York: Routledge, 1997.

West, Patricia. *Domesticating History: The Political Origins of America's House Museums.* Washington, D.C.: Smithsonian Institution Press, 1999.

Wexler, Laura. *Tender Violence: Domestic Visions in an Age of U.S. Imperialism.* Chapel Hill: University of North Carolina Press, 2000.

White, Deborah Gray. *Too Heavy a Load: Black Women in Defense of Themselves, 1894–1994.* New York: W. W. Norton, 1999.

Whites, LeeAnn. *The Civil War as a Crisis in Gender: Augusta, Georgia, 1860–1890.* Athens: University of Georgia Press, 1995.

———. "Rebecca Latimer Felton and the Problem of 'Protection' in the New South." In *Visible Women: New Essays on American Activism,* edited by Nancy A. Hewitt and Suzanne Lebsock, 41–61. Urbana and Chicago: University of Illinois Press, 1993.

Wiebe, Robert H. *The Search for Order, 1877–1920.* New York: Hill and Wang, 1967.

———. *Who We Are: A History of Popular Nationalism.* Princeton, N.J.: Princeton University Press, 2002.

Wilkins, Roger W. *Jefferson's Pillow: The Founding Fathers and the Dilemma of Black Patriotism.* Boston: Beacon Press, 2001.

Willard, Frances E., and Mary A. Livermore, eds. *A Woman of the Century.* 1893; reprint, Detroit. Mich.: Gale Research Co., 1967.

Williams, Lillian Serece. *Strangers in the Land of Paradise: The Creation of an African American Community, Buffalo, New York, 1900–1940.* Bloomington and Indianapolis: Indiana University Press, 1999.

Williams, Lillian Serece, and Randolph Boehm, eds. *Records of the National Association of Colored Women's Clubs, 1895–1992. Part 1: Minutes of National Conventions, Publications, and Presidents' Correspondence.* Microfilm; Bethesda, Md.: University Publications of America, 1993.

Wilson, Chris. *The Myth of Santa Fe: Creating a Modern Regional Tradition.* Albuquerque: University of New Mexico Press, 1997.

Wilson, Woodrow. *A History of the American People.* 5 vols. New York: Harpers, 1902.

Winegarten, Ruthe. *Black Texas Women: 150 Years of Trial and Triumph.* Austin: University of Texas Press, 1995.

Wolcott, Victoria W. *Remaking Respectability: African American Women in Interwar Detroit.* Chapel Hill: University of North Carolina Press, 2001.

Wood, Clara L., ed. *History and Register, Idaho State Society, Daughters of the American Revolution.* Caldwell, Idaho: Caxton Printers, 1936.

Wood, Mary I. *The History of the General Federation of Women's Clubs for the First Twenty-Two Years of Its Organization.* Norwood, Mass.: Norwood Press, 1912.

Zeiger, Susan. *In Uncle Sam's Service: Women Workers with the American Expeditionary Force, 1917–1919.* Ithaca, N.Y.: Cornell University Press, 2000.

Zelinsky, Wilbur. *Nation into State: The Shifting Symbolic Foundations of American Nationalism.* Chapel Hill: University of North Carolina Press, 1988.

Zimmerman, Martha Rosenberger, comp. and ed. *Centennial History of the Illinois State Organization, National Society Daughters of the American Revolution.* N.p., 1991.

Unpublished Works

Blair, William. "Reburying Caesar, with Plenty of Praise: The Politics of Ladies Memorial Associations in Postwar Virginia." Paper delivered at the Douglas Southall Freeman and Southern Intellectual History Conferences, University of Richmond, February 22, 2002.

Clark, Kathleen Ann. "History Is No Fossil Remains: Race, Gender, and the Politics of Memory in the American South, 1863–1913." Ph.D. diss., Yale University, 1999.

Cumberbatch, Prudence Denise. "Working for the Race: The Transformation of the Civil Rights Struggle in Baltimore, 1929–1945." Ph.D. diss., Yale University, 2001.

Delegard, Kirsten Marie. "Women Patriots: Female Activism and the Politics of American Anti-Radicalism, 1919–1935." Ph.D. diss., Duke University, 1999.

Feimster, Crystal Nicole. "'Ladies and Lynching': The Gendered Discourse of Mob Violence in the New South, 1880–1930." Ph.D. diss., Princeton University, 2000.

Hickel, Karl Walter. "Entitling Citizens: World War I, Progressivism, and the Origins of the American Welfare State, 1917–1928." Ph.D. diss., Columbia University, 1999.

Jensen, Kimberly. "Minerva on the Field of Mars: American Women, Citizenship, and Military Service in the First World War." Ph.D. diss., University of Iowa, 1992.

Johnson, Joan Marie. "'This Wonderful Dream Nation!': Black and White South Carolina Women and the Creation of the New South, 1898–1930." Ph.D. diss., University of California at Los Angeles, 1997.

Kachun, Mitchell A. "The Faith That the Dark Past Has Taught Us: African-American Commemorations in the North and West and the Construction of a Usable Past, 1808–1915." Ph.D. diss., Cornell University, 1997.

LaGanke, Lucile Evelyn. "The National Society of the Daughters of the American Revolution: Its History, Policies, and Influence, 1890–1949." Ph.D. diss., Case Western Reserve University, 1951.

Morgan, Francesca Constance. "'Home and Country': Women, Nation, and the Daughters of the American Revolution, 1890–1939." Ph.D. diss., Columbia University, 1998.

Sallee, Shelley Kathryn. "Inventing 'the Forgotten Child': The Whiteness of Child Labor Reform in the New South." Ph.D. diss., University of Texas at Austin, 1998.

Shields, Elizabeth. "A History of the United States Army Nurse Corps (Female): 1901–1937." Ed.D. diss., Columbia University Teachers' College, 1980.

Sneider, Allison Lee. "Reconstruction, Expansion, and Empire: The U.S. Woman Suffrage Movement and the Re-Making of National Political Community, 1870–1900." Ph.D. diss., University of California at Los Angeles, 1999.

Stott, Kelly McMichael. "From Lost Cause to Female Empowerment: The Texas Division of the United Daughters of the Confederacy." Ph.D. diss., University of North Texas, 2001.

Index

Bruce, Josephine Beall Wilson, 24–25
Brundage, W. Fitzhugh, 3
Buel, Elizabeth Cynthia Barney, 83, 202 (n. 15)
Buffalo, N.Y., 103, 121
Buford College (Tenn.), 204 (n. 32)
Burleson, Albert, 112
Burroughs, Nannie Helen, 123
Butler, Selena Sloan, 61, 75

Cabell, Mary Virginia Ellet, 45, 49–50
Calhoun, John C., 186 (n. 104), 209 (n. 91)
California, 30, 46, 51, 65, 72, 84, 136, 149–50, 159–60, 186 (n. 111), 189 (n. 133), 220 (n. 18)
Cambridge, Mass., 99, 224 (n. 54)
Campbell, Susie S., 115–17
Canton, Ohio, 104
Capitalism, 50–54, 82–83, 106–7, 132–34, 138, 152, 159
Carby, Hazel V., 92
Carney, William H., 26
Carr, John Foster, 202 (n. 15)
Carr, Mary L., 186–87 (n. 113)
Carter, Mary D., 115
Catholics. *See* Religion: Roman Catholicism
Catt, Carrie Chapman, 109
Cedar Hill. *See* Douglass, Frederick
Cedar Rapids, Iowa, 159
Cemeteries, 28, 34, 52, 105, 133, 161
Charleston, S.C., 23, 28, 30, 37, 113, 145, 186 (n. 104)
Chicago, Ill., 49, 51, 68, 119, 122, 140, 146, 149, 229 (n. 93), 233 (n. 7)
Child labor reform, 81–85, 94, 98, 131–32, 202 (n. 14)
Children and youth, work among, 2, 9, 21, 39, 41, 55, 70, 86, 111, 201 (n. 7), 204 (n. 34); by black women, 9, 23–27 passim, 37, 60–62, 68, 74–75, 82, 102–4, 123, 129–31, 147, 150; by white women, 11, 23, 35, 37, 40, 67, 83–90 passim, 95–96, 99, 104, 111, 143, 151, 162, 172 (n. 32), 202 (n. 16), 204 (n. 33), 206 (n. 49), 213 (n. 42), 223–24 (n. 48), 236 (n. 31)
Children of the American Revolution, 206 (n. 49)
Children of the Confederacy, 11, 35, 95–96, 143, 162
Children of the Republic, 206 (n. 49)
China, 212 (n. 23), 220 (n. 18)
Chipeta (Ute leader), 64, 195–96 (n. 30)
Cincinnati, Ohio, 81, 88, 189 (n. 131), 206 (n. 49), 229 (n. 93)
Civic nationalism: white, 11–15, 83–84, 151, 179 (n. 35); African American, 15, 20–26, 37, 74, 80–81, 91, 99, 119–25, 146–48, 156–57, 161, 175 (n. 51), 199 (n. 78)
Civilization, 3, 79, 102, 109; defined by white women, 15–16, 58, 62, 64–67, 71, 83–84, 88–90, 104–5; defined by black women, 58–59, 61, 72–75, 199 (n. 76); defined by men, 59, 67, 92, 97; and gender distinctions, 66, 88–90
Civil rights movement, 5, 13, 98–99, 117–18, 147, 151–55 passim, 160–61, 171 (n. 28), 180 (n. 38); women within, 16, 25, 74, 79–80, 90–93, 101–2, 119–25, 146–49 passim, 152, 161
Civil War, 6, 10, 15, 17, 19–21, 42–47, 54–55, 58, 77, 96–98, 107, 157, 161, 173 (n. 38), 177 (n. 12); commemoration of Union struggle, 21–22, 26–27, 37, 39–41, 86, 142, 161; commemoration of women's service to Confederacy, 32, 96–97, 181 (n. 43);

Cunningham, Sumner Archibald, 32, 67, 96–97, 182 (n. 65), 209 (n. 92)

Czolgosz, Leon. *See* McKinley, William

Darling, Flora Adams, 44–45

Daughters of Revolution, 159

Daughters of the American Revolution: membership figures, 11, 237 (n. 34); racial exclusion by, 12, 152–56, 189 (n. 131), 232 (n. 122), 233 (n. 1); and United Daughters of the Confederacy, 13, 30, 44, 46–47, 71, 87, 94, 113–15, 142–45, 174–75 (n. 49), 189 (n. 134), 208 (nn. 76, 78), 215 (n. 61), 227 (n. 71); social composition of, 42–43, 50–54, 162, 191 (nn. 151–54), 236 (n. 32); formation of, 43–49, 190 (nn. 147, 149); and North-South reunion, 45–46, 85–86, 142–45, 190 (n. 47); organizational structure of, 47; and marriage, 49–50; uses of genealogy by, 50–51, 187 (n. 115), 191 (n. 151); and capitalism, 50–54, 133–34; antiradicalism within, 51, 82–83, 106–7, 132–42, 151, 158–59, 162–63; and Spanish-American War, 58, 62–63, 68–69, 192–93 (nn. 1, 3), 197 (n. 47); and civilization, 58, 64–66, 71, 83–84, 88–90; and Philippine-American War, 58, 65, 68–69, 71; and female fertility, 62, 141–42, 159–60, 194 (n. 18); and empire, 62–66, 68–69; and Native Americans, 64, 136, 174 (n. 43), 195–96 (nn. 29–30), 222 (n. 35); and westward expansion, 64–66, 84, 196 (n. 33), 220 (n. 18); and military culture, 68–69, 133; Anglophilia within, 69–70, 198 (n. 57); and organized labor, 82–83, 202

(nn. 14, 16); support for progressive reform, 82–86, 132, 162, 201–2 (n. 13); and naturalization, 84, 105; and Mormons, 87–88, 205 (n. 47); outreach to African Americans, 89–90, 117, 206 (n. 55); and World War I, 104–11, 125–26, 132, 213 (n. 42); on government actions during Red Scare, 106–7, 110–11, 213 (n. 47); and military preparedness, 108, 110–11, 213 (n. 38); pre-1923 peace activism of, 108–10, 132; rightism (opposition to reform), 126–28, 132–34, 137–38, 155–56, 158, 162–63, 218 (n. 1); and national defense, 127–28, 133–42, 151; and Sheppard-Towner Act, 132, 136–37; and consumer culture, 133–34, 159, 221 (n. 26); opposition to peace activism, 135–41; resignations from, 136, 139, 222 (n. 37), 225 (n. 56); and surveillance agencies, 137–38, 141, 225–26 (n. 61); National Defense Committee, 138–41, 155, 159, 163, 223 (n. 46); expulsions from, 139, 224 (n. 54); and far right, 139–41, 233 (n. 7); and racial segregation, 151, 216 (n. 76); and eugenics, 159–60, 235 (n. 21); and Ku Klux Klan (formed 1915), 213 (n. 43); use of "general" by, 214 (n. 53); and spider-web charts, 226 (n. 62). *See also* Americanization; "Doubtful speakers" lists; Girl Home Makers' Clubs; Historic preservation; Monuments; State-based nationalism; U.S. flag; Woman suffrage

Daughters of the Republic of Texas, 171 (n. 25), 179 (n. 29)

Davidson, Nellie S., 154–55

Davis, Jefferson, 35, 36, 116, 151, 183 (n. 72)

L'Ouverture, Toussaint, 61–62
Loyalty. *See* Americanization; Patriotism; Treason
Loyalty oaths, 32, 209 (n. 88), 223–24 (n. 48)
Lusitania (ship), 110
Lyles, Mrs. T. H., 26–27, 180 (n. 38)
Lynchings, 22–24, 72, 90–91, 120, 124–25, 147–48, 155, 199 (n. 78)
Lyons, Maritcha, 92

MacFarland, Mary Perley, 224 (n. 54)
"Madonna of the Trail." *See* "Pioneer Mother of the Trail" statues
Maine, 61, 227 (n. 68)
Maine, USS, 72
"Mammy" statue (proposed), 145–46
Manifest destiny, 2, 63–66
Manila, the Philippines, 62, 68, 197 (n. 47), 200–201 (n. 5)
Manliness, 5–6, 51, 55, 92–93, 169 (n. 4)
Marriage, 7–9, 29, 38, 45, 49–51, 59, 80, 84, 86–89, 94, 105–6, 134, 159, 172 (n. 31), 190 (nn. 145, 149), 203 (n. 19)
Marvin, Fred R., 139–41, 225 (n. 60)
Maryland, 38, 39, 55, 113–14, 182 (n. 61), 214 (n. 58), 216 (n. 81)
"Maryland, My Maryland," 55
Masculinity, 3, 5–7, 10, 49, 57, 66, 92–93, 104, 108, 117, 129, 138, 149, 160
Masculinization of women's nationalisms: among African Americans, 16, 80, 90–93, 117, 128–30, 148–50; among whites, 16, 93, 101, 107, 111, 116, 128–29, 135, 137, 142–43, 158–59
Massachusetts, 22, 24–26, 37, 39–40, 46, 62, 70, 73, 84–85, 93, 99, 119, 135, 139, 171 (n. 28), 174 (n. 46), 178

(n. 14), 188–89 (n. 130), 192 (n. 163), 203 (n. 20), 210 (n. 3), 224 (nn. 52, 54)
Massachusetts Public Interests League, 221 (n. 32)
"Massive resistance," 161–62
Matricide, cultural, 158
Matthews, Victoria Earle, 25, 27, 92, 103
Maxwell, Lucia Ramsey, 141, 226 (n. 62)
Mayflower. See Pilgrims
Mayflower Descendants, General Society of, 43
McClintock, Anne, 3
McComb, Miss., 95–96
McCord, Louisa Cheves, 28, 181 (n. 43)
McDowell, William Osborne, 43–44
McGee, Anita Newcomb, 61
McKinley, William, 32, 42, 68, 83, 96
Mead, Lucia Ames, 138, 144, 224 (n. 50)
Mellon family, 50
Memorial Day, 12, 21, 38, 40–41, 186 (n. 100)
Memphis, Tenn., 33, 45, 121, 175 (n. 51)
Menominee, Mich., 88
Merritt, Emma Frances, 74–75
Mexican Americans, 11, 46, 65, 84, 220 (n. 18), 221 (n. 24)
Mexican War. *See* U.S.-Mexican War
Mexico, 65, 72, 108, 196 (n. 33)
Michaels, Walter Benn, 158
Michigan, 67, 88, 117, 139–41, 151, 225 (n. 56), 236 (n. 32)
Military Intelligence Division. *See* U.S. Military Intelligence Division
Military preparedness: notions of, 108, 110, 113, 126–27
Military service. *See* Warriors, perceptions of

Milwaukee, Wis., 51, 138
Mink, Sarah C., 40
Minneapolis, Minn., 50–51, 141
Minnesota, 26–27, 41, 50–51, 64, 79,
    88, 141, 148, 180 (n. 38), 204 (n. 32),
    209 (n. 87), 227 (n. 68)
Minor, Anne Rogers, 135–36
Minor, Charles Landon Carter, 227
    (n. 72)
Mississippi, 22, 25, 32, 38, 64, 94–97,
    106, 113, 116, 213 (nn. 43, 47)
Missouri, 35, 40, 49, 60, 85, 114, 133,
    150, 189 (n. 134), 195–96 (n. 30), 201
    (n. 9), 209 (n. 87), 214 (n. 58), 215
    (n. 61), 219 (n. 4)
Monroe Doctrine, 71, 136
Montana, 30, 131
Monuments, 3, 5, 7; regarding Civil
    War, 11, 21–22, 26–28, 34–36, 45,
    94, 96–97, 111, 115, 145, 183–84
    (n. 75), 227 (n. 68); proposed by
    United Daughters of the Confeder-
    acy, 11, 33–36, 94, 96–98, 111–13,
    115, 145–46, 150–51, 161–62, 183–
    84 (nn. 67, 70–71, 75), 231 (n. 113);
    proposed by African Americans,
    21–22, 26–27, 68, 80–81, 93, 149,
    197 (n. 46), 200 (n. 4); regarding
    African Americans, 21–22, 33,
    68, 80, 93, 97, 145–46, 149, 183
    (nn. 70–71), 200 (n. 4), 216 (n. 76);
    regarding white men, 34, 36, 111,
    115, 151, 183–84 (n. 75); proposed
    by Daughters of the American
    Revolution, 45, 63, 66, 68, 118, 133,
    141, 177 (n. 3), 195–96 (nn. 29–30,
    33, 37), 197 (n. 47), 216 (n. 76), 227
    (n. 68); regarding white women,
    45, 94, 96–97, 133, 177 (n. 3), 196
    (n. 37), 227 (n. 68); regarding black
    women, 80, 145–46, 200 (n. 4); re-
    garding American Revolution, 93,

133, 195 (n. 29); regarding World
    War I, 118, 216 (n. 76); regarding
    "white" or "American" babies, 141
Moral authority, 2, 5, 9, 12, 15, 101,
    107, 138
Mormons. See Religion: Mormonism
Moss, Arlene Nichols, 133
Motherhood, 2, 6–7, 32, 36, 60–61,
    66–67, 86, 89, 104–6, 129, 133–34,
    150, 160, 206 (n. 54)
Mothers' pensions, 132
Mount Vernon (Va.), 19–20, 25, 103
Mount Vernon Ladies' Association,
    19–20
Museums, 3, 52; Mount Vernon (Va.),
    19–20, 25, 103; Frederick Douglass
    Home (D.C.), 20, 25–26, 102–4;
    Confederate White House (Va.), 34;
    Oliver Ellsworth House (Conn.),
    48; Independence Hall (Pa.), 48, 52,
    64, 179 (n. 29); Homestead National
    Monument (Neb.), 64; Lapwai Mis-
    sion (Idaho), 64; The Alamo (Tex.),
    72, 179 (n. 29); Roosevelt Cabin
    (N.D.), 135; Paul Revere House
    (Mass.), 192 (n. 163)

Nashville, Tenn., 29, 204 (n. 32), 209
    (n. 92)
Natchez Trace Parkway, 64
Natchitoches, La., 183 (n. 71)
National Afro-American Council, 90
National American Woman Suffrage
    Association, 12
National anthem. See "Star-Spangled
    Banner, The"
National Association for the Advance-
    ment of Colored People, 16, 98,
    124, 128, 147, 151, 155, 217 (n. 94),
    218 (n. 100), 229 (n. 93); and black
    women, 86, 91–92, 97, 99, 102, 120,
    148–49, 180 (n. 38), 206–7 (nn. 57,

66), 229 (n. 93), 230 (nn. 101, 103); formation of, 90–92

National Association Notes, 61, 86–87, 171–72 (n. 28)

National Association of Colored Graduate Nurses, 120

National Association of Colored Women, 8–9, 22–23, 27, 130, 161, 172 (n. 32); civil rights protests by, 8, 22–23, 91–92, 98, 120, 124, 146, 148, 152, 171–72 (n. 28), 230 (n. 101); membership figures, 8, 119, 171 (n. 27); conservative turn, 8–9, 171–72 (n. 28); and black history, 9, 42, 80–81, 82, 102, 149–50; and museums, 20, 25–26, 102–4, 210 (n. 2); precursors of, 22, 27; social composition of, 22, 178 (n. 14); formation of, 22–23, 47, 177 (n. 12), 219 (n. 4); and libraries, 23; and schools, 23, 82; and commemoration, 27, 80–81, 102–4, 180 (n. 38); on progress of women, 61, 80, 129; and progressive reform, 82, 131, 201 (n. 9); and polygamy, 87; and *The Birth of a Nation*, 98–99; and World War I, 119–21, 123; and Red Scare, 123; and International Council of Women, 124–25, 152; and National Association for the Advancement of Colored People, 148, 230 (n. 101); and red-baiting, 152. *See also* American and "Negro" nations; Black nationalism; Civic nationalism: African American; Frederick Douglass Home; International Council of Women of Darker Races; Woman suffrage; *and names of local clubs*

National Colored Women's Congress (Atlanta, Ga.), 27

National Conference on the Cause and Cure of War, 138–39

National Congress of Mothers, 143

National Consumer League, 85

National Council for the Prevention of War, 138

National Council of Negro Women, 161, 210 (n. 2)

National Council of Women, 132, 136, 138, 222 (n. 34)

National defense: concept of, 127–28, 137, 139, 141, 144, 151. *See also* Daughters of the American Revolution; Women's Patriotic Conference on National Defense

National Flag Conference (1923), 143–44

Nationalism, men's, 6–7, 43–44, 59–61, 66–67, 96–97, 137–38, 140–41; and female fertility, 5–7, 57, 59–60, 77, 150, 160, 231 (n. 111)

Nationalism, women's: and country, 1, 13, 30–31, 156; definitions of, 1–2; and female fertility, 2, 60, 141–42, 150, 159–60; distinctively feminine forms of, 3, 5, 15, 21, 34–35, 41, 67, 80–81, 89, 104, 134; and feminism, 3, 14, 87, 105–6, 129–30, 176 (n. 59); centered on women, 3–4, 15–17, 24–27, 35–36, 41–42, 48–49, 55, 60–61, 65–68, 80–90, 93, 99, 102–7, 129–34, 156–59, 169 (n. 4); centered on men, 5, 11, 16, 101–2, 107–17, 134–42, 148–50, 159; and Civil War, 5–6, 15, 19–55, 142; and U.S. state, 7–8, 17, 57–59, 81–82, 107–11; and African Americans and the state, 13, 15, 73–75, 81–82, 119–25, 148, 201 (n. 9); effects of war on, 57–59, 67–70, 71–75, 101–26, 132; and empire, 57–77, 124, 136; and peace activism, 108–10, 212 (n. 36); and democracy, 157–58. *See also* Black nationalism; Civic nationalism; Masculinization of women's nationalisms; Neo-Confederate nationalism; Patriotism; Race-based nationalism; State-based nationalism; Transnationalism

National League for Women's Service, 126

National patriotism, 12, 15, 23, 37–41, 70, 107, 147, 171 (n. 25)

National Society of the Colonial Dames of America, 43, 171 (n. 25)

National Society of the Daughters of the American Revolution. *See* Daughters of the American Revolution

National Training School for Women and Girls, 123

National Woman's Party, 87, 213 (n. 40)

Native Americans, 11, 19, 38, 41, 46, 64, 115, 118, 136, 173 (n. 39), 174 (n. 43), 195 (n. 29), 196 (n. 37), 222 (n. 35), 236 (n. 32)

Nativism. *See* Immigration

Navy League, 110, 113

Nebraska, 64

Neff, Elizabeth Hyer, 89

Negro History Week, 6, 131

"Negro National Anthem, The (Lift Ev'ry Voice and Sing)," 147–48

Negro World, The. See Universal Negro Improvement Association

Neo-Confederate movement. *See* Sons of Confederate Veterans; United Confederate Veterans; United Daughters of the Confederacy

Neo-Confederate nationalism, 10–11, 15, 29–31, 66–67, 70–71, 80, 93–97, 102, 161–62; and American na-

tion, 30–31, 70–71, 112–17; and U.S. state, 58, 71, 79, 112–17; and 1920s rightism, 142–45

Neve, Felipe de, 65

Neverdon-Morton, Cynthia, 152

New Hampshire, 44

New Haven, Conn., 48, 69, 139, 225 (n. 56)

New Jersey, 43, 93, 141, 217 (n. 93), 224 (n. 54)

New Mexico, 174–75 (n. 49), 191 (n. 151), 221 (n. 24)

"New South": notions of, 29, 40, 181 (n. 49)

New Spain: commemoration of, 64–65, 72, 189 (n. 133), 221 (n. 24)

New York, 25, 27, 38, 40, 51, 66, 69, 80, 89, 92, 98, 103, 109–10, 120–22, 125, 133, 141, 144, 151, 158, 179–80 (n. 35), 189 (n. 139), 190 (n. 149), 200 (n. 4), 204 (n. 32), 230 (n. 105), 237 (n. 34)

New York Age. See Fortune, T. Thomas

New York City, 89, 109–10, 121, 125, 141, 144, 151, 158, 190 (n. 149), 204 (n. 32), 230 (n. 105)

Niagara Movement, 26, 90; and female auxiliary, 90–91

North Carolina, 24, 32–33, 48, 64, 67, 72, 114, 140, 189 (n. 134), 210 (n. 98), 216 (n. 76)

North Dakota, 134–35, 195–96 (n. 30)

Nurses: African American, 16, 58, 120–22, 125, 193 (n. 2), 217 (n. 89); in World War I, 16, 106, 120–22, 217 (n. 89); in Civil War, 41, 181 (n. 43), 186 (n. 107); in Spanish-American War, 58, 193 (nn. 2–3); in Universal Negro Improvement Association, 125

Princeton, N.J., 93
Progressive reform, 7, 15–16, 79–99,
    131–32, 135–38
Puerto Rico, 57, 62, 70, 93
Pulaski, Tenn., 95, 111
Pullman family, 51

Race-based nationalism: white, 1,
    9–13, 28–41, 45–47, 54–55, 67,
    69–70, 84–86, 88–90, 98, 117–18,
    142–44, 151–52; African Ameri-
    can, 13–14, 74–76, 125, 146–47
Race riots. See Pogroms
"Race suicide," 57; and white Ameri-
    cans, 6–7, 59, 62, 65–67, 104,
    141–42, 159–60; and African
    Americans, 7, 59–61, 150, 160
"Race women," 9–10, 152
Racial discrimination. See Exclusion,
    racial; Jim Crow; Segregation, racial
Randolph, Janet Weaver, 34
Reactionaries. See Antiradicalism;
    Conservatism; Rightism
Reconciliation, sectional. See Reunion,
    North-South
Reconstruction, 13, 21, 26, 32, 34,
    45, 95–98, 115, 142, 151, 161, 177
    (n. 12), 209 (n. 88), 232 (n. 117)
Red-baiting, 96, 107, 128, 134–42 pas-
    sim, 150–51, 154–55, 222 (n. 37),
    226 (n. 141), 232 (n. 119)
Red Cross, 110, 112–13, 119–20, 193
    (n. 3)
Red Scare, 107, 110–12, 115, 123, 132,
    142, 213 (n. 47)
Reinterments. See Cemeteries
Relief Society, 205 (n. 47)
Religion, 2, 39–40, 98, 119, 121, 145,
    147; Protestantism, 1, 8, 12, 29,
    46, 62–66, 87, 111, 174 (n. 47), 194
    (n. 19), 229 (n. 93); Roman Catholi-
    cism, 46, 64–65, 72, 181 (n. 46); Ju-

daism, 46, 181 (n. 46); Baptism, 72,
    75, 123; Mormonism, 87–88, 91, 95,
    106, 205 (n. 47); Quakerism, 139
Republican motherhood, 4, 36, 128
Republican Party, 32, 34, 50–51,
    61–63, 72–73, 85, 192 (n. 159)
Respectability, female, 9, 129, 158, 219
    (n. 4)
Reunion, North-South, 2, 15, 20–22;
    as framed by white women, 10,
    12–13, 20, 28–31, 33–37, 39–47,
    50, 54–55, 85–87, 89–90, 112–16,
    142, 150–52, 157, 161–62, 236
    (n. 32); based on race, 10, 12–13,
    20, 29–31, 33–47, 50, 54–55, 65,
    85–87, 89–90, 97–99, 150–52, 157,
    162, 236 (n. 32); based on loyalty, 10,
    17, 20–22, 80–81, 86, 96; as framed
    by black women, 13, 17, 20–22, 26,
    74, 80–81, 92–93, 121; as framed
    by neo-Confederates, 20, 29–31,
    33–37, 70–71, 79, 86, 112–16,
    143–46, 150–51, 161
Richmond, Va., 21–22, 34, 36, 111,
    189 (n. 134)
Rightism, 109, 127–28, 131–45, 148,
    151, 155–56, 159, 218 (n. 1), 223–24
    (nn. 46, 48, 53), 226 (n. 62), 233
    (n. 7), 234–35 (n. 19), 237 (n. 35)
Robert E. Lee's birthday, 95
Robeson, Paul, 152
Rogin, Michael, 99
Roosevelt, Eleanor, 17, 155, 158
Roosevelt, Franklin Delano, 155, 158,
    162
Roosevelt, Theodore, 6, 59, 63, 83, 135
Roosevelt Cabin (N.D.), 135
Rose, Laura Martin, 95, 113, 214
    (n. 53)
Rose of New England Women's
    League (Conn.), 26, 68
Ross, Mrs. I. N., 81

Truth, Sojourner, 25, 80
Tubman, Harriet, 24–25, 80, 200 (n. 4)
Turner, Frederick Jackson, 66
Tuscaloosa, Ala., 178 (n. 15)
Tuskegee Institute, 120, 219 (n. 11)
Tuskegee Woman's Club (Ala.), 219
(n. 11)

Uncle Tom's Cabin. See Stowe, Harriet
Beecher
Union patriotism, 12–13, 17, 21–22,
37–38, 86, 156
Union veterans, 5, 12, 26, 38, 41–42,
50, 61, 98. *See also* Grand Army of
the Republic
United Confederate Veterans, 28, 96,
113, 183 (n. 71), 197 (n. 41)
United Daughters of the Confederacy,
12, 80–81; membership figures, 10,
29, 143, 173 (n. 39), 181 (n. 45), 197
(n. 41), 227 (n. 74), 235 (n. 29); social
composition of, 10, 29–30, 43, 49,
173 (n. 39), 174 (n. 45), 181 (n. 46),
190 (n. 145); and U.S. state, 11, 31,
34–35, 96, 112–16, 143–46, 151;
and scholarships, 11, 85–86, 112,
144, 204 (n. 32); and World War I,
11, 112–16, 144, 216 (n. 81), 228
(n. 79); overlap with Daughters of
the American Revolution, 13, 30, 44,
46–47, 71, 87, 94, 113–15, 142–45,
174–75 (n. 49), 189 (n. 134), 208
(nn. 76, 78), 215 (n. 61), 227 (n. 71);
precursors of, 28; formation of, 28–
29; admission requirements, 28–29,
181 (n. 44); and class, 29, 43, 87, 111;
and "New South," 29, 181 (n. 49);
organizational structure of, 30;
moderate and militant wings of,
30–31, 71, 96; and "nation," 30–31,
113–14, 116, 182 (n. 60); and slavery, 33, 145–46, 182 (n. 61), 183

(nn. 67–68, 70–71); and grave
maintenance, 34; conservatism of,
34, 36, 49, 142–45; and holidays,
34, 95, 114, 183 (n. 72); and Ku Klux
Klan (formed 1866), 34, 95–96, 98,
210 (n. 98); and history textbooks,
35; and schoolchildren, 35, 96, 184
(n. 77), 236 (n. 31); and commemoration of white women, 35–36,
96–97, 184 (n. 80); on women's "political" activism, 36, 66, 95, 145; and
marriage, 49, 190 (n. 145); within
neo-Confederate movement, 66–67,
161, 197 (nn. 41, 43), 209 (n. 88);
and Spanish-American War, 70–71;
criticism of Philippine War, 71;
and progressive reform, 80, 93–95,
208 (n. 76); and southern mountain
people, 85–86, 204 (n. 33); and
polygamy, 95; and Reconstruction,
95, 115, 151, 209 (n. 88); and red-
baiting, 96–97, 144, 209 (n. 87);
and *The Birth of a Nation*, 98; and
Ku Klux Klan (formed 1915), 111;
and Woodrow Wilson, 112, 115–16;
and U.S. flag, 114–15, 143–45; and
peace activism, 115, 144, 212 (n. 30),
215 (n. 67); and Abraham Lincoln,
142, 227 (n. 72); and American Legion, 143–44, 228 (n. 79); on "national defense," 144–45, 228 (n. 83);
Crosses of Honor, 184 (n. 82); and
Columbia University, 204 (n. 32);
use of "general" by, 214 (n. 53).
See also Children of the Confederacy; Jim Crow; "Mammy" statue;
Monuments; Neo-Confederate nationalism; Race-based nationalism;
Reunion, North-South; Woman
suffrage
U.S. Bureau of Investigation (Department of Justice), 128, 141

U.S. Children's Bureau, 81, 82, 85, 94

U.S. Congress, 7, 25, 32–34, 41, 50, 52, 63, 68, 72, 85, 87–88, 97–98, 103, 110–11, 115, 131–33, 138, 140–41, 146, 149, 183 (n. 74), 191 (n. 150), 203 (n. 20)

U.S. Daughters of 1812, 228 (n. 78)

U.S. Education Department (proposed), 131, 136

U.S. flag: Pledge of Allegiance to, 6, 39; and Woman's Relief Corps, 12, 37, 39–41; and African Americans, 15, 21, 23, 26, 74, 93, 121, 175 (n. 51); and Daughters of the American Revolution, 30, 48, 51, 63, 66, 84, 105, 107–8, 134, 143, 192 (n. 159), 215 (nn. 60–61); and World War I, 105, 107, 111, 114, 214 (n. 58); and international peace, 108; and neo-Confederates, 114–15, 143–44

U.S. Flag Code, 143–44

U.S. Marines, 73, 124, 218 (n. 100)

U.S.-Mexican War, 65, 196 (n. 33)

U.S. Military Intelligence Division (Department of War), 123, 128, 137–38, 141, 223 (n. 46), 225–26 (n. 61)

U.S. Treasury Department, 216 (n. 76)

U.S. War Department, 61, 105, 120, 137, 141, 143, 223 (n. 46)

U.S. Women's Bureau, 81

Universal Negro Improvement Association, 13–14, 16, 130, 219 (n. 2); membership figures, 13, 173 (n. 53); popularity in U.S., 13–14; flags, 14, 147; African Black Cross Nurses, 125; formation of, 125; and World War I, 125; and civil rights movement, 125, 229 (n. 93); government surveillance of, 128; and International Council of Women of Darker Races, 130, 146; and progressive re-

form, 131; and class, 146, 229 (n. 93); and National Association of Colored Women, 146, 229 (n. 93); and patriotism, 146–47; women within, 149, 231 (n. 107); and red-baiting, 151–52. *See also* American and "Negro" nations; Black nationalism; Civic nationalism; Garvey, Marcus Moziah; Jacques Garvey, Amy; Race-based nationalism

Upperville, Va., 115

Utah, 87, 95

Valley Forge (Pa.), 64

Vardaman, James K., 97

Versailles, Treaty of, 115–16, 132

Veterans. *See* American Legion; Confederate veterans; Union veterans; Warriors, perceptions of

Victoria (queen of Britain), 61, 69–70

Virginia, 19–22, 29, 34–36, 38, 43–45, 60, 71, 91, 94, 97, 111, 113, 115, 131, 171 (n. 25), 183 (n. 72), 187 (n. 115), 188 (n. 129), 189 (n. 134), 191 (n. 153), 195–96 (n. 30), 214 (n. 58), 227 (n. 72)

Voice from the South, A. See Cooper, Anna Julia

Waco, Tex., 40, 68, 121, 200–201 (n. 5)

Wadesboro, N.C., 216 (n. 76)

Walker, Flora Bredes, 125–26, 135–38, 140–41, 155, 159, 234–35 (n. 19)

Walker, Madame C. J., 103

Walworth, Ellen Hardin, 19–20, 44–45, 50, 87, 190 (n. 149)

Walworth, Reubena Hyde, 69

War of 1812, 52–53, 93

Warriors, perceptions of: white male warriors, 2, 5, 11, 26–28, 34–45, 49, 51–55, 58, 64, 67–68, 70–72, 95–96, 98, 104–5, 107–9, 112–16,

124–26, 128, 137, 140–42, 150, 159, 162; female warriors, 19, 24, 69, 80, 96–97, 106, 126, 133; African American male warriors, 21–22, 26, 58, 61–62, 67–68, 72, 75, 92–93, 117–22

Washington, Booker T., 8, 27, 74, 86, 90, 102, 118, 129, 197 (n. 50)

Washington, D.C., 17, 22, 24–25, 38, 42–47 passim, 62, 67–68, 74–75, 81, 85, 87, 91, 102, 109, 117, 123, 138, 144–46, 151, 191 (n. 150), 195 (n. 29), 202 (n. 14), 208 (n. 78), 213 (n. 38), 215 (n. 67), 227 (n. 71); racial segregation in, 97–98, 152–56, 236 (n. 32)

Washington, Eugenia, 43–44, 190 (n. 149)

Washington, George, 19–20, 44, 48–49, 65, 93, 115, 134, 142, 159, 191 (n. 153). See also Mount Vernon

Washington, Margaret Murray, 8, 27, 61, 86–87, 130–31, 171–72 (nn. 28, 32), 219–20 (nn. 11, 12), 229 (n. 93)

Washington, Martha Custis, 49, 134, 191 (n. 153)

Washington Crossing the Delaware, 159

Washington Disarmament Conference (1921–22), 132, 215 (n. 67), 221 (n. 21)

Washington State, 64, 125–26, 196 (n. 37), 215 (n. 67)

Wells-Barnett, Ida B., 22–23, 25, 72, 74, 90, 91, 92, 122–24, 193 (n. 2), 207 (nn. 66, 70)

West Point, N.Y., 133

West Virginia, 27, 149, 183 (n. 71)

Westward expansion, 64–66, 72–73, 135, 179 (n. 29)

Wheatley, Phillis, 25, 80

White, George Henry, 72

Whitman, Narcissa Prentiss, 66, 196 (n. 37)

Wiles, Alice Bradford, 68, 197 (n. 50)

Wilmington, N.C., 32

Wilson, Woodrow, 97–99, 102, 109, 111–12, 115–16, 123

Windsor, Conn., 48

Wisconsin, 51, 138

Wittenmyer, Annie, 186 (n. 101)

Womanliness, 9, 61, 117, 169 (n. 4)

Woman's Christian Temperance Union, 12, 174 (n. 47), 201–2 (n. 13)

Woman's Era, 73, 90, 171–72 (n. 28)

Woman's Era Club (Boston), 73, 99, 174 (n. 45), 178–79 (nn. 14, 23)

Woman's Loyal Union (Brooklyn, N.Y.), 25

Woman's Peace Party, 109–10. *See also* Women's International League for Peace and Freedom

Woman's Relief Corps, 8, 12, 172 (n. 31); and North-South reunion, 10, 12–13, 37, 39–41, 47; African Americans within, 10, 12–13, 38–40, 97, 119, 179–80 (n. 35), 185 (nn. 94, 97–98); membership figures, 12, 137, 235 (n. 25); and Civil War, 37, 41, 86, 179–80 (n. 35); formation of, 37–38; and Union veterans, 37–38, 41, 70, 185 (n. 90), 186 (n. 111); social composition of, 38, 41; membership requirements, 38, 160; and immigration, 39, 111; and history textbooks, 41; and "literary" programs, 42, 186–87 (n. 113); and Spanish-American War, 70; and southern mountain people, 86, 204 (n. 34); and polygamy, 87; and World War I, 101, 111; and women's naturalization, 105; and progressive reform, 131–32; and peace activism, 132, 222 (n. 34); and "national de-

Gender and American Culture

Women and Patriotism in Jim Crow America, by Francesca Morgan (2005).

Relative Intimacy: Fathers, Adolescent Daughters, and Postwar American Culture, by Rachel Devlin (2005).

The Freedom of the Streets: Work, Citizenship, and Sexuality in a Gilded Age City, by Sharon E. Wood (2005).

Home on the Rails: Women, the Railroad, and the Rise of Public Domesticity, by Amy G. Richter (2005).

Worrying the Line: Black Women Writers, Lineage, and Literary Tradition, by Cheryl A. Wall (2005).

From Welfare to Workfare: The Unintended Consequences of Liberal Reform, 1945–1965, by Jennifer Mittelstadt (2005).

Choice and Coercion: Birth Control, Sterilization, and Abortion in Public Health and Welfare, by Johanna Schoen (2005).

Closer to Freedom: Enslaved Women and Everyday Resistance in the Plantation South, by Stephanie M. H. Camp (2004).

Masterful Women: Slaveholding Widows from the American Revolution through the Civil War, by Kirsten E. Wood (2004).

Manliness and Its Discontents: The Black Middle Class and the Transformation of Masculinity, 1900–1930, by Martin Summers (2004).

Citizen, Mother, Worker: Debating Public Responsibility for Child Care after the Second World War, by Emilie Stoltzfus (2003).

Women and the Historical Enterprise in America: Gender, Race, and the Politics of Memory, 1880–1945, by Julie Des Jardins (2003).

Free Hearts and Free Homes: Gender and American Antislavery Politics, by Michael D. Pierson (2003).

Ella Baker and the Black Freedom Movement: A Radical Democratic Vision, by Barbara Ransby (2003).

Signatures of Citizenship: Petitioning, Antislavery, and Women's Political Identity, by Susan Zaeske (2003).

Love on the Rocks: Men, Women, and Alcohol in Post–World War II America, by Lori Rotskoff (2002).

The Veiled Garvey: The Life and Times of Amy Jacques Garvey, by Ula Yvette Taylor (2002).

Working Cures: Health, Healing, and Power on Southern Slave Plantations, by Sharla Fett (2002).

Southern History across the Color Line, by Nell Irvin Painter (2002).

The Artistry of Anger: Black and White Women's Literature in America, 1820–1860, by Linda M. Grasso (2002).

Too Much to Ask: Black Women in the Era of Integration, by Elizabeth Higginbotham (2001).

Imagining Medea: Rhodessa Jones and Theater for Incarcerated Women, by Rena Fraden (2001).

Painting Professionals: Women Artists and the Development of Modern American Art, 1870–1920, by Kirsten Swinth (2001).

Remaking Respectability: African American Women in Interwar Detroit, by Victoria W. Wolcott (2001).

Ida B. Wells-Barnett and American Reform, 1880–1930, by Patricia A. Schechter (2001).

Taking Haiti: Military Occupation and the Culture of U.S. Imperialism, 1915–1940, by Mary A. Renda (2001).

Before Jim Crow: The Politics of Race in Postemancipation Virginia, by Jane Dailey (2000).

Captain Ahab Had a Wife: New England Women and the Whalefishery, 1720–1870, by Lisa Norling (2000).

Civilizing Capitalism: The National Consumers' League, Women's Activism, and Labor Standards in the New Deal Era, by Landon R. Y. Storrs (2000).

Rank Ladies: Gender and Cultural Hierarchy in American Vaudeville, by M. Alison Kibler (1999).

Strangers and Pilgrims: Female Preaching in America, 1740–1845, by Catherine A. Brekus (1998).

Sex and Citizenship in Antebellum America, by Nancy Isenberg (1998).

Yours in Sisterhood: Ms. Magazine and the Promise of Popular Feminism, by Amy Erdman Farrell (1998).

We Mean to Be Counted: White Women and Politics in Antebellum Virginia, by Elizabeth R. Varon (1998).

Women Against the Good War: Conscientious Objection and Gender on the American Home Front, 1941–1947, by Rachel Waltner Goossen (1997).

Toward an Intellectual History of Women: Essays by Linda K. Kerber (1997).

Gender and Jim Crow: Women and the Politics of White Supremacy in North Carolina, 1896–1920, by Glenda Elizabeth Gilmore (1996).

Delinquent Daughters: Protecting and Policing Adolescent Female Sexuality in the United States, 1885–1920, by Mary E. Odem (1995).

U.S. History as Women's History: New Feminist Essays, edited by Linda K. Kerber, Alice Kessler-Harris, and Kathryn Kish Sklar (1995).

Common Sense and a Little Fire: Women and Working-Class Politics in the United States, 1900–1965, by Annelise Orleck (1995).

How Am I to Be Heard?: Letters of Lillian Smith, edited by Margaret Rose Gladney (1993).

Entitled to Power: Farm Women and Technology, 1913–1963, by Katherine Jellison (1993).

Revising Life: Sylvia Plath's Ariel Poems, by Susan R. Van Dyne (1993).

Made From This Earth: American Women and Nature, by Vera Norwood (1993).

Unruly Women: The Politics of Social and Sexual Control in the Old South, by Victoria E. Bynum (1992).

The Work of Self-Representation: Lyric Poetry in Colonial New England, by Ivy Schweitzer (1991).

Labor and Desire: Women's Revolutionary Fiction in Depression America, by Paula Rabinowitz (1991).

Community of Suffering and Struggle: Women, Men, and the Labor Movement in Minneapolis, 1915–1945, by Elizabeth Faue (1991).

All That Hollywood Allows: Re-reading Gender in 1950s Melodrama, by Jackie Byars (1991).

Doing Literary Business: American Women Writers in the Nineteenth Century, by Susan Coultrap-McQuin (1990).

Ladies, Women, and Wenches: Choice and Constraint in Antebellum Charleston and Boston, by Jane H. Pease and William H. Pease (1990).

The Secret Eye: The Journal of Ella Gertrude Clanton Thomas, 1848–1889, edited by Virginia Ingraham Burr, with an introduction by Nell Irvin Painter (1990).

Second Stories: The Politics of Language, Form, and Gender in Early American Fictions, by Cynthia S. Jordan (1989).

Within the Plantation Household: Black and White Women of the Old South, by Elizabeth Fox-Genovese (1988).

The Limits of Sisterhood: The Beecher Sisters on Women's Rights and Woman's Sphere, by Jeanne Boydston, Mary Kelley, and Anne Margolis (1988).